THE SCOTTISH
REVOLUTION 1637–1644

THE SCOTTISH
REVOLUTION 1637–1644

The Triumph of the Covenanters

DAVID STEVENSON

DAVID & CHARLES : NEWTON ABBOT

0 7153 6302 6

Set in 11 on 13 pt. Garamond
and printed in Great Britain
by Ebenezer Baylis & Son Limited
The Trinity Press Worcester and London
for David & Charles (Holdings) Limited
South Devon House Newton Abbot Devon

To
My Parents
In Gratitude

Contents

Contents

9

List of Illustrations

MAPS

Preface

The purpose of this book is to provide a political history of the period; I believe that lack of such a work is probably one of the main reasons why this period of Scotland's history has been so neglected—in accordance with G. R. Elton's dictum that 'political history must come before any other and has always done so. The study of history began as political history. . . . It need not stop there, but unless it starts there, it will not start at all'.[1] The absence of an adequate political history of mid-seventeenth-century Scotland has made research on other aspects of it very difficult.

That the period has been neglected hardly needs stressing. Indeed it even lacks a generally accepted name or label, often being vaguely referred to as 'the civil war period', borrowing the name (and even the war) from England, or in terms of the rivalry of Argyll and Montrose. Both are misleading and inadequate. To talk of the covenanting period recalls to most people the years after 1660 when the covenanters were a tiny minority, not the years when they ruled Scotland; this in itself is a clear indication of the neglect of the earlier period. I have therefore coined the term 'The Scottish Revolution'. This obviously risks the charge of trying to jump on the fast-accelerating bandwagon of revolutionary studies without a valid ticket, but I believe the term is justified, and hope this book will help to demonstrate its appropriateness.

Though it is primarily a work on Scottish history, I hope it will also make some contribution to the study of aspects of English history, especially the part played by Scotland in English affairs. As Gilbert Burnet put it, 'the first beginning and rise of the Civil Wars having been in Scotland, from whence they moved Southwards, there can be no clear understanding of what followed until these first disorders be truly stated'.[2] The subject also has some interest for the general study of mid-seventeenth-century revolutions, yet Scotland's revolution has been largely ignored. Thus Roland Mousnier lists obscure as well as famous revolts and revolutions from all corners of Europe and beyond, but makes no mention of Scotland. He even quotes Robert Mentet on the origins of the seventeenth-century revolutions without realising[3] (or at least without thinking it worth mentioning) that this was a former Scots minister, Robert Menteith, who had settled in France in the 1630s. But of course much of the blame for this refusal to consider the significance of events in Scotland must lie on Scots historians who have failed to make these events intelligible to outsiders.

Any study of the covenanters must include a good deal of religious history, but I have tried to avoid the error of Buckle, and many others before and since (clerical and anti-clerical), the belief that 'the real history of Scotland in the seventeenth century is to be found in the pulpit and in the ecclesiastical assemblies'.[4] Far too much so-called political history of seventeenth-century Scotland has been little more than church history. I have sought to redress the balance by emphasising the importance of laymen, secular motives and civil institutions in the complex events of the time.

There is almost no aspect of the rule of the covenanters which does not cry out for further research. If this book manages to provoke some interest in it by showing that there was more to it than the dreary and irrational antics of backward and fanatical Scots obsessed by dark religion, then it will have served its purpose.

D.S.

University of Aberdeen

CHAPTER ONE

The Rule of Charles I in Scotland and the Causes of Discontent, 1625–1637

SCOTTISH SOCIETY

When James VI died in 1625 he was the first Scottish king since 1390 to leave an adult heir to succeed him, and Scotland was enjoying a period of peace and stability which contrasted sharply with the periodic anarchy of the sixteenth century.[1] The nobility and the kirk, the two great interests in the land that had rivalled his power in his early days, had come to support his regime. The problems of chronic disorder in the Highlands and on the Borders seemed to have been cured, the violence of personal and family feuds and rivalries throughout the country to have been greatly reduced. The Scottish parliament—which in any case had never achieved anything like the power and influence of its English counterpart—had been brought firmly under royal control. Ruling Scotland from London through the privy council in Edinburgh, James had smugly boasted in 1607 'This I must say for Scotland and truly vaunt it: here I sit and govern it with my pen: I write and it is done: and by a Clerk of the Council I govern Scotland, which others could not do by the Sword'.[2] Though by this time an absentee monarch, James had had many years of personal experience of Scottish political life in his youth; this had taught him the skills of a politician and the limitations of his power. His son Charles had had no such training in the realities of royal power in Scotland, yet assumed that he too could govern by the pen.

The contrast between the old king, James, wise (or at least cunning), flexible and experienced in Scots affairs, and Charles, young, rash, ignorant of Scotland, heedless of growing opposition, is a commonplace which has behind it a basis of truth. The story of James' reign (in Scotland) is one of triumph over difficult circumstances, his son's reign a story of difficult circumstances exacerbated by political ineptitude in the king. Charles I inherited a fairly orderly and loyal kingdom of Scotland in 1625; less than thirteen years later the great majority of his Scots subjects of all classeshad united in opposition to him.

The keystone of the arch of Scottish society was the king, and one might say that this keystone had been seriously loosened by the absentee monarchy brought about by the union of the crowns of 1603. Yet at first the union seemed to have enhanced the king's position. By that time James had gone far towards restoring royal power in Scotland after the confusion of his long minority. The union helped him to continue this process by freeing him from fear of his over-mighty Scots subjects, by placing the great resources of England at his back, by the vast increase in prestige and stature which the English crown brought him. Yet already at the time of his death it was becoming, perhaps not obvious but at least discernible, that the changes in the way Scotland was governed, and indeed in Scottish society itself, brought about by the union were potentially dangerous to the monarchy. Some of these changes were perhaps inevitable consequences of union, others followed from changes in royal attitudes and policies which were strongly influenced by the move from Edinburgh to London.

The English court, as inherited from the Tudors, was a very different institution from that of Scotland. James' court prior to 1603 had been small, poor (often humiliatingly so) and informal, almost homely. The Scots king was very much first among equals among his nobles, who treated him with little subserviency or awe. The richness and ceremonial of the English court provided a contrast that was balm to James' vanity. Though he always retained something of his Scots informality, and allowed his new court to decay at times into vulgarity and sordid scandal, he none the less loved the deference and flattery with which the English treated a monarch. He encouraged this exaltation of kingship and the spread of theories of absolute monarchy by divine right, theories which he had dreamed of in Scotland but which never had won much acceptance there. His son carried this tendency further. He created round himself a court of elaborate formality and ceremonial which suited his withdrawn and fastidious nature and insulated him from his subjects. Scots coming to court increasingly found that they had to adopt formal English manners if they were to hope for royal favour and avoid being sneered at as uncouth. Yet if they did adopt such manners this created a barrier between them and their countrymen when they returned home. Charles' dislike of the familiarity natural to his Scottish subjects was most clearly seen during his visit to Scotland in 1633. He was clearly ill at ease and found the behaviour of many Scots offensive. 'Upon which the Lord Falkland was wont to say, "that keeping of State was like committing adultery, there must go two to it", for let the proudest or most formal man resolve to keep what distance he will towards others, a bold and confident man instantly demolishes that whole machine, and gets within him, and even obliges him to his own laws of conversation.'[3] If he found his Scots subjects boorish, they found him haughty and unapproachable.

The absentee monarchy created similar difficulties for the Scottish officers of state. Though they visited the court they had not the frequent personal contact with the king which might have built up understanding between them. The one exception to this was Sir William Alexander (Earl of Stirling, 1633), secretary of state from 1626 until his death in 1640, who normally resided at court. But his long residence at court left him out of touch with Scots affairs and feelings, and this applied also to nearly all the other Scots who spent much of their time at court and had most personal contact with the king.[4] The Earl of Clarendon later recalled that when Charles I visited Scotland in 1633 'it evidently appeared, that they of that nation who shined most at the Court of England had the least influence in their own country',[5] though he excluded the Marquis of Hamilton from this generalisation. The king either did not notice or at least did not see it as dangerous that those with most influence in Scotland had little contact with him, for he made no attempt to widen the circle of those in whom he confided concerning Scots affairs.

Thus the union of the crowns deprived the Scots of the presence of their kings and made their kings increasingly alien to them, out of touch with Scottish feelings and opinions. These changes naturally most affected those who had been most closely associated with the king in governing Scotland, the nobility. In structure the society of Scotland was still essentially feudal, based on the holding of land from the king in return for service to him. The estates of the realm were composed of those who held land directly from the king as tenants in chief and had the right and duty to be represented in parliament to advise and assist the king in governing. There were three estates, those of the lay tenants in chief (nobles and lesser barons or lairds), the clergy, and the royal burghs.

In all but name the nobles and lairds were by the early seventeenth century separate estates, but technically they remained one as they shared a common origin. Originally all lay tenants in chief had had the duty of attending parliament personally, but in time the greater tenants had been created lords of parliament, attending personally, while the lesser men had come to elect representatives to attend for them.[6] The nobility of Scotland was a surprisingly large estate, and one which was growing fast. Scotland had perhaps one fifth of the population of England (very approximately 1 million to 5 million) and was much the poorer country, but the number of nobles in each was about the same. In 1603 Scotland had between 50 and 60 nobles, and England 55. By 1641 this had risen to about 105 nobles in Scotland and 121 in England.[7] The largest group of these new creations, which almost doubled the size of the Scots nobility in forty years, comprised the lords of erection, men who had come into possession of large areas of former church land which James VI had erected into temporal lordships for them—an action which had gone a long way to win him their support. Other new titles went to junior branches of existing noble families, many more were given as rewards for loyal service to the crown, some to families in which such service in various offices had become hereditary.[8] The 'inflation of honours' represented by this unprecedentedly fast growth in the numbers of nobles naturally caused some resentment among the older nobility, especially as James and Charles tended increasingly to rely on such 'new men' in governing the country. Such officials of relatively humble origins were often prepared to regard service to the crown as a full-time occupation, whereas the greater nobles inevitably spent much of their time running their estates—and even had they had the time, they seldom had the inclination to concern themselves with the bureaucratic routine of administration.

The social importance of the use and promotion of 'new men' should not be exaggerated, however. While it brought new blood to the nobility, this hardly represented a revolutionary change. For kings to favour lesser men on whose loyalty they could rely rather than great magnates was common, though certainly James' very success in restoring royal power and extending the machinery of government led to his employing and promoting more such men than his predecessors. Moreover most such 'new men' did not come from entirely outside the ruling classes but from families of lesser landowners, or lairds. With reference to the great increase in size of the Scots nobility it is worth noting that the practice of selling peerages, common in England in this period, was almost unknown in Scotland. The only known instance is that one of the six Englishmen granted Scots titles, Sir Thomas Fairfax, paid £1,500 sterling for the title of Lord Fairfax of Cameron.[9] The newly created lesser title of baronet of Nova Scotia, however, was sold freely.

The nobility of Scotland as a whole believed that they had a right to share power with the king. As the greatest of his subjects they were his natural and traditional advisers. In the past factions of nobles had often been able to defy the king or dictate his actions. By grants extorted from previous kings many had come to possess powers rivalling those of the king himself. Grants of regality gave them power to try all criminal cases except treason. In the many baron courts nobles and lairds had jurisdiction over a wide variety of lesser cases. Even the post of sheriff, the king's chief financial, administrative, judicial and military representative in the shires, was often held hereditarily by a great local family. Commissions as king's lieutenant had frequently given sub-regal powers in Argyll and the Isles to the Earl of Argyll, and to the Marquis of

Huntly in the North East. In addition the Earls of Argyll held the office of justice general hereditarily until 1628, and even after that date remained justices general of Argyll and the Isles. The holding of justice ayres, royal circuit criminal courts, was irregular. In these circumstances royal power in the shires was often little more than nominal. Restoration of central and royal power thus inevitably entailed curbing the powers of the nobles and aroused their opposition. James had the sense to avoid any major confrontation with the nobility and consolidated his power gradually. His success in increasing his power lay more in the winning of the support of the nobility for his regime than in any direct attack on their power.

James was undoubtedly helped in curbing the nobility by the union of the crowns; the nobility suddenly found that their traditional methods of bringing pressure to bear on the crown were no longer effective. To put it cynically, one might say that they regretted that threats of violence, of kidnapping or bullying the king could no longer be used successfully, but more legitimate means of influencing the king, by personal petitioning, advice and argument, had also largely disappeared. Few could afford to spend long at the extravagant English court, or had much wish to stay there and be ridiculed for their poverty and accent. A few of course adapted, becoming anglicised courtiers more at home in London than Edinburgh, but for most Scots nobles the union of the crowns meant primarily the sudden disappearance of the institution which had been at the centre of their social and political lives, the Scottish court. It was some time before this became clear, for many of the nobles had had high hopes of the effects that having a Scots king on the English throne would have on them. They had hoped for rich pickings in offices and pensions, and at first some got them. But soon English jealousy forced the king to limit his favours to his countrymen, and the king himself became anglicised. The Scots found that instead of their taking over the English court, it had absorbed their king and largely excluded them. They had hoped to help rule England in Scotland's interests, but it soon became clear that this had been to expect the tail to wag the dog, and that in fact the opposite was happening.

In these circumstances it was inevitable that discontent should rumble among the nobility. They had little contact with a king who was increasingly alien, and were unable to influence him, while royal policy was directed at undermining their power. The ineffectiveness of this discontent for many years is perhaps a measure of how long it took for the nobility to realise the change in nature of their position brought about by the union of the crowns, and to adapt to this new situation.

Though convenient for the purposes of generalisation, it is of course an over-simplification to speak of the nobles as if they formed a homogeneous body. They were a diverse group, ranging from great magnates, with almost regal power on their vast estates, to Lord Somerville, so poor that he did not use his title since he could not live in a style befitting it. The division between the older nobility and the many recent creations has already been mentioned, but it does not appear to correspond to any clear division in political opinions; new nobles tended quickly to adopt the prejudices and outlook of their long-established colleagues. However, it is noticeable that a disproportionately large number of the older nobility—perhaps a fifth—were Roman Catholics, and were thus largely excluded from public life. These included great nobles like the Marquis of Huntly (living in France), the Earl of Argyll (living in London) and the Marquis of Douglas.

The other part of the estate of lay tenants in chief was equally diverse. All men holding land freehold from the king worth more than 40s of old extent (a traditional valuation) who were not nobles were entitled as 'small barons' to take part in electing commissioners from the shires to parliament. These lairds throughout the country numbered several thousand men, some more wealthy than many a noble, others little richer than the better-off tenant farmers.

The estate of small barons had since the mid sixteenth century become more active in public affairs than previously, and had played a leading part in bringing about the Reformation. Yet on the whole they were still far more dependent on the nobility than their English counterparts, the gentry. Family and feudal ties remained stronger than in England, and lairds often deferred to the noble head of their family or 'name'. Many, as well as holding land direct from the crown, also held some as sub-vassals of nobles, who thus had claims over them as feudal superiors. Paradoxically the English gentleman often paid more outward respect to a noble (in accordance with English formal manners) than the Scots lairds (used to more easy-going and familiar Scots ways) did, yet it was the lairds who were the more dependent. Increased contact with England after the union of the crowns led some of the Scots nobles to feel that they should be treated with more respect and deference by their inferiors in Scotland. The eldest sons of earls had begun, in English fashion, to take the courtesy title of lord instead of being content with the plain old Scots designation of master. Such snobbish affectations on the part of nobles naturally offended lairds and others of lesser rank, just as the aloof formality of the king offended the nobles—who were none the less trying to ape it. One of the reasons for the fifth Earl of Montrose's early popularity was his easy and courteous manner when dealing with inferiors. Patrick Gordon of Ruthven explained the changing attitudes of some of the nobles at length:

> once that Inglish diuell, keeping of state, got a haunt amongest our nobilitie, then begane they to keepe a distance, as if there ware some diuinitie in them, and gentlemen therefor most put of there shoes, the ground is so holy whereon they tread; but as he is ane euill bread gentlemen that vnderstandes not what distance he should keep with a noble man, so that noble man that claims his dewe with a high looke, as if it did best fitte his noblenes to slight his inferiours, may well gett the cape and knie, but neuer gaine the heart of a freborne gentleman . . . It is true that in Ingland the keepeing of state is in some sorte tollerable, for that nation (being so often conquired) is become slavish, and takes not euill to be slawes to there superioures.
>
> But our nation, I mean the gentre not the commones, haueing neuer beene conquired, but always a free borne people, ar only wine with courtesies, and the humble, myld, chearefull, and affable behavioure of there superioures.[10]

However, the gap between the nobility and the lairds was far from unbridgeable; as landowners, part of the ruling élite, they had more interests in common than at variance.

The representatives of the clerical estate in parliament consisted of the two archbishops and eleven bishops (twelve after the creation of the diocese of Edinburgh in 1633). One of James VI's greatest successes in Scotland had been the assertion of royal control over the kirk. In the years after 1603 he had finally broken the power of the Melvillians, the extreme presbyterian followers of Andrew Melville who had insisted that the kirk should not be subordinate to the crown but should be supreme in its own sphere, that of spiritual matters. James had revived the powers of the bishops and through them gained control of the hierarchy of presbyterian church courts—kirk session, presbytery, synod and general assembly. Bishops had become *ex officio* moderators of the synods, with power to appoint moderators of presbyteries and control the admission of ministers to parishes. Church government in Scotland thus combined elements of episcopacy and presbyterianism;[11] the two systems were not yet generally regarded as entirely incompatible, and this mixed system of government was acceptable to the majority of Scotsmen—including ministers, for there is relatively little sign of friction between the two elements in the church courts.[12] Thus to try to make a clear distinction between 'episcopalians' and 'presbyterians' in this period is unrealistic; it was only to be Charles' determination to exalt the former elements in the kirk at the expense of the latter that in the end convinced many that the two were incompatible. By identifying the bishops too closely with his policies in both church and state he made it inevitable that an attack on the policies would develop into an attack on the bishops. James had had the sense to avoid testing the compatibility of the two elements too far; he removed the most controversial cases from the now episcopally dominated presbyterian courts. To discipline ministers and laymen who opposed royal religious policies a new court, the court of high commission, had been established on the English model in 1610.[13]

James' control of the kirk had been far from unlimited, however. When he had turned from changes in church government and discipline to changes in the worship of the kirk he had met with far more opposition than he had expected. He managed to

force a general assembly in 1618 and parliament in 1621 to accept
the Five Articles of Perth (concerning details of liturgical practice), but the bitter opposition aroused by their supposed papist
tendencies showed the king the limitations of his power. Rather
than reopen the question of relations between kirk and state, and
thus perhaps undermine his achievement of having brought the
kirk under royal control, James wisely conciliated his Scottish
subjects by making little attempt to enforce the Perth Articles
and by promising that he would not introduce any further 'ceremonies', thus abandoning plans to introduce a new liturgy in
Scotland.[14] It is overstating the case to say that James left 'a
church at peace' in Scotland on his death,[15] but it is perhaps also
misleading to say that he initiated the process leading to the overthrow of royal control of the kirk in 1638.[16] James started down the
path that led to revolt against his son, but had the sense to turn
back when he saw the strength of the forces he was arousing
against himself.

At the time of Charles I's accession most of the parish ministers
of Scotland—there were between 900 and 1,000 parishes—were
willing to accept the kirk as it then was. Many, perhaps even most,
disliked the Perth Articles and evaded or refused to implement
them, and many had little love for bishops. But very few of them
were ready to take action to bring about a change; the number of
dedicated presbyterians was very small though 'their enthusiasm
and sense of mission had, if anything, grown over the years' since
James had brought the kirk under royal control.[17] The number of
ministers punished by the court of high commission for opposing
royal policy was fairly small;[18] so long as ministers unhappy at the
state of the kirk did not make a nuisance of themselves they could
usually escape persecution. Indeed even the small minority whose
opposition was open managed to survive, and by the 1630s had
come to form what may be called a radical party within the kirk,
analogous to the virtual church within a church formed by the
English puritans. The ministers involved came mainly from the
South West—men like Samuel Rutherford (minister of Anwoth,
Kirkcudbrightshire, until banished to Aberdeen by the high commission in 1636) and David Dickson (minister of Irvine). Others

from the same area like John Livingstone, John McLellan and Robert Blair were driven by persecution to leave Scotland and work among the Scots settlers in Ulster, but they returned frequently to preach and meet with sympathisers before retreating again to safety. All these men had close links of friendship, and some of marriage, with Edinburgh laymen like the merchants John Mean and William Rig of Atherny who had been in trouble in 1619–24 for holding conventicles or private prayer meetings. James VI had ordered the suppression of the conventicles but in 1624 the chancellor, Sir George Hay, leniently defined them as private meetings held in time of public services—a good example of how the king's ministers could water down unpopular policies. Under this definition prayer meetings at all other times were not persecuted, and they appear to have become widespread at least in Edinburgh and the Western Lowlands. Thus the king's radical opponents managed to establish and extend an organised party within the kirk through personal ties and conventicles, and persecution was too inefficient to prevent this, while at the same time being irksome enough to inspire it.[19] But it should be stressed that such radicals continued to regard the kirk as essentially a true and godly kirk, whatever its corruptions. They had no thought of separating from it. Rutherford sums up their attitude rather startlingly by calling the kirk his 'whorish mother', his 'Harlot Mother';[20] it remained his mother, and therefore he owed it his love and his best efforts to redeem it from its prostitution. Except for Roman Catholics, indeed, there was general acceptance that the kirk was the true reformed kirk; those who desired to reform it wished to do so from within, not to secede from it.

Support for royal religious policy was strongest in Aberdeen and the North East, and in the universities; Catholicism was also stronger in what has been called 'Scotland's Conservative North'[21] than elsewhere in the country, though isolated pockets of it remained in the South as well, especially where there was the protection of a local Catholic noble (like the Earl of Nithsdale in the shire of Dumfries). Of the great clans of the Highlands only the strongest of all, the Campbells, was strongly committed to Protestantism. In parts of the North West there can have been very little organised religion at all (some parishes had been without ministers since the Reformation) but the old faith lingered on, encouraged by Catholic missionaries (Franciscans from Ireland and Scots Jesuits) and distrust of Protestantism as the religion of the hated Lowlanders.

The bishops were among the most trusted of Charles' Scottish servants and advisers, and the king consistently advanced them and those of the ministers who supported his religious ideas in both secular and ecclesiastical power and status. For the king such a policy had many advantages. Appointed by him and dependent on him, the bishops had not the independence of royal favour which so many of his lay councillors had. Though many of Charles' bishops (especially those that he had inherited from his father) were unhappy at his religious innovations, for religious reasons as well as through fear of the opposition that they would arouse in Scotland, they all obeyed him. Thus by increasing their secular powers Charles demonstrated the position that he felt was due to them through their place in the church while at the same time adding to his administration men on whose fidelity he could rely. That obedience was not the only quality necessary in councillors and administrators did not seem to occur to the king. Take, for example, John Spottiswood, Archbishop of St Andrews. Though known to have little enthusiasm for Charles' religious policies, he was made president of the exchequer in 1626, and the king ruled that he should have precedence before all other subjects in Scotland; previously such precedence had belonged to the chancellor, and the holder of that office, Sir George Hay, steadfastly refused to cede his precedence to the archbishop.[22] In 1635, after Hay's death, the king made doubly sure that his archbishop would have precedence by making him chancellor, thus appointing to the highest office of state 'an old unfirme man'[23] aged seventy who would obey, but without zeal. Far from bringing the archbishop the respect that Charles intended, the appointment earned him the hatred of those who believed that clerics should not accept lay offices, and the jealousy of the nobility.

In 1634 Charles ordered that all bishops and the most suitable ministers were to be made justices of the peace.[24] Two years later four out of sixteen commissioners named in a new commission of exchequer were bishops, whereas only one was a noble,[25] a striking contrast with the commission of 1626 in which only two commissioners had been bishops and eight nobles.[26] The number of bishops on the privy council rose from six in 1625 to nine in 1637 and they attended more regularly in the 1630s than before, taking an increasingly large part in the council's activities.[27] Whereas many of the bishops appointed by James VI had been content (like Spottiswood) with a relatively humble position in church and state, those appointed by Charles tended to have (like their king) more exalted ideas about the respect and powers due to a bishop.

The third estate was that of the burgesses of the royal burghs (burghs holding charters from the king as tenants in chief) plus a few of the larger ecclesiastical burghs (like Glasgow and St Andrews) which joined the royal burghs in contributing to taxes and shared with them a monopoly of foreign trade. These fifty or so burghs sent representatives to parliament and enjoyed a large measure of internal self-government by magistrates and council, who tended to form a self-perpetuating oligarchy since they elected their own successors. Most of the burghs were very small. Perhaps only Edinburgh had many more than 10,000 inhabitants, and only half a dozen more than 5,000. By the standards of the greater English boroughs most of the Scots burghs were small and poor, but to say that Edinburgh was 'destitute of mercantile spirit' and Scotland 'without merchants' is absurd.[28] Moreover, poor as they were, the Scottish burghs in some ways played a more important part in national life than the boroughs of England. The English boroughs had no national organisation, and most of the men who represented them in parliament were not merchants but gentry, often with little or no interest in the borough's welfare. In Scotland on the other hand a convention of royal burghs met annually to consider matters of common interest, and the commissioners for burghs who sat in parliament were usually active merchants, though some of the smaller burghs were dominated by powerful local families. The well-organised Scots burghs were to take a leading part in opposing Charles I, while the English boroughs, each jealously guarding its own interests, provided little leadership for or against the king.[29]

Those who made up the three estates of Scotland, the tenants in chief, numbered only a few per cent of the population of Scotland. Those of no estate included many men of substance, such as feuars of crown lands (holding their lands in perpetuity in return for payment of a fixed annual feu only to the crown) and the greater sub-vassals, holding land from nobles and lairds. Those who actually farmed the land usually had no hereditary interest in it, holding by short leases or as tenants at will with no leases at all. Below them were the landless (or almost landless) labourers who worked on the land of others, and those in the burghs who had not the status of burgesses. Scotland was a poor country, and the conditions of life even of the tenant farmers were often miserable; the landless were even worse off, and the large numbers of poor without regular employment or maintenance were often on or over the brink of starvation. Yet except in years of unusually bad harvest there was little sign of social unrest, for the great majority stoically accepted their lot in life. Those few who did not strove to rise out of their class rather than to improve the lot of their fellows in it. Society was on the whole conservative and changing only slowly, but it was not entirely static or without tensions. As always, some were prospering, others declining. The have-nots envied the have-gots; the have-gots feared the masses of have-nots. In the burghs merchants and craftsmen squabbled endlessly. Lairds resented the pretensions of the nobles. But such divisions cannot be called 'causes' of the revolt against Charles I; they were rather the usual background tensions present in every society. Indeed it was Charles' unhappy achievement to unite almost all classes and groups in Scottish society against him in spite of their conflicting interests. The causes of the revolt were 'social' only insofar as a variety of motives led Scottish society to unite to an unusual extent against its head.

The society so far discussed has been the society of the Lowlands, of southern and north-eastern Scotland. There were of course many important local differences in society and customs within the Lowlands, but it is true to say that the great majority of

Lowlanders felt themselves to have more in common with each other than with the Gaelic speakers of the North and North West. The Lowlander usually thought of the Highlander as a savage, an alien, Irish in language and culture, given to stealing, disorder and cruelty. The division of the ruling élite into feudal estates, so important in the Lowlands, had little or no meaning in the Highlands. There were virtually no burgesses, few ministers, few nobles even, for few of the clan chiefs had yet been ennobled. Feudal landholding was not yet universal; chiefs held their lands and ruled through older claims to authority, ancestry and conquest, and had little need of charters from the king granting them lands or jurisdictions. But the extension of royal power in the Highlands by James VI had brought with it an extension of feudal landholding. This caused much confusion and unrest. Many Highlanders owing traditional clan loyalty to a chief found that another chief or noble was the feudal superior of the land on which they lived; to which was their loyalty due? How, for example, could Camerons in Lochaber reconcile loyalty to their feudal superior, the Marquis of Huntly, with loyalty to their chief, Cameron of Locheil, the ties of feudalism with the ties of kinship (actual or mythical)?

The differences between Highland and Lowland society should not be exaggerated, however. There were areas where the two overlapped, and in both society was bound together by basically the same ties, partly feudal, partly of kinship, though in general the latter tended to be the more important in the Highlands, the former in the Lowlands.[30] The differences which caused friction between Highlands and Lowlands were as much linguistic and cultural as social.

THE GOVERNMENT OF SCOTLAND

Charles I, like his father, ruled Scotland through the privy council in Edinburgh. It was a method of government adequate for routine administration of the country at times when there was little or no organised opposition to the regime, but inadequate to deal with any crisis. The competence of the council was extremely wide though indefinite. Its main functions were executive, to implement the king's policies, but it had also legislative powers, though it was usual to have its legislation (unless it was only of a temporary nature) confirmed by parliament. It supervised the activities of most central and local royal officials 'as a sort of discipline committee of the civil service'.[31] The council's judicial powers were extensive if rather vague; it was especially concerned with cases relating to the public peace and cases in which other courts were unable to provide remedies. In short, 'The council was a convenient instrument of the royal will: it was the mainspring of executive action; the repository of the residual equitable juris-diction of the crown; and the guardian of the peace'.[32] The Scottish privy council had of course many similarities with the council of England,[33] but there was one all-important difference between them; in England the king was often present at the meet-ings of the council and it could take an active part in discussing and making policy, and in advising the king, whereas the Scottish council after 1603 received instructions from a distant king who seldom asked its advice or gave it any discretion in important matters. It carried out the fiats of an absentee monarch, 'very often merely putting into effect policies shaped elsewhere'.[34] Often in-deed the king neglected even to give the council information as to the reasons for or ultimate aims of the instructions and policies it was ordered to carry out, and many councillors became deeply suspicious as to what the king's intentions were. This undermining of the confidence of his councillors by not deigning (or daring) to confide in them was one of the reasons why the imposing façade of the power of Charles' Scots council collapsed so quickly once it was challenged in 1637. 'Among the lay councillors in Scotland . . . it is doubtful if a single one knew the king's mind and under-stood his motives'.[35]

Charles' secretiveness was naturally resented by the Scots nobles who believed that their rank entitled them to a greater share in the government of the kingdom. Many of course had seats on the council and indeed Charles increased the number who had when in 1626 he reconstructed it. The privy council that he inherited from his father contained nineteen nobles and eldest sons of nobles who did not hold office, whereas the councils Charles appointed in

1626 and 1631 each had twenty-seven such members out of totals of forty-seven and forty-six respectively.[36] But membership of the council did not give the nobles what they wanted, opportunities to advise the king and assist in policy-making. Consequently few of the non-office-holding nobles attended council regularly, they 'did not respond to the king's invitation to resume active participation and the reconstructed council of 1626 often found it difficult to form a quorum'.[37] The nobles had little interest in helping to execute orders from Whitehall on which they could have little influence and which the king seldom bothered to explain to them. Charles has been criticised for omitting from his council 'too many of the Scots lords who felt that they had a right to sit on it',[38] such as the Earl of Montrose; but, as we have seen, over half the council already consisted of nobles who were not officers of state. By contrast the English council could muster only three peers not holding office out of thirty members in 1625, and five out of forty-two in 1630.[39] Therefore, as few of the Scottish nobles attended the meetings of the council regularly, the king may be forgiven for seeing little point in adding more of them to it, especially as the Scots council was already larger than the English. There is no reason to suppose that any of the nobles who joined the opposition to the king in 1637 would have been prevented or much discouraged from doing so by membership of the council; indeed many of those who were members did oppose him.

The real criticism of Charles' policy as to the part of the nobility in his regime was that, on or off the council, few of them were encouraged to feel that they had an important part to play in government or that their interests were respected by the regime. The king could have responded to the lack of interest of the nobles in his council by making it more attractive to them. This could have been done by taking the trouble to explain his policies to it and giving it more discretion, or by encouraging them to take part in the government in other ways. Such a policy would have been difficult, and perhaps dangerous; no king remembering the powers of the Scots nobles before 1603 could be entirely happy at the idea of giving them more power and influence. But it would probably have been less dangerous in the long run than to let many of them feel that they were not given the place in the regime that was their due, and to lose all sense of identity with the king's government.

It was not only to the nobles that the rule of Charles I from England seemed alien, imposed from afar and taking no account of Scots opinions. In 1640 Charles' ambassador in Paris was to note 'The Scots have never come much to me: they take me, I thinke, to be Ambassador of the King of England only',[40] and in many other ways Charles seemed to his Scots subjects to be primarily king of England—and, moreover, to be determined to change Scotland's place in Great Britain from 'North Britain' to 'North England', so many of his innovations in Scotland were based on English practice. 'The best policy he could devise for Scotland was to make it as like his ideal of England as was possible.'[41] This led many in Scotland to believe that the king's Scottish policies were unduly influenced by his English advisers. In fact both James VI and Charles I were very careful to see that the English council did not discuss Scots affairs, not out of any scrupulous regard for Scots independence, but to keep control of Scots affairs in their own hands and prevent any increase in the English council's powers and competence. This was reasonable, but James and his son unwisely went further; not only was the English council not consulted about Scots affairs, but the king refused even to inform it of what his policies were in Scotland or what was happening there. Viscount Wentworth later complained 'I never was much in Love with the way of King James his keeping of all the Affairs of that Kingdom of Scotland amongst those of that Nation, but carried indeed as a Mystery to all the council of England; a Rull but over much kept by our Master also', and claimed that the troubles in Scotland might have been prevented if the English council had had knowledge of Scots affairs.[42] Of course Charles did discuss Scotland with a few of his most trusted English advisers, especially and fatally with William Laud (Archbishop of Canterbury, 1633), but the king's secretiveness and insistence that his English right hand should not know what his Scottish left hand was doing proved a great weakness; the disturbances in Scotland in 1637 came as a surprise to his English councillors,[43] and many of them feared that the king's reluctance to inform them of events hid designs and policies that he dared not reveal.

In 1626 Charles made a number of changes in the administrative machinery and courts of Scotland. Most of these reforms were justifiable, but introducing them all at more or less the same time, after only a minimum of consultation with those concerned, and with little attempt to justify or explain them, led to their arousing much opposition that could have been avoided with a little care and forethought.

The main change was the separation in membership of the court of session (the central civil court) and the privy council; all ordinary lords of sessions were removed from the council, and for the future it was ruled that none of the ordinary lords of session should be nobles. In theory this was reasonable; the councillors would be able to concentrate on the work of the council, the lords of session on their judicial duties, and the influence of the nobles on the court of session would be reduced. But those who were removed from the council or court of session naturally resented the changes, and though the session would no longer be burdened with nobles with little knowledge of the law, the council was deprived of the experience and learning of lords of session who had been among the most regular attenders of council meetings.[44]

Another of the changes planned by the king also affected the council; he ordered the establishment of a council of war, perhaps to bring Scotland into line with England, where such a council had first been appointed in 1621 as a small body of experts and members of the privy council with whom the king could discuss information and plans concerning war which were too secret to be confided to the full privy council.[45] The idea of having such a body in Scotland was greeted with deep suspicion, especially by the nobility who evidently feared that the king intended to use a small council of war made up of men dependent on him to supersede in part the privy council; a majority of the privy council were nobles, while only six of the seventeen councillors of war were.[46] If this had in fact been the king's intention he soon abandoned it, for the Scots council of war confined itself to overseeing routine preparations for war and was never more than a subcommittee of the privy council. It continued to meet occasionally for several years but then, being a novelty, it very properly 'evanished', as Sir James Balfour noted with satisfaction.[47]

Balfour is less correct in calling another of Charles' commissions a 'new iudicatorey' and novelty; this was the commission for grievances,[48] of which Balfour claimed 'the wyssest and best sighted not onlie fearid, bot did see that this new commissional courte was nothing els bot the starchamber courte of England under ane other name, come doune heir to play the tyrant'.[49] In fact James VI had appointed such a commission in 1623,[50] but it probably was true that both monarchs intended the commission to develop into a Scottish star chamber, a prerogative court for checking abuses and corruption among the powerful which could also be used to suppress any opposition to the crown. The star chamber's ecclesiastical counterpart in England, the court of high commission, had already been introduced to Scotland, and the nobility were determined that a star chamber should not be permanently established in Scotland. In the face of their opposition Charles gave way and the commission never met. The king's creation of a new officer of state, the president of the council, also met with opposition. One earl refused to accept appointment to the office and another denied the king's right to create new officers of state (an opinion which the king called seditious). The king insisted on his right but, as with the council of war, having introduced an innovation in spite of opposition the king soon abandoned it; when the president of the council was dismissed from office in 1633 no new president was appointed.[51] A new commission of exchequer issued in 1626 also contained innovations in that it appointed a permanent exchequer,[52] whereas previously it had been normal to appoint commissioners separately each year, though experiments had been made with a permanent exchequer in the later sixteenth century.

In spite of all the opposition the king aroused in making these administrative reforms, most of them were soon accepted. But what continued to rankle was the way in which the king had introduced them, with little consultation of those concerned or regard for tradition. Scottish suspicion of anything that could be classified as an 'innovation' might be very exasperating to the impatient young king, but a wiser man would have taken more account of it. After the changes listed above, all introduced in 1626, Charles made few alterations in the administrative machinery, and most of the attention he gave to Scottish affairs in the next ten years was focused on his act of revocation and his religious policies.

THE REVOCATION

As the result of the long series of royal minorities in previous centuries it had become accepted that between the age of twenty-one and the end of his twenty-fifth year the king might pass an act of revocation, revoking grants and gifts of royal property made to nobles and others during his minority. Charles decided on a far more sweeping revocation which would revoke all gifts of both royal and kirk property to subjects made since 1540, whether or not made during royal minorities. The amount of property this involved was huge. Former kirk property now held by laymen and property still remaining to the kirk was responsible for paying half of taxations raised by parliament, which suggests that something approaching half of the income derived from land in Scotland came from such property. The great majority of this was in the hands of laymen and fell within the scope of the revocation. Thus if carried out in full Charles' act would have brought about revolutionary changes in landholding throughout Scotland, mainly at the expense of the nobility. Yet, as we shall see, the king's intentions were really comparatively moderate; much of the land concerned was to be confirmed in lay hands, and compensation was to be given for that surrendered to the crown. But he failed to make this clear from the start; he introduced and carried through the revocation without adequate consultation with those most concerned, and insisted that they declare their willingness to surrender completely their property to the crown though he had no intention of taking full advantage of such surrenders. He seems to have done this simply as a demonstration of his power, to begin his reign in a way that would show his determination to exact obedience from his subjects in all things. He probably believed that a moderate settlement following on the sweeping surrenders of property rights would bring him the gratitude of those concerned. Instead the act brought him the lasting distrust of most of his Scots tenants in chief. A revocation was bound to be unpopular with those who had benefited from the gifts being revoked, but the tactless way in which Charles carried it through, without quieting the fears of those whose estates seemed threatened, greatly increased the strength of opposition. Admittedly there was a very good reason for the original act being introduced with haste and without consultation; Charles came to the throne in March 1625 and had to introduce his revocation by the following November, for he would then reach the age of twenty-five and thus lose the right to pass such an act. But having hurriedly introduced the act in October 1625 there was no reason why he should not have taken time to explain his intentions and still fears raised by his action.

What did the king hope to gain by his revocation? First, a settlement of the confused matter of the teinds (tithes), and the establishment of machinery for making greater provision for the clergy out of them, as well as bringing some financial benefit to the crown. Second, the reduction of the power and influence of the nobles and other great landowners over lesser men through the possession of hereditary offices, of tithes, and of feudal superiorities of former crown and church lands. Third, he hoped that such changes would increase his revenue in Scotland and changes were to be made in the terms on which some lands were held of the crown. A summary of the final settlement of the revocation, as ratified by parliament in 1633, will make it clear how the king hoped to achieve these objectives.[53]

First, the teinds. These were of course the tenth parts of the produce of the land which were supposed to be devoted to the support of the clergy; responsibility for paying them rested with the heritor or life-renter; that is, with those who possessed their land hereditarily or for life. The right to collect the great majority of teinds was no longer held by the clergy, having fallen into the hands of landowners, known in this capacity as the titulars of teinds. Only a small part of the teinds went directly to the ministers, and the payments they received from the titulars as part of their stipends represented only a small fraction of the total value of the teinds collected by the titulars. The right to collect teinds from a given piece of land had thus become a form of property in the land, often separate from its ownership, which could be bought, sold or leased. Actual collection of the tenth of each crop was carried out by the agents of the titulars or, where the titular had leased out collection, to the tacksman (leaseholder) of teinds. Collection led to endless petty dispute and disorder throughout the country; to have to pay teinds to a minister was seldom popular; to have to pay them to a titular or tacksman who performed no religious function was often bitterly resented. Ownership of the teinds and the amount due was often disputed, and the right of collection gave the titulars many opportunities to exercise petty tyranny and undue influence over heritors and life-renters, especially if the landlord and the titular of teinds were the same person.

As to the matter of making adequate provision for the ministry out of the teinds, commissions set up by James VI had already had much success in this, making settlements parish by parish which increased payments due from titulars to ministers. Indeed it was one of Scotland's prides that, though a much poorer country than England, her parish clergy were on the whole much better paid than their English counterparts.[54] But Charles determined on a general settlement of the teinds instead of continuing in this piece-meal fashion. The revocation decreed that all teinds were to be valued; they were to be reduced to a fixed sum in money or grain due from each piece of land instead of being a proportion of the crop. The principle was laid down that 'each man should have his own teinds', that is, each heritor should have the right to the teinds for his own land. In order to bring this about, after the teinds of a parish had been valued the heritor or life-renter would have the right to buy his own teinds from his titular at nine years' purchase (nine times their annual value). There were to be two exceptions to this rule. First, the part of the teinds due to the minister as part of his stipend would still be payable to him; how much this should be would be fixed by the commissioners of teinds, who had the right to allocate a stipend and review it from time to time in order to check its adequacy. Secondly, an annuity of 6 per cent of the value of teinds was to be payable to the crown.

The settlement of the teind question was one of Charles' most farsighted and lasting achievements; the machinery for settling stipends and valuing teinds lasted with little alteration until the twentieth century. But at the time it was inevitable that this settlement should be bitterly opposed by those whose vested interests were threatened. Certainly the titulars would receive payment for the teinds they gave up, but there was no compensation for their simultaneous loss of power and influence over those whose titulars they had been, for their loss of prestige. Superficially those who stood to gain most by the settlement were the clergy. Yet some of the most determined opposition came from the bishops, on whose subserviency the king could normally rely, and they probably had the support of many ministers. This seeming paradox is easily resolved; since the Reformation the reformed kirk had kept in view the ultimate goal of having all teinds restored to kirk use. In view of the strength of the lay vested interests involved this was unrealistic, but while no final settlement of the teind problem was reached the clergy could still dream of an ultimate restoration of all teinds. Charles' settlement confirming most teinds in lay hands might make provision for increasing stipends, but it made achievement of such an ultimate ambition impossible. The bishops would have preferred to continue having two birds in the bush but instead were given one in the hand. Moreover, that the king himself should benefit financially from the settlement (through his annuity of teinds) was disillusioning to those of the clergy who had looked to him to uphold the kirk's right to its former property.

For similar reasons the bishops were also in agreement with the nobility in opposing the act of revocation's settlement of the question of other kirk property alienated to laymen, though of course their motives for opposition were very different; the nobles feared the settlement because it increased royal power at their expense, the bishops because it was the crown and not the kirk which was to benefit.

By 1625 nearly all the land which had formerly been owned by the church had passed into lay hands. The process had begun before the Reformation and had accelerated after it. Many of those who benefited most had had their lands erected by the crown into temporal lordships. These lords of erection had feued out much of their new land, but though thus alienating the actual possession of their lands the lords had retained feudal superiority over them. The feuars were their vassals, and by their feu charters they often owed various obligations as well as the annual feu duty to the grantor. A considerable part of the power and influence of many nobles thus rested on their position as superiors of former church and crown lands. By the revocation Charles cancelled the grants of these lands to the lords of erection. The lords were to be allowed to retain (in return for feu duties payable to the crown) possession of those parts of the lands that they had not feued out. But they were to give up to the crown possession of feudal superiority over the lands they had feued out. In future the feuars of these lands would be directly dependent on the crown, to whom they would pay their feu duties. For the loss of these duties the lords of erection would be compensated by the crown at ten years' purchase. But, as with the teinds, there was to be no compensation for the loss of the more intangible benefits which the feudal superiorities had brought the lords. Influence over a large class of landholders was to be transferred from nobility to the crown. The nobles were forced to accept this, but they did so grudgingly and never forgot or forgave the king's action.

The third main change brought about by the revocation was that it gave the king the right to revoke grants of hereditary offices and pensions. Reduction of hereditary offices had already been begun by James VI, and Charles now took general power to revoke such grants. Again compensation was offered, but again this took no account of the loss of power involved for those who surrendered office. Finally the revocation provided for changes in tenure of many lands held of the crown. Most land had originally been held by the tenure of 'ward and relief', the traditional feudal tenure whereby land was held in return for military service and a variety of 'casualties' or occasional payments. But many had persuaded previous monarchs to change their tenure, either to 'taxed ward' whereby the casualties were commuted for a fixed money payment, or to 'blench', involving a nominal annual payment for the land. These changes were damaging to crown finances and the king now claimed the right to return such tenures to the old ward and relief.

It is a measure of Charles' incompetence as a politician that he received no gratitude for the revocation even from those who stood to benefit by it. It appears never to have occurred to him that if he were to implement a revocation that entailed an attack on the political power of the nobility, he would be well advised first to make sure of the firm support of other powerful interest groups in the country. The clergy would benefit by increased stipends, but Charles saw no need to emphasise this to them or to try to ensure that they would agree to the settlement. Lesser landholders, it was thought, would gain by the decrease of the power of the nobility over them as titulars of teinds and feudal superiors, and Charles expected their support; but he made little attempt to win such aid or to ensure that he had it before acting. Therefore most of the lesser men, whose gratitude Charles had expected, joined in opposing the revocation, deeply disturbed by the attack on property rights which it involved. From first to last over his revocation the king conjured up far more opposition and suspicion than was necessary by failing to explain what he was trying to do or to reassure those who thought his actions high-handed. As in implementing some of his other policies, Charles seems to have assumed that as he had the right to demand obedience from his subjects, there was no need to explain his actions or make obedience pleasant. Moreover, though he had won recognition of his right to buy for the crown superiorities of kirklands and hereditary offices, he was in no position to take full advantage of this right, nor was ever likely to be. For implementation of these parts of the revocation required very large capital expenditure by the crown in payment of compensation, and such capital was not available. Thus to a large extent Charles earned himself the bitter resentment of the nobility, by insisting on the principle of revocation, without having the resources to put these principles into practice and thus benefit from them. A few superiorities were purchased, a few hereditary sheriffs bought out, but this did little to outweigh having created mistrust and 'induced a sense of insecurity in nearly every landholder in Scotland'.[55] The whole bungled affair of the revocation 'in effecte was the ground stone of all the mischeiffe that folloued after, both to this Kinges gouerniment and family; and whoeuer wer the contriuers of it, deserue they and all ther posterity to be reputted, by thir three kingdomes, infamous and accursed for euer', for it led to 'the alienatione of the subiects hartes from ther prince, and layed opin a way to rebellion'.[56] And the main contriver of this fatal policy had in fact been the king himself.

Charles failed through the revocation to gain the support of lairds and lesser men against the nobility. He also failed to persuade the lairds to support his policies by offering them a larger share in governing the country than previously. He had removed 'the nobilitie and officers of estate from the places of the session advancing thereto only the gentry',[57] and lairds had formed the majority of his council of war. Charles continued his father's policy of appointing justices of the peace and sheriffs drawn mainly from the gentry.[58] But though some lairds were no doubt flattered at being given a part to play in the government that they had not played before, it was obvious that the king's main interest was in increasing his own powers and that he was more concerned to limit the powers of the nobility than to advance the lairds. It did not take an over-suspicious mind to suspect that once the king had emasculated the nobility to his satisfaction he would have little time for any pretensions that the lairds might have to any real power in government.

The revocation failed to bring about any significant improvement in the king's financial situation. Gifts of royal property had reduced ordinary crown revenue to less than £16,500 sterling per annum by the early years of Charles' reign, an amount totally inadequate to pay for the administration of the country (even though the union of the crowns had freed those revenues of the burden of supporting a resident royal court), as pensions alone almost equalled ordinary revenue. Extraordinary taxation, agreed by parliament, had become regular to supplement ordinary revenue,[59] but such taxes led to much discontent, as the old belief that a king should be able to live on his ordinary revenues except in emergencies died hard. The extraordinary taxes were therefore 'regarded as extortionate, and . . . had a serious influence on the outbreak of the rebellion'.[60] The king's religious policies were the main cause of complaint in the parliament of 1633 but dislike of extraordinary taxes was joined with religion as one of the chief grievances.[61] Suspicions were also aroused by the king's efforts to increase his ordinary revenues. Increases in the impost of wines and in most customs duties caused resentment not simply because they were increases but because they were imposed without the consent of parliament or the convention of estates, which had come to be regarded as necessary for such increases. However, Charles did not need to resort in Scotland to extra-parliamentary taxation as he did in England, for in Scotland he was never without taxes agreed by parliament.[62]

RELIGIOUS POLICIES AND THE GROWTH OF OPPOSITION

The most important of all the king's policies in alienating the trust and support of his subjects were his innovations in the liturgy and discipline of the church; mistrust and anger at the act of revocation was mainly confined to the landowning classes, whereas the religious changes affected the whole population. The Church of Scotland in 1625–37 had many merits. Pluralism and non-residence among ministers were virtually unknown, while in England they were still common.[63] Stipends were often inadequate, but they compared favourably with those of England. The average Scottish minister was probably also better educated and more conscientious than his English counterpart. But in the king's eyes the Church of Scotland was greatly inferior to the Anglican church, for it lacked a proper liturgy, its worship proper ceremony and ritual, its bishops a suitably exalted status.

Rather surprisingly, considering his later impatience, Charles at first followed his father in not insisting on absolute obedience to the Five Articles of Perth. In 1626 he instructed the Scottish bishops that ministers who had been ordained before the introduction of the Articles and had refused to obey them, 'especially that concerning geniculation' (kneeling to receive the elements at communion), might be allowed to ignore the Articles for 'a tyme till they be better resouled',[64] though he did attempt to make the Edinburgh ministers kneel at communion.[65] It is possible that the delay by the king in enforcing the Articles or introducing further innovations was connected with the difficulties he had in the early years of his reign with parliament in England and over the revocation in Scotland; he had little time to devote to religious reforms and the Scottish bishops had no wish to take any initiative in introducing changes for which few of them saw any need.

Charles first turned his attention to liturgical reform in Scotland in 1629, but while Laud urged the king to introduce the English prayer book to Scotland without alteration most of the Scots bishops had grave doubts as to the wisdom of this. The king inclined to agree with Laud but, faced with the reluctance of the Scots hierarchy, he delayed deciding the matter for several years; it was not until 1634 that he ordered the Scottish bishops to suggest alterations that should be made to the English prayer book before it was imposed in Scotland. This action was probably the result of the king's visit to Scotland the previous year. He had met with more opposition than he expected and his reaction to this (unlike his father's) was a strengthening of his determination that Scotland should have a new liturgy. While in Scotland he had used the English prayer book and ceremonies for his own worship and that of his court. He had insisted on acts being passed in parliament acknowledging his right to dictate the apparel of churchmen and ratifying all former acts concerning religion.[66] A petition of some ministers to the king and parliament outlining the grievances of the kirk was read by the king but then suppressed and ignored.[67]

A supplication was drawn up in name of members of parliament concerning religious and other grievances but was not presented to Charles, since he made it clear that such action would earn his displeasure. The following year, however, it was brought to his notice, and Lord Balmerino was arrested after a copy (with alterations by him) was found in his possession. Balmerino was tried for lease-making (slandering the king or his council) and sentenced to death—though he was found guilty only on the least important charges against him, and that only on the casting vote of the Earl of Traquair (the treasurer depute) as foreman of the jury. Balmerino was eventually pardoned by the king, in November 1636,[68] the whole object of the trial having been to terrify opposition into silence. But opinion in Scotland was deeply disturbed by the injustice of the verdict. So staunch a royalist as William Drummond of Hawthornden, the poet, was shocked into protest at the prosecution of Balmerino, even though he had no sympathy with the supplication that had caused the trouble.[69] If the act of revocation had made many Scots fear for the safety of their property, the condemnation of Balmerino made them fear for their lives. If possession of a copy of a supplication to the king was regarded as treason, then it might be concluded that united and direct opposition to the king was the only policy possible other than complete submission to the royal will.

It was well known in Scotland that a new liturgy was being prepared and there were rumours of even greater changes to come. It was said that the king intended to appoint abbots to the pre-Reformation abbeys who would have seats in parliament[70] and join with the bishops in ensuring its obedience to the king. Rumours circulated that the powers of the court of high commission were to be greatly increased to ensure submission to the king and bishops.[71] In doctrine Arminian ideas were being adopted by many of the younger bishops and their supporters (mainly under English influence) and this seemed to have official approval. Samuel Rutherford's banishment to Aberdeen was the result of his publishing a work in Amsterdam attacking Arminianism as well as of his opposition to the Five Articles of Perth.[72] Fears that Arminian tendencies were undermining strict Calvinist predestination may have been exaggerated (as in England)[73]—'Arminian' tended to become a loosely used term of abuse for all religious trends which were disliked—but the fear was nonetheless real and influential.

Yet the covenant or federal theology which predominated among those opposed to Arminianism could also undermine predestination. God's covenants could be interpreted as conditional contracts requiring some positive reaction from man as the price of salvation. However, whether or not interpreted in this way, the federal theology with its emphasis on God's gift of grace and the response it deserved from man in life and action was to prove of great power in justifying men in opposing the king. Further developments in covenant ideas which led to Scotland being seen as a nation enjoying a special relationship with God, to the Scots being seen as a chosen people, successors to the Israelites, gave men confidence that resistance could succeed, however unlikely this might seem in worldly terms.[74]

To many Scots the king's efforts to reform the kirk and bring it into line with the Church of England added up to a policy leading eventually to a return to Catholicism. Even some Scottish Catholics believed this and looked forward to the restoration of their religion in the near future.[75] Rumour inconsistently credited Charles with attempting to reconcile the kirk to both the Lutherans and popery.[76] The atmosphere in which the king's secretive bungling could lead to widespread acceptance of such extravagant rumours was provided by events on the Continent. The Thirty Years War, seen simply as a contest between Protestantism and Catholicism, the forces of good and evil, strongly influenced opinions in Scotland. Stories of Catholic persecution and atrocities, of how by force and by guile popery was seeking to subvert true religion, encouraged hatred and superstitious dread of Catholicism in Scotland. Many in Scotland as in England thought it shameful that Charles had failed to intervene in the war to support the Protestant cause, and feared that he secretly designed to lead the kirk to Rome. In retrospect this may seem absurd, but Charles' handling of religious policy in Scotland made it seem all too likely at the time.

A new book of canons imposed by the king on the church in January 1636 added to fears of his ultimate intentions. Mainly concerning the behaviour and conduct of ministers, the canons embodied the Five Articles of Perth. Many of the new canons were bound to offend Scots susceptibilities, being based on the English canons of 1604. General assemblies, presbyteries and kirk sessions were nowhere mentioned by name—did this mean that the king intended to abolish them? No minister or reader was to 'be permitted to conceive prayers *extempore*';[77] the church which 'had once claimed to overrule at almost every turn the policy of the state, was now reduced to praying only in the words prescribed to it by the King',[78] but the new liturgy from which the prayers were to be read was not completed for more than a year after the introduction of the canons, so it was impossible to obey this order. Perhaps the most sinister of the canons as an indication of what might be expected from the king in the future was that which laid down that no minister should be allowed to preach in a parish other than his own without a licence from his bishop.[79] This order —paraphrased by John Row as 'Christ's minister may not preach Christ's trueth, if a loun minister neare by him have taught lies, except the Bishop give him leave so to doe'[80]—is the first sign of licensing of preachers in Scotland. In England since the time of Elizabeth preaching had been strictly controlled and only a minority of ministers, men of known loyalty to official religious policy and the crown, were licensed to preach. These restrictions on preaching in England had been intensified under Charles I; his puritan opponents claimed that a minister who did not preach was no true minister, an opinion which would have been generally accepted in Scotland. The canon suggests that if the king had his way preaching would eventually be similarly restricted in Scotland —it was well known that the bishops, the 'unpreaching prelats',[81] held 'that there was too much preaching in the land'.[82]

In October 1636 the king ordered the Scottish privy council to issue a proclamation commanding use of a new prayer book, which was then nearly completed after two years of consultations between the king, the Scottish bishops and Laud. Though based on the English prayer book it contained many alterations in what the king did not consider essentials designed to make the book more acceptable to Scottish opinion, mainly inspired by the Scottish bishops. Considering these changes, 'it might have seemed a proper deduction that by far the greater part of the book of 1637, and almost all the parts of it in regular use, would be reasonably acceptable, provided—and it is an important qualification—that the merits of the book received serious attention'.[83] Its merits never did receive such attention; 'Had the book been immaculate in its kind, had it been the work of a joint-committee of Cherubim and Seraphim, it would not have been accepted in Scotland.'[84] The way the book had been compiled, with much bustling of bishops to and from London and with the advice of Laud, but without consulting any Scots laymen or the ministers, prejudiced the Scots against it in advance. So did the way it was imposed, by royal prerogative alone (like the canons). But most important of all in ensuring that the merits of the book never got a fair hearing was the fact that it was taken as symbolic of the whole religious policy of the king and his father. It might not in itself contain anything warranting rebellion, but as the latest in a long series of changes and innovations in the 'creeping episcopalianism of the Stuarts'[85] it was deliberately chosen by those most opposed to royal policy as an issue on which to make a stand. The fact that many of those who protested at the prayer book had never read or even seen it is thus no evidence that their opposition concealed non-religious and less worthy motives than they pretended. Knowing that their king would never rest content until he had by piecemeal innovations brought the Church of Scotland into conformity with the Church of England—or even that of Rome as many feared—they found in the prayer book, tactlessly imposed before mistrust generated by the introduction of the book of canons had subsided, an issue which would unite most of the country.

Yet in spite of all the religious innovations thrust on a reluctant ministry, the scope of the grievances expressed by most of the ministers in 1637 (or at least of those which they felt were sufficiently serious to demand action) was very limited. They wanted the new liturgy withdrawn, and perhaps the canons as well, and the secular powers of the bishops limited. As events were to prove, even long after the first resistance to the liturgy had appeared, most ministers would have been content to retain episcopacy and even the Five Articles of Perth. They wanted reform, not revolution; 'Bishopes I love; but pride, greid, luxurie, oppression, immersion in saicular affaires, was the bane of the Romish Prelats, and can not have long good sucess in the Reformit'.[86] But the king's failure to make any concessions or alternatively to suppress the opposition to the liturgy before it became widespread played into the hands of the extremists—ministers and laymen—who were prepared for revolution.

How much demand there was in Scotland before the troubles for constitutional changes is hard to say. Certainly there was some, especially after the 1633 parliament when it had been clearly seen how the king dominated parliament through the bishops, and that he recognised no right to vote or petition against his policies. But it is going too far to deduce the existence (and by implication, the extent) of constitutional discontent before 1637 from the constitutional revolution carried out in 1640–1,[87] for much that was done in 1640–1 was done to safeguard concessions won from the king which it was believed that he would go back on unless he was restrained by constitutional reforms which would have been virtually unthinkable in 1637 and before. The revolutions in both Scotland and England began with demands for changes in royal policies, which led to demands that advisers responsible for the former policies should be replaced, and ultimately to demands for control by parliament of policy and officials; the demands widened as distrust of the king's good faith in maintaining the concessions that he had granted grew, and it is not legitimate to infer the nature of discontent before the troubles from changes made several years after the troubles began. In Scotland in 1637 desire for constitutional changes went no further than desire for the removal of churchmen from secular power, and in particular from their domination of parliament, and a vague desire that parliament should be freer from royal manipulation than that of 1633 had been.

The importance of economic grievances and distress in Scotland in the 1630s is impossible to judge in the absence of any study of the economy in the period. The modest growth of trade and prosperity which had taken place under James VI had, however, probably come to an end. The 1620s and '30s in England saw economic stagnation or decline, and the same is probably true of Scotland. Disastrous harvests in England caused by bad weather have led to 1620–50 being called 'probably among the most terrible years through which the country has ever passed'.[88] Scottish historians are naturally reluctant to rely on English evidence, but bad harvests in the two countries usually coincided. It therefore

Map 1 (above): Scotia Septentrion.

SCOTIA Septentrion.

SEPTENTRIO

DEUCA
Orcades Insule
LEDONIUS

OCEANUS

GERMANICUS OCEANUS

Strathnavernia

Murray fyrth

ROSSIA

Loquhabria

MORavia

Hebrides Insule

Maria

Buquhania

Miliaria Scotica

OCCIDENS · ORIENS

MERIDIES

Page 50 MAPS OF SCOTLAND from William Camden's *Britannia*
(Amsterdam 1639): (*above*) Northern Scotland; (*below*) Southern Scotland

Map 2 (below): Scotia Australis

SEPTENTRIO

ROSSIA

Hebrides
Insule
DEU

CALEDONIUS
OCEANUS

Loquhabria

MORavia

Lorna

Perthia

Germanicum

Marcia

Cliddesdaill

Arren

Mare
Hiberni

Pars Hibernie

Miliaria Scotica

SCOTIA Australis

PARS ANGLIÆ

OCCIDENS · ORIENS

MERIDIES

seems likely that there was a great deal of economic distress in Scotland at this time,[89] and that this may have contributed to popular unrest and willingness to support resistance to the king.

Some causes of discontent were specific to the burghs. There was indignation among them, for example, at patents and monopolies granted by the king, though this was not nearly so vocal as in England, and the extraordinary parliamentary taxes on annual rents (interest payments) fell most heavily on the burghs, especially on Edinburgh. The king also heaped other burdens on the capital —building a new parliament house and two new churches, and increasing ministers' stipends.[90] He had no more respect for the burgh's constitution than for other traditional rights and liberties. In 1634 he interfered in the elections of the magistrates and council,[91] and two years later he recommended that in future the burgh be ruled by 'a constant council', annual elections being abandoned as they 'breid inconstancie in government', and that merchant companies be established as in London, because without them 'all persounes indistinctlie run to trade without ordour'.[92] Burgh government was thus to be reformed to make it more amenable to central control. Another minor cause of discontent which mainly affected the burghs was the issuing of copper two-penny pieces or 'turners' by the Earl of Stirling by warrant of the king; far too many of the coins were struck and their value fell sharply.[93]

Thus there was a wide variety of causes of discontent in Scotland in the 1630s, most of them being discontents with the rule of Charles I, centring on his religious policies. All these discontents contributed to some extent to the conception and growth of the troubles which began in 1637. Some of the discontents were common to many regimes—grumbles at high taxation, the mutterings of nobles who feel that they are insufficiently regarded by their king. Others were inherited by Charles from his father—the hatred of the Five Articles of Perth, for example. The failure of Charles I in Scotland lies in the fact that he made all the difficulties facing him, all the discontents of his Scots subjects, far deeper than necessary by his secretiveness, tactlessness and arrogance. He consistently refused to take account of the opinions and feelings of his subjects. Convinced of the rightness of his religious and other

policies, and of his duty to impose them, he would have regarded
it as a betrayal of his trust to change them in the face of opposition
by subjects who had, as he believed, no right to oppose him.

As a man Charles had many attractive qualities; he was deeply
religious, a faithful husband, a great patron of the arts, but he had
few qualities of a good ruler. His religion included belief in his
own divine right, a belief which gave him arrogance as great as
that of his presbyterian opponents who numbered themselves
among the elect. His 'enthusiasm for reforming the Church was
quite as irrational as that of Knox and Melville for establishing
its power'.[94] His insistence on principle in the face of the realities
of politics became at times dangerously like the obstinacy of the
stupid. He had no liking for the sort of routine hard work which
might have given him a better understanding of the many difficulties facing him, and had a tendency to ignore or dismiss as
irrelevant unpleasant facts such as the extent of opposition to him.
He was, as Laud said, 'more willing *not* to hear than to hear'.[95] He
seldom saw the need for tact when introducing innovations; service was the duty of subjects, so he took it for granted. As a king
he was obeyed and even respected, but he was little loved until the
misfortunes which he had done so much to bring on himself made
him pitied. So long as the letters to the privy council by which he
ruled were obeyed, he ignored or did not see the growing resentment in Scotland at his policies, the many grievances which would
require little encouragement to unite in opposition to him.

It has been remarked that the whole experience of the seventeenth century in Scotland shows 'that ecclesiastical issues alone,
and ministers and their followers alone, could never bring about a
revolution'.[96] James VI had worked to ensure that the interests of
the nobility and of the ministers, two of the strongest interests in
the country, did not coincide. Charles never realised the necessity
for this, and his act of revocation and the settlement that followed
it proved 'decisive in convincing the Scottish aristocracy of the
virtues of presbyterianism, to which they had hitherto been sin-
gularly blind'.[97] As in England a few years later (and in the Calvinist risings in France and the Netherlands in the sixteenth
century), revolt based on religious and other grievances gained

power to shake the throne only through the support of the nobility.[98] If the Scots nobles had remained loyal to the crown, hatred of Charles' religious innovations among the ministers and their lay supporters might have led to disturbance and disorder, but not to the revolution which in fact took place in 1637–41.

An indication of how little Charles expected that the introduction of the new prayer book would cause a crisis in Scotland is that he made no attempt to prepare his administration to deal with opposition. After the administrative changes he had made in 1626 he had lost interest in such matters. Since he required little more of his servants in Scotland than that they should obey his orders without question, able men were deterred from entering his service. No judge of men, Charles employed men of little ability or spirit, and never allowed them much initiative. Of the officers of state the Earl of Traquair, promoted from treasurer depute to treasurer in 1636, was by far the most prominent. It was said that he 'now guides our Scotts affairs with the most absolute sovereigntie that any subject among us this fourtie yeares did kyth', and he was expected by the bishops to enforce conformity to the king's wishes with 'horrible fynes'.[99] Traquair worked hard, and with some success, to increase the king's revenues and carry out his orders, perhaps seeing himself as the exponent of 'thorough' in Scotland. But he had no more liking than most of the other Scots nobles for bishops, and it never seems to have occurred to him how important religious policy was to the king, or how dangerous these policies were. Moreover through his defects of character he did the king more harm than good. Quick-tempered, tactless and arrogant, he seems positively to have enjoyed creating alarm as to the king's intentions by dropping dark hints, and to have exaggerated the extent to which he was in the king's confidence.[100] His squabbles with the Bishop of Ross (who had been his rival for the office of treasurer) weakened the administration. He enjoyed lording it over the king's other servants; the chancellor, the Archbishop of St Andrews, was said to be terrified of him.[101] Over seventy years old, unhappy at the king's religious innovations, and little interested in affairs of state, the archbishop was no more than a cipher though he held the highest offices both in church and state. The one officer of state who was resident at court, the secretary, was little better; the old and insolvent Earl of Stirling was 'little esteemed in the Court, and not at all employed in Affairs, except in matters of course'.[102]

The keeper of the privy seal, the Earl of Haddington, had long lived in virtual retirement and died in May 1637 (being replaced by the Earl of Roxburgh). All these three, chancellor, secretary and keeper, had risen to eminence under James VI and had been continued in office or promoted by Charles though he knew that they did not support his religious or other policies with any enthusiasm. They well illustrate the justice of C. V. Wedgwood's remark that 'the position of several of King Charles's ministers, both in Scotland and in England, was not only unprecedented but unique in the history of the British Isles. Their advice and opinions were systematically overruled or disregarded by the king, but he kept them in his council and expected them loyally to support and carry out his policy.'[103] Sir Thomas Hope of Craighall, the king's advocate, was another official who had little sympathy with the king's religious policy. Though he had taken a leading part in drawing up the act of revocation and in prosecuting Lord Balmerino, he was no friend of the bishops and was soon to prove willing to help those opposed to religious innovations. Of all the officers of state Sir John Hay, the clerk register, was the most consistent supporter of the king's policies and the bishops; he was said to have proposed executing Lord Balmerino after his trial without consulting the king. Closely associated with Hay was Sir Robert Spottiswood, president of the court of session and son of the chancellor. Of the other officers of state, Sir James Galloway (master of requests) supported the king's policies but had little influence. Sir James Carmichael (treasurer depute), and Sir John Hamilton of Orbiston (justice clerk) both seem to have been moderate men anxious to avoid trouble, supporting neither the king nor his opponents with any vigour when the troubles began.

It took little ability on Traquair's part to dominate the council and officers of state. He seems to have made poor use of his pre-eminence except in satisfying his own vanity, by boasting of his own powers and influence with the king. Instead of allaying fears as to the king's intentions he aroused them. To a council already weak and irresolute, lacking the king's confidence and increasingly divided between supporters and opponents of the bishops, he added confusion.

Not surprisingly there are signs of administrative decay in the years immediately preceding the troubles. Close scrutiny of the roll of sheriffs to be appointed each year, a feature of the earlier years of the reign, ceases after 1635.[104] In 1636 the privy council complained that many of those nominated as justices of the peace 'slights and neglects this service and hes not accepted the charge upon them nor keeps thir Quarter Sessions'[105] (though it may be that in this the situation was no worse than in previous years). The work of the commission for valuation of teinds was suspended by the king in October 1636, restarted in December, and again suspended in July 1637.[106] Far more serious was the state of the Highlands and the Borders. Disorders in these areas had broken out in the last years of James VI's reign. Charles had made little attempt to deal with the problem and disorder had increased steadily, 'a growth of crime which only the preoccupations of an absentee King had rendered possible'.[107]

Thus on the eve of the troubles in Scotland the administration was in no condition to meet the crisis thrust upon it by a king who refused to recognise the difficulties involved in imposing his policies.

CHAPTER TWO

The Prayer Book and the National Covenant, 1636–February 1638

THE ORGANISATION OF RESISTANCE AND THE PRAYER BOOK RIOTS

The organisation of the opposition to Charles I's policies in Scotland before 1637 is hard to trace, but it seems likely that after the 1633 parliament, if not before it, various groups of discontented ministers, lairds, nobles and others met irregularly and informally to lament the state of affairs and discuss remedies, and that some of them had contacts with those opposed to the king in England. Samuel Rutherford's correspondence, for example, shows him to have been in touch with a wide circle of Scots nobles, lairds, burgesses and ministers, many of whom were to be conspicuous supporters of the covenant. The inner rings of this circle comprised the radical party in the kirk. Its exact part in stirring up opposition to the king is obscure but undoubtedly it was a major one, providing through its conventicles a loose underground organisation to co-ordinate the activities of the king's enemies. The radical ministers quickly established themselves after the troubles began as among the most influential men in the kirk, though working in co-operation with more moderate ministers who had objected to conventicle-holding and had previously taken little part in actively opposing the king.

The meetings and discussions of the king's opponents were naturally kept secret (expecially after the trial of Lord Balmerino), and after the troubles began the covenanters on the one hand were anxious to portray the revolt against the prayer book as a spontaneous rising, while on the other hand royalists claimed that the troubles were the result of a secret conspiracy by some nobles for selfish ends, disguised as religious zeal. Thus John Spalding claimed that the malcontents in Scotland and England had signed 'ane clandestyne band' to overthrow the bishops and the royal prerogative in both kingdoms.[1] This was not so, but there seems little reason to doubt the story that the Scots opponents of the bishops had a resident agent in London in the person of Eleazar Borthwick (who had formerly been minister to a Scottish congregation in Sweden), or that Borthwick returned to Scotland in February 1637 with encouraging news for the discontented as to the result of his efforts to gain sympathy and support for them in England.[2] There were also close contacts between Scottish malcontents and radical Scottish ministers who had settled in Ulster, many of them having gone there in the 1620s to avoid the Five Articles of Perth and the supervision of the Scottish bishops. In the 1630s their positions became increasingly difficult. Some of them were deposed and excommunicated, and fled back to Scotland in 1636 and 1637,[3] bringing with them stories of persecution to add to the fears aroused in Scotland by the king's innovations.

The meetings of the discontented grew in frequency after the introduction of the book of canons in January 1636; 'The Puritanes this year, who afterward wes called Covenanters, had some quiet meittings',[4] and lamenting the situation gave way to resolution to make a stand against the next innovation expected, the new prayer book. Organisation of resistance to the new liturgy was given time and a suitable atmosphere in which to develop by prolonged delays and uncertainties in introducing it. On 15 November 1636 the privy council considered a letter from the king ordering the publication and practice of the new prayer book; the council had not yet seen the book and showed no enthusiasm for imposing it. It issued a proclamation that each parish should buy two copies of the book by Easter 1637 but gave no order for using it.[5] A copy of the book was produced for inspection by the council on 24 November, but this cannot have been the version finally approved by the king as printing it was not completed until April 1637.[6] A new proclamation on 20 December renewed the order for each parish to buy copies of the book by Easter and ordered that it should be used, though without specifying when use of it was to begin;[7] it was probably hoped that it would be brought into use gradually as each parish bought copies, the whole country using it by Easter.[8] If this was what was intended it was rendered impossible by the delays in completing the printing of the book. However, two at least of the bishops—Ross and Dunblane—began to use a prayer book before Easter 1637 'that by their example they might beginne the practice, and commend it to others';[9] Ross said in May 1638 that he had used the English prayer book in his cathedral for the previous three years.[10] It had also been in use at the royal chapel at Holyroodhouse and in one of the colleges at St Andrews for several years, and at all the services which the king had attended in Scotland in 1633.[11]

Completely unaware that the innovations that he had already introduced were leading to a crisis, Charles early in 1637 ordered the use of a new translation of the psalms in all churches in Scotland, for no more religious reason than that the translation was partly the work of his father.[12] This piece of pointless meddling must have gone far to convince any Scots who still needed convincing that the king would not rest from his endless innovating until he had changed the Church of Scotland out of all recognition.

Active opposition among ministers to accepting the prayer book had already shown itself. At a meeting of the synod of Edinburgh late in 1636 parts of the book had been read and many objected to them as containing popish errors.[13] Meetings called specifically to decide on the tactics of resistance are first heard of early in 1637, when there were many 'private meetings, and the godly's often speaking one to another . . . in all the corners of the land, but especially in Edinburgh'.[14] At a meeting said to have been held in April 1637 Alexander Henderson (minister of Leuchars) and the radical David Dickson, representing the discontented ministers of Fife and the West respectively, conferred with Lord Balmerino and Sir Thomas Hope of Craighall, the king's advocate, and got their approval in opposing the prayer book. The two ministers then met in a house in the Cowgate with various Edinburgh 'matrons'. It was decided that women should lead the protest when the prayer book was first used in Edinburgh, and that afterwards men would take over the demonstration.[15]

While such secret plans were being made there was also increasing open opposition to the prayer book. When the synod of
Edinburgh met on 31 May, in the Trinity (or College) kirk, the
bishop urged the ministers to receive and use the prayer book, and
he read out parts of the book which had not been available at the
last synod. During this reading several of the ministers walked out
of the meeting and did not return until it was finished. Later seven
ministers refused to receive copies of the book, as it had not been
approved by an assembly of the kirk and contained popish and
other errors. After angrily denouncing these ministers the bishop
agreed that they should be given time to consider whether they
would receive the book or be deprived of their charges.[16] Elsewhere in Scotland in May other synods were held for encouraging
use of the prayer book. At Dunblane the bishop gave ministers
until Michaelmas (29 September) to decide whether or not to
accept it; as the time allowed by the Bishop of Edinburgh was
similar, it would seem that some of the bishops had agreed among
themselves in advance that if they met with opposition they would
put off imposing the book until that date. Meanwhile 'some of the
unconforme pairtie makes it their text daily, to shew the multitude
. . . how that it was nought bot the Mass in English'.[17]

On 6 June 1637 the best-documented of the meetings of ministers opposed to the prayer book took place, evidently in Edinburgh; nine ministers who are named, including Alexander
Henderson and David Dickson, and some others who are not
named, attended and decided that a treatise should be written and
printed against the prayer book. This work was to be completed
by the end of September—the time at which it was then believed
that the book would first be imposed in Edinburgh. Arrangements were made for calling another meeting if necessary, and
arguments to be used against the book were noted. They decided
that 'the weill affected in Edinburgh' should, the first time the
prayer book was read, 'go to the kirk and quhen the service
beginneth to be read all to start up and go foorth, and altymes
thairafter absent thaimself therfrom'.[18] On the same day Dickson
conferred with Archibald Johnston of Wariston (a brilliant
and fanatically religious young lawyer) about 'praeparation for

subsequent tryels'; they met again in Edinburgh a month later and 'advysed about the danger for not receaving the Service book', and on this occasion they were joined by John Livingstone.[19]

The failure of large numbers of ministers to buy prayer books as ordered led the privy council on 13 June to proclaim that letters of horning[20] would be issued against those who failed to buy and use the book since some ministers 'does what in thame lyes to foster and enterteany distractioun and troubles in the Kirk',[21] but the council was content to leave the matter of when the book was to be imposed to the bishops—together with the opprobrium that would inevitably fall on those who imposed it. The king was later to claim that 'no symptoms of any considerable opposition did appeare' to the prayer book before the riots of 23 July,[22] and it is quite possible that he was so out of touch with Scottish affairs that he really believed that this was true. His Scots councillors and bishops knew that to inform him of difficulties and opposition would only bring them his displeasure. He refused to accept the concession made by the bishops who had given their ministers until the autumn to consider the prayer book, and insisted that it be used before then.[23] Therefore the Bishop of Edinburgh ordered intimation to be given in all churches in and near Edinburgh on Sunday, 16 July, that the prayer book would be used in all these churches the following Sunday, 23 July. It was hoped that the successful introduction of the book in Edinburgh would prove a good example to the rest of the country. The court of session's term ended on 31 July and the many judges, lawyers, nobles, lairds and others in Edinburgh on legal business would then return to their homes, spreading (as was intended) news that the new liturgy had been accepted in Edinburgh. Many of the ministers read the intimation on 16 July unwillingly; Andrew Ramsay (Greyfriars) and Patrick Henderson (reader at St Giles) refused to read it.[24]

This warning a week in advance that the prayer book would be used in Edinburgh was (as Archbishop Laud and others afterwards realised)[25] a tactical error; 'The whole body of the Towne murmures and grudges all the week exceedingly; and who can marvell, discourses, declamations, pamphlets, every where against this course; no word of Information, in publick or private, by any to account of, used for the clearing of it.'[26] The week's warning gave those opposed to the new liturgy time to arrange a reception for it which would give the dispersing lawyers and their clients very different news to take home from that which the bishops intended.

It was agreed among the Edinburgh ministers who were willing to read the prayer book that they should all start to read at the same time, the intention being to prevent any who might protest at the liturgy making a nuisance of themselves at more than one kirk, as they might have done if it was read at different times. On the morning of 23 July[27] many members of the privy council, the two archbishops and eight or nine of the bishops, and the lords of session assembled in St Giles with a large congregation. As soon as the dean began to read from the new prayer book those who objected to its use, especially the women, began to shout insults at the bishop and dean 'calling them traitors, belly-gods, and deceivers'. Many got to their feet, throwing stools and protesting, and left the kirk. They continued to riot outside while inside the service continued. When the bishop left the kirk after the service he was pursued and stoned by the mob (the women again taking a leading part). The dean, whom the mob were even more eager to find as having been the actual reader of the 'popish' prayer book, wisely remained in the kirk, shutting himself up in the steeple.[28]

In the Tolbooth kirk (meeting in the partitioned-off west end of St Giles) the liturgy had met with a similar noisy reception, though David Mitchel managed to finish the service.[29] In Greyfriars kirk James Fairlie was forced to give up reading by curses and threats, and like the bishop he was pursued home by a mob of cursing women, 'he also cursing them'.[30] Henry Rollock of the Trinity kirk, who had previously shown more enthusiasm for the prayer book than any other Edinburgh minister, had second thoughts about it. No doubt his known liking for the book had led to his congregation being packed with a particularly enthusiastic band of would-be demonstrators. He 'very wisely, resolved to halt a little' before starting the service, waiting until he heard how the liturgy was being received in the other kirks. When he heard of the tumults he made no attempt to read the prayer book as he had promised, thus disappointing the potential rioters in his audience.[31]

At the afternoon service in St Giles the new liturgy was read without incident, though the kirk was surrounded by mobs of demonstrators; the doors were well guarded but the rioters do not seem to have made any determined attempt to enter. At the end of the service the Bishop of Edinburgh was again attacked and forced to flee to Holyroodhouse in the Earl of Roxburgh's coach, which was stoned all the way there. Whether afternoon services were held in the other Edinburgh kirks and how the prayer book was received in the kirks around Edinburgh in which it was to have been read is uncertain, but the hatred aroused by the book had been made clear in the most important kirks, the very places where the bishops had hoped to demonstrate its peaceful acceptance. This uproar 'in al historie wil be remarqued as the faire, plausible and peacible wealcome the service book receaved in Scotland' noted Wariston with satisfaction.[32]

That the demonstrations in Edinburgh on 23 July were well organised cannot be doubted, nor that Alexander Henderson and David Dickson played a leading part in organising them. They had contacts with the nobles and other laymen who were soon to take over the leadership of the opposition to the liturgy, but these nobles and lairds remained in the background until a 'spontaneous' popular demonstration of religious zeal created a situation in which they could claim to be acting as representatives of widespread opposition which they had not themselves instigated. Exactly as had been agreed at the meetings in April and June preparing opposition to the liturgy, women had taken a leading part in the riots, and the demonstrators had first protested and then left their kirks when the liturgy was read, and had not entered the kirks for the next service. Perhaps the throwing of stools and stones was not premeditated by the organisers, and the demonstration thus more violent than they had intended.

Accounts of the riots state that the women who began them were 'rascal serving women', women of the meaner sort, 'serving maids', and the few women arrested in connection with the riots were servants,[33] but they were probably led by their betters. The women who took part in the meeting in April were described as 'matrons', which is not a word that would be applied to servants, and another account says that women 'of all sorts' participated in the disturbances.[34] The woman later credited with having taken the lead in the demonstration in St Giles, Barbara Hamilton,[35] was the wife of John Mean, the merchant associated with the radical party, who had nearly twenty years of opposition to bishops and ceremonies behind him. The rumour that some of the 'women' were apprentices or other men in disguise[36] seems to be false—it would have been an unnecessary complication, as there was no shortage of women willing to take part.

In reacting to the events of 23 July the privy council showed itself to be divided and irresolute. The chancellor and other bishops wrote to the king in secret, informing him of the riots, without consulting the lay councillors; they laid the blame for the disturbances largely on Traquair, stating that he had failed to take any precautions against trouble and had avoided being in Edinburgh on 23 July. On the other hand when the council, dominated by Traquair and other lay councillors, wrote to the king it blamed the 'imprudent precipitation' of the bishops in imposing the prayer book for the riots. The council seemed more alarmed by what the king's reaction to the riots might be than by the riots themselves—its letter to the king was not sent until 26 July, and in it the seriousness and significance of the riots was minimised.[37] Traquair explained his absence from Edinburgh on the day the prayer book was read by claiming that he had been attending the marriage of a kinsman,[38] but it may well have been that he wished to avoid being associated with its first reading.

The day after the riots the council (meeting at Holyroodhouse lest there be further disturbances in Edinburgh) issued a proclamation forbidding gatherings or meetings that might lead to disturbances, and speaking against the government or prayer book, on pain of death. The burgh of Edinburgh was made responsible for preventing disorders, investigating the riots, and punishing those responsible.[39] The baillies of Edinburgh, anxious to avert the king's wrath, promised to do all that they could to punish the rioters and find men willing to read the prayer book in the kirks,[40] but in practice they did little, doubtless fearing to provoke further disturbances. The Bishop of Edinburgh suspended the ministers who had refused to read the prayer book, and banned all prayers and sermons in the kirks on weekdays.[41] On 29 July, the eve of the first Sunday since the riots, the chancellor and some of the other bishops demonstrated their lack of enthusiasm for the new prayer book and fear of the consequences of imposing it by recommending to the council that no further attempt should be made to read the new liturgy until the king's pleasure was known, and that use of the old form of service according to the book of common order should likewise be forbidden. The council agreed to this, and for several weeks there were no services in Edinburgh except for sermons on Sundays.[42]

PETITIONS AND SUPPLICATIONS

The king's reaction to the news of the riots of 23 July was, predictably, one of cold anger. In a letter which reached the council on 4 August he gave strict orders that those responsible for the disturbances should be tried and punished and that the council should give full support to the bishops. In another letter he instructed the bishops to 'continue as you have begun without any intermission till the work be fully settled'.[43] The council ordered consultations with the burgh council about reintroducing the prayer book, but decided that to have it used again immediately would be unwise and lead to further riots. A committee of councillors was set up to try those who had taken part in or encouraged the riots,[44] but this was little more than a gesture to please the king.

Outside Edinburgh a few bishops (such as Ross and Dunblane) used the prayer book in services and even managed to persuade a few of their ministers to do so,[45] but this was exceptional. They continued to try to make their ministers buy copies of the book, charging them to do so by letters of horning under the privy council proclamation of 13 June.[46] The next round in the campaign against the book therefore took the form of petitions to the council by some of the ministers charged to buy copies, asking that the letters of horning issued against them be suspended, with

letters from nobles and lairds to the council supporting the petitions and denouncing the prayer book. This was organised by
David Dickson. By about 20 August petitions had been procured
from three ministers in Fife (including Alexander Henderson) and
from ministers in the presbyteries of Ayr, Irvine and Glasgow,
together with a number of supporting letters. The letter from the
Earl of Rothes asking the council 'to help keip bak such an un-
sound piece of work' as the prayer book is probably typical of the
letters,[47] and the Fife petition typical of the petitions; it condemns
the prayer book as introduced without warrant of general assembly or parliament, undermining the liberties of the kirk, containing many errors and being an innovation.[48]

The four petitions and the letters were presented to the privy
council on 25 August.[49] The chancellor was strongly opposed to
making any concessions to the petitioners as the council had
received another letter from the king the previous day, again
demanding that the rioters be punished and the prayer book imposed. But the Earl of Southesk and other nobles on the council
argued that although the petitions were few in number 'a great
many of the best of the countrey resented' the imposition of the
book.[50] The council compromised by making a concession to the
petitioners without admitting that it was doing so; it declared that
the proclamation of 13 June under which the letters of horning
had been issued against the petitioners only enforced the buying
of the prayer book, not the use of it.[51]

In order to explain the necessity of this concession and excuse
the failure to impose the new liturgy the council now decided that
it must tell the king the truth about how widespread opposition to
the book really was. It therefore wrote explaining that it was faced
by 'the clamor and feares of your Maiesties subiects, from diuersse
pairts and corners of the kingdome'; there was a 'generall grudge
and murmur of all sortes of people' against the book, which the
council did not dare to impose. He was begged to summon some
of his councillors and bishops to him to explain the situation, and
the council arranged to meet again on 20 September to hear his
answer.[52] As Traquair explained to the Marquis of Hamilton, 'we
durst no longer forbear to acquaint his Majesty' with the extent

of the opposition (Traquair seems to have regarded telling the king the truth as a last resort only to be used when all else had failed). He asked Hamilton to try to see that, if the king did summon some of the bishops to consult with him, those chosen should be moderate men, as some of the bishops 'are so violent and forward . . . that their want of right understanding how to compass business of this nature and weight, does often breed us many difficulties'.[53]

When the news that the council would meet on 20 September to receive the king's instructions spread, those opposed to the prayer book began to prepare to meet in Edinburgh to give in petitions to the council. There was 'much trafficking throughout the country, for drawing numbers to Edinburgh against the next council diet'.[54] This activity was much intensified by news of a visit to Scotland by the Duke of Lennox to attend his mother's funeral. He was the king's cousin and one of those closest to him, and it was hoped that he could be persuaded to represent the hatred of the prayer book to the king.[55] Attempts were made to persuade the burgh of Edinburgh to join the petitioners against the prayer book.[56] This was a very important matter, because few of the burghs would join the agitation until they were given a lead by Edinburgh. The baillies of Edinburgh had twice written to Archbishop Laud apologising for the riots of 23 July and promising to do their best to get the new liturgy accepted,[57] but they had failed to punish those responsible for the riots and had shown little enthusiasm for the prayer book. The king therefore ordered them to elect Sir John Hay, the clerk register, as their new provost. Of all the officers of state Hay was the one most in favour of the prayer book, and the king expected that he would be able to keep the burgh firmly under his control and prevent any further disturbances. Instead the burgh was insulted at being ordered to elect as provost a man whose opinions were widely detested.[58]

On 20 September about twenty nobles, a large number of lairds (especially from Fife), commissioners from many parishes in the West, between eighty and a hundred ministers, and commissioners from a few of the burghs assembled in Edinburgh. Among the twenty nobles who assembled at this time, the first open meeting

Page 67 A CONTRAST IN LAWYERS: (*left*) Sir Robert Spottiswood, 1596–1646, President of the Court of Session, 1633–41; (*below*) Sir Thomas Hope of Craighall, died 1646. King's Advocate 1626–46. By George Jamesone

Page 68 CHARLES I, with Edinburgh in the background. Probably issued in connection with one of his visits to the burgh (1633 and 1641). By Cornelius van Dalen.

of nobles opposed to the prayer book, were nearly all those who were to emerge in the months ahead as the lay leaders of the agitation. Doubtless many of them had, like Lord Balmerino, been involved in or known of plans to oppose the prayer book before this time, and several had, like Balmerino again, long histories of opposition to the king. The Earl of Rothes had been prominent in opposing the Five Articles of Perth in the parliament of 1621 and as an opponent of the king in the 1633 parliament: Lord Loudoun and Lord Lindsay also had opposed the king in 1633, as a result of which patents creating them earls had been suspended by the king. The prominence of the Earl of Sutherland among the leaders seems to have been the result rather of the fact that he was first in precedence among the nobles who opposed the prayer book than of his ability. Among the more important of the other nobles who attended the meeting on 20 September were the Earls of Cassillis, Home and Lothian.

A meeting of nobles on the previous day had drawn up a general petition against the prayer book as illegally introduced and containing errors, and this was given in to the clerk of the privy council together with about sixty-eight local petitions from parishes, burghs and presbyteries. When the Duke of Lennox came up from Holyroodhouse to attend the meeting of the privy council in the Tolbooth he found the petitioners drawn up outside its doors, the nobles and lairds lining the north side of the road, the ministers the south. All greeted him respectfully as he passed.[59] This was a far more impressive demonstration of the strength of the opposition than the riots of 23 July. Less than two months after the riots which had acted as a spark to inflame the latent opposition to religious innovations, a fifth of the nobility of Scotland, many lairds and perhaps a tenth of the ministers had met in a disciplined and orderly manner to demonstrate their determination to oppose the prayer book.

The king's reply to the council's letter of 25 August showed that it need not have been so shy of telling him the truth as to the extent of the opposition to his policies, because now that he had been told he simply ignored it. He coldly complained that his former directions had produced 'but very small effect' from the

5

council. The suggestion that some councillors and clergy should be sent to confer with him he scornfully rejected as unnecessary and because it would make it seem that he had either 'a very slacke councell or very bad subjects'. He was satisfied with neither the privy council nor the burgh of Edinburgh, as none of the rioters had been punished to terrify the others into obedience. He ordered the council to see the prayer book read in Edinburgh and the bishops to impose it in their dioceses.[60] The king was putting the council in an impossible position; to all reports from Scotland he simply replied that the prayer book must be enforced, but without explaining how this was to be done or showing any recognition of the difficulties involved.

At the end of the council's meeting on the morning of 20 September the petitioners found that their general petition had not yet been considered, so they retrieved it from the clerk and Traquair helped them to rewrite it 'and made it very smooth. He wold not advyse us to irritate any.'[61] Traquair's motive for this extraordinary action was probably that he thought that as he could not stop the petitioners he should at least see that their petition was in moderate terms that would not enrage the king unnecessarily. Frustration at the king's refusal to take any account of the realities of the situation in Scotland probably made him feel more sympathetic to the aims of the petitioners than he had been previously. Whatever his motives his help must have greatly encouraged the petitioners—who were already receiving advice from another of the officers of state, lord advocate Craighall.[62]

When the council re-assembled on the afternoon of 20 September the rewritten general petition was handed in and the council gave it, two of the local petitions, and a list of the rest to the Duke of Lennox to take to the king, entreating him to 'remonstrat to his Majestie the trew estat of the bussiness with the manie pressing difficulties occurring therein'.[63] The council then rose without taking any action to implement the king's orders, the opponents of the prayer book being again left free to organise opposition and stir up hatred of the book in the weeks of waiting for the king's next letter to the council. Their hopes that Lennox would intervene with the king on their behalf were disappointed; he had little interest in Scots affairs, having 'the manners and nature and heart of an Englishman'.[64]

It was at about this time that Robert Baillie first began to fear that civil war was a possibility, and he recalled with dread the religious wars in Holland and France in the previous century; 'no man may speak any thing in publick for the King's part, except he would have himself marked for a sacrifice to be killed one day. I think our people possessed with a bloody devill, far above anything that ever I could have imagined.'[65] Such extreme fears and hatreds were probably at this time still largely confined to the West and Fife—the great majority of the petitions presented to the council on 20 September came from these areas.[66] The ministers who had gathered in Edinburgh on 20 September realised that this limitation of the agitation to a few districts was a weakness, and at a meeting the following day they took steps to remedy it. Four ministers were commissioned to go to specified areas of the Lowlands (outside Fife and the West) and persuade ministers and others there to join in the petitioning.[67] This plan for spreading the agitation was greatly helped by the decision of the burgh council of Edinburgh to join the petitioners. Having unwillingly obeyed the king's order and elected Sir John Hay as provost on 19 September, the council indicated the mood in which it had obeyed by ordaining three days later that it should be explained to the privy council that the burgh council would not help to impose the prayer book as it had formerly promised, as the arguments of the nobles, lairds and ministers who had met in Edinburgh had 'alienated their mynds' from the book.[68] The new provost was not present at this meeting of the burgh council; he naturally disapproved of the decision but failed to get it altered and on 26 September the burgh's petition against the book was given to the privy council.[69] The news of Edinburgh's decision 'had such influence on the boroughs, that whereas the most part of them had formerly lain by, very shortly after, all of them (Aberdeen only excepted) came in to the cause: and indeed, being once engaged, turned the most furious of any; so that neither their own ministers, nor any other that disliked the course, could be in safety among them'.[70]

The king's answer to the council's letter and the petitions of 20 September was not at first expected until the beginning of November, but then it was rumoured that the council was to meet on 17 October to receive letters from him. Some attempt was made to keep this secret, presumably to prevent crowds gathering, but Johnston of Wariston discovered the plot and hurriedly wrote summoning the other petitioners to Edinburgh.[71] As a result Edinburgh was more crowded than ever before when the council met on 17 October. Several hundred local petitions were given in to it, and the nobles, lairds, burgesses and ministers who had assembled each held separate meetings to discuss the situation.[72] The king's instructions to the council were as uncompromising as ever, but at least he was more specific than before about what action he wished to be taken. The council was ordered to declare its meeting dissolved so far as the affairs of the kirk were concerned, thus preventing it making any concessions or receiving petitions against the prayer book. All the petitioners that had gathered in Edinburgh were to be ordered to leave within twenty-four hours, and the king showed his displeasure with Edinburgh by ordering that the privy council and court of session should leave the burgh and sit first at Linlithgow and then at Dundee. The council duly issued proclamations implementing these orders,[73] but the petitioners showed little intention of obeying the order to leave Edinburgh. The nobles among them met and (angry at the king's attitude) resolved to draw up a new petition or supplication, and they instructed the lairds and ministers to remain in Edinburgh while this was being done. The leading part in organising protests at the prayer book had been taken at first by the ministers, and this was the first occasion on which the nobles as a body had openly taken the initiative.[74]

The presenting of the new supplication on 18 October was delayed for several hours by violent rioting against the privy council's proclamations issued the day before. Whether these riots were incited by the petitioners is impossible to say, but little if any incitement can have been necessary. To hatred of the prayer book and of the provost imposed on them was now added anger at the king's removal of the privy council and court of session as motives inducing the inhabitants of the burgh to riot. In confused disturbances Traquair, the Bishop of Galloway and the provost were roughly manhandled by the mob, which forced the provost and burgh council to agree to appoint commissioners from the burgh to join those of other burghs among the supplicants. The supplicants denied all responsibility for the riots. The rioters at one point invited the lairds (who had requisitioned a room in the Tolbooth to meet in as they could not find a room elsewhere big enough for them all) to join them, but on the advice of the nobles the lairds refused.[75] After the rioters had dispersed, the privy council (which had retreated to Holyroodhouse) issued a proclamation condemning the disorders. It gave the supplicants permission to remain in Edinburgh for another twenty-four hours,[76] as it was obvious that they were going to stay whether the council liked it or not, but the council refused to accept a copy of the supplication as the king had forbidden it to do so.[77]

The new supplication was signed that evening in turn by nobles, lairds, burgesses and ministers. It differed from the previous petitions in that it attacked not only the prayer book but also the book of canons and, more significantly, the bishops, who were denounced for introducing canons and a liturgy full of errors, abusing the king's trust, and arousing discord between the king and his subjects.[78] This widening of the scope of the quarrel to include a direct attack on the bishops was the work of the nobles and a few of the leading ministers. When the supplication was brought to the meeting of ministers for signature many of them were reluctant to support such an attack. The nobles soon persuaded them of the necessity of this, and indeed according to Robert Baillie many of the ministers proceeded to sign the supplication on the recommendation of the nobles alone, without even reading it.[79] The signatures on the supplication clearly indicate that by this time the agitation against the king's religious policies had spread throughout the Lowlands; the 482 signatures are those of approximately 30 nobles, 281 lairds, 48 burgesses (representing about 36 burghs, including all the more important ones except Aberdeen and St Andrews) and 123 ministers.[80]

Having signed the supplication the petitioners returned to their homes, arranging to meet again in Edinburgh on 15 November; some took with them copies of the supplication to be signed locally.[81] The privy council was left with the unenviable task of explaining and excusing these events to the king. Traquair wrote in despair to Hamilton 'I am in all these things left alone, and, God is my witness, never so perplexed what to do. Shall I give way to this people's fury, which, without force and the strong hand, cannot be opposed?' To oppose the people might lead to 'more danger than I dare adventure upon' without the king's warrant.[82] This neatly sums up the dilemma of the privy council; the king sent orders to be enforced, but would give no indication that he was prepared to sanction the use of force which would be necessary if he was to be obeyed, and he would place all the blame on the council if he was not obeyed.

There now ensued another lull in this crisis by monthly instalments, while the king was informed of the situation and given time to try again to rule Scotland by letters to the privy council. The council tried to meet at Linlithgow (as the king had ordered) at the beginning of November, but not enough councillors appeared to form a quorum. As for the court of session, the provost and baillies of Linlithgow demonstrated their support for Edinburgh by claiming that they could not find lodgings for the judges, and that the palace was not in a fit condition for them to sit in. The judges therefore had to return to Edinburgh and the session did not sit at all until the following February.[83] The council first sat at Linlithgow on 14 November to decide how to deal with the meeting to be held in Edinburgh the following day by the supplicants. It must have been clear to all present that the removal of the council from Edinburgh had been a mistake. The king had in effect abandoned the capital (just as he was to abandon London in 1642) to the supplicants, who could now meet there and plan their future actions without interference. Admittedly the council had had little success in the past in restraining the supplicants when it had met in Edinburgh, but at least it had been able to keep in close touch with their actions and plans, and some of the more moderate councillors had been able to restrain them to a limited extent. The council in Linlithgow realised how isolated it was from events and therefore commissioned Traquair, and any other councillors who were willing, to go to Edinburgh to do their best to prevent any disorderly meetings taking place, and to negotiate with the leaders of the supplicants to dissolve their meetings and return home; if they refused they were to be charged in the king's name to do so.[84]

Later that day (14 November) Traquair, the Earl of Lauderdale and Lord Lorne met the supplicants in Edinburgh, but they refused to return home, claiming that their meeting was legal and necessary. They alleged that during the meeting of the council on 18 October Sir John Hay and the Bishop of Galloway had proposed that the supplicants should choose a few commissioners to petition the council peacefully.[85] It is quite possible that the provost and the bishop, badly shaken by the riots, had made some such proposal, without considering its consequences, and that the supplicants chose to read far more into this than had been intended, to take it as an official authorisation to them to meet to choose commissioners. They now claimed that this was why they had gathered in Edinburgh. Eventually Traquair and the two other councillors agreed that the supplicants should choose a few commissioners to remain in Edinburgh, and promised that they should be told when news of the king's intentions arrived, so that they could summon the other supplicants to assemble.[86]

The next day, 15 November, four nobles and three each of the lairds, burgesses and ministers met again with Traquair and some other councillors[87] and desired that the supplicants might have permission to hold meetings in the shires to choose commissioners to assemble in Edinburgh to hear the king's answer. The councillors protested that they had no power to authorise this, but Sir Thomas Hope of Craighall again showed his sympathy with the supplicants by giving it as his opinion that lairds had a right to meet to choose commissioners to parliament, to a convention of estates, 'or for any publict bussiness'. Having gained this approval for their plans from the king's own legal adviser, the supplicants agreed to disperse, leaving behind in Edinburgh a few commissioners to keep them informed of events.[88]

Just as the supplicants had distorted the meaning of remarks made in council in October as authority to meet in Edinburgh in

November, so the king's advocate's opinion and the fact that the other councillors present had not contradicted it soon became distorted into belief among the supplicants that elections to a sort of informal convention of estates had been 'countenanced by the counsell'. It was agreed that future meetings of the supplicants in Edinburgh should be attended by all the nobles, one minister from each presbytery, two lairds or barons from each shire, and one or two burgesses from each burgh.[89] In fact this plan was never adhered to exactly, as far more ministers and lairds usually flocked to Edinburgh for meetings than it allowed for, but the famous 'Tables' which later became the instruments through which the covenanters governed the country had their origin in the electing of commissioners by the supplicants which began in November 1637. The word Table was probably used as a convenient synonym of council or committee with less formal and official connotations than the latter words, thus trying to avoid giving the impression that the covenanters were usurping the government of the country.[90] Any meeting, council or committee of the supplicants was at first likely to be called a 'Table', but later use of the word was usually confined to describing small permanent committees of nobles, barons, burgesses or ministers, or to joint committees of all four. Such permanent committees did not evolve until 1638, and contemporaries who (writing a few years later) claimed that they appeared in 1637 were ante-dating later developments.[91] It was at these meetings in the middle of November that the Earl of Montrose first joined the supplicants. A talented and extremely ambitious young man, almost from the moment he joined the supplicants he appears among their leaders in signing petitions and making protests but, essentially a man of action, he took little interest in the detailed work of drafting documents or deciding tactics.

At the end of November the commissioners who had remained in Edinburgh were informed that the king was sending instructions to Scotland with the Earl of Roxburgh, and that the council was to meet at Linlithgow on 7 December.[92] The nobles and commissioners of shires, presbyteries and burghs were therefore summoned to Edinburgh. A specimen formal commission had been drawn up and distributed, to be signed by electors, giving their commissioners power to join with others to await the king's answer to the petitions and do everything lawful to further them.[93] Roxburgh and Traquair managed to persuade representatives of the nobles and commissioners not to come to Linlithgow when the council met, but in order to obtain this concession they had to promise that the council would give the supplicants a hearing within a few days.[94]

One would have thought that the riots of 18 October would have convinced the king of the need for fast and decisive action to regain control in Scotland before matters got completely out of hand. Instead he had written to Traquair ordering him to see that the rioters were punished as 'such an exorbitant cryme doth require',[95] which was impracticable, and the royal letters to the council brought by Roxburgh and read on 7 December were equally unhelpful. Far from being stung into action by the riots, the king used them as an excuse for further delay; he had been going to answer the petitions given in to the council in September, he explained, but out of resentment at the riots he had decided to defer doing so. He gave orders that all councillors should be summoned to attend council meetings; the numbers attending had fallen sharply as most of the bishops feared to appear and many of the lay councillors had no wish to take their seats at such a difficult time. To satisfy the fears of his subjects he ordered the council to issue a proclamation declaring his abhorrence of all the superstitions of popery.[96] Needless to say, this did not settle the crisis when proclaimed by the council.

Meanwhile in Edinburgh the commissioners of the supplicants were meeting. The nobles chose Johnston of Wariston and four other advocates to advise them as to how they could proceed against the court of high commission (which they held to be illegal) and the introducers of innovations in religion, and to demonstrate the legality of their holding of peaceful meetings to advance a just cause. They feared that the king might try to take legal action against all or some of them, and wished to have advocates briefed ready to answer any charges against them.[97] To avoid large and confused meetings the nobles decided that they would not consult with the whole bodies of the lairds, burgesses and ministers who had assembled but with four representatives of each, who were to relay the advice and decisions of the nobles back to the main bodies —from this time onwards some such arrangement as this was made at all the main meetings of the supplicants. On 9 December Rothes, Montrose, Lindsay and Loudoun and one of the lairds had a meeting with Traquair and Roxburgh in Holyroodhouse. The two officers of state tried to persuade the supplicants to return the controversy to the state it had been in before 18 October, by petitioning only against the prayer book (not against the bishops and book of canons as well), and by not all signing one general supplication like that of 18 October but presenting several local supplications, since the king regarded a general supplication as a mutinous combination. These proposals were referred back to the other supplicants, who rejected them two days later after much debate. Commissioners were sent to inform Traquair and Roxburgh of this and to give them notice that they intended to give in a declinator against the bishops to the council the following day[98] —that is, a formal declaration of their refusal to submit to the bishops (as members of the council) acting as judges of their grievances as they were parties interested in the case.

The council was most reluctant to receive such a document, and it was not until 21 December, after several meetings at Dalkeith and much argument,[99] that the council was persuaded to accept it. Twelve commissioners appeared before the council. One of them, Lord Loudoun, made a speech explaining their grievances; they concerned alterations in religion and public worship, 'the most soleme action of ws all cretures in earth'. They were working to preserve true religion, for the salvation of their souls, and the lawful liberty of subjects. They wanted action taken against guilty bishops. He pointed out, as proving the necessity for a declinator if their grievances were to be given a just hearing, that there were so many bishops on the council that they could form a quorum on their own, without any lay councillors being present.[100] Loudoun then gave in to the council a petition complaining at the way their former complaints had been dealt with, copies of the supplications of 20 September and 18 October, and the declinator, and took instruments on the delivery of these papers (i.e. had a formal narrative of what he had done authenticated by a notary or clerk as a record of his action); presumably it was feared that the council might later claim that it had not formally accepted the papers. After further speeches by ministers the council stated that the matters contained in the papers presented were of such importance that they would have to inform the king of them before replying. Most of the supplicants agreed to return home to await the king's reply, but a few were left in Edinburgh to draw up a narrative or 'historical information' of events since the introduction of the prayer book to justify their proceedings.[101]

THE MAKING OF THE NATIONAL COVENANT

News of these events, and especially of the declinator, at last decided the king that the situation in Scotland was serious enough to require summoning Traquair to court for consultations.[102] When the supplicants heard of his intended journey to the king they were anxious that he should take a copy of their historical information with him for the king. Typically, he compromised by refusing to take it himself but agreeing that Sir John Hamilton of Orbiston, the justice clerk, who was accompanying him, should carry it.[103] Traquair must have faced his visit to court with some trepidation; he had failed to implement many of the king's orders in the last few months, and he had several times helped or encouraged the supplicants in an effort to retain the friendship both of them and of the king, 'but it was already growne difficult to keep the King and them too'.[104] When he reached court he found that the bishops and his other enemies had not failed to report his dealings with the supplicants to the king. His advice, in favour of moderation and compromise, was rejected in favour of the chancellor's, that the supplicants would disband if the king threatened to proclaim them traitors unless they did so. But, astonishingly, the king insisted that Traquair should return to Scotland to implement an uncompromising policy to which he had shown that he was opposed.[105]

Traquair arrived back in Scotland in the middle of February 1638. He met Roxburgh in Edinburgh and arranged a meeting of the privy council at Stirling on 20 February. He refused to divulge the contents of a proclamation that he had brought from the king, but, as he later wrote, 'little or nothing is done at court . . . whereof they have not . . . got some intelligence'.[106] Johnston of Wariston seems by this time to have built up a remarkably efficient intelligence service through which news from highly placed English and Scottish friends of the supplicants at court was sent to him and distributed by him. On 16 February he was 'given intelligence of the main points of the proclamation'.[107] Many of the supplicants had gathered in Edinburgh, and the news that the king's attitude was as uncompromising as ever soon spread among them. They decided that a meeting should be held at Stirling, and wrote urging as many other supplicants as possible to join them there on 20 February.[108] Traquair and Roxburgh tried to dissuade them from going to Stirling, but failed. The two nobles had written to Hamilton in this context that if 'we cannot prevail by fair meanes, to work the wished effect' they would try other methods.[109] What they meant by this soon became clear. The meeting of the council and issuing of the proclamation had been arranged for 20 February but at about two o'clock on the morning of 19 February Traquair and Roxburgh secretly left Edinburgh for Stirling, intending to have the proclamation issued there before any of the supplicants could arrive and protest. Through the indiscretion of a servant of Traquair, however, news of his and Roxburgh's departure reached Lord Lindsay, and he and the Earl of Home at once set out for Stirling, arriving in time to make a protestation at the proclamation, and take instruments on it. From what we know of Traquair's previous attempts to keep on good terms with both king and supplicants it is possible that his servant's 'indiscretion' was contrived—especially as, of all places to be indiscreet, the servant chose an inn which was a well-known meeting place of the noble supplicants and where Lord Lindsay was lodging.[110]

In the proclamation the king made no concessions, and he took the responsibility of having composed and approved the prayer book on himself—whereas the supplicants had tactfully blamed it on the bishops. He denounced the petitions against the prayer book and the supplication of 18 October as much injuring his royal authority, and the meetings of the supplicants as deserving his highest censure. But, as he believed that they had acted out of 'ane preposterous zeale and not out of anie disloyaltie or disaffection to soveraintie', he would forgive all who on hearing of the proclamation would return home and behave as dutiful subjects. All meetings of supplicants in the future were forbidden on pain of treason, and any who were in Stirling were to leave within six hours.[111] The protestation by Lindsay and Home on behalf of the other supplicants complained that in spite of their declinator bishops had taken part in judging their supplications. They demanded that their grievances should be presented to the king and be tried before the ordinary courts, and that the bishops should be tried for the crimes of which they had been accused.[112]

Many other supplicants crowded into Stirling later on 19 February, but the following day they agreed to return to Edinburgh on the council's threat to dissolve its meeting unless they did so. The council approved the proclamation—there had not been time for it to meet and approve the proclamation in advance of publication (as was usual) the previous day—but at least two of those present would not sign it; Craighall refused to do so on a technicality and another councillor on the grounds that he had not been present when it was proclaimed.[113] In a letter sent to the council with the proclamation the king admonished it for its past weakness and explained that the reason for his uncompromising proclamation was that 'we can never conceave that the countrie is trueli quyet when regall auctoritie is infringed, for, altho it may have a seeming settlement at first, it cannot so long continue when the King's true auctoritie is not truelie preserved'.[114] The proclamation was repeated at Linlithgow and Edinburgh on 21 and 22 February, and in both places was immediately followed by a protestation.[115]

Many of the supplicants had been very reluctant to leave Stirling, regarding their return to Edinburgh as a retreat. They were bitterly disappointed and angry at the king's continued refusal to consider their grievances, and at Traquair's attempt to issue the proclamation before they could reach Stirling. Far from being intimidated by the king's threat that any further meetings would be

regarded as treason, they decided on holding a larger meeting than
any of the previous ones. On 22 February Rothes drew up a letter
of advertisement to be sent to nobles, lairds and others who had
not yet joined the supplicants: 'We have heir in present consideration the most important bussiness that ever concerned this nation.'
Religion, liberties, lives and fortunes were threatened by the
prayer book, canons, and court of high commission, and the supplicants' enemies were attempting to deprive them of the right to
seek ordinary legal remedies for their grievances. Those to whom
the letter was sent were begged to come immediately to Edinburgh
for consultations and to decide whether to join the supplicants or
not. Loudoun and David Dickson sent similar letters to those
known to favour the supplicants, summoning them to Edinburgh.[116]

A committee of four each of the lairds, burgesses and ministers
was chosen to sit with the noblemen, and on 23 February they
decided on the necessity for a band of union to be sworn by the
supplicants. Previously they had confined themselves to petitioning the king, but under threat of being proceeded against for
treason they felt the need for some band between them to stand
together. As to the form of the band of union, it was agreed that it
should be 'the renewing of the old Covenant for religion'.[117] This
was the confession of faith signed by James VI in 1581 (known as
the king's confession or the negative confession), the signatories
of which bound themselves to uphold the true religion of the
Church of Scotland and oppose popery and superstition.[118] Who
first suggested that this confession should be renewed is uncertain; it may well have been Johnston of Wariston, who had been
studying it the previous September,[119] but it must have occurred
to many in the months of agitation against the prayer book that
the old confession had some relevance to the situation.

While suitable additions to the confession were being drafted,
ministers were set to preach in Edinburgh kirks of the need to
renew it. One of them (Henry Rollock) seemed, to one of his
audience at least, to suggest that the new covenant would 'make
use forswear Bishops and Ceremonies', and some of the supplicants were now saying openly that the Five Articles of Perth and

government of the kirk by bishops should be abolished, a further widening of the scope of the dispute with the king.[120] The drawing up of the additions to the old confession was entrusted to Johnston of Wariston and Alexander Henderson, and their work was revised by Rothes, Balmerino and Loudoun. Meanwhile, on 23 February, Traquair had come to Edinburgh to reason with the supplicants; instead of a few supplicants appearing before the privy council, the treasurer was now almost in the position of a supplicant before the Tables. While the council sat in useless exile in Stirling the supplicants virtually ruled the country from the capital. Traquair begged them to submit to the king, but he had lost all credit with the supplicants for his part in issuing the proclamation on 19 February and his advice was rejected.[121]

26 and 27 February were spent in making further alterations to the new covenant. Some opposition to it was found, especially among the ministers, two or three hundred of whom met in the Tailors' Hall in the Cowgate, and several changes had to be made to conciliate moderate opinion among them. The ministers then accepted the new covenant unanimously, but it was clear that the nobles and other leaders of the supplicants were ready to support more far-reaching changes in religion than the body of the ministers who opposed the prayer book; briefly it had seemed that the covenant might divide the supplicants instead of uniting them.[122]

The national covenant was first signed in Greyfriars kirk on 28 February. The lairds assembled there and were addressed by Loudoun and Alexander Henderson, after which Johnston of Wariston read out the covenant. A few doubts raised by some of the lairds having been answered, the nobles arrived and signed, followed by the lairds. The next day nearly three hundred ministers and the commissioners for the burghs signed, followed on the two succeeding days by the people of Edinburgh.[123] It was decided that copies of the covenant should be provided for 'ilk shire, balzierie, stewartry, or distinct judicatorie' to be signed by the principal persons of the area, while copies for each parish should be signed by all who were admitted to the sacrament there.[124] John Livingstone rode to London with letters and copies of the covenant, which were delivered to friends of the covenanters at court by Eleazer Borthwick.[125] After the signing of the covenant most of the covenanters who had gathered in Edinburgh returned home, many of them taking copies of the covenant with them for signature locally. Before they dispersed it was arranged that six nobles and a few commissioners from each shire should remain to await the king's reaction to the covenant, and that elections should be held to choose commissioners for future meetings. Each parish and burgh was ordered to keep lists of those who signed the covenant and of those who refused to do so.[126]

The national covenant opens with an explanation stating that it is the confession of 1581 'now subscribed in the year 1638 by us noblemen, barons, gentlemen, burgesses, ministers and commons under subscribing; together with our resolution and promises ... to maintain the ... true religion, and the King's Majesty, according to the confession aforesaid and acts of parliament'. There follows the 1581 confession and a long summary of acts of parliament against popery, papists and superstition. The final section is the most important and original part of the covenant. The signatories bound themselves to adhere to and defend the true religion, to forbear the practice of innovations, and not to give approbation to the present government of the kirk until the 'kirkmen' had been tried in free assemblies and parliaments. This was not to imply any diminution of the king's powers; 'on the contrary, we promise and sweare, that we shall, to the uttermost of our power, with our meanes and lives, stand to the defence of our dread Soveraigne, the Kings Majesty, his Person, and Authority, in the defence and preservation of the foresaid true Religion, Liberties and Lawes of the Kingdome: As also to the mutual defence and assistance, every one of us another in the same cause of maintaining the true Religion and his Majesty's Authority'. They swore that they would not 'suffer ourselves to be divided or withdrawn by whatsoever suggestion, allurement, or terrour from this blessed and loyall Conjunction', and to suppress any 'divisive motion'. Renewing their covenant with God, they promised to try to keep themselves and all those under them 'within the bounds of Christian liberty, and to be good examples to others'.[127]

The national covenant, it has been said, was 'essentially a constitutional, and not a revolutionary document',[128] and this is certainly true of its form and wording, since it largely consists of the 1581 confession and citations of acts of parliament. The final section is at several important points carefully moderate in tone—though also carefully vague so that it could bear differing interpretations as circumstances might require. Thus religious innovations were not to be practised, but they were not condemned as unlawful, and no attempt was made to define the innovations referred to. Similarly, though approbation of the existing form of kirk government was withheld, the form was not specifically rejected. Bishops are not mentioned, those to be tried being called simply 'kirkmen'. Yet it is clear that the compilers of the covenant, and its most fervent supporters, opposed episcopacy (on the Melvillian ground that it was incompatible with the principle of parity of ministers) and regarded the covenant as condemning it. The fact that they refrained from making such condemnation explicit is an indication of how slow the opposition to the king's religious policies was in adopting an exclusively presbyterian outlook. Even when the new covenant was first signed many hoped for a settlement introducing some form of limited episcopacy, combining the best features of both forms of church government. A clear attack on episcopacy would therefore have divided the country instead of uniting it. Months more of experience of the king's intransigence was needed before moderate covenanters were convinced of the necessity for a presbyterian polity. In other words, 'It is quite plain that the attack on episcopacy was only a secondary development in a revolt which had broken out over quite different issues'.[129] The covenant made no attempt to make good what was traditionally the greatest weakness in Calvinist political thought; the covenanters bound themselves to defend both true religion and the king's authority, but ignored (because they could not answer) the question of what they should do if the two conflicted. They promised to support the godly magistrate but as yet ignored the problem of a magistrate who refused to be godly, whereas the whole trouble was that Charles I would not (in the eyes of the covenanters) be godly, though of course it was already clear that

6

in practice they were willing to defy the king if he would not adhere to and defend the true religion.

One respect in which the national covenant differed notably from that of 1581 was that whereas the latter was simply a covenant between the individuals who accepted it and God, the national covenant bound the individuals who accepted it to each other as well as to God. Indeed it could be argued that, at first at least, the most important aspect of the national covenant was that it bound together those who had been supplicating into a body of men sworn to support and stand by each other. It had been the need for such a band of union after the proclamation of 19 February that had led to the drawing up of the covenant. Publicly the covenanters refused to acknowledge this double character of the covenant, in binding individuals to each other as well as to God; they denied that it was in any way 'a private league of any degree of subjects among themselves'. The reason for this insistence was to avoid their covenant falling within the scope of an act of parliament of 1585 forbidding private bands. They admitted that it was more than a covenant of individuals with God and defined it as 'a publict covenant of the collective bodie of the kingdom with God for God and the King'.[130]

But details of the contents of the national covenant are of little more relevance to the enthusiasm with which it was greeted than the contents of the prayer book are to the bitter opposition to it. Just as the prayer book was a symbol of all that was disliked in the king's policies, so the national covenant became symbolic of united opposition to religious and other innovations. Within a few weeks of the first subscribing of the covenant it was being signed throughout the Lowlands (except in parts of the North) amid a wave of popular enthusiasm. Nearly all the nobility, except Catholics and members of the privy council (to whom it was not offered), signed, as did all the burghs except Aberdeen, Crail and St Andrews—and although the burgh council of St Andrews would not sign, most of the inhabitants did.[131]

Traquair complained that he had known all along that to issue the proclamation of 19 February would be unwise, but even he can hardly have expected such an extreme reaction to it by the supplicants as the national covenant, introduced in direct defiance of the king and adding to former demands refusal to accept the government of the kirk unless free assemblies and parliaments were allowed. Traquair no longer saw the slightest hope of establishing use of the prayer book. In spite of all his efforts to retain the friendship of both sides he now found himself hated as much as the most unpopular of the bishops, 'But I shall not foolishly give occasion of offence to any',[132] a resolution indicating that he no longer had any intention of even trying to carry out the king's impractical policies.

While the covenant was being signed in Edinburgh the privy council met in Stirling (1 March). The meeting had been called by the chancellor and other bishops, but only one bishop attended the meeting. The letter which the chancellor wrote excusing his absence was almost an announcement of his retirement, in that the advice he gave, 'to lay aside the booke and not to presse the subjects with it anie more, rather than to bring it in with suche trouble of the church and kingdoms as we see', was bound to be unacceptable to the king. The council declared that the cause of its meeting was to represent to the king 'the trew estat of the countrie be occasion of the Service Booke, Booke of Canons and the Hie Commission', and the following day passed a similar resolution that the 'causes of the generall combustion' were fears of innovations in religion introduced 'contrare or without warrant of the lawes'. On 3 March it decided that it could do nothing further towards settling the 'combustions' since the proclamation of 19 February was being ignored, and that the justice clerk should be sent to the king to explain to him 'the trew estat of maters heir'. Orbiston was to show the king that the troubles had been caused by religious innovations contrary to law, and to beg him to take trial of the grievances of the covenanters.[133] In the absence of the bishops the lay councillors clearly had no intention of defending their master's policy and were willing to recommend virtual surrender to the covenanters.

CHAPTER THREE

The Glasgow Assembly,
March–December 1638

HAMILTON'S MISSION

Even the signing of the national covenant and the clearly stated opinion of the council that religious innovations should be withdrawn did not convince Charles of the need to take quick and decisive action in Scotland. Incredibly, it was not until early June, when another three months had passed, that the Marquis of Hamilton arrived in Scotland as the king's commissioner to try to settle the crisis. The king's immediate reaction to the council's news and opinions was seen in a letter which the justice clerk presented to the council from him on 24 March. He expressed surprise at the state of affairs in Scotland and at the council's advice, for while he conceded that it could perhaps 'see more than we can' the action it advised would overthrow the church government established by his father, and he was sure that this was not what was really meant. He therefore requested that Traquair or Roxburgh (or both) be sent to him to explain the intentions of the council. Both were sent.[1] The council can have had little hope that they would manage to persuade the king to accept its advice, so determined did he seem to ignore bad news.

Lord Lorne also set out for England early in April to advise the king, probably at Charles' request; Traquair had instructed the justice clerk to consider with Charles 'if it shall not be necessary to send for Lorne. I need not enlarge this point, the reasons are sufficiently known to yourself.'[2] Unfortunately these reasons remain obscure. Born in 1607, Archibald Campbell, Lord Lorne, had been in effect head of his clan since his father, the seventh Earl of Argyll, had left Scotland and become a Catholic in 1617.

He has been well described as 'a man equally supple and inflexible, cautious and determined'.[3] Throughout his career he was to show remarkable caution and reluctance to declare himself openly, punctuated by surprising bursts of outspokenness, and this was well illustrated in 1637–9. Most of the Campbells were strongly opposed to the king's innovations, and there is no doubt that at heart Lorne agreed with them—he had had a violent quarrel in 1637 with the Bishop of Galloway over religious and other matters.[4] Yet he continued to sit on the council, had joined in none of the agitation and supplications, and had not signed the covenant. His refusal to commit himself to the covenanters until he was convinced that they were likely to succeed was partly the result of his temperamental caution, but he was also probably influenced by fear that if he appeared in open opposition to the king while his father was still alive then they would cancel his father's resignation of his lands to him. Not until October or November 1638 when his father died and Lorne succeeded him as eighth earl was this possibility removed. Meanwhile Lorne endeavoured to remain on friendly terms with the covenanters (though his visit to court in April was against their wishes[5]) while not antagonising the king.

Before Traquair left for court he was given by the covenanters a paper entitled 'The Least that can be asked to setle this churche and Kingdome in a solid and durable Peace', drawn up by Wariston and Alexander Henderson and revised and approved by the leading covenanting nobles.[6] These articles showed a further increase in the changes demanded, based on the covenant. Simply withdrawing the prayer book, canons and high commission was no longer enough, it was stated; experience had shown that it was necessary for the kirk to be secured by acts of a free general assembly and parliament. There must be some guarantee that innovations removed would not be reintroduced. General assemblies must meet yearly, or at least at set times, and the powers of bishops must be curtailed. The assembly should be allowed freedom to censure the bishops, and urging of obedience to the Five Articles of Perth must cease.[7]

The three councillors had arrived at court by 8 April, and on that day Lorne talked privately with the king for an hour and a half. With the king's permission Lorne had 'verie frie conference' with him and spoke plainly of Scotland's grievances and his own dislike of the Articles of Perth and the misgovernment of the church by the bishops. It is hard to decide which is the more surprising; that Lorne was for once so outspoken, or that his frankness did not lose him the king's trust, though the latter was probably due to the fact that the king had always been willing to ignore disagreement with his policies from his advisers provided they would obey him, and Lorne had not yet publicly opposed him. Typically, Lorne's own account of his interview with the king to Lord Loudoun was 'so generall and ambiguous as I could nott know his meaning'. Lorne further puzzled his contemporaries by returning to Scotland in May in the same coach as Traquair and the Bishop of Galloway 'as good friends',[8] whereas few Scots at that time were willing to be seen even talking to a bishop for fear of the general dislike and suspicion such an action would bring them. Why had Traquair suggested that Lorne be sent for to court, and why had the king granted such a long private interview? Though there seems to be no contemporary evidence for it, it is possible that Traquair had suggested that Lorne might be a suitable person to be sent to Scotland as the king's commissioner to settle the troubles. In retrospect, once he had become leader of the covenanters, such an idea doubtless seemed too absurd to entertain, but in April 1638 it would not have seemed so ridiculous. Lorne was one of the most powerful nobles in Scotland, yet the king could expect to have an unusual amount of influence over him since his father was still alive. Lorne had shown no sign of joining the covenanters and had on several occasions tried to get them to moderate their demands, yet was still respected and trusted by them to a far greater degree than any other Scottish noble of comparable standing. Thus there was much in favour of appointing him as a mediator between king and covenanters; but, if this was considered seriously, his clear statement of his religious sympathies to the king and a warning from his father that he was not to be trusted[9] led the king to appoint the Marquis of Hamilton as his commissioner to Scotland instead.

Traquair was sent back to Scotland in May with a letter to the council announcing this decision and ordering the council to meet at Dalkeith on 6 June to advise and assist the new commissioner.[10] While the king was making these arrangements with little indication that he saw any need for haste, the covenanters were using the respite to consolidate their hold on the country. A delegation sent to Aberdeen failed to persuade the burgh council to sign the covenant on 16 March,[11] but elsewhere there was little resistance to it. It was widely signed in St Andrews, the only other major burgh in which there was strong resistance, after a sermon by Alexander Henderson in which he explained that what had been added to the 1581 confession 'is nothing but ane interpretation of the former part', and that even those who did not sign and swear the covenant were bound to it by their baptism. To the argument that it was an illegal combination against the king he replied 'when your neighbour's house is burning, ye will not run to the king to speir if ye should help him or not', and similarly when religion was in danger there was no need to consult the king before going to its rescue. Increasing pressure was put on those who refused to sign the covenant, especially ministers. David Mitchel, an Edinburgh minister, lamented on 19 March that he and others like him dared not venture into the streets as they were followed by gentlemen with drawn swords who muttered threats and curses.[12] Six weeks later Mitchel and others claimed that new moderators were being elected by the presbyteries to replace the constant moderators nominated by the bishops, new ministers were being admitted to charges without the bishops being consulted, while ministers who still would not sign the covenant were reviled and abused, and found that they could not get their stipends paid. A few weeks later it was reported that such ministers were being deposed.[13] Though perhaps exaggerated, these laments were substantially true; many presbyteries, for example, were deposing their constant moderators as Mitchel claimed.[14]

The North had been slower and more hesitant than the rest of the country in accepting the covenant, so on 26 March letters were sent summoning the nobles, lairds, ministers and others of the North to a meeting at Inverness on 25 April with commissioners from Edinburgh. In spite of the efforts of some of the bishops the meeting was well attended, those present including the Master of Berriedale (heir to the Earl of Caithness) and forty of his friends and vassals, the Earl of Sutherland and the gentry of Sutherland, Lord Reay and his men, the gentlemen of the name of Ross, Monro, Fraser and Mackenzie, and some of the Grants. Andrew Cant, minister of Pitsligo, and an advocate, had been sent from Edinburgh to satisfy religious and legal doubts about the covenant. All present agreed to sign the covenant though the ministers at first showed some reluctance. The following day the inhabitants of the burgh of Inverness signed, though the provost and two councillors refused to do so as most of the Grants and Mackintoshes had not signed and their burgh being 'invyroned amidst the Hieland', they wished to keep on good terms with these clans.[15]

Another meeting was summoned at Forres on 28 April,[16] at which some of the gentry of the district and 'all the bodie of the toune' signed the covenant; the ministers of Forres presbytery hesitated but, as at Inverness, were persuaded by the laymen to sign. The performance was repeated at Elgin on 30 April, but only three ministers agreed to take the covenant. The burgh council signed, though their request that they should add to it a clause permitting them to kneel at communion was refused.[17] As this summary of the covenanters' signature-gathering tour in the North is taken from their own account of it, it probably exaggerates somewhat the amount of support for the covenant in the area, but it does not try to hide the fact that many ministers had grave doubts about or were opposed to the covenant, and it is substantially supported by the account of the royalist John Spalding.[18] By the end of May the only areas of Scotland in which the covenant had not been widely signed were the western Highlands and Isles north of Argyll, and the shires of Aberdeen and Banff, where resistance was led by the Marquis of Huntly and the Gordons. Elsewhere the minority which supported the king's religious policies was demoralised by his long delay in making any public declaration of his attitude to the covenant; 'this long boggling and irresolution (for so people do take it) makes many doubtful whether he be disposed to break the same' and thousands signed who would have continued to refuse to do so if the king had given them a lead.[19]

When it became known early in May that the king was sending Hamilton to Scotland as his commissioner, the covenanters drew up articles to regulate their conduct in negotiating with him, so that they would present a united front. No answers were to be given in matters of public importance without common consent and advice. For preparing and discussing matters to be negotiated, a committee chosen by lairds, burgesses and ministers was to sit with the meeting of the nobles. If Hamilton said that the king would grant their legal desires but that episcopal power and the Five Articles of Perth were established by law, it was to be replied that abuses of episcopacy were contrary to law, that the Articles should 'be rightlie interpret', and that a free assembly and a parliament must be held as part of any settlement.[20]

Hamilton did not leave for Scotland 'till he saw all our countrey-men, which the court in any way might spare, sent home before him'.[21] The clerk register, the president of the court of session and a 'multitude of our Scottish Lords'—the Earls of Morton, Linlithgow, Kellie, Mar, Kinnoull and Haddington and Lord Almond —returned to Scotland. Most of these nobles were men with no very strong religious feelings who either usually lived in England or had gone there to avoid deciding for or against the covenant. The covenanters rightly feared that they were sent to Scotland to use their influence over their friends, vassals and dependants against the covenant, and therefore laid down 'that we will depend on no man who is of ane adverse judgement, or about a contrarie employment in the matter of our covenant and consciences'.[22]

The result of this decision was seen as soon as Hamilton arrived in Scotland. He had written to his friends and vassals and many other leading nobles and lairds to meet him at Haddington, to accompany him to Dalkeith in a manner befitting the king's commissioner. 'Many would gladly have done him the honour', but the covenanters' ruling was obeyed;[23] a paper written by Wariston and David Calderwood had been distributed beginning bluntly 'Such Noblemen as are not joyned in Covenant with us, whether they favour our cause or not, are not to be attendit at this tyme'.[24]

Hamilton therefore had to do without his grand entry to Dalkeith, and interest in his arrival was further diverted by another circumstance; a few days before a ship with arms and ammunition for Edinburgh castle had arrived at Leith, but the covenanters had refused to allow the munitions to be carried to the castle. Traquair had therefore had them taken secretly by night to the king's house at Dalkeith.[25] The covenanters denounced this as arming one of the king's houses against them. Guards were placed on Edinburgh castle to prevent any further attempt to bring ammunition to it, and wild rumours circulated of a Catholic rising. Armed covenanters crowded into Edinburgh to protect the burgh. Thus when Hamilton arrived at Dalkeith and displayed his commission to the council on 6 June the covenanters were in no mood to submit to the king or compromise.[26]

Until this time Hamilton had played little part in Scottish public affairs. Born in 1606 he had led the life of a courtier rather than of a statesman. But in 1631–2 he had led a British military force in Germany under the King of Sweden in the Thirty Years War. The expedition had achieved little, but Hamilton's part in it and his subsequent negotiations (up to 1637) with Sweden in favour of Charles I's nephew, the Protestant Elector Palatine, had associated him closely with the Protestant cause on the Continent. This gave the covenanters some trust in him. He was the only leading Scottish noble well known to and trusted by the king who was not distrusted by the covenanters. Since he had taken so little part in Scottish politics, he was not discredited by being identified with the king's unpopular policies.[27] The appointment of Hamilton as king's commissioner was therefore an astute move by Charles, though Hamilton himself had no wish to return to his native land, even with the status of the king's personal representative.[28] It was easy to deduce from Traquair's experience that the middle-man between king and covenanters was likely to end up distrusted and disliked by both, and he was more at home and better known in London than in Edinburgh. The king gave Hamilton two proclamations and discretion to have proclaimed whichever he thought fit. Both declared that the prayer book and canons would be imposed only in a fair and legal way, and that the court of high commission would be rectified. The first version went on to promise pardon for what was past provided that all seditious bands—the signed copies of the covenant—were surrendered; all who did not renounce the covenant would be declared traitors. The second version said nothing about surrendering covenants but threatened that unless testimony of obedience was given force would be used to restore order. The choice was one of wording rather than content; both demanded obedience under threats in return for concessions so vague that it would be easy for the king to interpret them into meaning whatever he wanted once he had regained control in Scotland.

The king's instructions to Hamilton show that he did not fully understand the difficulties likely to face his commissioner. Any who protested at whichever proclamation was made were to be considered rebels and their leaders arrested. Any body of covenanters which gathered in Edinburgh or elsewhere was to be dispersed, by force if necessary. He empowered Hamilton to raise forces in Scotland, though it was obvious that any attempt to do so would have met with the swift assembly of far greater forces of covenanters. Acts of council enforcing use of the prayer book might be suspended and practice of the Articles of Perth cease, and the king's willingness to call a general assembly and parliament once order was restored made known, but Hamilton was also to indicate that if subjects did not return to obedience the king would bring forces from England to exact it.[29] In fact the king had already begun preparations to raise forces in England and send arms and ammunition to his Scottish castles. Hamilton's task was as much to gain time and prevent open rebellion by keeping negotiations going, until the king was ready to crush the covenanters, as to work genuinely for a negotiated settlement.

Hamilton had got only as far as Berwick on his way to Dalkeith when he was informed that the covenanters would not be satisfied with the vague concessions that they had heard the king was offering, and were talking of summoning a general assembly and parliament themselves if the king would not. He wrote to the king to urge him to hurry the preparations to send an English army and fleet to Scotland,[30] but in the meantime he began his negotiations.

The covenanters requested him and the council to come to Holy-roodhouse as more convenient than Dalkeith, and he agreed on condition that he was given a fitting reception and that the guards around Edinburgh castle were removed. This was done, though a private watch was retained on the castle[31] and the reception of Hamilton was turned into a demonstration of the power of the covenanters rather than of respect to the king's commissioner. He was met by thirty nobles 'at the end of the Sands betuixt Leith and Musselburgh, the gentry standing all in ranks along the sea-side till verie neir the end of the sands, being a myll and ane half long; and at the eastmost end of Leith Links ther stood above 600 ministers, by whose ranks the Commissioner past', while between Edinburgh and Leith 20,000 people waited.[32]

On 12 June representatives of the covenanters went to Hamilton at Holyroodhouse and inquired as to the king's intentions. He replied that this would be made known by a proclamation, where-upon the covenanters indicated that they would make a protesta-tion after the proclamation. Hamilton's entreaties and threats failed to make them alter this decision. He had already decided to use the version of the proclamation which did not specifically require the giving up of all copies of the covenant, since he saw no hope of its being obeyed and Craighall and many other lawyers had stated that the covenant was justifiable by law.[33] But which-ever proclamation he used he was bound by the king's instructions to arrest the leaders of any protest against it. Any attempt to do this would clearly have led to open rebellion, and Hamilton there-fore withdrew (on 14 June) his order for issuing the proclamation on finding that there were covenanters waiting to protest at it. In fact there had been much argument among the covenanters them-selves as to the necessity for a protestation. Some of the nobles (including Cassillis and Lothian) had argued against one, but after consulting lawyers and receiving threats from the lairds that they would issue a protest on their own if necessary, the nobles had agreed to one.[34]

On hearing Hamilton's first pessimistic reports from Scotland the king virtually abandoned hope of a peaceful settlement. Hamil-ton was to continue negotiating and try to get the covenanters to return to their homes by lulling their fears—'flatter them with what hopes you please'—though he was not to consent to an assembly and parliament unless the covenant was renounced. Hamilton's main aim was 'to win time'; 'so long as this Covenant is in force . . . I have no more Power in Scotland than as a Duke of Venice; which I will rather die than suffer'. The covenanters were not to be declared traitors until the English fleet had sailed for Scotland; meanwhile Hamilton was to try to secure Edinburgh and Stirling castles.[35] Two weeks of complex negotiations followed Hamilton's decision to make no proclamation, but brought a settlement no nearer—not surprisingly, as he was simply playing for time. At the beginning of July he left for court for further consultations (which would provide a convenient excuse for several more weeks of delay). He promised to represent the covenanters' demands to the king, on their agreeing in return to dissolve their meetings in Edinburgh and not reassemble until he returned.[36]

Hamilton had barely left Edinburgh when he received an order from the king to issue a proclamation. This began (like the two proclamations which Hamilton had not issued) with promises not to press the prayer book or canons except in a fair and legal way and to rectify the high commission, but went on (as the two earlier versions had not) to promise that the king would call a free assembly and parliament at his convenience, and ended with demands that his subjects return to obedience.[37] Now that the king had determined on the need to use force against the covenanters he saw no need to alarm them with threats of force or of being proclaimed traitors, as he had been ready to do a month before. As required by the king, Hamilton returned to Edinburgh and had the proclamation published on 4 July. Before doing so he assured the covenanters that it contained concessions which should fully satisfy them, but when they heard it they were bitterly disappointed by its vague promises. They had ready a protestation 'of so large a tenour as to answer any thing they could suppose might be contained in a Proclamatione', and they read this and took instruments on it. Afterwards Wariston rewrote the protestation when he had studied the proclamation and knew more clearly what he was protesting against, and the new version was printed as if it was the protest that had actually been made. Hamilton managed to persuade all the councillors present except Lorne and Southesk to sign an act ratifying the proclamation, but the covenanters persuaded a majority of them to repent having done so, and these councillors forced Hamilton to tear up the act before it was entered in the register of the council by threatening to sign the covenant unless he destroyed the act.[38]

June 1638 saw some important changes in the organisation of the covenanters. On about 5 June a meeting of the nobles decided that they should choose a president each day; 'to eschew the speaking of many at once' it was ruled that none should speak without obtaining leave of the president.[39] So that most of the crowds of covenanters who had gathered in Edinburgh could leave, commissioners from each shire and burgh (together with assessors) were to be elected to remain in the capital, being replaced at intervals by elected substitutes. Those who remained in Edinburgh would number about 600 men, who in turn would elect a few representatives to sit with the nobles on a central committee or table. These meetings were dissolved when Hamilton left for England in July, and arrangements were then made for two or three nobles to remain in Edinburgh in turn for two weeks at a time until he returned.[40] This constant changing of commissioners probably had two motives behind it. First, it spread the burden both of the work of agitation and of the expense of staying in Edinburgh. Secondly, it involved as many as possible of the nobles, lairds and burgesses who were active covenanters in the leadership and organisation of opposition to the king, thus encouraging them in their loyalty to the cause and avoiding it seeming that the covenanters were led by a small faction, which might have given rise to jealousies among those who felt excluded from the leadership. This was doubtless also the reason why the meeting of the nobles chose a president daily instead of for longer periods. From 9 June to 6 July 1638 ten nobles sat as president,[41] and of the fourteen nobles delegated to attend in Edinburgh in turn until Hamilton returned only two had acted as president in the preceding month. Of course this appearance of co-operative leadership was in part a façade behind which power and decision-making remained in the hands of a few men who emerge most clearly in matters of importance like the negotiations with Hamilton; Rothes, Montrose and Loudoun, or at least one of them, are almost invariably present and take the leading part in such talks, other nobles and any lairds, burgesses and ministers present often being little more than observers. Even in the nobles' meeting with its variety of presidents, Rothes acted as clerk and was accepted as a sort of residual president when for some reason no president was elected,[42] and there is little doubt that usually he and a few others effectively controlled the meetings.

By July 1638 both king and covenanters were arming openly. Both probably began secret preparations for war soon after the covenant was first signed, the king raising men in England to invade Scotland, the covenanters buying arms in Holland for defence. Typically, Charles was hopelessly optimistic as to the size of the forces he could muster and the speed at which he could have them ready. Thinking in terms of an English invasion, he made little real attempt at this time to persuade his supporters in Scotland to rise in arms for him. Hamilton had some hope of help from Huntly and his Gordons, from the Ogilvies, and from the Western Highlands and Isles; in August Sir Donald Macdonald of Sleat met the captain of Clanranald, Macdonald of Glengarry and the whole name of Clan Donald, and all swore to live and die in the king's service,[43] but Hamilton warned the king that they would act only out of hatred for the Campbells, not through loyalty to the crown.[44] The covenanters seemed little worried by fear of a royalist rising in the north. With much exaggeration they claimed that the Forbeses, Frasers, Grants, Mackenzies, Mackays, Mackintoshes, Macleans, Macdonalds and Inneses, as well as all the Campbells to a man, had zealously signed the covenant. As for the Gordons, many of them were dependent on the covenanting Earl of Sutherland rather than on Huntly, who was written off as being practically bankrupt.[45] The king hoped to gain some help from his army in Ireland and from the Catholic Randal Macdonnell (or Macdonald), Earl of Antrim, and his clansmen from Antrim. Until the early years of the century Macdonalds had occupied Islay, Kintyre and other lands in Scotland, from which they had been driven by the Campbells. It was now widely rumoured that Antrim had offered to invade Scotland on the king's behalf if Kintyre was restored to them, and that the king had agreed to this. Certainly Charles approved Antrim's offer of help, but it is not clear whether or not he promised to deprive Lorne and the Campbells of part of their lands to pay Antrim. The rumour that he had was not effectively denied, and there was little doubt that any expedition to Scotland by Antrim and his Macdonnells would turn into an attack on their old enemies the Campbells, whatever the king might wish. By accepting help from the Macdonnells the king gave Lord Lorne an additional motive for eventually joining the covenanters,[46] and the fact that the Macdonnells on whom the king relied for help were Catholics greatly damaged his cause in Scotland.

Charles' plan of campaign at this time was probably a naval blockade of Scotland to cut off all Scottish foreign trade and prevent arms being imported, followed by Antrim's invasion of the West and the seizure of Edinburgh and Leith by an English army. He was not short of advice: Sir William Monson rather wildly suggested that the king should construct a fortified line from Glasgow to Stirling and abandon all Scotland north of it 'where it is not fit for civil men to live', while the Lowlands were incorporated into England.[47] Viscount Wentworth, lord deputy of Ireland, was more realistic but similarly insistent on the necessity of anglicising Scotland once it had been subdued; it should be governed, like Ireland, by an English deputy, and perhaps English law introduced.[48] With rumours of these and similar plans current many Scots who had no great love for the covenant must have decided to support it against the king as the only alternative seemed to be, not a return to Scotland as it had been before the troubles, but the reduction of their country to a dependency of England.

Raising forces in England proved far more difficult than Charles had expected. There was no enthusiasm for a war with Scotland. Part of the trouble was Charles' failure to explain the situation in Scotland or to justify his conduct there, so that the covenanters' interpretation of events was widely accepted. It was not until 1 July 1638, some time after he had decided that the use of force against the covenanters would probably be necessary, that he first officially informed the English privy council of the troubles of Scotland. Even then he told it little if anything that was not common knowledge[49] and did not use the council's help and advice in his preparations for war. No doubt he argued that troubles in Scotland were not the business of the English council, but it was English resources that were to be used to subdue Scotland; at the end of July he gave orders that up to £200,000 sterling be spent on preparations for war.[50]

The covenanters' preparations seem to have been more effective. By early July a system of beacons to be lit to give warning of invasion had been established: this was revealed when a covenanting laird who was staying in Edinburgh panicked on hearing a rumour that ships of the English navy had been sighted in the Firth of Forth and tried to light them.[51] At about the same time instructions were sent to the shires from Edinburgh, ordering that two lairds of each parish should compile lists of the names of all able-bodied men and what arms, ammunition and horses they had. Rolls were also to be made of those who had not signed the covenant and what estates, arms and provisions they had. The name of any 'that hes beine abroad and is able to doe any seruice in warres' were to be noted—the first sign that the covenanters were aware of the wealth of military experience with which those many Scots who had served in Germany in the Thirty Years War could provide them. Meetings of nobles and lairds of Perth on 17 July and of Argyll on 2 August[52] ordered the implementation of these instructions.

The covenanters made another attempt to bring Aberdeen into conformity with the rest of the country. On 20 July Montrose, Lord Coupar, some lairds and ministers arrived at the burgh and began to urge subscription of the covenant. The magistrates and council had a few days before they renewed their previous decision not to sign and could not be persuaded to change their minds.[53] Preaching by the covenanting ministers produced only forty or fifty signatures, and two local ministers would sign only with a declaration that they did not condemn the Five Articles of Perth or episcopal government as unlawful.[54] Opposition to the

7

covenant was largely inspired by the 'Aberdeen Doctors', a group of ministers connected with Aberdeen and its universities who supported Arminian tendencies and the king's religious policies; a paper war of pamphlets between the Doctors and the covenanters was soon in progress. Thus though they had some success in getting the covenant signed in the country round Aberdeen,[55] the covenanters' mission was a failure in the burgh itself. But their activities were slowly eroding resistance. Why, demanded an indignant royalist, did not the king clearly denounce the covenant, so that they could cite his denunciation as their reason for not signing, for many were wavering and would soon sign unless they were encouraged to continue their refusal.[56]

PREPARATIONS FOR THE ASSEMBLY

When, in the middle of August, Hamilton arrived back at Holyroodhouse from court, he found the state of affairs worse than before. Training of men for war by the covenanters was well under way, and a few days before a convention of burghs at Stirling (to which Aberdeen had not been invited to send a commissioner) had ratified the covenant and had ordered that no burgh was to admit any man as a burgess or magistrate, or send any commissioner to future conventions, who had not signed the covenant.[57] Moreover, in their efforts to win signatures to the covenant in Aberdeen and elsewhere the covenanters had claimed that Hamilton had declared his satisfaction with their proceedings before he had left for court, and many had believed this.[58]

Hamilton brought with him new instructions from the king, dated 27 July. To demonstrate his Protestantism and willingness to defend the reformed Church of Scotland Charles ordered Hamilton to try to persuade the council and the covenanters to sign the confession of faith of 1560, with a band added binding the signator to maintain the confession, the king's person and authority, and the laws and liberties which the country enjoyed under the king's sovereign power. Hamilton seems to have disapproved of this rival to the national covenant and to have made no attempt to get it signed.[59] The king further instructed Hamilton to summon a general assembly. He was to endeavour to get the covenanters to concede that bishops should have seats and votes in the assembly, that the moderator should be a bishop, that the Articles of Perth should be held as things indifferent and not condemned, and that as few restrictions as possible should be placed on episcopacy. But notwithstanding these instructions Hamilton was 'by no means to permit a present Rupture to happen, but to yield any thing though unreasonable, rather than now to break'.[60] The king still hoped that his forces would be ready to overthrow the covenanters before the assembly met. Hamilton presented the covenanters with a list of demands that they must agree to before he would indict (summon) an assembly: restoration of ministers and moderators of presbyteries who had been deposed or suspended by the covenanters, that all moderators of presbyteries should be members of the assembly, and that no layman should have any part in choosing commissioners to the assembly. Finally, the covenanters were to agree to dissolve all their meetings and stop pressing men to sign the covenant.[61]

A committee of covenanters drafted an answer to these demands on 17 August. Most of Hamilton's demands, it was claimed, concerned ecclesiastical matters, so only the assembly itself could decide them, and the assembly of 1606 which gave all moderators of presbyteries seats in assemblies 'was never reputed by the Church to be a lawfull nationall Assemblie', while in elections of commissioners to the assembly 'the order of our church discipline' gave elders a vote.[62] These answers were presented to the Tables the following day for approval. The ministers objected strongly to the claim that elders should have a part in electing commissioners from the presbyteries, as for elders to have seats in presbyteries was an innovation. Faced with the united insistence of the lay covenanters that they concede this point, they gave way and withdrew their objection, 'yet that question is like to make us trouble; for sundry of the brether are very jealous of the gentrie's usurpation over them'.[63]

After seeing the covenanters' answers rejecting his demands, Hamilton reduced the conditions on which he would summon an assembly to two: that laymen should have no part in choosing commissioners from the presbyteries, and that the assembly should not interfere with matters (such as the Articles of Perth) settled by acts of parliament except through petitions to parliament, a meeting of which would be summoned after the assembly.[64] When these also were refused Hamilton asked for time to go to consult the king. After much argument the covenanters reluctantly agreed to this, promising not to elect commissioners to the assembly (as the lairds had proposed) until 20 September, by which time Hamilton was to return.[65]

This was agreed on 25 August, and Hamilton left Edinburgh on the same day. Near Dunbar he met with Traquair, Roxburgh and Southesk, and they drew up and signed articles of advice to the king. They urged him to abandon completely the prayer book and canons and 'the unbounded power of Bishops in the High Commission (never yet warranted by Law)', describing the Articles of Perth as being 'withstood by the most considerable part of the Subjects of all qualities, both Laity and Clergy'. They recommended that the king should order the signing of the 1581 negative confession, the basis of the national covenant, with an additional band of his own. This, they believed, would restore confidence in the king and quiet the disorders.[66] Needless to say, the king did not welcome this advice. Hamilton found that he 'did utterly disrelish the Proposition' that the negative confession should be renewed, and recalled his father saying that he regretted having signed it. Hamilton admitted that it would strain his own conscience to sign it, but said that it was 'the Idol of Scotland' and he saw no other way to satisfy the Scots. At length the king gave way to this and other recommendations and on 9 September he signed new instructions to Hamilton, empowering him to 'absolutely revoke' the prayer book, canons and court of high commission. Practice of the Articles of Perth was to be forbidden, and when parliament met the king would agree to the rescinding of the act ratifying them. The privy council and all subjects were to sign the 1581 negative confession and the king would accept limitations on episcopal government. Hamilton was to indict an assembly and a parliament, and though he was to do all he could to prevent laymen taking part in elections in presbyteries this was not to be made an essential condition of holding an assembly.[67]

There is little doubt that in agreeing to these instructions the king was still simply playing for time. Greater concessions than before had to be offered as a longer delay was required, since it was becoming clear that he would not be able to raise sufficient forces to act against the covenanters until 1639. Nothing in Charles' conduct before or after September 1638 supports the idea that he had any intention of permanently honouring the promises he authorised Hamilton to make in his name.

Though a few presbyteries broke the promise made to Hamilton before he left Edinburgh on 25 August that they would not hold elections of commissioners to the general assembly before 20 September, the leading covenanters tried to see that the promise was kept. However, no sooner had Hamilton left Edinburgh than they began preparing for such elections. On 27 August directions were drawn up, 'publik for presbyteries . . . and privat for trustie persons'.[68] The public directions to the presbyteries ordered that each should send one baron or elder and up to three ministers to the assembly, and each burgh in the presbytery one burgess (with two from Edinburgh), as had been laid down in an act of assembly of 1597. One elder from each kirk session was to be present and vote in the presbytery when the elections were held. If any of scandalous life or erroneous doctrine (ie non-covenanters) were elected, then the best affected elders were to come to the assembly and protest against them. The elections were to be held on 21 to 25 September, whether or not Hamilton had by then summoned an assembly.[69] The private directions were to be distributed to trusted covenanters only. Information against the bishops was to be collected in each presbytery, not only as to their errors in doctrine and government of the church but also as to any faults in their private lives. The evidence discovered was to be sent to Edinburgh so that charges against them could be prepared.[70]

The most controversial points raised by these directions from the covenanters as to how elections were to be conducted were the order that elders should sit in presbyteries and vote in the elections, and the question of the composition of the assembly. When presbyteries had first been established in and after 1581 it had been intended that they should include elders as well as ministers,[71] though there were to be fewer of them than ministers.[72] But in practice elders had seldom if ever attended the meetings of presbyteries, which thus came to be composed entirely of ministers.[73] Consequently when in 1638 the covenanters demanded that one elder from each kirk session should attend and vote in presbyteries, many ministers regarded this as an innovation just as scandalous as those introduced by the king, while the covenanters could claim that what they proposed was merely the completion in membership of presbyteries as they had originally been planned by Andrew Melville.

The exact composition of a general assembly was also debatable. It had originated as an assembly of the estates, including nobles, representatives of the small barons or lairds, burgesses and ministers. Later, however, Andrew Melville and other presbyterians had insisted that a true general assembly was not a meeting of estates but a meeting of representatives of church courts, of ministers and elders alone.[74] They had failed to get the assembly reformed in keeping with this belief, and barons and burgesses continued to sit in it; as already mentioned, the act of 1597 stipulated that three ministers, one commissioner in the name of the barons of the shire, and one commissioner from each burgh, should attend assemblies from each presbytery.[75] Though the covenanters claimed in 1638 to be upholding this act, they in fact altered the position of the nobles and lairds in the assembly. In accordance with the instructions the covenanters circulated, all the nobles and lairds who sat in the Glasgow assembly and the covenanters' later assemblies were elders and members of presbyteries, and all were elected by their presbyteries. Previously nobles and small barons who sat in assemblies had not necessarily been elders, and the small barons had usually been elected by their fellow lairds in their shires. The new arrangements altered this, but the change was little more than a gesture towards the Melvillians. Not only did elders at most serve for only a few years at a time (Melville had argued they should hold office for life, like ministers), but many of the new 'ruling elders' who represented their parishes in presbyteries and the general assembly were not in fact 'session elders', elders in the kirk session of the parish they represented. Two distinct types of elder were thus emerging. Elders at the parish level, concerned entirely with petty local affairs, tended to be lesser men, tenant farmers and small heritors. Larger landowners and more powerful men had neither the time nor the taste for such matters; but they usually reinforced the kirk session when the election of a ruling elder to sit in the presbytery was held. Melville and his followers had taught that all ministers were equal, whatever level in the hierarchy of presbyterian church courts they might reach, and that a similar equality should exist among elders. Lay covenanters were now insisting on the introduction of a hierarchy among elders, men of differing social rank serving at the appropriate points in the hierarchy of courts. Only those parish elders who were highest up the social ladder, and men who thought service as a parish elder beneath their dignity, had much chance of serving as ruling elders in the presbyteries. And only the greatest —in secular terms—of the presbytery elders had any chance of election to the general assembly. Thus the lay covenanters adapted the Melvillian church polity, which had been intended to challenge existing lay society, so that instead it reflected the structure of that society.[76] This the Melvillians were forced to accept, for they knew that their only hope of achieving anything lay in co-operation with society as it existed, even though it was their ambition ultimately to alter that society towards greater godliness.

The conversion of barons elected by shires into elders elected by presbyteries left the burgesses isolated as the only remaining members of the assembly (except the commissioners from universities) who were not elected by a church court. The burgh commissioners were usually elected by the burgh magistrates and council, sometimes in consultation with the kirk session (or sessions) of the burgh. Yet some were unwilling to admit that the burgesses in any way represented their estate, since this would contradict the principle that the assembly should consist entirely of representatives of church courts; they insisted that the burgesses sat as elders from the burgh kirk sessions,[77] though without explaining why such sessions should have special representation. The conversion of the assembly from a meeting of the estates into a meeting of representatives of the church courts was thus as much a matter of redefining former types of members who continued to attend as of making any real changes in membership. The ministers proved unable to resist lay influence in ecclesiastical courts. Lay covenanters might pay lip service to the ideal of the two swords, of the independence of church and state in their own spheres, but in practice they had shown themselves determined not to implement the theory, insisting on strong lay representation in the superior church courts.

Apart from allowing the claims of the king's commissioner and of representatives of the universities to sit in assemblies, the covenanters insisted that only those mentioned in the 1597 act had the right to sit. This was designed to exclude from membership of the assembly a variety of extra types of member which James VI had added to assemblies in the latter part of his reign in his endeavours to control them. In the assemblies of 1606–18 (which covenanters were now claiming had been unlawful) James had increased the numbers of those on whose votes he could rely by appointing several king's commissioners each with a vote, by giving these commissioners several 'assisters' or assessors who likewise had votes, by summoning various nobles, lairds and (in the case of the 1618 assembly at least) ministers to sit and vote who had no commissions from presbyteries. Moreover some presbyteries had been allowed to break the 1597 act by sending more than three ministers to assemblies, while probably as the result of royal discouragement few presbyteries sent commissioners for the barons to these assemblies, and few burgh commissioners attended.[78] By insisting on excluding from the 1638 assembly the various kinds of royal nominee, the covenanters greatly reduced the influence the king could hope to exert in the assembly.

Hamilton returned to Edinburgh for the third time in mid September, and on 21 September the privy council approved proclamations embodying the concessions the king had agreed to, ordering signature of the negative confession, and summoning an assembly to meet at Glasgow on 21 November 1638 and a parliament at Edinburgh on 15 May 1639. Glasgow was chosen for the assembly as considerable opposition to the covenant had appeared there and it was near to the centre of Hamilton's influence, his estates in Clydesdale. The proclamations were issued on 22 September and the council signed the negative confession of 1581, with the addition of an anti-Catholic band of 1589, and approved the appointment by Hamilton of commissioners in each shire to enforce the subscription by all subjects of this 'king's covenant' as it soon became generally known.[79]

Wariston's dismayed reaction to these concessions was typical of that of most of the leaders of the covenanters. When he was told of them (by Lord Lorne) the day before they were proclaimed he 'was dasched thairwith, thinking that they had never light on so aparant ane meane to devyde and ruyne us'.[80] The problem was that the king's concessions were superficially fair, even generous, so if they were rejected as insufficient to satisfy the covenanters' grievances, many moderate men would rally to the support of the king. Yet Wariston and his colleagues were convinced that the king was insincere and not to be trusted, that he would ignore his promises as soon as the forces that he was known to be raising were ready. In this of course they were right: the very day the concessions were proclaimed Charles wrote to Hamilton mentioning the sending of cannon north to Hull,[81] and the king greatly disliked the king's covenant he had ordered his subjects to sign: it was merely a weapon to divide and embarrass his enemies. Consequently it was decided to meet the proclamations with yet another protestation, which was quickly written by Wariston after hurried consultations with Rothes, Loudoun and Alexander Henderson. Since the real reason for rejecting the concessions—distrust of the king—was not openly expressed, the protest was not an impressive document and must have seemed to many who did not share its authors' lack of faith in the king to be unreasonable, trying to find fault and ambiguities in the king's concessions. Many reasons were listed for not signing the king's covenant and to demonstrate that to do so would be a betrayal of the national covenant.[82]

Willingness by the covenanters to accept the king's concessions at their face value was strongest among the ministers. Many of them were deeply disturbed by the insistence of the laymen that elders should sit and vote in presbyteries. Therefore when the lay covenanters asked a meeting of ministers to send a few of their number to join in the protest against the proclamations, the meeting replied that it saw no need for any protestation, and would certainly not agree to one until they had read and considered it. The laymen duly read their protestation 'of the Noblemen, Barons, Gentlemen, Burrowes, Ministers, and Commons' after the proclamations, while the people (doubtless well briefed) cried 'God, saive the King: bot awaye with bischops, thes traitors to God and man, or any uther covenant bot our auin'.[83] A few ministers assisted in the protest but no representatives from their meeting were present;[84] the lay covenanters now had the initiative and were prepared to ignore the views of the body of the ministers if they thought this necessary. However, the protestation and other papers distributed by the covenanters generally had the desired effect, and except in parts of the North East the king's covenant was not widely signed. The magistrates and council of Glasgow welcomed the proclamations and refused to allow the protestation against them to be read, and several Glasgow ministers and members of the university supported them in this, but they abstained from signing the new covenant.[85]

Hamilton himself contributed much to the failure of the king's covenant by appointing (to the king's amazement) many of the leading covenanters as commissioners to enforce subscription. He justified his action on the grounds that many of them would not dare to disobey the order to impose the king's covenant and would therefore return to obedience to the king, that it would cause divisions among the covenanters since those named would become objects of suspicion to their colleagues as they would seem to support the new covenant, and that the common people would be deluded into signing the new covenant by believing that the leaders of the covenanters approved of it.[86] In fact by this clumsy attempt to outwit the covenanters Hamilton merely ensured that most of the commissioners named would take no action at all to get the covenant signed. In spite of all his efforts in the following two months (up to the time the general assembly met), nearly all reports spoke of general resistance to signing; even on his own estates he had little success. It was later estimated that in all 28,000 signatures to the king's covenant were gathered, 12,000 in the sheriffdom of Aberdeen through the efforts of Huntly and many more in Forfar.[87] Ironically, many of the king's staunchest supporters were as reluctant to sign as the covenanters, since they believed that the 1581 confession could be interpreted as condemning many of the religious innovations which they supported. Six of the Aberdeen Doctors, the provost, baillies and many inhabitants of Aberdeen would sign only with reservations stating that by signing they did not abjure (among other things) the Articles of Perth and episcopal government.[88]

This matter of the interpretation of the king's covenant was also raised when Hamilton requested the lords of session to sign it; four of them refused to sign on the grounds that they could not accept that religious innovations since 1581 were reconcilable with the confession of that year, as Hamilton had declared to them that the king had interpreted it. True interpretation could be decided only by the general assembly.[89] The reason that Hamilton had found it necessary to explain what the king understood by the confession was that Craighall, the king's advocate, had declared it inconsistent with such innovations. He and other members of the council who favoured the covenanters had signed the king's covenant, and he declared himself stupefied by the decision of the covenanters to resist it, urging them all to sign.[90] His motive for this was that he believed that the covenanters would gain far more by obeying the king by signing, and then declaring that they believed that they and all others who had signed were bound to renounce episcopacy as it was contrary to the 1581 confession. They could then go on to destroy episcopacy and innovations in the king's name. The refusal of most of the covenanters to sign much reduced the effectiveness of Craighall's plot, but even so the king's interests and policy had been greatly damaged when he had sprung his trap. Craighall had waited until the end of October before doing this, to give the king's supporters time to sign his covenant; he then informed Hamilton that he and all others who had signed had sworn to abolish episcopacy.[91] Hamilton was evidently taken by surprise by Craighall's announcement, though when the privy council had signed the king's covenant Craighall had clearly indicated that he had some such idea in mind. With the support of Lord Lorne, Craighall had proposed that Hamilton should add to the act narrating that the council had signed the king's covenant a statement that the council had signed the 1581 confession of faith contained in it 'according as it [ie faith] was then profest within this kingdome'.[92] Hamilton had foolishly agreed to this without considering its significance, and it now added strength to Craighall's interpretation.

Though most convenanters continued to refuse to sign the king's covenant they quickly adopted Craighall's interpretation of it and used it as evidence that king and council had agreed to abolish all innovations since 1581. 'The subscryveing of the King's Covenant by the counsell was so cunninglie turned, by slight of hand, that it became the soveraigne ingyne to overturne Episcopacie'.[93] The blame for the whole bungled affair lies squarely on Hamilton. He had persuaded the reluctant king to accept it, and it had been his idea to appoint covenanters to enforce it. It probably never occurred to him that many of the king's most loyal supporters, after waiting for well over a year for some encouragement and leadership from Charles, would be demoralised and embittered by being ordered to sign what appeared to many of them to be little better than the national covenant. Charles believed as much as his father in 'no bishop, no king' and had told Hamilton that he believed that few of those who opposed episcopal government did not also secretly oppose monarchy,[94] and Hamilton the courtier had dutifully echoed this sentiment back to the king—he thought that the covenanters would abolish episcopacy but that their main intention was to destroy the monarchy.[95] Yet between them they contrived and imposed a king's covenant which gave the covenanters an opportunity to claim that they had approved the abolition of episcopacy. That Craighall's interpretation of the king's covenant as condemning episcopacy was historically dubious (to say the least) was no consolation in the circumstances.

Preparations for the assembly continued during the controversy over the king's covenant. There was still much ill feeling between ministers and the lay covenanters over the insistence of the latter that one elder from each parish should take part in presbytery elections, and Hamilton worked to widen this rupture to the king's advantage.[96] A few elections had been held before the assembly had been indicted on 22 September; that for Peebles presbytery was said to have been,[97] and the commission to one of the ministers from Penpont presbytery is dated 19 September,[98] two days before the covenanters had ordered the elections to begin. Many more were completed before the end of September, but though staunch covenanters were usually elected there was much tension between ministers and elders, and some presbyteries refused to make elections until October or November.[99] In Glasgow the presbytery delayed the election when elders appeared and demanded to be allowed to sit and vote. Only after a delegation of leading covenanters arrived from Edinburgh did the presbytery admit the elders and make the election.[100] Royalists claimed that, in many of the elections in presbyteries, since one minister and one elder from each parish was present, the ministers were inevitably in a minority once the ministers on the leet (list of candidates) for election as commissioners to the assembly had withdrawn.[101] Quite apart from the fact that this would suggest that ministers must for similar reasons have formed the majority of the electors when barons or elders were being elected, it appears that only in a relatively small number of cases did as many elders as ministers attend the presbyteries for the elections, doubtless because many kirk sessions were reluctant to make the innovation of sending elders.[102] Probably more accurate were Hamilton's complaints that non-covenanting ministers were excluded from the presbyteries, and abused and threatened,[103] but he made little attempt to prevent the elections being conducted in the way that the covenanters had directed, for he saw the abuses in the elections as a weapon. He was convinced that he would have to dissolve the assembly to prevent it going further in reforming religion than the king was prepared to accept even as a delaying tactic, and the more illegalities and irregularities that he could show to have taken place during the elections, the better excuse he would have for his action.[104]

The covenanters were determined that the bishops should not sit in the assembly, and one of the means they adopted to prevent this was fear. In a remarkably sinister letter of 26 October 1638 to

Wariston ('Deare Christian Brother and couragious Protestant') from 'your owne whome you know, G.' it is related that upon a rumour that the Archbishop of St Andrews was coming to Scotland preparations were made 'how he might be intertained in such places as he should come unto' as it was 'altogether inconvenient that he, or any of that kind, should show themselves peaceably in public'. The news of St Andrews' visit had proved false, but the Bishop of Brechin was said to be in Edinburgh and Wariston was advised to see 'that, in a private way, some course may be taken for his terror and disgrace if he offer to shew himself publicly'. Meanwhile 'we are going to take order' with the chief supporters of the bishops.[105] With such a campaign of systematic terrorisation in progress it is hardly surprising that so few were willing to appear in open opposition to the covenant. Effective control and government of the country was in the hands of the covenanters and the king and Hamilton were powerless to protect their supporters.

In October the Tables sent out further instructions concerning the assembly. All nobles who had signed the covenant were to attend. Four to six gentlemen from each presbytery were to accompany their commissioners to the assembly to act as their assessors —to sit in the assembly and advise them but not to vote. Each burgh commissioner was to have up to six assessors. Gentlemen not chosen as assessors could attend voluntarily and the gentlemen of each presbytery were to see that no minister was deterred from attending the assembly by lack of money.[106] Thus not content with intruding elders into the presbyteries and ensuring that a large proportion of members of the assembly would be laymen, the covenanters arranged for large numbers of lay assessors to attend to overawe any opposition. On the other hand they were very reluctant to admit the right of the king's commissioner in the assembly to have assessors, or at least that such assessors should have votes, and there was no possibility that they would allow the bishops to sit. It was clear to Hamilton that an attempt would be made to abolish episcopacy, especially after Craighall, 'a bad and most wicked instrument', had interpreted the king's covenant as requiring this.[107] On 24 October a bill or complaint against the archbishops and bishops was given in to Edinburgh presbytery in the name of all covenanters, and as intended the presbytery referred the complaint to the assembly and cited the bishops to appear before it for trial. So that the bishops could not complain that their judges were also their accusers, none of those who signed the complaint were members of the assembly. The complaint itself detailed the errors and illegalities of the bishops in doctrine, in government, and in introducing innovations, demanding that they be punished.[108]

Hamilton ordered all privy councillors to accompany him to the assembly to help defend episcopacy. Craighall refused and was forbidden to go to Glasgow; instead Hamilton took Sir Lewis Stewart, advocate, with him to Glasgow as his legal adviser, though Stewart complained that if he defended episcopacy he would lose all his legal practice.[109] By proclamation Hamilton forbade any but members of the assembly and their personal servants to gather in Glasgow;[110] the covenanters protested at this and then ignored it, for they were determined to attend in strength to discourage opposition and prevent any attempt to dissolve the assembly by force. On 16 November the noble covenanters of the western Lowlands arrived in Glasgow accompanied by great numbers of their friends and vassals, and the rest of the nobles, lairds and ministers and their friends and servants appeared the following day after holding a meeting in Edinburgh. They expected to meet with far more opposition in the assembly than in fact materialised; right up to the time it met they believed that some of the bishops and the Aberdeen Doctors would appear and give trouble.[111] As for Hamilton, he expected no good at all from the assembly, but felt it necessary to let it meet even if he then had to dissolve it, in order to demonstrate that the king had kept his promise to hold an assembly. He knew that even if he did forbid it to meet the covenanters were ready to hold it without him.[112]

The covenanters made final preparations for the assembly on 19 November. Representatives of the nobles, lairds, burgesses and ministers met and decided that Alexander Henderson, 'incomparablie the ablest man of us all' should be elected moderator and that Wariston 'was a nonsuch for a Clerk'. In what detail the covenanters arranged in advance how they would conduct themselves in the assembly is hard to say, but it is probable that fairly detailed plans had been made at the meeting in Edinburgh, though knowledge of such plans was confined to the leading covenanters. Obviously their plans must have been flexible, as much depended on Hamilton's behaviour once the assembly met, but that the assembly on the whole went according to plan is indicated by Wariston's later statement that it had 'proceided publikly according to the treatise of proceidings in privat'.[113]

THE ASSEMBLY

On the morning of 21 November such great crowds gathered in and around Glasgow cathedral that the members of the assembly had much difficulty in getting to their places; 'hudge numbers of people, ladies, and some gentle women' filled the cathedral.[114] It had been usual for the moderator and clerk of the previous assembly to act until new elections were held, but as the Archbishop of St Andrews had moderated in the 1618 assembly, John Bell (an old Glasgow minister) acted as moderator as a man acceptable to both Hamilton and the covenanters. Thomas Sandilands acted as clerk as deputy for his father who had been clerk in 1618. Proceedings opened with 'a very good and pertinent sermon' by John Bell (which unfortunately few could hear) and prayers. In the afternoon Bell wished the assembly to elect a moderator but Hamilton insisted that his commission as the king's high commissioner to the assembly should be read first, and this was done. The commission was remarkable in being sealed with both the great seal and the privy seal; a short time before the Archbishop of St Andrews had, at the king's insistence, surrendered the chancellorship (in return for a promise of payment of £2,500 sterling). The king had given Hamilton custody of the great seal but had not made him chancellor, and it was perhaps feared that the covenanters might have challenged the validity of Hamilton's commission, if it had been authorised only by a seal which was in his own keeping.[115] Hamilton made a moderate speech, as he knew that the assembly was in no mood to take any threats or rebukes from him; he made his real feelings clear in a letter he wrote to the

Page 117 A CONTRAST IN CLERICS: (*left*) John Spottiswood, 1565–1639. Archbishop of St Andrews 1615–39; (*below*) Samuel Rutherford, 1600–61.

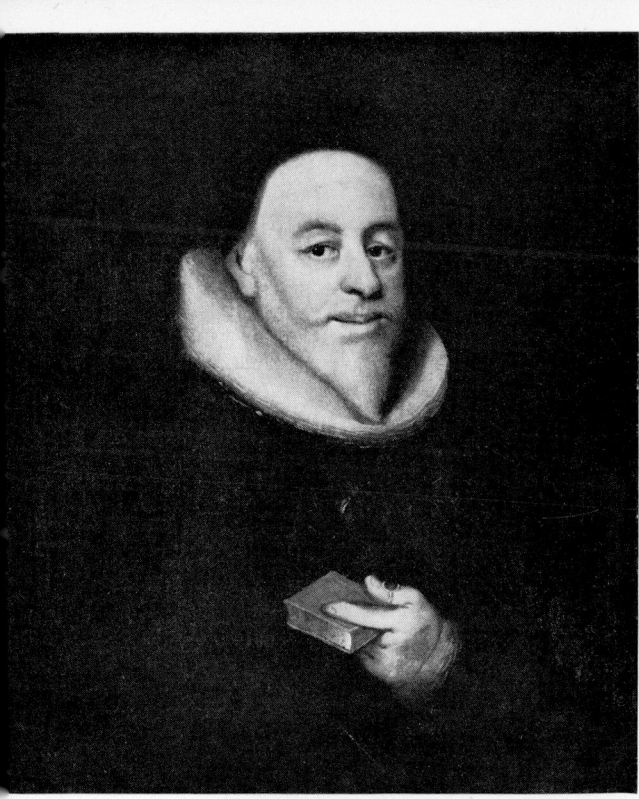

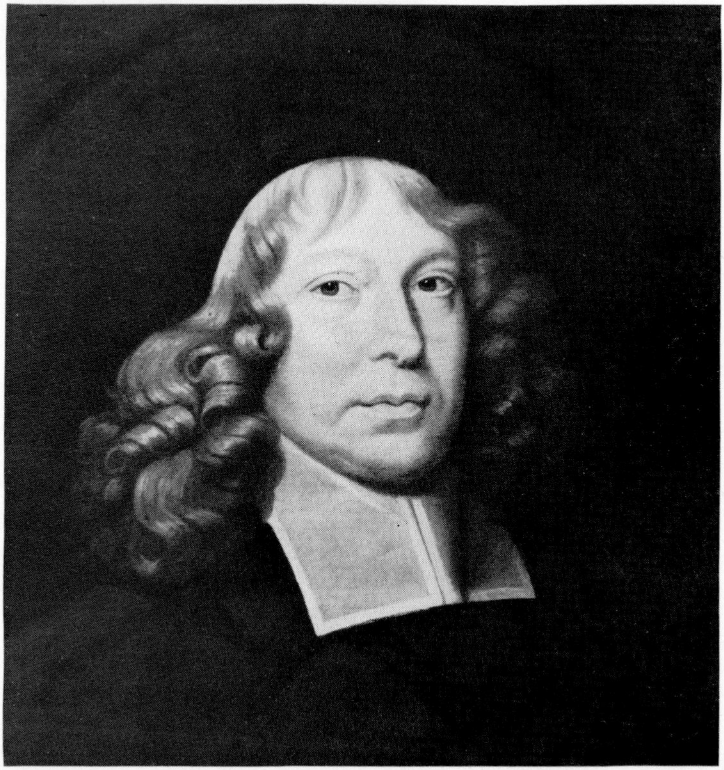

PUBLICA SALUS NUNC MEÆ· MERCES.

PRO FŒDERE, REGE, ET GREGE.

1640.

Set here a Merchant, who for's Countries good,
Leaves off his Trade, to spend both Wealth and Blood;
Tramples on Profit, to redeem the Fate,
Of his decaying Church, and Prince, and State.

Such Traffick, sure none can too highly prize,
When Gain it self is made a Sacrifice.
But Oh! how ill will such examples move,
If Loss be made the recompence to Love.

Page 118   WILLIAM DICK OF BRAID, the richest Edinburgh merchant,
pours out his wealth in 1640 to help the covenanters resist the king's fleet in
the Firth of Forth and a royal garrison in Edinburgh Castle. A fanciful
print from *The Lamentable Estate and Distressed Case of the Deceased Sir
William Dick* [1657]. British Museum

king the following day in which he related with contempt that many of the members of the assembly were illiterate (which was not true), and that most totally lacked learning, and warned that nothing but disobedience could be expected from them.[116] After Hamilton's speech the commissions to members of the assembly were given in to the clerk and the assembly rose for the day.[117]

The next day (22 November) John Bell again proposed that a moderator be chosen, but Hamilton first delayed until a letter from the king had been read, and then (supported by Traquair and Sir Lewis Stewart) argued that the validity of the commissions given in the previous day must be tried before the assembly took any decisions; the assembly could not act as an assembly until its membership had been decided. 'This was a ready way to turne the Assemblie upside down, to put us in a labyrinth inextriable; for, before the constitution of the Synod [assembly], the Commissioner should have so drawn in the deepest questions, such as the power of Elders . . .'.[118] Hamilton was claiming in effect that he should be able to decide who should be members of the assembly before the assembly was formally constituted. After much argument Hamilton abandoned this claim, though (copying the covenanters' own tactics) making protestations, which were in turn protested against by the covenanters. He then demanded that a declinator and protestation by the bishops against the assembly should be read, but this was also refused. Finally, he tried to insist that before a moderator was elected his right as king's commissioner to have assessors not only to advise him but also to vote in the assembly be recognised, but it was decided that they should not have power to vote. Hamilton's excuses for delay having been exhausted, the election of a moderator then took place, and Alexander Henderson was chosen, few if any voting against him.[119]

The assembly turned in its third session on 23 November to electing a clerk. Hamilton recommended Thomas Sandilands, but Wariston was elected. Before relinquishing his place Sandilands produced the registers of the general assemblies since 1590, but nothing was known as to the whereabouts of the earlier registers until Wariston produced them, five volumes covering 1560 to

8

1590. This production by Wariston was important for the covenanters, as the volumes produced by Sandilands dealt with a period
when the church had been increasingly subordinated to the king,
and therefore precedents could be found in them tending to prove
that past assemblies had been limited in power and independence,
whereas Wariston's five volumes covered the period of the kirk's
greatest power and freedom, and precedents extracted from them
would be of much value to the covenanters. Wariston, never one
to minimise the importance of his own actions, claimed that the
production of the registers was the turning point of the assembly,[120] but there can be little doubt that its course would have been
little different without them, though they certainly made it easier
for the assembly to justify its actions as 'restoration and not
revolution'.[121] The rest of the session passed in renewed arguments as to whether the bishops' declinator should be read or
not.[122]

The meetings on Saturday 24 November and Monday 26
November were taken up with trying the commissions to the
assembly. As had been laid down in the covenanters' instructions
of 27 August, wherever non-covenanters had been elected, covenanters had come from the presbytery concerned to protest. Out
of a total of about 112 commissions presented, about 13 were
questioned, by no means invariably because they elected non-
covenanters; the commission from Glasgow university, for example, was rejected because it elected four commissioners instead of
one (as the other universities had done). Rival versions of the
presbytery of Aberdeen resulted in two commissions, and that of
the covenanting presbytery was accepted, but even if the other
had been allowed only one of the three ministers named in it had
dared to come to Glasgow. Most of the other disputes were similarly settled in favour of the covenanters or referred to trial by
committees.[123]

With a moderator and clerk elected and the commissions examined, 'Now at last we fand the Assemblie, to our great joy, fullie
constitute, and so we went on to our busines'.[124] On 27 November
Alexander Henderson asked that he should be allowed some assessors to help and advise him in the discharge of his weighty duties

as moderator, and four ministers and eleven elders were appointed. All were members of the assembly so there was no difficulty over whether they should have votes or not. This had doubtless been arranged in advance, and the moderator's assessors included many prominent covenanters. They were in effect the Tables under another name and, meeting with the moderator between sessions, they effectively controlled the business presented to the full assembly. Such appointing of assessors to the moderator had been common in earlier assemblies, and had developed by the beginning of the seventeenth century into what was known as the 'privy conference' in which the moderator and prominent members (mainly supporters of royal religious policy) had decided what business should be presented to the assembly to be voted on; it had been becoming by 1618 the counterpart of the lords of the articles who controlled parliament for the king.[125] The covenanters now took over this useful device for their own ends. After choosing the moderator's assessors the assembly was at last ready to proceed to reform the kirk. That it had taken six days to reach this stage was an indication of Hamilton's success in carrying out the king's policy of delay.

Now that it was too late for the claims and objections in the bishops' declinator and protestation to affect the constitution of the assembly, its reading was allowed; 'some did smyle, others laugh and jeere, at it, whilst it was a readinge',[126] and no attempt was made to consider the points it raised about abuses and innovations in elections and about membership of the assembly. Two protests against the assembly were also read. Since it was obvious that they would have no effect whatever on the assembly, Hamilton would have been well advised to have suppressed them, for nothing could have demonstrated more clearly the lack of organised opposition to the covenant than the fact that he had been able to produce only two protests; the covenanters themselves had feared that there would be many more.[127]

After the session of 27 November Hamilton decided to dissolve the assembly the following day.[128] Now that it was formally constituted he knew it would not be long before it proceeded to actions which he could not sanction by his presence, even with protestations. In a long and gloomy letter to the king he complained that 'so unfortunate have I been in this unlucky country, that though I did prefer your service before all worldly considerations, nay, even strained my conscience in some points, by subscribing the negative confession; yet all hath been to small purpose; for I have missed my end, in not being able to make your Majesty so considerable a party as will be able to curb the insolency of this rebellious nation, without assistance from England, and greater charge to your Majesty, than this miserable country is worth'. He even seems to hint that he expected a martyr's death from the covenanters; this might be the last letter he would write to the king, and he requested that his sons be brought up in England and his daughters 'be never married in Scotland'—'next Hell I hate this place'. He advised the king to subdue the country by using his navy to cut off its trade. Huntly should be appointed as his lieutenant in the North and Traquair or Roxburgh (or both) in the South, so that those who opposed the covenant would have some foci of resistance to which to rally and form an army. In future Scotland must be governed by a commissioner or deputy, as there must be some one person on whom responsibility lay;[129] Hamilton had seen the folly of expecting a spineless and divided privy council with no initiative to rule.

By the time the assembly met on the morning of 28 November the rumour had spread that Hamilton intended to dissolve it. The moderator asked the assembly to vote on whether or not it was competent to judge the bishops. Hamilton intervened, outlining the concessions the king had made and stating that the assembly could discuss only the matters that the king had summoned it to discuss. He complained that he had not found the respect due to the king's commissioner, and declared that, considering the papers that the Tables had sent out to influence elections to the assembly and the conduct of the elections, 'I can give no consent to any thing that is heir done'. There followed a long and increasingly bitter argument, between Hamilton on the one hand and Rothes and Loudoun on the other, over the elections and the membership and powers of the assembly. This broadened into a general attack by Hamilton on the usurpation of power by the covenanters.

Eventually he declared 'that nothing done heir in this Assembly shall be of any force to bind any of his Majestys subjects; and I in his Majesties name discharge this court to sit any longer'.[130] He then rose and left, the dignity of his exit being somewhat marred by the fact that the cathedral door had been locked and the key concealed so that it had to be broken open. Rothes made a protestation against his departure, and this was supported by all but a few members of the assembly, which then declared that it should continue to meet and that it was competent to judge the 'pretendit' archbishops and bishops.[131]

After leaving the assembly Hamilton held a meeting of the privy council to draft a proclamation confirming and justifying his dissolution of the assembly and ordering all its members to leave Glasgow (which only about half a dozen members obeyed).[132] The proclamation was met with the usual protest by Wariston.[133] Argyll had refused to attend the meeting of the council or to sign the proclamation; he had not left the assembly with Hamilton as his other assessors had done, thus for the first time openly siding with the covenanters.[134] He received a warm welcome from the assembly, and was allowed to sit and speak in it though not to vote. He was greeted not only as the most powerful of the Scottish nobility but also as one who (it was thought by the covenanters) still had the favour of Hamilton and the king, and some hoped that he could act as mediator. Argyll told the assembly that in signing the king's covenant he had bound himself to the 1581 confession in the same sense as it had originally been signed—which of course Craighall had declared to exclude episcopacy—and in the next few days seven other privy councillors (the Earls of Wigton, Kinghorn, Galloway and Mar, Lords Almond and Napier, and Sir Archibald Stewart of Blackhall) made similar statements.[135]

Now that Hamilton was no longer present to obstruct it, the assembly turned to reforming the church. After a few days mainly taken up with preparing acts, it passed an act on 4 December declaring the six general assemblies of 1606 to 1618 unlawful and null, as they had been dominated by the king and the bishops.[136] Two days later an act condemned the prayer book and the book of canons as unlawfully compiled, introduced without warrant from the kirk, and full of popish errors, while the court of high commission was denounced as illegally erected without consent of assembly or parliament.[137]

On 8 December the assembly voted that episcopacy had been abjured by the 1581 confession of faith and should be removed out of the kirk. Wariston records that he had heard that 'many scores' came to the assembly on 8 December determined to vote for the retention of episcopacy,[138] but this rumour was almost certainly untrue. Very few members wished to vote against removing episcopacy from the kirk, but there was a large minority of members who did not wish it to be declared abjured, since they believed that episcopacy 'such as it was in the ancient church, and in our church dureing Knox's dayes, in the person of the superintendents' was not unlawful though it was expedient to remove it from the kirk. Some at least of the leaders of the covenanters were willing to tolerate this attitude, and when Wariston as clerk called the roll of members' names in taking the vote on the question of whether by the 1581 confession episcopacy ought to be abjured and removed more than fifty members answered simply 'removed' instead of 'abjured and removed'. Yet in recording the vote Wariston marked all as having voted 'abjured and removed' (there were no votes against both parts of the motion) on the grounds that 'for answering affirmative to one part of the question, and negative to none, they ought to be taken as affirming the whole'.[139] All except Robert Baillie accepted this dubious proceeding and agreed to being thus counted as abjurers, and the act of assembly declaring episcopacy abjured and removed consequently states that the vote was unanimous except for one 'hesitation', presumably Baillie's.[140]

On 10 December the Five Articles of Perth were also declared abjured and removed,[141] and between 7 and 13 December all fourteen archbishops and bishops were deposed as episcopacy was illegal. Eight of them were also excommunicated and the rest suspended from acting as ministers until they submitted to the assembly and repented; they also were to be excommunicated if they did not submit. Seven ministers were deposed.[142] The church was to be governed in future by kirk sessions, presbyteries, synods and general assemblies, with the powers they had had in 1581, and the holding by ministers of any civil place or power was forbidden.[143] Finally, on 20 December, acts were made affirming the kirk's power to summon assemblies annually, summoning one to meet in Edinburgh on 17 July 1639, and banning the printing of any works concerning religion without licence from Wariston, who had been appointed advocate or procurator of the kirk as well as clerk of the assembly.[144] It was ordered that the national covenant should again be signed and sworn, this time with the addition of what became known as the Glasgow Declaration. This made explicit points which had been left vague when the covenant had been written nine months before, explaining that the covenant bound its signatories to abjure episcopacy, the Articles of Perth, and the civil powers of churchmen. Commissioners were appointed to represent to parliament articles from the assembly asking it to ratify the liberties of the kirk, and a supplication to the king was approved, begging him to agree to such a ratification.[145]

The assembly then dissolved itself (20 December). In the three weeks since Hamilton had left, it had ordered revolutionary changes in the government of the church and consequently in the balance of power in Scotland. Nothing had been done to define the place of the king in the kirk, but it was clear that he would be given very little part in controlling its activities. The abolition of the bishops and banning of churchmen from holding civil office deprived Charles of the services of some of his most loyal servants. The authors of this revolution were mainly laymen, supported by leading ministers, and the changes made were far wider than many ministers wished or felt were wise; Robert Baillie was typical of many in wishing that the Articles of Perth and episcopacy had been removed but not declared unlawful,[146] but few ministers dared to express such views openly. Lay covenanters had dominated the elections to the assembly, and though the ministers formed a majority in the assembly (about 140 out of a total membership of about 240)[147] it had been elders such as Rothes and Loudoun who had played the most prominent part in the assembly. Most of the ministers can have had little chance to open their mouths except when voting. Many must have feared that the kirk had exchanged domination by king and bishops for that of nobles and lairds.

After Hamilton had issued his proclamation dissolving the assembly on 29 November he had left Glasgow, issuing another proclamation from Holyroodhouse on 19 December annulling all acts of the assembly and denouncing its proceedings and those of the Tables.[148] The king approved his actions and authorised him to make Huntly his lieutenant in the North and Traquair or Roxburgh in the South if he thought it was absolutely necessary, but he urged Hamilton to continue to make promises to the covenanters to prevent open rebellion until forces were ready to invade Scotland in February or March 1639. Hamilton left for court to report to the king on 28 December, leaving Traquair in charge of the king's affairs in Scotland,[149] even though Traquair had already shown that he was liable to return to his old policy of trying to conciliate both king and covenanters. On 21 December he had exhibited a royal letter to the lords of session forbidding them to grant any letters of horning or other execution for exacting obedience to the acts of the assembly, but the next day he had stated that he was quite willing to suppress the letter if it gave any offence.[150]

CHAPTER FOUR

The First Bishops' War and the Treaty of Berwick, January–July 1639

MILITARY PREPARATIONS AND FIRST SKIRMISHES

By careful control of elections before, and scrutiny of membership during, the assembly, by terrorisation of their opponents outside the assembly and the presence of threatening crowds while it sat, the covenanters had pushed through their programme for the reform of the government and worship of the kirk, going further than many ministers wished. It is all too easy to assume that the outcome of the assembly was a foregone conclusion, but this was not how the covenanters themselves had viewed the situation; they had been in the event much more successful in silencing opposition than they had expected. In carrying out reform of the kirk without the king's consent they had gone further in defying him than ever before; their success in having reform accepted by the assembly in spite of Hamilton's attempt to dissolve it greatly increased their prestige. The step from demanding reform by the king to carrying out reform without him was a momentous one. The last months of 1638, as the covenanters had faced up to the necessity for such a step, had been a time of great tension. Decisive action by the assembly, making it clear that a policy of directly defying the king was to be followed, relaxed tension by reducing uncertainty. War was virtually inevitable. The covenanters would be satisfied by nothing less than the ratification of the acts of the assembly, while the king was determined to restore his authority. The prospect of war might be terrible but in some ways it was easier to bear than uncertainty. Indecisive and rather demoralising negotiation could now be replaced by constructive action.

At the beginning of January 1639 Rothes, Montrose, Balmerino and other leading covenanters held a meeting in Edinburgh which drafted a letter and detailed instructions to be sent round the country. The Earl of Argyll was present at this meeting and signed the letter; from this time onwards his voice was one of the most influential in the counsels of the covenanters. Remarkably he still did not sign the covenant, and it appears that it was not until April that he could be persuaded to sign,[1] so strong was his reluctance to commit himself fully to one party. But he showed no hesitation in joining in the covenanters' military preparations, especially those against the threat of an invasion from Ireland led by the Earl of Antrim; while in Edinburgh at the beginning of January he bought arms from an Edinburgh merchant, David Jonkin, and commissioned him to buy a fully armed frigate for him in Holland.[2]

The letter sent out by the meeting in Edinburgh related that Scotland was menaced by armies being raised to convert her liberty into slavery, and that it was necessary to use all lawful means to prevent this. The instructions began by outlining an administrative framework which was to be established to simplify the spreading and implementing of news and orders from Edinburgh. Each shire was to meet as soon as possible and choose two commissioners (or only one for small or remote shires) to go to Edinburgh and remain there for three months, after which they were to be replaced. The shire commissioners thus gathered in Edinburgh were to meet daily for consultations, to receive news, and to send orders and advice to their shires. Their expenses were to be paid by their shires, and in addition each shire was to pay in turn for the watch which was now being kept on Edinburgh castle. Each shire was also to choose one commissioner to remain in the shire to receive directions from the commissioners in Edinburgh and report them to meetings of one commissioner from each presbytery in the shire. The presbytery commissioners were in turn to pass on the information and orders they received to one commissioner for each parish in the presbytery. This parish commissioner, with the help of the parish minister, was to be responsible for execution of the orders originating from Edinburgh.

Shire committees of war were also to be established. These were to consist of the one commissioner from every presbytery already mentioned together with three or four other men from each presbytery. The main tasks of these committees were to be listing all those aged between sixteen and sixty in each parish who were able to bear arms, and what arms they had or were willing to buy, choosing from among these men those who were to be ready to serve as soldiers if necessary, and seeing that they were properly armed and trained. The committee was also to appoint officers; local gentlemen were to serve for three-month periods and then be replaced, thus spreading the burden of service and reducing jealousies among those who believed they had a right to be officers but were not appointed at first. However, to prevent the general lack of military training among those who thus thought they had a natural right of command, by virtue of property or ancestry, having a disastrous effect on military efficiency, certain ranks were reserved for skilled soldiers who were to be sent for from Holland and Germany—lieutenant-colonels, sergeant-majors, lieutenants and sergeants—while the colonels, captains and ensigns were to be nobles or gentlemen. The country was divided into quarters, each of which was to have an army organised and ready to come together for defence when necessary. Finally the instructions ordered the valuation of the rents of all parishes to be made so that the cost of the armies and other public expenses could be distributed equally.[3]

Of course these elaborate instructions were not carried out to the letter. In many areas other arrangements were made for raising soldiers and communicating with Edinburgh which were more suited to local conditions, but within a few weeks systematic efforts to train men were being made throughout most of the country,[4] and there was some body or committee existing in most shires to receive directions from the Tables. Few openly opposed military preparations. Most opponents of the covenant reluctantly concurred, paying their share of the expenses, rather than expose themselves to the hostility of covenanters, against which the king could offer them no protection. Many determined with Drummond of Hawthornden that:

Give me a thousand Covenants, I'll subscrive
Them all, or more, if more ye can contrive
Of rage and malice . . .
I'll not die martyr for a mortal thing:
Enough to be confessor for a King![5]

It was probably the same meeting which issued the instructions to the shires that sent a general call to Scottish Protestant officers in service abroad to return home to protect their country and religion; in February Sir James Lumsden begged for permission to leave the Swedish service, as 'I have received from the Scottish Estates, the authority placed by God and Nature over me, a peremptory call home, which I cannot disobey as a cavalier who loves his honour'.[6] Soon sufficient veteran officers had returned home to form a trained nucleus in the covenanters' forces. The motives of these officers who came home in 1638–40 and joined the covenanters are usually represented as religious zeal and nationalistic fervour, and certainly in many cases these were the main reasons, but there were others. When Alexander Leslie, the most famous of these officers, having risen to the rank of field marshal in the Swedish service, retired from it in 1638 he did so, it appears, to put himself at the disposal of Charles I who was contemplating sending forces to Germany to help his nephew, the Elector Palatine.[7] Only after the abandonment of this project did Leslie join the covenanters, late in 1638, becoming almost at once their chief military adviser. Similarly when James Turner, best known as a persecutor of covenanters after the Restoration, left Germany in 1640 to take part in the Second Bishops' War he was indifferent as to which side he joined; since the first ship he could get a passage on was going to Scotland rather than England he became a major in the forces of the covenant. He had, as he later explained, 'swallowed without chewing, in Germanie, a very dangerous maxime, which militarie men there too much follow; which was, that so we serve our master honnestlie, it is no matter what master we serve' and that 'I wronged not my conscience in doeing any thing I was commanded to doe by these whom I served'.[8] That many other Scottish officers held similar views is suggested by the fact that when in May 1639 a ship carrying about twenty of them to join the covenanters was captured by the king's ships, they all immediately offered to fight for the king instead.[9] Robert Monro, major-general of the Scottish army in Ireland from 1642 to 1648, was also said to have offered first to serve the king but, getting little encouragement, to have joined the covenanters.[10] Turner, Monro and their like were professional soldiers who welcomed a civil war in their native land as it gave them an opportunity to return home while continuing to make their living in the only way they knew, a somewhat paradoxical form of patriotism.

The fact remains, however, that though some of the Scottish officers trained in the Thirty Years War joined Charles I's armies in the Bishops' Wars, far more served the covenanters. This was partly the result of patriotism and militant Protestantism, but probably equally important was the fact that the covenanters quickly realised the importance of gaining the aid of such professional soldiers and actively solicited their help.

While preparing for war the covenanters continued to justify themselves by more peaceful means. George Winrame of Libberton left Edinburgh on 7 January with the assembly's supplication to the king and other papers to present to him or Hamilton, but though he stayed in London for some weeks he could not get a hearing or reply.[11] Instead the covenanters learnt the king's intentions (if they had any doubts left about them) from a letter written by the king to the nobility of England on 26 January. In this Charles announced that he was raising an army to resist any invasion from Scotland and required the nobles and forces raised by them to attend him at York on 1 April for defence of England.[12] The covenanters replied by issuing an Information addressed to all good Christians of England, dated 4 February, blaming the troubles on the prelates, affirming their loyalty to the king and denying any intention of invading England. They asked that their case might be judged by the parliament of England and talked of the two nations in one island which were 'once at variance, but now happily reconciled and tied together by the most strict Bonds, which We desire rather to encrease than diminish'.[13]

This apologia was said to have had a considerable effect on
opinion in England,[14] and in two respects it represented a widening of the covenanters' demands. For the first time their distrust of
the king led them to appeal beyond him to an English parliament;
and for the first time they went further than assurances of friendship for England by stating that they wished actually to strengthen
the bonds of union between the kingdoms. In the years ahead the
wish to strengthen the union was to emerge as one of the most
important of the covenanters' policies. The union of the crowns,
far from protecting Scotland as had been hoped, had enabled the
king to introduce unpopular policies from a safe distance. At first
the covenanters had sought only to change his policies, but his
refusal to do so led them on to re-think the union to protect themselves. To break the union completely and revert to independence was evidently unthinkable to the covenanters; apart from
anything else it would rouse English hostility, which the covenanters were realistic enough to see would be fatal to their cause.
Moreover destruction of the union of the crowns was virtually
impossible within their terms of reference; they could conceive of
no alternative to continued rule by their native Stewart dynasty
(however much they might limit its power) and obviously Charles
would not give up his English throne. Union therefore was inevitable, and the covenanters were also convinced that it was potentially beneficial to Scotland. Their answer to the failure of the union
of the crowns was not less union but more; permanent links between the parliaments to protect the liberties of the kingdoms from
the king, joint consultation to prevent misunderstandings and on
matters concerning both nations, free trade to promote prosperity.
Whether the covenanters had thought out this whole programme
for closer union by early 1639 is not clear, but, as the Information
shows, they had at least decided to seek closer union.

Charles answered the Information with a proclamation (27
February) denouncing the seditious practices of some Scots who
sought to overthrow regal power. This was regarded by the
covenanters as declaring them to be 'the foulest traitors and rebells
that ever breathed'[15] and was denounced by them in turn in a
remonstrance of 22 March lamenting that both the king's ears

were possessed by the false and spiteful misinformations of the late pretended bishops.[16]

Since war seemed unavoidable, an important part of the covenanters' propaganda was now concerned with justifying resistance to a king by his subjects. Naturally they turned to the writings of Scottish and foreign Calvinists and others on the subject. In January Wariston was making extracts from the works of Knox and Buchanan and drawing up reasons for resistance, and for a week in February he was 'busie on the question of defence'.[17] The question was one which troubled many, among them Robert Baillie and the Earl of Cassillis, who took much persuading of the legality of resisting the king. The covenanters therefore commissioned Alexander Henderson, 'our best penman' to write a paper on the subject, which he did, though 'somewhat against the hair [ie against his inclinations], and more quicklie than his custome is; so it was not so satisfactorie as his other wryts: for this cause, though read out in many pulpits, yet he would not let it go to the presse'.[18] In spite of Henderson's modesty his 'Instructions for Defensive Arms' is an interesting document, though unfortunately none of its arguments are developed at any length. It was regarded as worth printing in England on the eve of the civil war there to justify resistance to the king by parliament.[19]

The covenanters' standpoint as outlined by Henderson undoubtedly undermined royal power, temporal as well as spiritual, thus convincing Charles of how right he had been all along in believing that this had been their intention from the start. In fact it had rather been his insistence that this was their aim, and that therefore he could not compromise with them, that had eventually driven the covenanters to adopt such a position, a position of which few had dreamt eighteen months before when the first riots against the prayer book had taken place. Most of Henderson's arguments are old though in a new guise. The question at issue between the king and his kingdom is not, Henderson states, whether we should honour the king, or render to Caesar that which is Caesar's but 'whether honour should be given to evil and wicked superiors in an evil thing?'[20] Superiors wicked and evil in themselves should certainly be honoured and obeyed—they might be sent by God as a punishment. Only if such evil superiors ordered evil things, contrary to God, might they be resisted; indeed they then must be resisted, since clearly when the orders of God and man conflict, God must be obeyed. In such circumstances Henderson indicated that even private citizens have a right to resist, but added that it is far more justifiable if resistance is led by the inferior magistrates, those who have a natural part in ruling the kingdom; this was, he claimed, the situation in Scotland, where all (except for a few papists and their like) were standing to defence. Henderson proceeded to explain that there is a 'line and order of subordination wherein both magistrates and people are placed', a hierarchy from the ultimate superior, God, down through the chief magistrate and the various levels of inferior magistrates to the people. If the chief magistrate gives orders contrary to God, then he breaks this chain 'and goeth out of his order and line'. In these circumstances God became the immediate superior of the chief magistrate's subjects until the magistrate returned to his place in line. This assertion that the magistrate who steps out of the divine hierarchy and order of society (as, it is assumed, Charles had done) must be resisted is Henderson's main and most plausible argument, though he notes many more without explaining them, some general and some specific to the circumstances of 1639; the law of nature gives a right of self defence, there is a mutual contract between king and people exemplified in the coronation oath, Scottish history and acts of parliament ratify the authority of the estates, the national covenant binds its signatories to resistance in the circumstances. Moreover, claims Henderson, there is a difference 'between the king resident in the kingdom, opening his ears to both parties, and rightly informed; and the king far from us, in another kingdom, hearing the one party, and misinformed by our adversaries'. Henderson's paper well served its purpose, giving the covenanters ammunition for use in arguing with opponents or the unconvinced, and helped many to accept resistance to the king. But most were probably won over not by his abstract arguments but by the political realities noted in the last words of the paper: 'Except we stand fast to our liberty we can look for nothing but miserable and perpetual slavery'. There

Page 135 A CONTRAST IN KING'S COMMISSIONERS (*see next page*):
James, 3rd Marquis and 1st Duke of Hamilton, 1606–49. By Daniel Mytens,
1629

Page 136 A CONTRAST IN KING'S COMMISSIONERS (*see previous page*): John Stewart, 1st Earl of Traquair, *c.* 1600–59, treasurer, 1636–41

was no going back to the conditions of two years before, for unless the king was resisted he would introduce changes in Scotland just as revolutionary as any the covenanters would make, in order to assert his authority.

Henderson ignored the most difficult question of all: who was to judge what God's commands were and when the chief magistrate was 'out of line'? The covenanters assumed their own right, that of subjects and inferior magistrates, but even had the king accepted the 'line of order' argument he would never have admitted the right of subjects to judge and was hardly likely ever to adjudge himself out of line. The problem was insoluble. It had arisen in the debates between Mary Queen of Scots and John Knox, and indeed had been the basic problem in most sixteenth-century political controversy.[21] It was to be raised repeatedly by the king at the treaty of Berwick in June 1639 and in other treaties with his English and Scottish subjects in the next ten years. In practice the only answer was to be that he who had the power to impose his own interpretation was right.

Meanwhile preparations for that armed resistance which Henderson had written to justify continued. General meetings in Edinburgh in February and March ordered the raising of troops to guard the Borders, while in the North East forces were gathered in arms under Montrose to oppose the burgh of Aberdeen (which still refused to obey the orders of the covenanters) and the Marquis of Huntly. To pay these troops 200,000 merks were borrowed from William Dick of Braid, the richest Edinburgh merchant and the farmer of the king's customs and impost as well as provost of the burgh.[22] It was decided to send one William Colville to the United Provinces and France to explain events in Scotland and beg the States General and the King of France to mediate between the covenanters and their king (to whom they emphasised their loyalty), while Robert Meldrum (secretary to Alexander Leslie) went on a similar mission to the kings of Sweden and Denmark,[23] but though letters and instructions were drafted for Colville's journey[24] it was later thought expedient to abandon the plans. Such appeals to foreign powers, it was feared, might give rise to anti-Scottish feeling in England, and many covenanters were much

9

opposed to receiving help from Lutheran Swedes and Danes, let alone from the papist French.[25] Thus though there may have been some contacts between agents of the covenanters and those of Cardinal Richelieu before the end of the First Bishops' War, rumours that the Cardinal had promised help to the Scots—which were believed by Charles I—were probably unfounded.[26]

Since the Glasgow Assembly and Hamilton's departure for England the privy council had not made any pretence at interfering with the covenanters' activities; it met seldom and did little, for nearly all the councillors who were opposed to the covenant had fled to England or at least given up attending its meetings.[27] In the latter half of March a fluctuating group of moderate councillors began to try to persuade the king not to invade Scotland, and in this they were joined by some of the lords of session. They sent a letter to the king with the justice clerk, Hamilton of Orbiston, stating that an invasion of Scotland would be a remedy worse than the disease, and that matters of faith could not be settled by force. They begged him to reflect 'that bloodie warres have ever bein to harden the spirits of men to opposition in matters of conscience, and to increase their number'. Moreover many would fight to defend Scotland against an invading English army who were not covenanters.[28] On 11 April and again in the middle of May these councillors and lords of session resolved to go to the king and throw themselves at his feet to supplicate him to spare Scotland from his royal wrath, but they got no encouragement from the king, and the covenanters refused them permission to go to England;[29] both king and covenanters were determined on a military solution.

Predictably the war began in the North East, if the bloodless campaign of manoeuvring forces around Aberdeen in March 1639 can be called war. In January the burgh council of Aberdeen had indicated its determination to resist the covenanters by force if necessary by deciding to arm and train men. In these preparations the burgh had the approval of the Marquis of Huntly, and he and the burgh council prevented the acts of the Glasgow assembly and other papers of the covenanters being published in Aberdeen.[30] Huntly, the greatest nobleman in the North East, was a loyal supporter of the king, but as he had spent most of his life in France he was little known in Scotland, and he had no wish to play a leading part in public affairs, being no leader of men.

Meetings of covenanters and their opponents, and of various 'names' and other groups in the North East were soon being held to decide what attitude to adopt to the approaching conflict. The 'name of Forbes' held a meeting at Monymusk 'for thair awin bussiness' on 14 January. This was inspired by the covenanters and Huntly thought it necessary to convene a rival meeting of his friends and vassals at Kintore on 18 January.[31] The nobles and gentry of Inverness met on 31 January and agreed to obey the covenanters' instructions.[32] On the same day the Master of Forbes, Lord Fraser, James Crichton of Frendraught and several hundred others met at Turriff to choose commissioners to reside in Edinburgh. They agreed to meet again at Turriff on 14 February to report on what had been done.[33]

The first of a series of confrontations and bloodless trials of strength took place early in February at Inverness when several Fraser and Mackenzie lairds seized for their own use arms and ammunition sent by Huntly to Inverness castle.[34] More important was the confrontation at Turriff a week later. Huntly had heard of the meeting of covenanters which was to be held there on 14 February and on the advice of Sir George Ogilvie of Banff he had summoned his own supporters to meet there on the same day, hoping to overawe the covenanters into cancelling their meeting. Instead the covenanters accepted Huntly's challenge and occupied Turriff with about 800 armed horsemen. Huntly approached with many more men but withdrew once it became clear that the covenanters were prepared to fight,[35] a moral defeat that much discouraged royalists. If he was not willing to use force Huntly would have been much better advised to have ignored the covenanters' meeting, yet it seems clear that he had never intended to fight. He had recently received a letter from the king appointing him king's lieutenant for the North of Scotland but ordering him to keep this secret for as long as possible and not to take any aggressive action unless provoked, as the king's English forces were not yet ready and the covenanters would be able to concentrate all their forces

against him if he rose in arms too soon.[36] Encouraged by Huntly's
withdrawal, the covenanters prepared to occupy Aberdeen and
disperse his forces; attempts were made to negotiate with him, but
these came to nothing.[37] An army under Montrose and Alexander
Leslie marched north and met with no opposition, for Huntly
decided not to fight even in self-defence when thus provoked, and
disbanded his forces. Demoralised by this, Aberdeen abandoned all
thoughts of resistance and was occupied by the covenanters on
30 March, while those known for their opposition to the covenant
fled.[38]

Immediately before Montrose had moved north the covenanters
had in a series of bloodless assaults within a few days captured
every castle in the Lowlands that they feared might be held for the
king against them, except for the Earl of Nithsdale's castles of
Caerlaverock and Threave.[39] The half-hearted attempts of the king
and his supporters to garrison and supply the castles had usually
been thwarted by the vigilant covenanters. Sir Patrick Ruthven, a
professional soldier trained in Germany and a loyal supporter of
the king who had recently been appointed muster master general
of Scotland and captain of Edinburgh castle, refused to command
its garrison as he regarded the castle as indefensible.[40] Consequently it was manned only by a few demoralised men when on 21
March a force of covenanters led by Alexander Leslie blew up the
outer gate, broke down the two inner ones and occupied the castle
without a shot being fired.[41] Two days later the king's house at
Dalkeith was similarly seized; Traquair made no attempt to defend
it[42] and fled to England. Most of the small, ill-supplied and
mutinous garrison of Dumbarton castle and their commander
were rounded up when they unwisely left the castle to attend
church on 26 March.[43] The Marquis of Douglas' castles at Tan-
tallon and Douglas were likewise peacefully occupied. The island
of Arran was garrisoned by Argyll's forces as it belonged to the
Marquis of Hamilton.[44] Thus in the last ten days of March 1639
the covenanters deprived the royalists of virtually all the Lowland
houses and castles which might have served as centres of opposition to the covenant, while in the North Aberdeen was occupied
and Huntly's forces disbanded.

CONFRONTATION ON THE BORDER AND WAR IN THE NORTH

The king's preparations for war outside Scotland were also meeting with difficulties. At the beginning of the year he had a grandiose plan of campaign that looked very well on paper. Levies in England would raise 30,000 men which the king would lead to the borders. Five thousand men under Hamilton would land at Aberdeen to join Huntly, who would advance south after securing the North. The Earl of Antrim would land in Argyll with ten or twelve thousand men from Ulster, while Viscount Wentworth brought a fleet and more men from Ireland to land at Dumbarton, the fleet using Arran as a base.[45] But by early April this plan was in ruins. Far fewer men than the king had hoped had been raised in England, and many of those that had been collected lacked arms, training and discipline. With Huntly overawed and Aberdeen occupied Hamilton's force had nowhere to land and no army to join. Antrim's boasts of his influence and resources had proved to be out of all proportion to reality and his promised army never materialised.[46] Wentworth's men would not be ready until the end of June, and with Dumbarton castle and Arran occupied by the covenanters there was no safe base for them. He therefore begged the king to wait until 1640 before attempting to defeat the covenanters rather than risk failure by attacking with inadequate forces,[47] but the king would not listen.

In the face of all these setbacks the king and Hamilton remained optimistic; Hamilton's forces could be diverted to the Firth of Forth to harry the covenanters there while the king invaded from England. They approved a proclamation to be published in Scotland by Hamilton. This promised that the king would uphold the religion, liberty and laws of Scotland and the concessions that he had formerly granted, but stated that some seditious men in Scotland were trying to overthrow monarchical government. Those who submitted would be pardoned, except for nineteen leading covenanters who were declared guilty of treason and excluded from all hope of pardon. These included the Earls of Argyll, Rothes and Montrose, Lords Balmerino and Loudoun, Wariston and Alexander Leslie. Rewards were offered to any who brought the heads (or other certain proof of death) of any of these men to the king, though the ministers were to be degraded from their ministry by the church before punishment.[48]

This warrant to licence head-hunting, the assassination of their opponents, is a remarkable indication of how little understanding the king and Hamilton had of the situation in Scotland or of the state of public opinion there and in England. Neither had any liking for Scotland which they saw as backward and barbarous, and they assumed that such barbarity would be acceptable and effective there in terrifying the population into submission. The issuing of this proclamation would undoubtedly have united opinion in Scotland more firmly than ever behind the covenanters, while in England it would have been widely accepted as clear evidence that the covenanters were justified in resisting a king who was acting tyrannically. The precedent for a king promising rewards for assassination that would immediately spring to mind was Philip II of Spain's encouragement of the murder of William the Silent in 1584, and any covenanter who was thus killed would immediately have become a Protestant and national hero and martyr. The king was saved from making the disastrous miscalculation of issuing the proclamation by the justice clerk (who had brought him the letter from councillors and lords of sessions begging him to act moderately) and Sir Lewis Stewart. The king showed them the draft proclamation; they were horrified and, as he wrote to Hamilton, 'they have both been very instant with me to change some thing of it'. After discussion Charles had the proclamation rewritten and the first version suppressed.[49] The new proclamation (published at York on 25 April) opened like its predecessor with promises that the king would maintain concessions he had previously granted. None were excluded from pardon, but any who did not submit within eight days of the publication of the proclamation would have their lands and other possessions confiscated and distributed among those loyal to the king, while their vassals and tenants were encouraged to support the king by promises that if they did their rents would be greatly reduced once the rebels were defeated.[50]

Charles had arrived in York on 30 March.[51] He had already

appointed the Earl of Arundel (who was generally believed to be a Catholic) general of the forces he was raising in England, and on 7 April he appointed Hamilton general of the forces to be used against the rebels in Scotland,[52] though he presumably had authority only over the 5,000 men he was to take to Scotland by sea and forces raised in Scotland. Hamilton was at Yarmouth with a fleet taking aboard his men. He promised to do all he could to get the king's proclamation published in Scotland, or at least all he could with 5,000 untrained men, for his optimism was already crumbling; he admitted to being worried by the facts that only 200 of his men had ever held muskets before and that many of their officers had not appeared. The men would need at least a month's training once they landed from his ships before they could fight; 'I expected trained men, ueel armed and expert in the handling of them, who at our verie first landing might a been able to haue done service . . . It is true so long as we ar aboard we are safe, but that will not annoye the rebells as I intended'.[53] However, Hamilton's presence in the Firth of Forth even if he made no landing would force the covenanters to leave troops to guard against a potential landing and thus reduce the size of the army they could send to the Borders. Charles intended to reach Berwick with his army by the middle of May[54] and by that time Hamilton hoped to have had his proclamation published in Edinburgh and that the eight days given to the rebels in it in which to submit would have expired.[55] Things did not go according to plan. Hamilton's fleet entered the Firth of Forth on 1 May and anchored off Leith while the beacon fires of the covenanters blazed round the firth to give warning of his arrival. He found it impossible to get the king's proclamation published or any obedience given to him as king's commissioner and general.[56] To these difficulties was added the embarrassment of having his mother, a staunch covenanter, threaten to shoot him herself if he attempted to land; 'the Lady Marqueis of Hamilton rydis on the heides of hir troupes boith day and nycht with hir pistollis and carbine'.[57] By 7 May he was in despair and wrote to the king that there was no hope of the covenanters submitting peacefully and that it would be a work of great difficulty and vast expense to subdue them by force. However, if the king was still resolved to use force, Hamilton would raid and burn the coastal towns, thus forcing the covenanters to keep large forces on both sides of the firth while the king attacked from the south, but this would have to be done quickly as the provisions of his fleet were running out—though on the other hand a few days' delay would be necessary, as his men still did not know how to fire their muskets! The king's army was not yet ready to attack, and therefore he ordered Hamilton to revert to the policy of the previous year—to negotiate with the covenanters to fill in time until his preparations were completed. This Hamilton did, though neither he nor the covenanters can have regarded the papers which passed back and forward between them as anything but an excuse for delay.[58] In fact the king was now uncertain as to whether he should attack or not; first Wentworth and now Hamilton had advised that the covenanters were too strong for the forces he had at his disposal. Irresolutely he changed his mind from day to day. On 23 May he instructed Hamilton to send two of his three regiments back to England as he feared they would be needed to meet an invasion by the covenanters, but by 2 June he could write to Hamilton 'now I set you loose' to attack the covenanters with what forces he had left. Finally two days later he informed Hamilton that he had decided to remain on the defensive and ordered him to return to England.[59]

While Hamilton had been away the king's hopes had been undermined and had eventually collapsed. Only about half the 30,000 men he had called for had been assembled, and most of them were far from enthusiastic or well trained. Few of the English nobles whom he had summoned to York were in favour of war.[60] This was partly the king's own fault, for while the covenanters bombarded the English nobles and army officers with letters justifying themselves, denying that they had any quarrel with England and blaming the King's evil advisers for their troubles,[61] the secretive king did not deign to explain to them his intentions and policies towards Scotland. 'The king for divers dayes had privat consultation with his Scotch Councel and others but no English was ever admitted'.[62] Charles still held that Scottish affairs were not the business of his English subjects, even though he expected

them to invade Scotland for him to impose his policies. His discouragement at the weakness of his own forces and rumours of the
strength of the covenanters is reflected in a proclamation he issued
at Newcastle on 14 May. This related that he intended to be in
Berwick soon and would give his Scottish subjects all satisfaction
in parliament as soon as the disorders were quieted. Provided
they swore all temporal and civil obedience to him (a phrase so
vague and open to differing interpretations that the covenanters
had always been willing to give such promises) he had no intention of invading Scotland, but the covenanters must keep their
troops at least ten miles north of the border.[63] Clearly the king was
now more concerned to keep the covenanters out of England than
with plans to defeat them in battle. But on 30 May the king joined
his army which was camped at Birks (three miles west of Berwick),
and once with the army, which now numbered perhaps 21,000
men, he became more optimistic and sent some troops to publish
his proclamation of 25 April at Duns.[64] The covenanters had
obeyed the king's injunction that they should keep their forces
ten miles north of the border, but they regarded themselves as
freed from any obligation to continue to do so by this invasion
and sent forces to occupy Kelso. On 3 June Charles sent about
3,300 men to drive them out, but they found themselves greatly
outnumbered by the Scots and hastily retreated back into
England. The effect of this on morale was disastrous, and the
ephemeral confidence instilled into Charles by the experience of
being (for the first time in his life) at the head of an army evapo-
rated; it was the day after the retreat that he announced to Hamilton his determination to remain on the defensive. His army lacked
discipline and training, money was running out and few in England had any desire to fight the Scots. When the covenanters' main
army advanced to Duns Law on 5 June few in the king's camp
thought it could be resisted. Therefore when the Scots sent a
supplication asking for negotiations the king agreed.[65]

Great as was the relief of the king's advisers when negotiations
began, it was probably exceeded by that of the leading covenanters,
for the advance of their army to Duns Law had been largely a bluff.
The reports of its strength and condition which much influenced

the king were the result of propaganda and concealed serious
weaknesses which, had he known of them, would have made him
far less willing to negotiate. Since their triumphs in March the
covenanters' preparations for war had not gone smoothly, and
resistance to them in the North East had not been as effectively
discouraged as they had hoped. After the occupation of Aberdeen
on 30 March Montrose marched north in pursuit of Huntly. They
met on 5 April and Huntly signed some sort of undertaking that
he would adhere to the 1581 confession of faith, would defend the
authority of the king and the liberties, religion and laws of the
kingdom, and would allow his followers to sign the covenant.[66]
Montrose then returned to Aberdeen where a meeting of northern
covenanters discussed the settlement. Many were dissatisfied with
his conduct, believing that he had not extracted sufficient guarantees and promises from Huntly as to his future good conduct.
They therefore invited Huntly to attend their meeting in Aberdeen, giving him an assurance signed by Montrose and others that
he would be allowed to leave freely afterwards. Huntly came with
his two elder sons, Lords Gordon and Aboyne. After several
meetings Montrose demanded that he should contribute a large
sum towards the expenses of the covenanters' army, and when he
refused this and other demands he was 'invited' to come to Edinburgh. On finding that he would be taken as a prisoner if he did
not go voluntarily he agreed, and he and Lord Gordon arrived in
Edinburgh on 19 April and were imprisoned in the castle the
following day; Lord Aboyne had promised to follow them south
but was persuaded not to do so by some royalist lairds.[67]

After this kidnapping of Huntly the covenanters in the North
East concentrated on the work of imposing the covenant, fining
their opponents and purging the ministry and universities.[68] But
the treatment of Huntly aroused indignation among royalists, and
rather than submit and sign the covenant Lord Aboyne, Sir George
Ogilvie of Banff and about 2,000 men gathered in arms to resist.
Aboyne suddenly disbanded his forces and left by sea to consult
the king but in spite of this setback Banff remained in arms and
was joined by Sir Thomas Urquhart of Cromarty, Sir John Gordon
of Haddo, Sir George Gordon of Gight and others, and the first

blood of the civil war was shed on 10 May when they attempted unsuccessfully to recover some arms (which had been seized by the covenanters) from a house defended by Lord Fraser and the Master of Forbes; one of Gight's servants, David Prat, was shot dead, the first of the many thousands who were to die in the civil wars of England, Scotland and Ireland in the next fifteen years. The royalists then determined to prevent a meeting of covenanters planned at Turriff from taking place. Early on the morning of 14 May they drove the covenanters who had already assembled there out of the burgh after a short fight and forced the inhabitants to sign the king's covenant.[69]

This 'Trot of Turriff' took the covenanters by surprise; after the removal of Huntly they had expected no further trouble and most of their forces had disbanded or moved south. Consequently there was no one to oppose Banff and his colleagues when, encouraged by their success, they marched on Aberdeen and occupied the burgh on 15 May. But though this encouraged other lairds and men to join them, their position was untenable. They had risen in arms to avoid being disarmed and forced to sign the covenant, but they had no plan of campaign and no idea what to do next, and would soon be faced with large forces of covenanters assembled to deal with them. They therefore abandoned Aberdeen after five days and after indulging in some plundering of the houses of prominent covenanters simply dissolved their forces and went home. The unfortunate burgh was reoccupied on 23 May by covenanters led by the Earl Marischal, who was joined two days later by more than 4,000 men led by Montrose and Kinghorn, while thousands more covenanters from the North converged on Aberdeen, only to find that the royalist 'army' had vanished, so they 'could hardlye tell wher to fynde ane enemye'. Most of the covenanters returned home while Montrose marched north to besiege the houses of the royalist lairds,[70] but before he could do anything he was recalled to Aberdeen by another sudden reversal of fortune. On 2 June several of the king's ships appeared off Aberdeen with Lord Aboyne and other royalists on board, including the Earls of Glencairn and Tullibardine, Sir Alexander Irvine of Drum and, surprisingly, Banff and several other of the lairds who

had just been in arms; they had set sail for England to escape
Montrose but had met Aboyne's ships carrying arms and ammunition sent by the king.

The covenanters feared that this had been timed to coincide
with a landing by Hamilton further south, so Montrose and
Marischal made no attempt to oppose Aboyne but marched south
with all their forces. Aberdeen again changed hands, the royalists
landing there on 6 June. Once Montrose and Marischal found
that there was no danger in the south they again marched north
with about 2,300 men. They found Aboyne awaiting them at
Bridge of Dee just south of Aberdeen with about the same
number of men on 18 June. An assault on the bridge that day
failed but it was stormed the next day; Aboyne fled, his forces
dispersed and the covenanters entered Aberdeen for the third
time—the day after the king had reached an agreement with the
covenanters at Berwick.[71]

Though little blood was shed, these disturbances forced the
covenanters to divert troops to the North at the very time when
they were anxious to concentrate their forces in the South to
oppose the expected invasion by the king. Nor were this and
Hamilton's fleet in the Firth of Forth the only diversions troubling
the covenanters. Many still feared a landing by Antrim in the West
and (though this did not become clear until later) the enemies of
the Campbells in the Western Highlands and Isles—including Sir
James Lamont, Macdonald of Sleat, MacLeod of Dunvegan,
MacLean of Duart, Sir James Stewart (sheriff of Bute) and Sir
Archibald Stewart of Blackhall—were ready to join any such invasion.[72] These plots in the West came to nothing as no army arrived
from Ireland, but there were other alarms in the area—measures
had to be taken to defend Islay when ships from the king's fleet
appeared there.[73]

The gathering of the main army of the covenanters was delayed
and hindered by troubles similar to those experienced by the king
—difficulty in raising the men ordered, lack of money, lack of
arms—though in one very important particular they had a great
advantage over the king: morale. For though they might be badly
fed, armed and trained, most of the officers and men at least had

enthusiasm for the cause for which they were preparing to fight. By the end of April the Tables in Edinburgh had sent instructions to the shires to send to the Lothians the fourth man—that is, a quarter of those aged between 16 and 60 who were able to bear arms—with arms or money to buy them. Any who refused were to have their estates confiscated and devoted to public uses.[74]

The parliament indicted by Hamilton in the king's name the previous September was due to meet on 15 May, but much as the covenanters wanted a parliament this was clearly not the time for one. With invasion by the king thought to be imminent, all attention needed to be devoted to military matters, and the inevitable arguments and disputes of a parliament would be a distraction apt to split the unity which the covenanters were so anxious to preserve. However, they prepared to hold the parliament lest the king should claim they had refused to let a parliament meet when he had granted them one. Charles did not realise this and believed that the covenanters wanted to hold a parliament. He therefore obligingly sent a commission to Craighall on 11 May to prorogue parliament until 23 July, and the covenanters gladly let this be done.[75] But they made use of the fact that a parliament had been summoned by getting those due to meet in it to gather in Edinburgh on 9 May, and this 'convention', as the covenanters called it, of 'noblemen, lords of parliament, commissioners of schyres, and commissioners of burrowes for the parliament' granted a commission to Alexander Leslie to be general of all the forces of the covenant, and promised obedience to him in everything respecting his duties.[76] The choice of Leslie as general was a wise one, not only because he was the best-known and most experienced Scottish soldier of his day, but also because the appointment of one of the nobles as general would have caused jealousies among the others. All the nobles agreed to obey him and give him precedence over them; as an outward sign of this he now (when present) signed all letters written by the covenanters before the nobles signed (in carefully formed, childish letters, as he could barely write). He admirably combined authority and tact so as to get himself obeyed without causing offence; 'we were feared that emulation among our Nobles might have done harme, when they should be mett in the fields; bot such was the wisdome and authoritie of that old, little, crooked souldier, that all, with ane incredible submission, from the beginning to the end, gave over themselves to be guided by him'.[77]

By the middle of May the failure of many of the men expected to join the main army of the covenant in the Lothians was leading to fears that it would be impossible to oppose an invasion by the king adequately, and therefore on 24 May new orders were sent out by the general and other leading covenanters with the army at Dunbar to the shires, renewing pleas that men be sent as previously ordered.[78] On 28 May an impassioned letter from the army demanded the sending of all forces possible to oppose the king's army: 'all that loves the good of this cause and their owne safetie' were to come in haste; 'let none stay at home when strangers ar hyred for three shillings a week to make us all slaves'.[79] Another letter stated bluntly that the Borders would be lost unless help was sent at once as 'we have no horsmen at all, ther is no provision of victuals and money'. Efforts in the next few days to provide food, money and men had little success.[80] On 3 June Wariston, Alexander Henderson, David Dickson and Robert Meldrum discussed the situation and concluded that the army could not advance, retreat or remain where it was. But (unlike the king's advisers in similar circumstances) they remained confident and took the remarkable action of drafting a document on which Dickson formally took instruments 'that whensoever God should give us a glorious outgate' none of the covenanters would claim any credit since only God's intervention could bring about victory. Thus the strength of the covenanters' faith gave them confidence even at a time when it seemed they were facing disaster. The next day (according to Wariston) the general himself acknowledged that this was a true summary of the situation.[81] Yet Robert Baillie's description of the army a few days later (when it was camped at Duns Law) states that it had sufficient food, and moreover that it was so well supplied that it would not have to worry about lack of food or money for several months to come.[82] This was certainly not true. The army's efforts to find food may have provided it with enough for a few days, but Baillie's belief in the existence of adequate supplies for the future is an indication of the success of the covenanters' propaganda, of a determined effort to convince their enemies of their strength and disguise the true situation.

THE TREATY

The bluff was successful, and the king was convinced that he was faced by an army similar in numbers to his own but much better supplied as well as superior in morale. He was therefore ready to negotiate with those he had come to conquer—though this did not prevent his secretly issuing commissions on 5 and 11 June to the Earl of Antrim and Sir Donald Macdonald of Sleat to be his joint lieutenants in the Western Isles and Highlands to attack the rebels.[83] On 6 June Robin Leslie, one of the king's Scottish pages, appeared in Duns and 'as it were of his own head' suggested that the covenanters should supplicate the king to negotiate with them. It is possible that his suggestion was secretly inspired by the king who was anxious to negotiate but wished to avoid the humiliation of making the first public move himself. The covenanters readily agreed to the proposal and the next day sent the Earl of Dunfermline to the king with a supplication humbly begging him to appoint some Englishmen well affected to the true religion and the common peace to negotiate with some like-minded Scots, so that all misunderstandings between the two kingdoms might be removed. The king's answer was brought to a meeting of nobles and lairds convened by the general the next day by Sir Edmund Verney, knight marshal of the king's household. He informed the covenanters that the king would do as they asked, but only if they would publish his proclamation of 25 April in their camp. The proclamation was read to the meeting but it was decided that it should not be published, and Verney was sent back to the king with this answer and a note of the reasons for the covenanters' refusal.[84]

Yet the next day, 8 June, the king sent a message to the covenanters stating that 'having understood of the obedience of the Petitioners in reading his proclamation' he granted their desire and would appoint six men to negotiate with their commissioners in his camp on 10 June. The explanation for this was evidently that

Sir Edmund Verney, a man sympathetic to the Scots and greatly desiring peace, had feared that the covenanters' answer would lead the king to refuse to negotiate. He therefore seems to have lied to the king, telling him that his proclamation had been published or that reading it was equivalent to publication, and suppressing the list of reasons the Scots had given him to present to the king explaining why they had not done so; well might Verney write 'I dare bouldly say I handled the business soe that I begatt this treaty'.[85] The covenanters sent denials to the English nobles that they had published the proclamation, but they did not inform the king, and if he heard of the denials he ignored them.

The treaty was delayed for one day by a Scots demand for a safe conduct for their commissioners, as the king felt that this was a reflection on his honour and refused to send one. Eventually the Scots accepted a verbal assurance from him, and the treaty of Birks or Berwick began on 11 June.[86] The Earls of Rothes and Dunfermline, Lord Loudoun and Sir William Douglas of Cavers (sheriff of Teviotdale) represented the covenanters. They expected to negotiate with English commissioners appointed by the king, but he entered as soon as the meeting began and took the leading part in the negotiations, his commissioners becoming little more than onlookers; he had appointed them because that was what the covenanters had asked, but he probably never had any intention of letting English and Scottish commissioners discuss a settlement by themselves, in effect sitting in judgement on his past actions. Rothes opened the proceedings by attempting to justify the conduct of the covenanters, but seeing that this was irritating the king and leading nowhere Loudoun directed attention to the 'humble desires' or demands of the covenanters which had been drawn up in advance. These were that the king would ratify the acts of the Glasgow assembly in parliament; that he would declare that in future all matters ecclesiastical would be determined by general assemblies and all matters civil by parliament, which would meet at set times every two or three years; that he would recall all the forces he had sent against Scotland; and, finally, that all incendiaries and informers who had caused the troubles through malice and for their own private ends should be returned to

Scotland for punishment, all proclamations inspired by them being suppressed.

The most novel and far-reaching of these demands is obviously the second, that in future parliaments and general assemblies should determine all matters civil and ecclesiastical respectively. The demand is so vague that it is impossible to know how wide the powers were that the covenanters intended at this time to give parliaments and general assemblies, and what authority they would leave to the king. Probably they themselves had not yet thought out the implications of the demand; they were determined to prevent the king withdrawing at some future date the concessions that they now insisted on his making, and thought they could best do this by insisting in general terms that he abandon the power to make alterations in kirk and state.

The king's reply to the demands was that it had always been his intention to protect laws and religion 'but the question will be at last, who shall be the judge of the meaning of those laws?', and again 'when I say one thing, and you another, who shall judge?' After a fruitless squabble over the legality of the Glasgow assembly the king asked whether the covenanters would be willing to state that all they desired was the enjoyment of their laws and religion, and that they would give him all civil and temporal obedience. They agreed and Loudoun wrote and signed a memorandum to this effect. Charles appears to have regarded this as a notable concession, though he himself had earlier shown that vague phrases without agreement on who should interpret them were useless.[87] A second meeting was held on 13 June, attended by Alexander Henderson and Archibald Johnston of Wariston as well as the other four Scots commissioners. As at the previous meeting, arguments over specific points led nowhere. Eventually the king declared that if the covenanters' full desires were only those contained in the memorandum he would accept them, and that he would answer their more detailed demands on 15 June.[88]

The answer he then gave was that he could not ratify the acts of the Glasgow assembly but that he was content that all matters ecclesiastical should be settled by assemblies of the kirk and all civil matters by parliament and inferior judicatories, and that assemblies and parliaments should meet yearly or so often as was necessary. If the covenanters dissolved their forces and meetings, restored his castles and property taken from royalists, then he would withdraw his fleet and army.[89] The Scots found this inadequate, for though superficially the king seemed to have made concessions, they were nearly all expressed in terms which would allow him to disclaim them if he wished. For example, ecclesiastical matters were referred to assemblies of the kirk, not specifically to general assemblies. Again, these assemblies were to meet yearly or so often as was necessary; did this mean they were certainly to meet yearly, or only if necessary? Wariston especially showed deep suspicion of the king's intentions; if the king had refused to ratify the acts of the Glasgow assembly or to accept its composition including elders, was not this an implicit pre-limitation on the next assembly and an indication that if it passed similar acts the king would refuse to ratify them? Indignantly the king 'answered that the devill himself could not make a more uncharitable construction or give a more bitter expression',[90] forgetting 'that this devilish interpretation of his actions was unquestionably correct'.[91] The Scots said that no settlement would be acceptable unless the king explicitly agreed to the removal of the bishops, and on their knees 'assured him that as long as he keiped them up . . . he wold never winne the hearts, nor keepe peace in this kingdome'. Charles would give no immediate answer, promising that he would reply on 17 June. But at the new meeting he offered no significant concessions.[92]

By now the covenanters were thoroughly alarmed; they had been negotiating for a week but a settlement seemed little nearer. The fear arose that perhaps after all the king had not agreed to negotiate through alarm at the strength of the covenanters but merely to delay a military decision for a few weeks until his own army was reinforced and that of the covenanters was forced to retire through lack of provisions. If there was to be a battle, the covenanters would prefer it to be as soon as possible, before the strength of their army was eroded by delay. It was therefore resolved that if at the next meeting with the king real progress was not made, the covenanters would break off negotiations, advance their army to the Tweed and 'lay down our leaguer within shott of cannon to the King's trenches'. This threat had the desired effect; at the meeting on 18 June the king was willing to make concessions, and articles of pacification were agreed and signed.[93] Or at least this was the account of events give by Robert Baillie; in fact the articles show that it was the covenanters who made most of the concessions, getting in return only vague verbal assurances from the king the meaning of which could never afterwards be agreed. Above all the covenanters consented to disband their army without getting the king to ratify the acts of the Glasgow assembly or accept the removal of the bishops, though these had been their main demands for the previous six months.

By the articles the covenanters agreed that, after the king published a declaration that had been agreed on, they would disband their forces and stop all work on fortifications. All property and castles belonging to the king and royalists which had been seized would be restored, and all royalists held as prisoners would be freed. The covenanters would hold no meetings not warranted by law. In return Charles undertook to withdraw his forces, release all Scots property and men and summon a general assembly and parliament to meet in Edinburgh on 6 and 20 August respectively.[94] In the declaration mentioned in the articles the king related that though he could not approve the acts of the pretended assembly at Glasgow, yet he would make good whatever Hamilton had promised as his commissioner the previous year, and for the future conceded that all matters ecclesiastical should be determined by assemblies of the kirk and civil matters by parliament and inferior judicatories. For settling the distractions of Scotland a free general assembly would meet at which the king himself intended to be present, and a parliament would ratify what was concluded by the assembly, settling other things conducive to peace and passing an act of oblivion. His intention in taking up arms, Charles declared, had been to maintain his royal authority, not to invade Scotland or innovate in religion and laws, as he had no intention of altering these.[95] As to the verbal assurances, the covenanters claimed that the king had explained that although his declaration 'contained hard expressions of the subjects of Scotland yet his Majesty declared that he had no such opinions of them' but his honour and credit with foreign nations required that he include them. Though he called the Glasgow assembly 'pretended' he would not insist that his subjects renounce it. Moreover he agreed that general assemblies should include an elder from each presbytery, and that by a free general assembly he meant one which could judge its own constitution and composition. He was also said to have objected that for him to agree to abolish episcopacy would be to prelimit the assembly, so he would leave it to the assembly to decide.[96]

These verbal promises by the king were soon to be the subject of bitter dispute, for the king was to claim that the covenanters' account of them was mainly false, though it is significant that he never attempted to explain what he had promised. His attitude was that the settlement was contained in the written articles and declaration, and that any verbal promises that might have been made were not part of it. It seems likely from this that in order to persuade the covenanters to accept the written settlement the king had made many informal promises which he intended to be kept secret and not committeed to writing (on the pretext that they contained matters which could not be made public as they reflected on his honour) and which he had no intention of keeping once the covenanters had bound themselves by the written terms. The covenanters on the other hand claimed that the 'vocall interpretations and expressions' were 'in our estimation . . . equall to that which was written'[97] and though they doubtless exaggerated what the king had promised it seems likely that their version of the promises was substantially correct. Neither king nor covenanters really believed that the vague and ambiguous articles signed and promises given would form the basis for a lasting settlement, but both were ready to accept such an unsatisfactory outcome to the treaty as both now believed that they had more to gain by returning to negotiations than by an immediate appeal to arms.

The terms of the king's declaration and the articles of pacification caused divisions among the covenanters as soon as they became known. As had been agreed with the king, the Scots army retired and disbanded on 20 June. One regiment remained in arms and the king's declaration was read to it, but immediately after the reading the Earl of Cassillis publicly declared that in accepting the declaration the covenanters still maintained the legality of the Glasgow assembly, 'whereunto all the people applauded that they did adhere to the assemblie, and bade hang the Bishops'. The covenanters had decided to make this announcement only after long arguments among themselves, in which those who were angry at the inadequacy of the settlement with the king prevailed. They also on the same day (20 June) sent Rothes and Loudoun back to the king to ask him not to garrison Berwick or fortify Edinburgh castle and 'to shew unto the English lords those conditions quhilk had past in word betwixt the King and us'; the covenanters had decided that it was necessary to reveal the king's secret promises in order to justify their acceptance of a written settlement which granted them so little of what they had asked. The two nobles got no satisfaction over Berwick or Edinburgh castle, but they claimed that the Earls of Pembroke and Holland, both of whom had been present at the treaty as English commissioners, accepted their version of the king's promises as correct.[98]

Wariston and the other Scots commissioners arrived back in Edinburgh on 21 June, 'wher we found many greived with our proceidings',[99] indignant that so little had been gained. The next day Hamilton received Edinburgh castle for the king, freeing Huntly from his imprisonment.[100] This handing back of the castle to the king, who immediately began provisioning and fortifying it, provoked an embittered 'Declaration of some of the Covenanters of Scotland to those Lords that gave way to the King to fortifie his castle at Edinburgh':

> Sirs, God lay it not to your charge for making a division of our sworne union, and causing the hartes of good people to faint, and rejoycing and encouraging the enemie. Drink as you brew. Looke for no assistance from us to put them out. God blest us so long as wee had a resolution to make a lawful resistance, but what can be expected of such needie yielding but a curse . . . Wee know your names; wee never refused night nor day to adventure for your defence and ours . . . Some of you by credulity, others by a slavish pretext of loyaltie, some through needy feare, some through

treacherie, others through their owne wickednesse will ruine
Religion, Lawes and Liberties. Henceforth wee resolve as private
Christians to suffer persecution . . . God give you more wisdome
and us Faith and Patience.[101]

The authorship of this declaration and what support it had are
unknown, but the feeling that the covenant had been betrayed—
though not the resolution therefore to suffer persecution passively
—was widespread among covenanters who were unaware of how
precarious the condition of the army at Duns Law had been. The
Tables circulated a letter indicating their disappointment with the
agreement which had been reached with the king, but begged that
covenanters should not listen to misinformations about what had
been done; unity, the 'strongest bullwark of defence against all
assaults and machinatiouns', must be maintained. Orders were
given that wherever the king's declaration was published it should
be met with a protest upholding the legality of the Glasgow
assembly.[102]

On 1 July a proclamation was issued by the privy council on the
king's orders summoning all archbishops, bishops, commissioners
and all others who had a right to sit in general assemblies to meet
in Edinburgh on 12 August.[103] The covenanters immediately protested that this indiction of the assembly should not be held to
acknowledge in any way the rights of bishops as they had been
abjured by the covenant and the previous assembly.[104] There was
also a revival of disturbances in Edinburgh; Traquair's coach was
stoned, he and several prominent royalists were manhandled.[105]

The king summoned fourteen leading covenanters to Berwick
to discuss his journey to Scotland to hold the assembly and parliament—or at least that was the reason he gave for summoning
them. But many saw the summons as 'a courte trape layed to
catche some of the pryme couenanters'[106]—why did the king need
to see so many of the leading covenanters at Berwick to discuss his
journey, and if they were to discuss other matters, then could not
this be more conveniently done once the king came to Scotland?
It certainly seems possible that Charles intended to kidnap the
leading covenanters, and he could have alleged many breaches of
the articles of pacification by them to justify his action—the dis-

turbances in Edinburgh, the protestation at the proclamation of
1 July, and so on.[107] The covenanters therefore delayed answering
the king's summons, calling a meeting on 13 July to consider it.
Deep divisions were revealed among the covenanters as to whether
the king could be trusted. Rothes (or so he later claimed) argued in
favour of obeying the king, and eventually a compromise was
agreed whereby only six of those summoned would go to Berwick,
including Rothes, Montrose, Lothian and Wariston. But many
opposed the sending of Lothian and, more especially, Montrose,
threatening to prevent Montrose leaving by force if necessary.[108]
Lothian was certainly a very lukewarm covenanter at this time,
and presumably there were fears that the king would be able to
persuade him to desert the covenant. The association of Montrose
with him indicates that he too was suspected of being susceptible
to the king's arguments; the beginning of Montrose's conversion
into a supporter of the king is usually said to date from his con-
versations with the king at Berwick, but this may indicate that his
covenanting colleagues feared that his enthusiasm for the covenant was waning even before the talks took place.

The six covenanters journeyed to Berwick on 16 July. Others of
those summoned by the king were said to have been prevented
from going by a force of covenanters led by Lord Balmerino. The
six who reached Berwick had talks with the king from 17 to 20
July, when they were sent back to Edinburgh with instructions
to return with the rest of the fourteen who had been summoned,
but only Loudoun and Lindsay appeared, bringing excuses for the
rest.[109] The king had sent to the Tables on 19 July a paper listing
eighteen breaches of the pacification by the covenanters, but in
reply they alleged six breaches of it by the king and stated that
they would never have agreed to his declaration on 18 June, with
its references to the Glasgow assembly as pretended and to their
loyal proceedings as disorders, if it had not been for his verbal
promises.[110] This uncompromising attitude and the refusal of
most of the covenanters he had ordered to come to Berwick convinced Charles that there was little point in his going to Scotland—
apart from anything else, it would be much easier to repudiate
promises made for him by a commissioner in an assembly than

any he made in person. He therefore left Berwick at the end of July. One of his first actions on reaching London was to question all those who had been present at the treaty of Berwick as English commissioners. They all agreed with him that the Scottish account of his verbal promises was mostly false, and on 11 August the king and the privy council ordered the burning by the common hangman of a paper containing the Scottish claims which had been widely circulated in England.[111]

What passed in the talks between the king and the covenanters who had gone to Berwick is not clear. Montrose is said to have given the king promises as to his future loyalty,[112] and the king claimed that Rothes had admitted that he was resolved to try to overthrow episcopacy in England and Ireland, and had not shown the respect due to a sovereign; Rothes replied that he had only said he would like to see episcopacy removed in these kingdoms, and that as for his rudeness he had been provoked by the king twice calling him a liar and equivocator,[113] insults which he had not the courtier-like docility beloved by the king to accept without comment. While the covenanters were at Berwick the king had ordered Hamilton to try to discover their intentions in private talks, if necessary speaking 'that language, which, if you were called to account for by us, you might suffer for it',[114] but Hamilton's simulated treasonable talk does not seem to have led to the discovery of any secrets. He had already advised the king again to prepare to subdue Scotland by war, posing the alternatives open to Charles as either to 'give way to the Madness' of the covenanters or 'of new to intend a Kingly Way' by use of force. The king had intended to send Hamilton back to Scotland as his commissioner, but he had argued that he was disliked and distrusted by the covenanters. Moreover, he added frankly, he wished to keep royal favour and whoever was sent to Scotland as commissioner at this time would have to do things which at heart the king found odious, and this would bring him his dislike.[115] Charles does not seem to have felt that this interpretation of his character was insulting, and agreed instead to appoint Traquair as his commissioner to the assembly and parliament.[116] He was probably just as unpopular with the covenanters as Hamilton but he could hardly claim to fear losing royal favour as the king already distrusted him (he had had him imprisoned at York for some days after he had let the covenanters seize the king's house at Dalkeith the previous March),[117] but there was no one more suitable available.

CHAPTER FIVE

The Failure of the Treaty of Berwick, July 1639—March 1640

THE GENERAL ASSEMBLY

The king gave Traquair detailed instructions on how to conduct himself in the assembly. He could accept elders as members, but was to protest if elders had sat in presbyteries during elections. If the worst came to the worst, he could (in effect) ratify the acts of the Glasgow assembly, but only on condition that they were passed as acts of the new assembly and did not mention that previous pretended one. He was by all means possible to avoid discussing the king's power, especially his sole right of calling and dissolving assemblies and his negative voice (the need for his consent to acts passed), unless he was convinced that they would be decided in the king's favour. If the assembly abolished episcopacy Traquair was to ensure that it was not declared unlawful, and in consenting to its abolition he was to announce that the king agreed to it only for satisfying the people, settling the disorders and other reasons of state (that is, only for political, not religious reasons), but he was to be careful to conceal the king's intentions in doing this—these intentions doubtless being to make the re-introduction of episcopacy easier when circumstances permitted. At the end of the assembly Traquair was to summon a new one to meet a year later at Aberdeen (or wherever else seemed best); by this he hoped to prevent the assembly making a general demand for yearly assemblies, which he thought would be greatly to his prejudice. Traquair could consent to signature of the 1581 confession provided it was not interpreted as abjuring episcopacy as a point of popery or as contrary to God's law. Finally, at the end of the assembly, he was to protest that he had received his instructions from the king so recently that he had not been able to consult the king about them, and that some matters had arisen as to which he did not know the king's pleasure, and therefore that if he had consented to anything contrary to the king's service the king should be allowed redress[1]—in other words, the king would not be bound by anything that Traquair had conceded in his name. Charles instructed the bishops not to attend the assembly, but he assured the Archbishop of St Andrews that 'though perhaps We may give way for the present to that which will be prejudicial both to the Church and Our Own Government, yet We shall not leave thinking, in time, how to remedy both'.[2]

The assembly met on 12 August in St Giles, and the following day elected David Dickson moderator. He was granted assessors and, as at the Glasgow assembly, elders outnumbered ministers among them. After some days spent in the reading of the acts of former assemblies and other evidence against episcopacy, innovations and other grievances,[3] an 'Act containing the Causes and Remedies of the bygone Evils of this Kirk' was passed. It declared that 'according to the constitutions of the Generall Assemblies of this Kirk' the prayer book and book of canons had been and still should be rejected as containing popish and superstitious errors, and that the court of high commission should also be rejected. The Five Articles of Perth were contrary to the 1581 confession and should no longer be practised, episcopal government and the civil places and power of kirkmen should 'be holden still as unlawfull in this Kirk', the assemblies of 1606–18 should be accounted unlawful and null, and in future general assemblies should be held yearly or as often as was necessary.[4] The act passed unanimously, with much show of emotion from older ministers who could remember the kirk before it had been dominated by the king and bishops. 'Old Mr. John Row', the historian, was in tears, as was John Wemyss who, when 'called on, could scarce get a word spocken for teares trickling doune along his gray haires . . . and yet withall smylling for joy, said—I doe remember when the Kirk of Scotland had a beautifull face' and rejoiced to see it restored.[5]

The act contained a few concessions to the king gained by Traquair; though the act in effect ratified all the more important acts of the Glasgow assembly the fact that it did so was not mentioned, since it had been agreed that it should neither be referred to nor matters decided in it be regarded as already settled.[6] But in many other ways the act was bound to offend the king. He was willing to abandon prayer book, canons, high commission, Perth Articles, even episcopacy, but not for the reasons given in the act. Thus he had agreed that episcopacy might be condemned as contrary to the constitutions of the kirk, but the act called it both unconstitutional and unlawful. The king argued that declaring episcopacy unconstitutional in the kirk would be relevant only to Scotland, but that to call it unlawful would imply that it must also be unlawful in other churches. What was against God's law in Scotland must be against it elsewhere, as puritans in England and Ireland would be sure to point out if he agreed to abolish episcopacy in Scotland as unlawful.[7] Later in the assembly Traquair tried to prevent the possibility of this calling of episcopacy unlawful in the act being applied outside Scotland by declaring that in accepting the act in the king's name it was to be understood that the kirk's prohibition of any practice in Scotland did not infer the censure of such practices elsewhere, but the assembly refused to agree that this was so. Apart from this Traquair consented to the act, though he declared (as the king had instructed) that the king agreed to the act against his own inclinations 'for settling the present distractions, and giving full satisfaction to the Subjects'.[8]

Another matter on which Traquair exceeded the king's instructions concerned subscription of the covenant. The assembly supplicated him and the privy council to pass an act ordering all subjects to take the national covenant, and the council did this on 30 August.[9] Traquair then told the assembly that as king's commissioner he must sign the covenant with a declaration added to it stating that he did so understanding it to be 'one in substance' with the 1581 confession signed by James VI. But he added that no other Scot would be expected to do this, and indeed that he himself as Earl of Traquair, not the king's representative, would sign the covenant without any limitation 'with all the rest of the subjects, even as Mr. Archbald Johnstoune subscryves, which I believe is strict enough'. The assembly allowed him to do this and passed an act ordering subscription of the covenant with the 'Glasgow Declaration' by all subjects.[10] Traquair's action was strictly in accordance with the letter of the king's last orders to him, which instructed him not to sign the covenant unless it was interpreted as being essentially the same as the 1581 confession,[11] but the king had clearly meant that he was not to agree to its being signed by anyone unless thus interpreted. Traquair probably knew quite well what the king wanted, but had reverted weakly to his policy of 1637–8 of trying to keep both sides happy and retain the favour of both.

Traquair promised that the first thing to be done in parliament would be the ratification of all the acts of the assembly, an announcement which the assembly greeted with 'clapping of their hands, and crying "God save the King"'. It wished to elect a commission to stay in Edinburgh to supplicate the king if necessary. This was obviously an attempt to establish a permanent ministers' Table with authority from the assembly, a thing the king had specifically warned Traquair to be on his guard against,[12] but after much argument he agreed that such a commission should be granted to the presbytery of Edinburgh, provided that it met only at the times when the presbytery normally met. Finally, the next assembly was summoned to meet in Aberdeen on 28 July 1640, and the asssembly was dissolved on 30 August.[13]

Traquair now had second thoughts about the consent he had given in the king's name to some of the acts of the assembly, and he therefore had qualifying declarations recorded in the register of the privy council. To the declaration he had already made in the assembly in assenting to the act of 17 August for remedying the evils of the kirk he now added that the king's consent was only to the Perth Articles, episcopal government and civil power of kirkmen being 'declared unlawfull within this kirk as contrare to the constitutions thereof'. He declared that 'whatever is allowed by me in this Assemblie is meirlie and onelie as an act of this Assemblie without anie respect or relation . . . to the last pretendit Assemblie at Glasgow'. Finally he made a general declaration (which the king had ordered him to make before the assembly itself) that if any act of the assembly that he had assented to wronged the civil power and authority of the king, then the king should be allowed redress.[14] The king was furious when he learnt what concessions Traquair had made, especially over episcopacy. Even to declare episcopacy only unlawful according to the constitution of the kirk (as Traquair had done in the privy council register) implied, wrote the king, that it was unlawful outside Scotland, 'for whatsoever is absolutely unlawful in one Church cannot be lawful in the other of the same Profession of Religion [ie Protestantism], but there may be many several Constitutions, and yet they all lawful'. He therefore ordered Traquair not to ratify the act in parliament unless the word unlawful was removed. He also forbade the rescinding of any acts of former parliaments in favour of episcopacy 'which may hereafter be of so great use to Us'.[15]

THE LORDS OF THE ARTICLES AND PARLIAMENT

Parliament met on 31 August, the day after the dissolution of the assembly; as agreed in the articles of pacification it had been prorogued on 23 July until 26 August, but then had to be again prorogued, first until 30 and then until 31 August as the assembly was still sitting.[16] The Scottish parliament in the early seventeenth century consisted (apart from the king or his commissioner) of five groups of members, the nobles, the clergy, officers of state, the small barons or commissioners of the shires, and the commissioners of the burghs.

The clergy had originally included abbots, priors and representatives of the lower clergy, but by this time they comprised only the archbishops and bishops.[17] Strictly speaking, the nobility and the commissioners of the shires formed one estate, the lay tenants in chief of the crown, but by an act of 1428 the smaller tenants in chief had been excused personal attendance in parliament on condition that they sent commissioners from each shire to represent them, while the larger tenants in chief had been personally summoned to parliament and had gradually become lords of parliament through creation by the king. In fact the 1428 act was largely ignored; the terms on which the small barons or lairds attended parliament in the seventeenth century were laid down in a new act of 1587, and apart from the technicality of their common origin they and the nobles formed separate estates. By the 1587 act each shire was to send two commissioners to parliament (with only one from the small shires of Kinross and Clackmannan). These commissioners were to be elected each year at the first sheriff head court held after Michaelmas, or at other times if it was more convenient, their electors being all the barons and free-holders (tenants in chief) who possessed land worth more than 40*s* of old extent per annum and were not nobles.[18]

The burgh commissioners to parliament were elected by the councils of the royal burghs and of a few episcopal burghs which contributed with the royal burghs to taxation. In and after 1621 each burgh sent one commissioner to parliament, except Edinburgh which sent two.[19] The existence of the convention of burghs reduced the interest that the burghs took in parliament, since the convention provided an assembly in which they could regulate their own affairs and through which they could negotiate with the king in matters concerning trade. The convention also regulated the conduct of the burgh commissioners in parliament. By the beginning of the seventeenth century it was usual for a short particular convention of burghs (as opposed to the annual general conventions of burghs) to be held immediately before a parliament met, and the commissioners to these conventions were very often the same men who were afterwards to sit in the parliament. In these particular conventions the matters likely to come before the parliament which affected the burghs' interest would be considered and the common policies to be supported by all the burgesses in parliament would be agreed.[20]

The final constituent group of parliament was the officers of state who sat *ex officio*. In 1617 James VI had agreed that not more than eight of them should sit in parliament, though which eight officers these should be was not fixed. The officers were also *ex officio* members of the lords of the articles, the committee which dominated parliament. The rest of the committee were chosen by election, the form of which had slowly developed until it was completely controlled by the king. The final form of election, used in 1621 and 1633, was that the bishops chose eight nobles, and these eight nobles then chose eight bishops. The sixteen nobles and bishops then combined to choose eight shire and eight burgh commissioners. The thirty-two men thus chosen, plus up to eight officers of state, composed the lords of the articles.[21] Since the bishops could be relied on to do the king's bidding and elect whichever nobles he wished, this method of election guaranteed subservient articles.

After the election of the articles on the first day of parliament the main body of members had nothing to do but await the outcome of their deliberations, for all matters and acts to be voted on by parliament were first examined by the articles, who had power to reject those of which they or the king disapproved (which thus never came before the full parliament). When the articles had finished drafting whatever acts they thought fit, the full parliament re-assembled to vote on them. The clerk register read out in turn a summary of each act, 'So first one wes red out in few words and licence gevin to such as wold, to speak in the affirmative or negative therof, but so as it wes to be done in few words'. After this the act was voted on by all members of parliament together (the parliament being unicameral) and passed or rejected by a majority. In the voting each shire had only one vote, even though it might have two commissioners present—'every Shyr had one voyce altho they had more Commissioners than one'.[22] Acts passed by a majority were presented to the king and he was petitioned to enact them as laws, which he did by touching the paper with his sceptre, or exercised his 'negative voice' by refusing to do so, 'a mark of suprem and full power and soverayntie', in which case they were rejected.[23] In fact probably only the more important acts were thus briefly debated and then voted on, the large number of minor and private acts being passed together. Even the very limited right to comment thus on acts drafted by the articles was being eroded by the king. In 1633 only one vote was taken to pass all the acts of that parliament and the king refused to allow members to give their reasons for opposing certain of the acts.[24]

This system whereby the full parliament met only to have lords of the articles chosen and then again to vote on the acts presented to it by the articles had resulted in increasing discontent, especially as the importance of the bishops in choosing the articles grew.

But Scotland had no strong national myth of free parliaments like England, and dislike of the system was little more than a reflection of hatred of the policies the system was used to impose. There is some sign of constitutional discontent after 1633, but little more than vague complaints that parliament is not 'free'. When pent-up grievances, mainly religious, led to the troubles of 1637 there is no sign that those leading the agitation thought of the holding of parliament as a necessary part of a settlement. Demands for a parliament first appeared in the national covenant, and in it and for many months afterwards all a parliament was required to do was ratify the acts of a general assembly. But by the time the parliament actually met, at the end of August 1639, things had gone much further. Firstly, a variety of different interests in the country were ready to take advantage of the king's weakness to demand remedies for non-religious grievances, changes that had nothing to do with the original resistance to the king. Secondly, and far more important, many of the covenanters were no longer willing to accept that after a religious settlement with the king had been reached the country should again be ruled as it had been before the troubles (except of course that there would be no bishops). If there was one thing that the experience of the past two years had taught them it was that the king could not be trusted, that, no matter what he promised, if they gave him back his power and returned quietly to their homes he would immediately begin the work of insinuating episcopacy and all its trappings back into the kirk—as his father had done—and of punishing those who had resisted him. For their own safety and that of their cause, many now insisted on having enough control over the regime to keep the king to his promises. They hoped to exercise this control through a remodelled parliament which would meet regularly and have much more control over its own activities than previous parliaments.

The parliament which met on 31 August 1639 consisted of Traquair as king's commissioner, fifty nobles (including one officer of state), three non-noble officers of state, forty-eight barons or commissioners of shires representing twenty-six shires, and fifty-two burgesses.[25] As we shall see, if a few more officers of state had attended, Traquair might have won over a majority of the lords of the articles. Of the commissioners for shires few if any were open royalists—Sir James Lamont sat for Argyll, but his plottings earlier in the year to join the projected invasion by the Earl of Antrim had not yet come to light. No doubt the elections were as efficiently organised by the covenanters as those to the general assemblies had been. Since virtually all burgh councils were by this time dominated by covenanters, the elections of commissioners to parliament from the burghs returned a solidly covenanting body of members.

The king made no attempt to influence the elections to the 1639 parliament (or assembly) since, as Traquair was told, the more irregular the elections were 'the more itt will conduce to his Majesties endes',[26] as it would make it easier to repudiate the parliament if necessary. Charles was anxious to ensure that parliament would continue to be dominated by the lords of the articles and that he should be somehow recompensed for the loss of the bishops (with their vital part in electing the articles). He had instructed Traquair that if the general assembly abolished episcopacy he was to try to get it to agree that the king should appoint fourteen ministers (or, if that was impossible, laymen) to replace the bishops in parliament and choose the nobles who were to sit on the articles. Traquair had not raised the matter in the assembly, presumably because he considered that there was no hope of it agreeing, and the king continued to press him to reach some agreement with the covenanters in the matter, that if the bishops were not replaced by royal nominees that the king himself should be allowed to choose the nobles to sit on the articles. If the covenanters would not agree, parliament was to be prorogued.[27]

On 31 August after the ceremonial 'riding of parliament', a procession of all members from Holyroodhouse, the parliament sat in the new parliament house which Charles had ordered to be built in 1632;[28] it was not yet completed but it had been used by the covenanters for their meetings for some months past. Traquair desired the nobles to retire with him into an inner room to choose the lords of the articles. This the nobles did and 'thair was a great contest amongst them, for the spaice of foure or fyve houres'. Traquair and some of the nobles argued that as the bishops 'ware out of the way' the right of choosing the eight noble lords of the articles belonged to the king, while most of the covenanters claimed that the nobles should choose them for themselves. Eventually a compromise was reached whereby it was agreed 'that thair sould be a list of the names of all estaites quha ware fittest to be on the Articles' compiled by the nobles and approved by Traquair, while to preserve the king's rights Traquair formally chose and appointed on the king's behalf the eight nobles already chosen and the eight nobles formally chose the sixteen commissioners of shires and burghs. Argyll protested in name of some of the nobles that this should not prejudice their rights in future parliaments, and asked that an act should be passed in the articles whereby in future nobles, shire commissioners and burgesses should each elect their own representatives to sit on the articles. Some of the commissioners for shires and burghs then entered and asked to be heard. They were told 'that thair was ane electioune alreadie maid' of lords of the articles, whereupon they protested that this should not prejudice their rights in future to elect their own lords of the articles. Huntly counter-protested, affirming the right of the nobles to choose shire and burgh commissioners to sit on the articles. Traquair and the nobles then returned to the outer parliament house where 'Dureing all this tyme thair was some little noyce and trubill in the hous moire than ordinarie' as the commissioners of shires and burghs argued over how the articles should be chosen. Traquair had the names of the lords of the articles read out and ordered them to meet with him daily; all the protests made in the inner parliament house were then repeated before the full parliament and it then adjourned.[29]

Though all but two of the nobles elected to the articles were covenanters they represented quite a wide variety of opinions. As well as the uncompromising Argyll and Rothes they included Montrose and Lindsay, both of whom would be willing to make some concessions to the king, and Marischal and Lauderdale, covenanters but far from fanatical. Southesk had signed the covenant but opposed armed resistance to the king, while Huntly's presence was a considerable concession by the covenanters. As for the barons and burgesses who sat on the articles, all were covenanters,[30]

though there were differences among them as to what sort of
settlement with the king would be acceptable. In the articles the
burgesses took little initiative, for though they had strong opinions
that they were willing to display in voting they evidently did not
regard it as their place to take a leading part in the argument and
debate on matters of general interest. The desires of the burghs as
given in to the articles were exclusively concerned with trade and
other matters of interest mainly to the burghs—the items of most
general importance being requests for reductions in customs
duties and the abolition of monopolies and patents.[31]

The instructions from the commissioners of the shires to those of
their number who sat on the articles were far more controversial
and significant. They demanded that each estate should choose its
own representatives to sit on the articles, that copies of all acts
passed in the articles should be distributed among the members of
parliament before the final day of parliament when they were
voted on, so that they might be considered. They asked that none
should vote in parliament except nobles and commissioners of
shires and burghs (thus excluding officers of state and any replace-
ments the king might demand for the bishops), for the abolition of
proxy votes and votes by foreigners (several Englishmen had been
given Scottish titles), and that no taxes should be granted except
by parliament. These demands for constitutional changes are interesting in that they do not require the abolition of the lords of the
articles but indicate how their power might be limited and far
more significance and importance given to the full parliament; the
articles were to be its servants, not its masters. The commissioners
of shires also demanded a variety of changes to remedy abuses in
the administration of justice and other aspects of government.
They asked that 'the nobilitie and gentrie by thair commissioneris
for shyris may have their publict meiting ance in the yeir to consult
upon suche matteris as may tend to the weill of the kingdome and
thair awne estates' and represent such matters to the privy council
and parliament. In other words, they wanted annual conventions
of nobles and of shire commissioners, on the model of the convention of burghs, a demand that in the circumstances the king
would be bound to regard as an attempt to perpetuate the Tables.[32]

On 2 or 3 September the commissioners for shires and burghs insisted on asserting their rights by electing their own lords of the articles, but showed their willingness to compromise by choosing those who had already been elected.[33] To do this they met in the parliament house, taking Traquair by surprise as he had not intended the estates to meet again until the lords of the articles had completed their deliberations, but there was little he could do, so in spite of his 'dislyke at the onusuall maner of proceidings, to sie them all conveined in the parliament houss',[34] Traquair and the lords of the articles began their deliberations on 4 September. They sat for about seven weeks, in which time they discussed a great number of proposals and acts; nearly all the acts which were to be passed in the parliaments of 1640 and 1641 had their origins in proposals which came before the articles in 1639. Traquair signed the covenant twice before the lords of the articles, once as king's commissioner with a declaration (later deleted by the articles) that his signature was limited by an explanation he would later make before parliament, and once as treasurer without any limitation. Acts were passed ratifying the acts of the general assembly concerning the remedies of bygone evils of the kirk and ordering subscription of the covenant, and on 24 September an act was passed rescinding all previous acts in favour of the civil power of kirkmen.[35]

Traquair worked hard to get such acts affecting the king's interests modified, and he had some limited success in this. Thus disputes over two different acts anent the constitution of parliament (one given in by the covenanters, the other by Craighall as king's advocate) led to a compromise act being passed which was unacceptable to some covenanting members of parliament who (led by Lord Loudoun) produced a new act before the articles and demanded that it should be passed instead.[36] The point at issue was evidently a demand by the shire commissioners (supported by most covenanters) that now the clerical estate had been removed from parliament the shire commissioners should be declared a separate estate to replace them, so that parliament would continue to be composed of three estates as was traditional.[37] They also demanded that each shire commissioner should have an individual vote, instead of only one for each shire, a proposal which Traquair condemned as something never before asked which would be very prejudicial to the king.[38] Many other acts were debated which would have diminished royal power in a variety of other ways.

'The time was spent thus in long and fruitlesse janglings' between Traquair and the articles.[39] He knew that the king, already angry at the concessions he had made in consenting to the acts of the general assembly, would never agree to ratify the assembly's acts in parliament, let alone all the new acts now being passed in the articles. He had indicated that he was more willing to accept a 'Rupture' with the covenanters than to accept their 'impertinent motions'.[40] But Traquair had had some success in dividing the covenanters, for many of them did not see the necessity for constitutional changes and accepted the argument that it was only just that the king should have power to appoint laymen to sit in parliament and choose the nobles to sit on the articles, in place of the bishops—Montrose and Lindsay were said to have been won over to this standpoint.[41] Traquair hoped that if the articles continued to meet for long enough he would wear down the opposition and gain the support of a majority for at least a delay in deciding the controversial matters concerning the constitution. By 4 October he believed that he had reached this position. He therefore proclaimed that parliament would meet on 8 October to vote on the acts presented to it by the articles.[42] On 5 October he demanded a vote in the articles on whether proposals for regulating the power of the lords of the articles should be remitted to the king for his consideration (as he wanted) or voted on by the present parliament (as most covenanters wished). Typically, Traquair had miscalculated; the voting was as follows:

	Refer to the king	Vote in parliament	Absent
Officers of state	4	0	0
Nobles	5	3	0
Shires	2	5	1
Burghs	1	6	1
Total	12	14	2

Traquair, 'being much moved, alledgit that ther ware too woices that ware not sufficiently cleired and desyred it myght be voyced againe: which was done. And fand that he haid lost the business be too woyces clearely',[43] and the act anent the constitution of the articles, giving each estate power to elect its own representatives, was passed.[44] He had come near to success. Only Argyll, Rothes and (surprisingly) Lindsay among the nobles voted against his desires, but the majority of the nobles and the four officers of state were insufficient to outweigh the votes of the shire commissioners—eager to be declared a separate estate—and the burgesses. After this failure Traquair had little hope of winning any major concessions. He did not dare hold the full meeting of parliament on 8 October, and between then and the end of the month he delayed the meeting eight times, on the final occasion until 14 November.[45] The articles continued to meet until 23 October, when Loudoun and some commissioners of shires and burghs, together with some commissioners of the general assembly, appeared and complained about 'the long dependence of this parliament occasioned by the intricacie and multiplicitie of business' and desired Traquair to bring it to a speedy conclusion.[46] On 1 November parliament commissioned Loudoun and Dunfermline to go to the king to ask him to consent to the acts passed in the articles, but Charles refused to see them on the grounds that their commission was not signed by Traquair, and they returned to Edinburgh.[47]

The king now instructed Traquair to prorogue parliament until 2 June 1640,[48] by which time he hoped to have subdued the covenanters by force. Even before he had left Berwick at the end of July he had written to Viscount Wentworth to come to England to advise him; as Wentworth had been advising him for months to avoid fighting the covenanters in 1639 and delay a decision till 1640 this seems a clear indication that the king had already determined on a new campaign against the covenanters. Wentworth arrived in London in September and, probably on his suggestion, a committee of eight privy councillors (Hamilton being the only Scot among them) was set up for Scottish affairs;[49]

the king had at last realised the folly of trying to use English forces against the Scots without consulting his English councillors.

On 14 November Traquair's order for the prorogation of parliament till 2 June 1640, since certain matters had been raised touching the king's civil authority and government and he needed time to consider them, was read to parliament. Craighall as king's advocate then ordered the senior clerk of parliament present, as representative of the clerk register, to declare the parliament prorogued, but he refused saying that while he was willing to read the order for prorogation as often as he was ordered to, he could do nothing more. Rothes then intervened and ordered him in the name of the estates to do nothing for which he would not be answerable to parliament itself, on pain of his life. The other clerk present also refused to prorogue parliament without orders from his senior, and Johnston of Wariston (though not a member of parliament) then read a protestation and declaration in name of the three estates (of which the commissioners for the shires were assumed to be one). The protest complained (with little regard for historical accuracy) that Traquair had taken it upon himself to prorogue parliament without the consent of the estates, a thing unprecedented and contrary to the laws, liberties and perpetual practice of the kingdom. Therefore the estates of parliament declared that the prorogation was contrary to the constitution of parliament and to the pacification of Berwick (for the king had undertaken to settle all matters civil in parliament). However, through their willingness to give all civil obedience to the king, they would only remonstrate against such illegal proceedings for the present, and appoint representatives of each estate, having power from parliament, to await the king's reply to their remonstrances and just demands. The estates then chose the committee to await the king's reply and dissolved.[50]

TOWARDS A NEW WAR

Many had expected that the parliament would continue to sit in spite of the prorogation,[51] but the covenanters had decided that it would be better instead to leave a committee of parliament, ostensibly simply to await the king's pleasure but which in fact with other leading covenanters formed a continuation of the Tables. Traquair was in some doubt as to whether parliament was technically prorogued or not. He tried unsuccessfully to get the record of the proceedings in parliament on 14 November altered, but Craighall assured him that the prorogation was legal even though the clerk had refused to co-operate. Traquair also had doubts as to whether those members of parliament who continued to meet in the parliament house still claimed to be a parliament. He called some of them before the privy council and declared that if they continued to sit and disobey the order for prorogation he would forbid them to do so under pain of treason, but that if they would dissolve their meeting the king would be willing to hear any whom they sent to represent their desires. The covenanters replied on 20 November that as those whom they had formerly sent to the king (Loudoun and Dunfermline) had not been heard they would not send again to him until they got his 'particular allowance' to do so, which they would ask for in a supplication. They denied that they had disobeyed the order to prorogue parliament,[52] and sent William Cunningham of Brownhill to the king with the supplication they had referred to, asking him to ratify the acts passed in the articles; they also wrote to Traquair (who had just left for court) asking him for 'more kyndly and wnpartiall dealling' than they had met with in the past.[53]

On 21 November, just before leaving Edinburgh, Traquair had removed from the privy council records the act by which on 30 August he and the council had signed the covenant at the request of the general assembly,[54] since the king was still angry that he had signed it.[55] As in 1637–8, Traquair's attempts to keep the favour of both king and covenanters had resulted in his losing the favour of both. He had shown little skill in dealing with the parliament or the assembly, but the king had well known before they met that the outcome of their meetings would almost inevitably be unsatisfactory. Yet he still blamed Traquair for their failure. When Traquair reached London and found himself in disfavour he busied himself in demonstrating his loyalty by denouncing the conduct of the covenanters and advocating the use of force against them.[56]

Meetings of the committee for Scots affairs on 27 November and of the privy council of England on 5 December heard Traquair's explanations of the situation in Scotland and agreed on the necessity for calling a parliament in England to raise money for war with the covenanters.[57] After his recent experiences with the Scottish parliament one would have expected the king to have rejected such a suggestion, but he urgently needed money and Wentworth convinced him that he could manage a parliament effectively. In Scotland the king's preparations for war were mainly confined to making Edinburgh castle defensible. Between 8 July and 16 November about 130 masons, wrights, smiths, quarriers and barrowmen were employed weekly on the fortifications, and work continued on a small scale until February 1640.[58] Judging by the fact that part of the castle walls fell down when guns were fired in celebration of the king's birthday on 19 November, the work was long overdue.[59]

The king replied on 11 December to the covenanters' supplication sent with Cunningham of Brownhill, giving them permission to send representatives to him to explain the reasons for their demands. Traquair returned to Scotland with this reply and found that many members of parliament were still meeting in the parliament house. He again ordered them to disperse on pain of treason once they had nominated commissioners to go to the king. They appointed Dunfermline, Loudoun, Sir William Douglas of Cavers and Robert Barclay, provost of Irvine, repeated the protestation of 14 November against the prorogation of parliament without its own consent, and broke up their meeting temporarily.[60] The covenanters had little hope that sending commissioners to the king would achieve anything, and those appointed in fact did not leave for London until February 1640. A meeting of the estates in the middle of January gave the commissioners additional instructions[61] but was more concerned with preparing for war than with negotiating. The meeting ordered subscription throughout the country of a band by which the signatory bound himself to pay his share of the common charges of defence and ordered valuation to be made of all rents;[62] the amount to be paid was later fixed at one tenth of the valued rents.

Early in February 1640, ships arrived in Leith with 100 English soldiers, ammunition and other supplies for Edinburgh castle and a letter from the king ordering the magistrates of Edinburgh to see them safely conveyed to the castle. This was done; the covenanters were evidently taken by surprise and feared that the governor, Sir Patrick Ruthven, newly created Lord Ettrick, would bombard the burgh unless they obeyed. Ettrick happily informed the king that he now had sufficient supplies to stand a six- or nine-month siege.[63] The covenanters summoned a meeting of as many nobles, commissioners to parliament and lairds as could conveniently attend for 10 March to discuss the situation and what was to be done. To emphasise the urgency of the situation they distributed with the summonses to the meeting copies of a commission granted by the king to the Earl of Northumberland to command the forces he was raising against Scotland.[64] After the meeting on 10 March the covenanters set a guard to watch the castle. Ettrick, believing that the shelters they began building for the guards were batteries from which to bombard the castle,[65] threatened to fire on the burgh unless they were removed. The covenanters refused, whereupon panic ensued as many inhabitants of the burgh tried to flee with their possessions. Some prominent anti-covenanters were arrested and others—including Southesk and Sir Lewis Stewart— were seized as hostages by the mob. Most, however, were soon released on signing the covenant,[66] since when Ettrick found that the covenanters were not preparing to bombard the castle he withdrew his threat. He had no wish to begin fighting so early in the year if he could avoid it as he could not expect relief from the king until the summer, and his confidence must have been somewhat undermined by the collapse at the end of February of long stretches of the castle's outer wall, and by the steady desertion of three or four Scottish soldiers from his garrison each night.[67]

The most important outcome of the alarm aroused among the covenanters by the reinforcing of the garrison of Edinburgh castle in February was that it finally decided the covenanters to send an agent to the king of France. They had been encouraged by contacts late in 1639 with the French ambassador in England, Pompone de Bellièvre, who was in favour of sending French help to them. Bellièvre reported that in return for such help some of the covenanters were willing to agree that they would not make a peace with Charles I in which their alliance with France was not recognised.[68] However, Cardinal Richelieu was opposed to involving France in any agreement with the covenanters; Bellièvre was therefore instructed not to meddle in Scottish affairs.[69] After the reinforcing of the castle garrison an undated letter to Louis XIII which had been written and signed by Alexander Leslie, the Earls of Mar, Rothes, and Montrose, and Lords Montgomery, Loudoun and Forrester some time before—probably the previous May— was produced and dated 19 February.[70] The letter explained that the bearer, M. Colville, was being sent to Louis XIII to ask him to intercede for them with Charles I and to justify their conduct. The letter was not sent until after the meeting of covenanters on 10 March, when William Colville was dispatched with it by sea to France.[71] He was instructed to inform Louis XIII and Richelieu of the great oppressions suffered by Scotland through religious and other innovations, especially through the court of high commission (which Colville was to claim surpassed the Spanish Inquisition in cruelty!). He was to show how their humble remonstrances to Charles had been met by an edict declaring them traitors and rebels with threats resembling those of the Turks, and encouraging their vassals and tenants to revolt against them. Their king was preparing to subdue them by force, and Colville was to beg for Louis XIII's intercession, claiming that this would be in France's interests, since Scotland's troubles were the result of the machinations of the pro-Spanish faction in England and part of the monstrous aggrandisement of the house of Austria, the Habsburgs.[72] William Colville, who had already been involved in the plan to write to Louis XIII in May 1639 which had been abandoned, was the brother of Sir Robert Colville of Cleish. Unfortunately, before he even left Scotland a copy of the letter he was carrying to Louis XIII was in the hands of Charles I and his brother James was a prisoner in the Tower of London.

For some reason the seven covenanters who had signed the letter sent with Colville had also signed another, undated, copy of the same letter—it may be that this other copy was signed first but was replaced because the covenanters had not signed it in order of precedence, as they did the copy that was actually sent. Whatever the reason, this other copy of the letter was signed but not used, and it somehow fell into the hands of a Lieutenant Dundas. It was handed on in turn to Colonel John Monro, Sir Donald Macdonald of Sleat and Traquair, who presented it to the king, probably late in February or early in March 1640,[73] though the king kept it secret until April. By coincidence, at about the same time James Colville was arrested. He had some weeks before boasted in Scotland that he could do the king good service if employed by him since he knew many of the chief covenanters, and news of his boasts had reached the king's ministers.[74] Whether James was simply a fool who could not resist boasting his knowledge or whether he was contemplating defecting to the king is not clear, but when he entered England in February to distribute copies of an Information the covenanters had drawn up he was arrested and sent to the Tower to discover what his boasted knowledge amounted to.[75] He found that he was believed to be the Colville mentioned in the letter to Louis XIII as its bearer.

Meanwhile the Scottish commissioners (Dunfermline, Loudoun, Sir William Douglas and Robert Barclay) had arrived in London and had been admitted to the king's presence for the first time on 20 February. The king had no interest in negotiating seriously as he was determined on a military solution in Scotland, but he heard the Scots as he had promised to do so. He met them several times in March but no progress was made, Charles raising a variety of objections to the form and content of their commission and instructions. As on previous occasions, Charles found the directness of the Scots in addressing their sovereign offensive, complaining that they 'did neglect a ceremony and complement', omitting the flattery he regarded as his due (the covenanters later explained that 'the Scottish are mor for realities in expressions of kyndness then of wordes and gesture').[76] The Scots commissioners gave in various papers explaining their desires but got no answer. Their instructions had directed them not to wait longer than 25 March at the latest, but the king ordered them not to leave London.[77] He had no intention of answering their demands, but he now had the copy of the covenanters' letter to Louis XIII and he hoped to use it to convince the English parliament when it met on 13 April of the necessity of war with Scotland. By keeping the Scottish commissioners in London until then he could ensure that when he did make the letter public he would be able to lay his hands on at least one of its signatories, Lord Loudoun.

Thus Charles confidently prepared for a new offensive against the covenanters. But his position was much weaker than it had been a year previously, before the First Bishops' War. Though that war ended in a treaty which both king and covenanters realised was little more than a truce, such a settlement had been in some ways a triumph for the covenanters. They had successfully defied the king, and their power in Scotland was unshaken, while Charles' failure to invade Scotland and defeat rebellion encouraged his opponents in England as well as in Scotland. Moreover, following this peace treaty which was in effect an admission of failure by the king, his and Traquair's miscalculations had led to a mishandling of the general assembly which gave the covenanters plausible grounds for claiming that the king had accepted their religious demands, confirming the reforms of the Glasgow assembly. The king's supporters could at least console themselves that Charles could hardly be less successful in the coming campaign than in the previous one. They were soon to be proved wrong.

CHAPTER SIX

The Second Bishops' War and the Treaty of Ripon, March–November 1640

RENEWED PREPARATIONS FOR WAR

In preparation for his revelation in parliament of the covenanters' negotiations with France, Charles wrote summoning Argyll, Balmerino and those who had signed the letter to Louis XIII to London to answer grave but unspecified charges.[1] Needless to say, they refused to obey.[2] On 11 April the king ordered the arrest of Lord Loudoun and the other three Scottish commissioners in London[3] and sent a copy of the covenanters' letter to Louis XIII to his ambassador in Paris, the Earl of Leicester. Charles was especially indignant that the letter 'was directed and endorsed *Au Roy*; which Title is not given by any, but by Subjects, to theire naturall Souveraigne; and indeed no Construction can be made of the Letter itself, but that they have given themselves to that King'. Leicester was to represent to Louis XIII how confident Charles was that he would not assist the Scottish rebels since 'the Ground of theire Rebellion is nothing but a meere Opposition to Civill and monarchicall Government, wherein the common Interests of Kings are highly concerned'.[4] Whether Charles really believed that the endorsement 'au roy' was an indication of the covenanters' intention of declaring themselves subjects of Louis XIII is doubtful, but this explanation of the endorsement had the virtue of making the letter seem far more treasonable than it really was. For certainly the covenanters themselves had no such intention, and if the endorsement had the connotation claimed by Charles they were ignorant of it. Indeed the ignorance of the French language and modes of address among the leading covenanters contrasted strangely with the close links and friendship between France and Scotland which they claimed existed and justified their request for French intercession. Loudoun had had to have the letter translated to him before he signed it and there were arguments over whether it and other French letters drafted by the covenanters made sense or not.[5]

The English parliament, soon to be known as the Short Parliament, met on 13 April 1640. The lord keeper outlined the king's intentions and desires; it was necessary to reduce Scotland to obedience by means of a powerful army, and for this money was urgently needed. 'This Summer must not be lost . . . lest by protraction here they gain time and advantage to frame their parties with Foreign States.' This hint at foreign negotiations by the covenanters was the cue for Charles to produce their letter to Louis XIII. It was read in French and English and the significance of the endorsement 'au roy' explained.[6] But these revelations were ignored by parliament, and Charles' hopes that they would horrify it into accepting the necessity of war with Scotland collapsed when the House of Commons insisted on concentrating on English grievances instead of voting taxes for war. All efforts to divert the parliament back to the purpose for which it had been summoned failed, and Charles therefore dissolved it on 5 May.[7] This left the king far less able to subdue the Scots than if he had never called an English parliament, for not only had it not granted the money vital for raising an army, it had demonstrated in the most public way possible that a large and influential part of English opinion would not support a war with the Scots.

The covenanters quickly published their own version of the origins of the letter to Louis XIII; it had been one of two letters to him drafted in April or May 1639 (which was probably true), but no letter had in fact been sent then or later (which certainly was not true).[8] They also printed part of the relatively innocuous instructions prepared for William Colville in May 1639, but made no mention of those which he had actually taken to France.[9]

Colville reached France about the beginning of April, and showed his instructions and the letter to Louis XIII to his contacts in the French government. He probably worked through Richelieu's almoner, the Abbé Chambre or Chambres,[10] better

CASTRVM EDINENSE quod & olim ARX PVELLARVM
The Castell of Edinborrough from the west Porte. by J. G.

Page 185 PRINTS BY JAMES GORDON, Minister of Rothiemay. 1640s:
(*above*) Edinburgh Castle; (*below*) Holyroodhouse

PALATIVM REGIVM EDINENSE,
quod & Cænobium S. Crucis.
The royal palace of holy rood-hous. by J. G.

known in Scotland as Thomas Chambers or Chalmers, for he was a Scottish Jesuit. He may have been employed by Richelieu to visit Scotland in 1637 and was appointed his almoner. He was in Scotland in 1638–9, the excuse for his journeys being the same as that later used by William Colville—ostensibly he was arranging the recruiting of men in Scotland for the French army. In fact his main business was probably to report to Richelieu on the state of affairs in Scotland and to make secret contacts with leading covenanters, assuring them of Richelieu's goodwill towards the covenanters.[11] There is virtually no evidence of Chambers' activities in Scotland, but by 1640 he was well known as the chief agent in contacts between Richelieu and the covenanters, being regarded by many as virtually the Scots ambassador in France,[12] an extraordinary alliance of Jesuit and extreme Calvinists. However, Chambers' influence did not alter Richelieu's cautious policy of welcoming the activities of the covenanters as an embarrassment to Charles I but not helping them or interceding for them. Consequently, though Colville was heard and his news considered, nothing was done to help the covenanters. When Charles made public their letter to Louis XIII Richelieu congratulated himself on having avoided any entanglements with the Scots[13] while Louis himself denied having any correspondence with them and promised not to favour them.[14]

The covenanters thus failed to get any help from France, but they were much more successful in gaining support in England. On 16 April they appealed to the parliament of England against their enemies, again emphasising (as in their Information of February 1639) their wish for friendship and closer union between the kingdoms. In particular they asked that commissioners of both parliaments meet to avert a quarrel between the two nations which their enemies were trying to stir up.[15] Whether or not as a result of such appeals, most of those in England who opposed the king's government looked on the Scots as their allies, and many nobles and others at court were willing to send news of events and plans of the king to the Scots, especially to Wariston 'who valued himself to have been the chief contriver' of this intelligence system. There were few court secrets that were not quickly known by the covenanters. Gualter Frost (later to be clerk of the council of state of the Commonwealth) carried letters to Scotland in a hollow cane on several occasions,[16] and on at least one of his journeys he acted on the orders of Lord Savile, the most unscrupulous of the English nobles who helped the Scots.[17] A man of no discernible principles, his guiding obsession at this time was hatred for the Earl of Strafford (as Viscount Wentworth had been created in January 1640), and he co-operated with the English puritans and the covenanters in the hope of bringing about his ruin. The evidence of Savile's dealings with the Scots early in 1640 is incomplete but there is no doubt that he talked with James Stewart (an Edinburgh merchant, later Sir James Stewart of Kirkfield) when the latter was in London at the beginning of 1640. Stewart distrusted Savile but eventually agreed that Frost should accompany him back to Scotland as his servant with a letter for the leaders of the covenanters. This was said to have been signed by some of those who were soon to be prominent in opposing the king in the House of Commons, with other forged signatures added by Savile. Unfortunately the contents of the letter are not known.[18]

The king suspected that the leading English parliamentarians were in touch with the Scots, and though the main reason for imprisoning the Scots commissioners in London on 11 April had been the letter to Louis XIII, a subsidiary motive had been to prevent them and members of parliament meeting while parliament sat. But while Loudoun was sent to the Tower (for signing the letter) Dunfermline, Cavers and Robert Barclay were released after ten days. Cavers and Barclay were soon rearrested (9 May) after reports that they had been conferring with members of parliament, but they denied any but the most casual contacts with them and were soon freed for lack of evidence, returning to Scotland with Dunfermline late in May.[19]

In spite of the failure of the Short Parliament to grant taxes Laud and Strafford still strongly advocated the subjection of Scotland by war. 'One Summer well employed will do it', while to remain on the defensive would be dishonourable and encourage discontent in England. The king was less resolute. Though determined eventually to overthrow the covenanters, he considered delaying a decision in Scotland, by reopening negotiations, until he had dealt with the disorders and increasingly open opposition to his policies in England, but he soon abandoned the idea. The raising of forces therefore continued, but the results were discouraging and at the end of June Northumberland, the commander-in-chief, wrote 'I must confess that our wants and disorders are so great that I cannot devise how we should go on with our designs for this year'. His conclusion, that 'We yet make full account of conquering Scotland before many months pass',[20] was a statement of his determination rather than of confidence of success.

In Scotland the preparations of the covenanters were more successful. Many of the foreign-trained officers who had served in their armies the previous year had been paid during the winter to induce them to remain in Scotland[21] and were busy training men by the spring. The Tables (by now becoming known as the committee of estates) sent orders to the shires in March 1640 for compiling lists of arms and ammunition available and of men able to bear arms,[22] while Thomas Cuningham, one of the Scottish factors at Campvere, sent home arms and ammunition.[23] A meeting of the estates in Edinburgh on 16 April approved a remonstrance to the English parliament maintaining the justice of their cause[24] and the following day reappointed Alexander Leslie as general with similar powers to those he had had the previous year, though it was now specified that in important matters he was to act 'with consent of the committee which shall be with him in the Armie';[25] such a committee had accompanied the army the previous year but it had not been mentioned in Leslie's commission. Later Lord Almond (a brother of the royalist Earl of Linlithgow) who had been trained in the Dutch service was appointed lieutenant-general and William Baillie and Robert Monro major-generals.[26]

In all the Lowlands only four castles were garrisoned for the king, his own castles at Edinburgh and Dumbarton and the Earl of Nithsdale's at Caerlaverock and Threave. In the North East there were no royalists in arms; Huntly and many of the other leading royalists had retired to England. But there was a good deal of sullen passive resistance to the rule of the covenanters which might have been transformed into a royalist rising if any leaders had appeared. The covenanters therefore decided that it was necessary to overawe the royalist areas and on 5 May Aberdeen was occupied by a force under the Earl Marischal, who began raising money and men for the covenanters' army. This force was joined on 28 May by a regiment under Robert Monro, who forced the magistrates of Aberdeen to make humiliating concessions.[27]

The date to which the Scottish parliament had been prorogued the previous November, 2 June, was now approaching. The covenanters seem to have decided by 9 May that it would meet, if necessary in spite of royal orders to the contrary, as on that date some of the burgh commissioners in Edinburgh wrote to the burghs asking them to send their commissioners to meet in Edinburgh a day or two before 2 June to discuss the parliament, as it was necessary 'to hawe everie thing done incumbent to ws, leist oure posteritie suld blame ws for neglect of what may conduce for preservatioune of oure religioun, lywes, and liberties'.[28] On 1 June the leading covenanters met to decide what should be done in the parliament. What was said and agreed at the meeting was never revealed, but there was certainly a wide-ranging discussion of what constitutional changes were necessary. The only account by a covenanter of the discussions occurs in a letter written by Wariston the following year, which refers to 'the speeches that passed in the meeting of Estates, the first of June, in the dispute whether to prorogate the Parliament, or to sit still notwithstanding of the King and Commissioner's absence, when Montrose did dispute against Argyll, Rothes, Balmerino, and myself, because some urged that, as long as we had a King, we could not sit without him, and it was answered, that to do the less, was more lawful nor to do the greater'.[29] The meaning of this appears to be that those who argued that parliament could not meet while there was a king who ordered it not to, were told that they could be held to be suggesting that it would be better to depose the king ('the greater') so that parliament could be held without disobeying him, than simply to hold it against his orders ('the less'), which was absurd. Certainly there was talk of deposition of kings in general terms at the meeting. Lawyers and ministers who had been consulted agreed that a king might be deposed for invading, deserting or selling his kingdom. There was probably no talk in more specific terms of actually deposing King Charles; a royalist, John Stewart younger of Ladywell, later stated that there was, that the covenanters debated the immediate deposition of the king but decided to delay it until parliament next met. This was almost certainly untrue.[30]

That there should by this time have been talk of deposing kings is hardly surprising. Though very few were ready to contemplate deposing Charles, it must have occurred to an increasing number of covenanters that if he would never concede their demands and honour his concessions (and this was coming to seem increasingly likely), then they would either have to give up their demands and submit, or deny his authority and depose him. The confrontation between king and covenanters had already lasted nearly three years, and there was the danger that if it continued much longer without any sign of a settlement religious enthusiasm would begin to wane while the high taxes needed to support the army made the covenant increasingly unpopular and desire for a return to normalcy grew; would it not be wisest to depose the stubborn and untrustworthy king before this happened? Probably such ideas were being whispered and hinted at by June 1640, but it is highly unlikely that they were openly discussed in the meeting on 1 June, and there is no sign that any consideration was given to how Scotland would be governed after such a deposition. There was talk of setting up a dictatorship but this was not seen as a replacement for the Stewart monarchy but as a short-term expedient for governing Scotland until a settlement was reached; the proposal was for one man to be given absolute power, superseding the ordinary magistrates for a limited period to deal with an emergency, like the early Roman dictators. As with the question of deposing the king, the evidence of plans for establishing a dictatorship comes almost entirely from rumours circulating among royalists, but this time the rumours seem to have a more solid foundation in revelations made by the covenanting Lord Lindsay who knew of but opposed the idea. There were suggestions that one dictator (probably Argyll) should be appointed, or two, one for the North (Argyll) and one for the South, or perhaps a triumvirate. The circumstance which some held made such appointments necessary was evidently that if (as was already being contemplated) the main army of the covenanters was to invade England, accompanied by many of the covenanting nobles, there would be need of a strong central authority to remain in Scotland and rule in their absence; could not this need be best supplied by appointing a 'dictator', or a general within Scotland with wide executive powers?[31] However, the question of such an appointment was not in fact brought before parliament, probably because the advantages of such a scheme would be outweighed by the jealousies and fears aroused by giving so much power to one or a few men. Government by committees might be inefficient in some ways, but it was very useful in preserving unity.

PARLIAMENT, THE SUBDUING OF THE NORTH, AND THE ASSEMBLY

Though the king at first thought of agreeing to let parliament meet, he eventually decided instead on a prorogation until 7 July.[32] But parliament was resolved to sit against the king's orders if necessary, and the covenanters were given an opportunity of claiming that they were not in fact disobeying him by the inefficiency or (more probably) the treachery of the lord advocate, for incredibly it was to Craighall that Charles entrusted the prorogation. He had known for nearly three years that Craighall was willing to use his official position to help the covenanters, and had in January 1640 confined him to his house of Craighall on the excuse of some minor misdemeanour but really to prevent his continuing to aid the king's enemies;[33] yet now the king decided that he was to be trusted.

The king ordered Craighall to have the parliament prorogued by authority of a commission he had granted (but which had not been used) under the quarter seal on 20 August 1639 to ten commissioners, empowering them to fence[34] and prorogue parliament as often as was necessary. Instead Craighall decided to use another commission, under the quarter seal, granted at about the same time, giving himself and three others power to act in parliament as king's commissioner in place of Traquair, if for some reason he had been unable to attend the 1639 parliament. When parliament assembled on 2 June 1640, Craighall asked his three colleagues to join him in proroguing parliament to conform to this commission, but two refused after reading the commission, declaring that it empowered them to act in Traquair's place only if Traquair ordered them to do so, which he had not done. Therefore, as the quorum named in the commission was three, Craighall could not act. Parliament claimed that there was no valid order from the king to prevent it sitting,[35] and assumed itself to be legally constituted.

Acts were passed electing Lord Burleigh president (the chancellor had normally acted as president in the past) and declaring that the present parliament held by the nobles, barons and burgesses and their commissioners comprised the true three estates of the kingdom and a complete and perfect parliament. This implicitly denied the right of officers of state to sit *ex officio* in parliament, and it was specifically declared that bishops or other churchmen had no place there. A declaration explained why it was necessary for parliament to meet; the pacification of Berwick had promised the settlement of all matters civil by parliament, but it had been prorogued the previous year before it could do this. Since then preparations for destroying Scotland by war had been made. It was necessary for parliament to sit so it could ratify the acts of the 1639 general assembly and settle other business conducive to the good and peace of kirk and kingdom. The fact that the king had sent no order for prorogation was stated to be a tacit consent and presumed allowance for parliament to meet; there was no intention of entrenching in the least on the king's authority.[36] Having delivered itself of this piece of hardly honest argument, parliament proceeded between 2 and 11 June to pass a series of acts memorable 'as exhibitting the reall grattest change at one blow that euer hapned to this churche and staite thesse 600 zeires baypast; for in effect it ouerturned not onlie the ancient state gouernment, bot fettered monarchie with chynes'.[37]

Most of the acts were based on acts passed or debated in the articles in 1639, which were revised by a committee elected by parliament.[38] One of the most important of the acts passed stated that frequent parliaments, such as were held before 1603, were necessary, especially since the king now normally resided outside the kingdom and subjects had not free and easy access to him with grievances and complaints. Therefore a full and free parliament was in future to meet at least once every three years and the king was to be supplicated to be present at all these parliaments.[39] As for the manner of proceedings in parliament, all matters and grievances were to be given in and debated in the full parliament; lords of the articles might be chosen if parliament decided that this was convenient, but even if they were, they would consider only matters referred to them by the full parliament. Each estate was to choose its own representatives to sit on the articles, and it was evidently intended that the articles of each estate should meet separately. In fact no lords of the articles were ever chosen under this act, though the 1640 parliament retained the old practice of voting on all its acts on the last day of parliament, as if they had then been presented by the articles.[40] It is not clear whether the shire commissioners had individual votes (or only one per shire) in 1640; the burgesses were strongly opposed to allowing them individual votes and Edinburgh burgh council ordered its commissioners 'to disassent therfra and rather to ryse then to sie such ane conclusioun pas in voice in parliament' as it tended to the overthrow of the estate of burgesses.[41] But either at this time or in the following year the shire commissioners were tacitly allowed individual votes, thus virtually doubling their voting strength.[42] Voting in parliament by proxy or by foreigners with Scottish titles who had not land in Scotland worth 10,000 merks per annum was forbidden.[43]

These acts concerning the constitution of parliament greatly altered its character. The removal of the bishops and the officers of state from membership and the changing of the lords of the articles from being the masters to the servants of parliament removed the members and institution on which the king relied to keep parliament subservient. But the important matter of what was to be the king's place in this new form of parliament was ignored completely as likely to provoke endless arguments and divisions.

To rule Scotland after parliament rose a committee of estates was appointed as the successor of the Tables. It consisted of twelve each of nobles, lairds and burgesses, most but not all of whom were members of parliament, and three ordinary lords of session. The act establishing the committee related that considering the preparations being made to invade Scotland, threatening kirk and kingdom, parliament was forced to take measures for lawful defence. It therefore appointed the committee to maintain the armies and order, direct and govern the whole kingdom, with full powers to do everything necessary for this. The committee was given authority to borrow money and raise taxes, to convene any meetings it thought necessary to give it advice, and to appoint and call to account all army and other officials. When convenient the committee was to split in two, one half remaining in Edinburgh while the other accompanied the army. Each part of the committee was to have full powers, except that the consent of both was to be necessary for engaging in war or agreeing to any settlement. Though Wariston was not a member he was ordered to attend the part of the committee that accompanied the army, since there would probably be a need for treaties and public declarations and he was best acquainted with such matters, an interesting testimony to how indispensable he had made himself to the covenanters. All general officers of the army were also given the right to be present at the meetings of the committees.[44] The members of the committee included nearly all the leading covenanters; the most notable exception was Argyll, since he was to remain in the North to guard the covenanters' interests there. Some whose loyalty and resolution was now doubted (such as Montrose) were given places on the committee, probably in the hope that this would induce them to continue to support the cause.

As to religion, the June 1640 parliament passed acts ratifying the acts of the 1639 assembly (the Glasgow assembly not being mentioned) and the national covenant. An act rescissory nullified all acts of parliament in favour of bishops and derogatory to the spiritual jurisdiction of the kirk (including the 1621 act ratifying the Five Articles of Perth).[45] Former acts against bands, leagues

and conventions among subjects were declared to have no relevance to the meetings and bands of the covenanters, all of which
were lawful. A new band was drawn up for subscription throughout the country binding signatories to uphold the legality of the
present session of parliament.[46]

In preparation for the coming war an act anent the common
relief gave detailed instructions for payment of the tenth penny
(one tenth of valued rents) as already ordered and for raising an
additional twentieth penny as a loan.[47] The governor and garrison
of Edinburgh castle were summoned to surrender, and on their
refusal the lives and property of Lord Ettrick and his officers were
declared forfeited for high treason.[48] For punishment of those
whom the covenanters held to be responsible for the troubles the
committee of estates was ordered to summon before the next
session of parliament all who had advised or assisted policies
destructive to the liberties of kirk and kingdom to answer for their
crimes. The main charges to be brought against them were ones of
lease-making; this had been the crime of slandering the king or his
council, but the covenanters now widened its definition to include
the activities and lies of 'all misinformeres raiseris and inter-
teaneris of jelousies suspitiones and divisiones betuixt the king
this kirke and kingdome', especially bad councillors who give
advice destructive to kirk and kingdom;[49] with such a definition
of lease-making few royalists would feel safe.

On 11 June, after issuing another declaration justifying itself
and disowning any intention of denying the king's temporal and
civil authority, parliament continued itself until 19 November.[50]
The committee of estates wrote to the Earl of Lanark as secretary[51]
explaining how, hearing nothing from the king to prevent it
meeting, parliament had sat and passed various acts, which they
enclosed and asked him to present to the king. The covenanters
did not ask for the king's formal consent to these acts, as this
might seem to imply that they accepted that he had power to veto
them by refusing his consent; neither did they explicitly claim that
acts of parliament were binding even if they had not received
royal consent, but simply assumed that this was so. The king
indignantly retorted that he had sent clear instructions for pro-

roguing parliament, Lanark adding 'if subjects there do assume the Power of making Laws, and rescinding those already made, what Act can be more Derogatory to that Regal Power and Authority we are all sworn to maintain'. This reply was brought to Scotland by Lord Loudoun who had been released from the Tower of London on promising to do all he could to get the covenanters to disband their forces,[52] a promise he seems to have made no attempt to honour.

While the parliament had been sitting Robert Monro had been strengthening the covenanters' hold on the North East with the help of the Earl Marischal. Many royalists were seized and sent to Edinburgh (where they were fined by the committee of estates) and their houses and castles occupied or made indefensible.[53] Early in July Monro and Marischal marched north, plundering the lands of the Gordons and other royalists, who offered no resistance. In mid August they moved to Banff to plunder the property of Sir George Ogilvie of Banff, returning to Aberdeen early in September.[54]

Further south the Earl of Argyll was similarly active in enforcing obedience to the regime. One of the first acts of the new committee of estates had been to grant him (on 12 June) a commission against 'the Earle of Atholl, the Lord Ogilvie, and thair complices and assistantis as weill in Atholl as in the braes of Angus, the Ferquharsounes, in the Braes of Mar, and thair complices and vtheris, our enemies and opposites, in Badzenoch, Lochaber, and Renoch', who had proved enemies to the country and its religion and awaited an opportunity to attack the covenanters or join invaders. Argyll was to pursue them with fire and sword until they were utterly subdued and rooted out or gave assurances for their future good conduct. The men for this punitive expedition were to be raised in the sheriffdom of Argyll, though the Earl of Argyll was given power to require the assistance of other shires if necessary.[55] Though Montrose was one of those that signed this commission he must have been bitterly disappointed by its terms, as it indicated how little he was trusted by most of the covenanters. He had himself been chosen by the shire committees of war of Perth and Forfar to command their forces and was thus the obvious person to be entrusted with action against the Ogilvies and anti-covenanters in Atholl. Instead Argyll had been called in and Montrose had been given no independent command. Monro had already replaced him as the enforcer of the covenant in Aberdeen and the North, and General Leslie and the committee of estates ignored his election to lead the forces of Perth and Forfar, appointing other officers to bring out forces from these shires in spite of his active opposition.[56] There had probably already arisen open hostility and rivalry between the cautious, reserved and stern Argyll, and the flamboyant and vastly ambitious Montrose. Argyll's commission now gave him a welcome opportunity to demonstrate his power in areas in which Montrose regarded his own interests as being involved.

This commission to Argyll enabled him to combine conveniently public and private interests, the suppression of royalists and the extension of his own and his clan's power. The head of the Ogilvies, the Earl of Airlie, had fled to England, but his eldest son, Lord Ogilvie, remained and had refused to sign the covenant. In May letters from him had been intercepted which indicated that a royalist rising was being planned, and that the Earl of Atholl had promised to join it.[57] Atholl had not yet openly opposed the covenant, though he had been rebuked for not obeying orders to send men to join the covenanters' army.[58] At the end of May Argyll warned his kinsmen to be prepared for a rising by the Stewarts and others in Atholl. He also announced that he was about to take possession of Badenoch and Lochaber. Some time before he had become cautioner for some of the debts of the almost bankrupt Huntly, and for the payment of the dowries of his daughters, Huntly agreeing that if Argyll had to make payments to his (Huntly's) creditors he should have the lands and lordships of Badenoch and Lochaber in recompense. Evidently Huntly had failed to pay his debts so Argyll now claimed these lands. This is a good example of how the Campbells made use of the financial embarrassments of their neighbours to increase their own possessions and powers; it seems that in this instance Argyll paid some of Huntly's debts before he had any need to do so in order to give himself a claim on the lands.[59] Argyll was thus planning a military expedition to assert his rights to Badenoch and Lochaber and to prevent any royalist rising by the Stewarts of Atholl long before he received his commission from the committee of estates to take such action. Though he wrote in May 'I wische heartilie I wer hindered of such imployments by the mens good behaviour in tyme',[60] in June he expressed a very different sentiment—'I should be werrie glad that the Athoill men wold draw to ane head and mak a stand for then I wold know quhair to find thame'.[61] He feared that the royalists would submit to him but rise later in the year when the covenanters had concentrated their forces on the Borders to oppose the king.

By 18 June, only six days after he had been granted his commission, Argyll had assembled 4,000 men, and between that date and 2 August he marched through Atholl, the Braes of Mar and Angus, Badenoch, Lochaber and Rannoch.[62] He met with little opposition, but the march itself was thought to be something of an achievement.[63] When (during this march) Argyll advanced towards the House of Airlie he found that Montrose, as a friend and neighbour of the Ogilvies, had taken matters into his own hands without authority. He had appeared at Airlie some days before with his own forces and come to some agreement with Lord Ogilvie whereby the latter was allowed to leave Airlie, taking his movable property with him while Montrose garrisoned the house. Montrose claimed that this was a military operation undertaken by him on behalf of the covenanters. But there is little doubt that in fact Montrose knew of Argyll's approach and acted to thwart him and help Ogilvie. To Argyll it was clear that Montrose had purposely helped an open enemy of the covenant escape arrest with some of his property (which should have been devoted to supporting the covenanters' forces) and without giving any guarantees for his future good behaviour—just as in May 1639 Montrose had made terms with Huntly which were later rejected by the other covenanters. Argyll had his revenge by expelling Montrose's garrison and destroying the house of Airlie.[64]

Montrose's dislike of Argyll and suspicion that he was acting to increase his own and his clan's power as well as to advance the covenant had led him, in conjunction with the Earl of Atholl, to send John Stewart younger of Ladywell to discover what bands Argyll and his followers were getting signed in Atholl and elsewhere, what evidence there was that Argyll had arranged for his commission to be granted to him, and whether he aspired to some form of supremacy above his equals. It was clear from these instructions what Stewart's employers suspected, and he seems to have played up to their suspicions by providing false evidence, greatly exaggerating whatever hints of Argyll's intentions he found and inventing facts when there were not even hints. When he reported that Argyll's soldiers sang (in Gaelic) in his praise since he would seize the gear of the Lowlanders and take the crown by force, and that they said 'they were King Campbells men, no more King Stewarts'[65] he was probably speaking the truth, but the exuberant shouts of clansmen on what they hoped would be a profitable plundering raid are no evidence of their dour chief's intentions. While in Atholl, Argyll summoned the Earl of Atholl and other leading men of the area to meet him at the Ford of Lyon, and what Stewart later claimed Argyll said at this meeting led to his own execution the following year. Probably, in trying to persuade the Atholl men to submit and obey the covenanters Argyll hinted that continuing to resist through loyalty to the king would bring about their ruin; kings might be deposed. Perhaps he also hinted that they would be wise to submit to him personally as he expected to wield a great power in the North in future. He certainly demanded subscription of bands of loyalty to the covenant.[66] But it seems inconceivable that Argyll, who was so careful to conceal his intentions and avoid incriminating himself, should have told this group of Atholl royalists, as Stewart said he did, that the king would be deposed by the next session of parliament, a dictatorship established, and other such extravagances.[67] Whatever Argyll said, he was not successful in persuading the Earl of Atholl and the other royalists present to support the covenant, and they were therefore arrested and sent south as prisoners.[68] Argyll's expedition to the North and East in June and July was successful in over-awing most of the Highland royalists, though some of the clans remained restless enough for him to appoint in

October two Campbell lairds to act against the Macdonalds of Lochaber and Glengarry, and the Robertsons.[69]

From 28 July to 5 August 1640 the general assembly sat in Aberdeen; the king had chosen the place the previous year, hoping that the royalism of the area would influence the assembly in his favour. Instead it gave the covenanters an opportunity to demonstrate how subdued the area was by holding their assembly there without any difficulty. The assembly differed considerably in composition from those of 1638 and 1639; now that most of the basic religious changes demanded by the covenanters had been made and there was no danger of any considerable party in the assembly trying to alter them, few of the leading covenanting nobles attended as elders. They were busy with the more urgent task of preparing for war and had little interest in the routine and internal business of the kirk which occupied most of the assembly's time, though some of the nobles of the North attended. It was now ministers who took the leading part in the debates. No king's commissioner was present, the assembly ruling that it could proceed without one 'according to their Liberties', and Andrew Ramsay was elected moderator.[70]

The most important debates were those concerning whether or not the holding of private prayer meetings or conventicles was compatible with the presbyterian system; this question led to violent and bitter arguments. As we have seen, many of the more radical ministers had held conventicles before 1637. After the troubles began these prayer meetings became more widespread, especially in the South West, and were encouraged or supported by many prominent ministers, including David Dickson, Robert Blair and Samuel Rutherford. But many other covenanters were strongly opposed to such conventicles, believing that they were liable to undermine family worship on the one hand and the worship of the parish in the kirk on the other. The spread of the meetings led them to fear the introduction of extreme sectarian and independent ideas into the kirk which would undermine the presbyterian government; they talked of 'Brownism', the 'Family of Love', the 'New England Way' and other such indisciplined perversions coming among them. Henry Guthry (minister of

Stirling), Alexander Henderson and David Calderwood had proposed that an act should be passed in the 1639 assembly against such conventicles, but in the interests of preventing open arguments among themselves at a time when they were trying to preserve unity to force concessions from the king this had not been done. Instead a private conference of ministers had reached some compromise whereby it was stated that prayer meetings might have been necessary in time of persecution and corruption but that they were no longer necessary now that peace and purity of the kirk had been restored. In spite of this conventicles had continued to meet and Henry Guthry now brought up the matter again in the 1640 assembly, gaining the support of most of the ministers and elders from the North for his demands that they be suppressed. David Dickson argued that to ban private prayer meetings would offend many of the covenanters' friends in England and thus hinder efforts to bring about religious uniformity between the kingdoms; the Earl of Seaforth replied that if such undermining of the kirk was the price of uniformity 'we will not buy it so dear'.[71] 'Presentlie all went to a heat and confused dinn';[72] the lack of noble elders to use their authority to keep the squabbling ministers in order was felt. Eventually the assembly decided against the prayer meetings, but the act passed against them was never published and was largely ignored by the radicals, who complained that such an act could only have been passed in an assembly held in the North with a larger than usual proportion of conservative ministers and elders from that area attending.[73] During the bitter debates on conventicles dispute between the moderates and radicals spread to include some points of worship. The radicals, partly through English puritan influence, partly through the critical attitude developed while opposing the king that all details of worship must be justified from scripture, wanted to purge the kirk of several traditional practices which they erroneously claimed were innovations. Moderates indignantly defended these well-loved practices.[74] It was therefore a deeply divided assembly which dissolved on 5 August, appointing its successor to meet in St Andrews on 13 July 1641.[75]

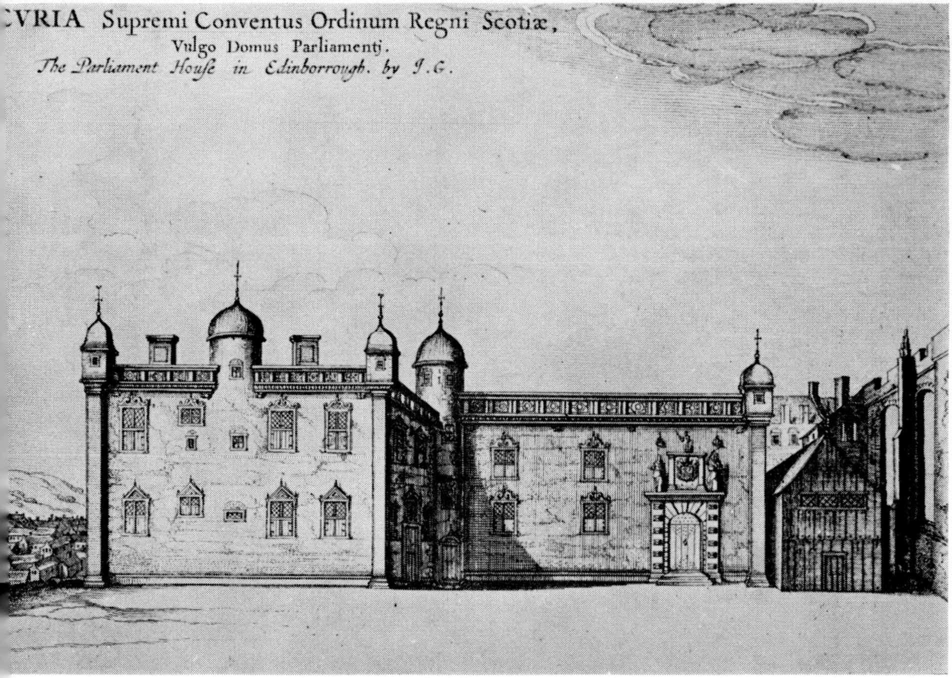

Page 203   PRINTS BY JAMES GORDON, Minister of Rothiemay. 1640s:
(above) Parliament House; (below) Heriot's Hospital

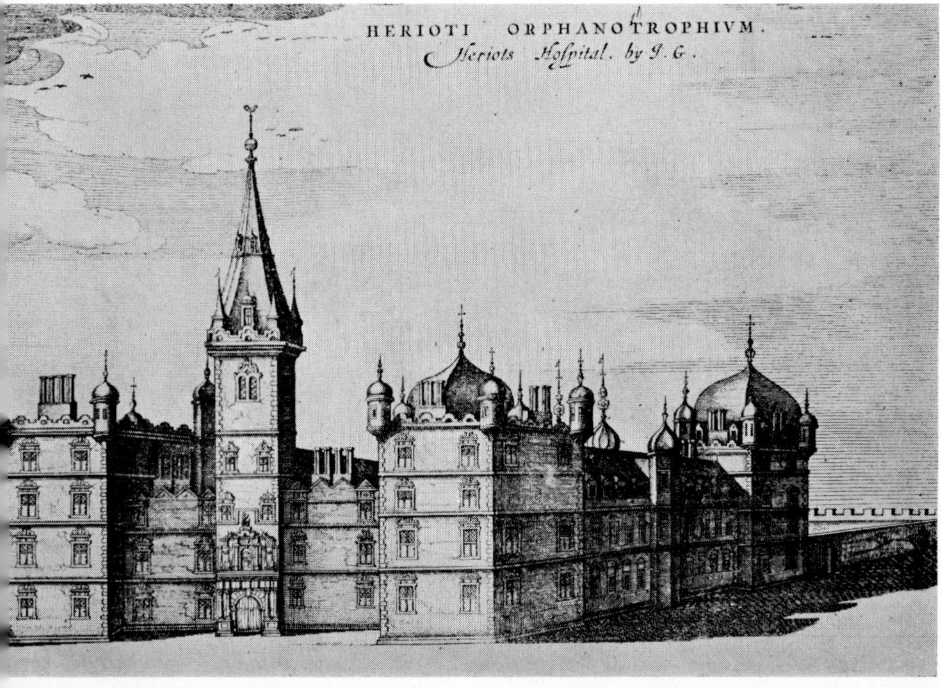

HERIOTI   ORPHANOTROPHIVM.
Heriots Hospital. by J.G.

General Leslie.

Page 204 A CON-
TRAST IN GENE-
RALS: (*left*) the
Professional. Alexande
Leslie, 1st Earl of
Leven, *c.* 1580–1661;
(*below*) the Amateur,
George Gordon, 2nd
Marquis of Huntly,
died 1649. After
Van Dyck

THE EXPEDITION INTO ENGLAND

All this time the main army of the covenant had been slowly assembling on the Borders. Troops had been arriving since the beginning of July[76] and by the end of the month the army had camped near Duns. There had been virtually no resistance to the raising of the army, though reluctance to provide money to pay and feed it was widespread and many of those ordered to serve in it tried to avoid doing so—as in the previous year every fourth man had been ordered to serve.[77] The problem was to keep the army together and adequately supplied. If it remained in Scotland, on the defensive, lack of supplies would probably soon force it to negotiate and accept terms as unsatisfactory as those of the Pacification of Berwick, for there was little chance that the king would invade Scotland and thus give the covenanters the opportunity to achieve a military victory. Since the king would not bring his army to Scotland, should not the covenanters enter England to force a decision?

The main danger of this was that it might rally English opinion behind the king to drive out the Scottish invaders, but many wer by now convinced that this risk would have to be taken if the stubborn and distant king was to be forced to concede their demands. Moreover it is possible that they were spurred on by messages from the king's English opponents urging them to enter England to uphold the liberties of both kingdoms, and threatening that unless the Scots thus helped them against the king, they would fight for the king against the Scots.[78] Whether or rot such earlier contacts had existed, the covenanters decided to try to get the English peers who opposed the king to invite them to enter England, and to promise to join them in arms if they did so. On 23 June Wariston wrote to Lord Loudoun in London asking him on behalf of the covenanters to try to arrange some such guarantees from the English.[79] Loudoun tried to do this through Lord Savile but failed. On about 8 July seven peers (including Savile) wrote to the covenanters stating that they could not invite the Scots into England or join them in arms, as that would be treason, but that they would help and support them in all other ways. This was too vague to be satisfactory to the Scots, even though Savile tried to

13

encourage them by claiming that though, out of regard for their honour, the peers had refused to give the guarantees asked, they had resolved that if the Scots invaded England they would gather a considerable body of men and send a remonstrance to the king demanding remedies for their own grievances and those of the Scots.[80] As the Scots still were not satisfied, Savile later in July forged his famous 'Savile Letter', signing it himself and forging the signatures of six other peers, containing the promises that the covenanters desired.[81]

With this encouragement the committee of estates and the army officers decided unanimously on 3 August to invade England and approved the distribution of a paper explaining their intentions[82] —they had no quarrel with England but were forced to act to defend their religion and liberties, and necessity was a sovereign law, above all other laws.[83] Another paper also urged that all men knew 'what is the great force of necessity, and how it doth justifie actions otherways unwarrantable', a crude argument but one which once accepted could be used to justify almost anything. The king, 'misled by the crafty and cruel faction of our Adversaries, began this years war, not we'. They were called to arms by divine providence and did not fight through disloyalty to the king or to enrich themselves, but for religion and to help the English to complete the reformation long prayed for by the godly in England —a clear bid for the support of the puritans. They were glad to give this help to their English brethren to repay the help the English had given them at the time of the reformation in 1560 'in freeing us from the French', a reference intended to allay the fears of any who believed the king's charges that the covenanters were willing to subject themselves to the French.[84]

Not all the covenanters were content with the decision to invade England, nor with other policies of the covenanting leadership dominated by Argyll. There were still rumours that it was intended to depose the king and appoint dictators. Moderate members of the committee of estates and army officers claimed that they were neglected in consultations and decision-making, and demanded changes in the composition of the committee.[85] Some of these malcontents, led by Montrose, met at Cumbernauld

House at some time in August and signed secretly the 'Cumbernauld Band'. This related that its subscribers had, out of duty to religion, king and country, signed the covenant, but that they now found that 'by the particular and indirect practiking of a few' the country and cause were suffering greatly. They therefore bound themselves to maintain the cause and the covenant and to do all tending to the safety of religion, laws and liberties of 'this poor Kingdom'. In these matters none would act without the consent and approbation of the other signatories of the band and (insofar as was compatible with the good of the public) they would protect each others' interests against all persons whatsoever. The band was signed (at Cumbernauld and later elsewhere) by the Earl Marischal, the Earls of Montrose, Wigton, Kinghorn, Home, Atholl, Mar, Perth, Galloway and Seaforth, and ten other nobles and eldest sons of nobles—including Lord Almond, the lieutenant general.[86] Though the wording of the band is so vague that it is impossible to know quite what it was meant to achieve, it is clear that Montrose was trying to create a party or faction to oppose Argyll and his supporters. It is also clear from the signatures that Montrose had at first a good deal of success in this, attracting moderate royalists such as Atholl as well as convinced covenanters like Marischal. But they did not form a very coherent or determined group. Most of them, unlike the militant Montrose, wanted a quiet life and to avoid committing themselves completely to either king or covenant, and the 'Banders' never became a significant political force, though they might have had more influence if the covenanters' invasion of England had not been successful.

The Scots had little to fear from the forces the king had managed to raise against them. The commander-in-chief, Northumberland, was lethargic while Lord Conway who commanded the forces in the north of England showed little energy or skill either in preparing to invade Scotland or to defend England, though this was not entirely his fault, for the orders sent to him were often vague and contradictory. It became clear that invasion of Scotland in 1640 was impossible, but the king dithered, reluctant to abandon plans for invasion but giving no indication of how they were to be carried out. Conway later complained that he had been promised

22,000 men but only about half of them ever appeared.[87] Not until August did the king and Conway seem to realise that a Scottish invasion was imminent; Charles did not leave London for York until 20 August.[88]

The Scots army also had its troubles. It had had to send a delegation to Edinburgh to beg the burgh to provide money and materials for tents which were urgently needed,[89] and orders had been given to execute one in ten of all deserters and forbidding all travelling without licence (except by 'persons of quality') to make desertion less common.[90] But these difficulties encouraged the covenanters to invade England rather than prevented them from doing so, since they increased the urgency of reaching a military decision soon, before their army deteriorated. Therefore the Scottish army entered England on 20 August—after the committee of estates had written to Lanark explaining that it was coming to present petitions to the king.[91] The army marched steadily south without meeting any resistance, reaching the Tyne at Newburn on 27 August. Conway's troops tried to prevent them crossing the river but fled the next day after a short fight; they were not pursued as the covenanters had no wish to cause ill feeling in England by inflicting unnecessary casualties. To the astonishment of the Scots, Conway withdrew his garrison from Newcastle, and the city, one of the richest in the kingdom, surrendered without a fight on 30 August.[92] The invasion had been more successful than the covenanters can have dared to have hoped; though Newcastle had been their main objective they had not expected to be able simply to walk into it. Conversely the success of the Scots was a shattering blow to the morale (never high) of the king's forces and advisers, and largely destroyed his prestige at home and abroad; in spite of his long preparations for war the invaders had occupied Northumberland and Durham with barely a shot fired except at Newburn.

Success in England also led to the fall of the few remaining royalist strongholds in the Lowlands. Dumbarton castle surrendered to Argyll on 27 August[93] and Caerlaverock in September after a long and bloody siege.[94] Edinburgh castle had been besieged since March and had sporadically bombarded the burgh.

Assaults on it by the covenanters had failed and it was still well supplied, but the garrison had suffered much from shortage of water and there was no prospect of help from the king. Lord Ettrick (who was too ill to walk) therefore agreed terms of surrender with Argyll on 15 September whereby he and his men were allowed to march to Leith with their arms, baggage and colours. Some blamed Argyll for allowing such generous terms, but there had seemed little chance of taking the castle by storm, its guns had killed nearly 200 people in the burgh and done much damage, and possession of the castle completed the covenanters' supremacy in the Lowlands.[95]

In spite of its initial success, the position of the Scots army in England was far from secure. Reinforcements were badly needed to garrison the area conquered while keeping a large enough army together to meet any attack by the king's forces, and an English garrison remained in Berwick and tried to disrupt the covenanters' communications.[96] It was thought safe to withdraw Robert Monro and his forces from the North East to police the Borders[97] but other reinforcements were hard to find and it soon proved impossible to supply the army's needs from Scotland.[98] That this would be so had been foreseen—indeed one of the arguments in favour of invading England had been that it would relieve Scotland of part of the burden of supporting the army, but it had been determined that at first most supplies should come from Scotland and those bought in England be paid for to create a good impression. The English were potential allies, not enemies, and plundering was harshly punished. But by mid September the Scots were forced to raise contributions in the area of England that they held to support the army. Though this was done in as orderly a manner as possible and most of the burden was put on Catholics and church property, it was hardly calculated to endear the invaders to the population.[99] Finally, and the most worrying of all the difficulties facing the covenanters once they had invaded England, none of the puritan peers whom they believed had promised to join them had appeared. 'If the English will now be beasts, and dastardlie cowards, they must lie without any man's pitie under their slavish servitude for ever' wrote Robert Baillie indignantly.[100] If the covenanters' friends in England did not soon assert themselves against the king the position of the Scots army might become hazardous.

However, the king's position was far worse. There seemed no possibility of raising forces sufficient to defeat the Scots in the face of a general unwillingness to provide men or money. Some of the king's ministers seriously discussed the possibility of the Scots army entering London within a month.[101] The leaders of the English opposition to the government took advantage of the king's embarrassment (as the covenanters had hoped they would) to demand remedies for their grievances; twelve peers petitioned the king to hold a parliament to try his evil counsellors and make peace with the Scots.[102] The covenanters sent their own demands to the king on 4 September; the committee of estates with the army at Newcastle petitioned him to repair their wrongs and losses with the advice and consent of an English parliament, and to settle a durable peace. The king replied that this was so vague as to be impossible to answer and asked for particulars of their demands, announcing that he had summoned a great council of peers to meet with him in York to help him in answering them. Meanwhile he hopefully ordered the Scots to advance no further into England.[103]

The Scots sent their detailed demands, though regretting that the meeting of the peers would delay the holding of a parliament 'which is conceived to be the only means of settling both Nations in a firm Peace', for they were determined to have more than just the king's word to guarantee a peace treaty. They asked that the king should publish the acts of the June 1640 Scottish parliament in his own name and that Edinburgh and other castles should be used only for the defence of Scotland. They required the restoration of all Scots ships and property that had been seized, and that the covenanters' losses and expenses should be repaid. 'Incendiaries' should be punished, all declarations against the covenanters recalled, and peace settled with the advice of the English parliament.[104] These, said the covenanters, were their full demands. This was far from true. They were rather the terms on which the covenanters would agree to a truce, a cessation of arms, while a detailed settlement of the constitutional and religious issues was negotiated. Montrose protested at this discrepancy between what the covenanters said they wanted and their actual plans for a peace which would leave the king virtually powerless in Scotland,[105] but his influence among the covenanters was greatly reduced when it was discovered that he was trying to open a secret correspondence with the king.[106]

The great council of peers met at York on 24 September. The king, giving way to almost universal pressure in England, announced that the English parliament would meet on 3 November, but he insisted that it would be dishonourable for him to disband his forces so long as the Scots army remained in England. Rather late in the day he tried to convince the peers that he had been justified in making war on Scotland by getting Traquair to tell them of the reasons that had led him to advise the king and privy council in favour of war, but the peers were unimpressed. They agreed that the king's forces should not be disbanded, but the sixteen peers whom they appointed to treat with the Scots were nearly all opponents of his government (they included all the seven peers who had written to the covenanters on about 8 July). The negotiations were to begin at Ripon on 2 October and it was agreed that six advisers or assisters appointed by the king should accompany the commissioners; four of these were Scots, the Earls of Traquair, Morton and Lanark, and Sir Lewis Stewart.[107] The king gave his instructions to the sixteen commissioners on 29 September. They were to take the articles of the pacification of Berwick as the basis of their treaty with the Scots, and keep as close to these articles as possible. The king would not publish the acts of the June 1640 parliament, since it had met without his authority, but he would consent to some of the acts if they were passed in a subsequent parliament. He agreed to the restoration of Scots goods and ships but rejected the covenanters' other demands.[108]

Charles was remarkably optimistic if he thought that the covenanters would agree to a peace based on the pacification of Berwick. Many of them had regarded that settlement as unsatisfactory even in the circumstances of June 1639, and now, when their army occupied the north of England, there was no chance of their again accepting such terms. As soon emerged, the covenanters were concerned at Ripon only to negotiate a cessation whereby the king agreed that their army should be paid by England and delay negotiation of a peace treaty until the English parliament met. If the king would agree to this and not to send any of his forces north of the Tees, then the covenanters would advance no further into England.[109] By involving the English parliament in the treaty they hoped to prevent the king's ever again trying to use the resources of England against his Scottish subjects. The depth of Scottish suspicion of the king by this time is illustrated by the fact that they refused to accept a safe conduct for their commissioners to go to Ripon signed by Charles alone, demanding that the English peers should sign it as well. Eventually they contented themselves with a letter from the English peers testifying that the king had signed a safe conduct in their presence.[110] At the treaty the previous year a safe conduct signed by the king had been exactly what the covenanters demanded, but they no longer believed it was adequate protection.

The Scots sent eight commissioners to Ripon: Alexander Henderson and Wariston, and two members of each estate, Loudoun, Dunfermline, Sir William Douglas of Cavers, Patrick Hepburne of Wauchton, John Smith (Edinburgh) and Alexander Wedderburne (Dundee).[111] When they met the English commissioners on 2 October they refused to negotiate in the presence of the six assistants appointed by the king, who were forced to withdraw. Loudoun stated that he and his fellow commissioners had no power but to ask for satisfaction of the Scottish demands. When the English suggested taking the pacification of Berwick as the basis of a treaty he replied that evils which had arisen since the pacification could not be cured by it. Discussion then turned to a cessation of arms to be agreed before a peace treaty. The main difficulty was the Scots' demand that their army should be supported at the expense of England, but eventually it was agreed on 17 October (after the king and peers at York had been consulted) that the Scots should have £850 sterling daily, and on 26 October articles of cessation were agreed on for (in the first instance) two

months. All acts of hostility were to cease and during the negotiation of a peace treaty (which was to be held in London) each army
was to retain what it possessed at the time of the cessation.[112]

The terms of the treaty of Ripon were humiliating for the king.
Not only had his rebellious Scots subjects successfully invaded
England, but he now agreed to pay their forces, while the fact that
an English parliament was necessary to provide the money to do
this would prevent his dissolving that parliament if it began to
question his policies or sympathise with the Scots. Though the
English commissioners at Ripon had done all they could to get the
amount of money demanded by the Scots reduced, many of them
must have been glad that the necessity for raising money would
make the king temporarily dependent on parliament. The Scots
commissioners and those of the English most favourably inclined
to them had had private talks at Ripon—at which the Scots had
reproached them for not joining the Scots army when it invaded
England, only to discover that the 'Savile Letter' was a forgery[113]
—and had probably discussed how the covenanters and the English parliament could best co-operate to force the king to concede
their respective demands. It is surprising that the king made no
attempt, or at least no very determined one, to take a personal part
in the treaty at Ripon. The previous year at the treaty of Berwick
he had managed to dominate the treaty personally though he had
appointed commissioners to negotiate for him, but at Ripon he
allowed his Scottish and his English subjects to negotiate directly
with each other, even though he knew most of the English concerned opposed his government and sympathised with the Scots.
Perhaps he hoped that peers sympathetic to the Scots could exact
more concessions from them than he or his supporters could. If so
he must have been disappointed. The great council of peers advised him to accept the cessation agreed at Ripon and he was in no
position to refuse to do so.[114]

CHAPTER SEVEN

The Treaty of London
and the 1641 Parliament,
November 1640–November 1641

NEGOTIATIONS IN LONDON

The committee of estates showed its confidence in the Scots commissioners who had negotiated at Ripon by appointing them all to go to London to continue the treaty there, with the addition of one member of each estate: Rothes, Sir William Drummond of Riccarton and Hew Kennedy (burgess of Ayr).[1] Four ministers were appointed to accompany them, Robert Blair, Robert Baillie, John Smith and George Gillespie, who were to carry the attack on the king's religious policies into England.[2]

The king seems at first to have believed that he could persuade the English parliament to react to the dishonour of having a Scottish army in occupation of the north of England by demanding its removal as soon as possible, but he soon found that he had misjudged its mood. When he referred in his opening speech on 3 November to the Scots as rebels who should be chased out of England this caused such offence that he felt obliged to explain away his reference a few days later, and the few members of parliament who copied the king in calling the Scots rebels were bitterly denounced by other members for doing so.[3] The Scots were too valuable an ally, in the view of most members of parliament, to be blamed for invading England; their presence would give parliament an opportunity to force concessions from the king that he would not otherwise have granted.

The Scots commissioners arrived in London on 10 November 1640, and the ministers among them soon busied themselves in preaching to large and enthusiastic congregations in a church put at their disposal by parliament. The Scots were much flattered by the puritans, being told that the English owed their religion, liberties and parliament to the Scots army, and fears were expressed that they would reach an agreement with Charles and withdraw from England before the English parliament could curb his power.[4] They first formally met the English commissioners (appointed by the king with the approbation of parliament) on 19 November; they were the same sixteen peers who had negotiated at Ripon.[5] The king himself attended the meeting but Rothes on behalf of the Scots refused to negotiate in his presence, as their commission authorised them only to treat with those appointed by the king and parliament, not with the king personally. Charles indignantly replied that the Scots had long asked to be allowed to present their grievances to him, yet were now refusing to do so; 'Away with trifles of law, but lett us goe on to bisines'. But the Scots refused to give way and the king attended no further meetings of the commissioners.[6] In the absence of the king all the proposals and demands of the Scots had to be sent to him through the English commissioners, while his replies also had to pass through their hands. This procedure inevitably led to delays, but it ensured that the English parliament was kept (through the English commissioners) in close touch with the negotiations at all times, and that the king could not make a quick peace with the Scots before parliament had time to squeeze concessions from him. Thus the treaty was not to be simply one between the king and the Scots (as the treaty of Berwick had been, with the English commissioners no more than onlookers); the covenanters were determined that the English parliament should be a party to the treaty and ratify it. Many personal meetings were held during the treaty between the king and the Scots commissioners, but these formed no part of the treaty itself.

The Scots made the basis of the treaty the demands contained in their letter of 8 September to Lanark. They thus kept to their promise that it contained all they asked for, but (as was to appear) they included in the vaguely worded eighth demand a variety of new claims of greater significance than all the first seven.

It asked that the king should, with the consent of the English parliament, 'condescend to all Particulars, which may establish a stable and well-grounded Peace, for enjoying of our Religion and Liberties, against all fears of molestation and undoing from year to year, as our Adversaries shall take the advantage'.[7] The vagueness of this was intended from the first as a means of justifying the addition of new demands, but at the beginning of the treaty it was not generally known what concessions the Scots would ask under it. This being so, by far the most important of their demands seemed to be the first, that the king should publish the acts of the June 1640 parliament in his own name. By doing this he would give his consent to the religious changes brought about by the 1638 and 1639 assemblies, to triennial parliaments, and to parliament without bishops or officers of state, free from the control of lords of articles. He was therefore expected to oppose the first demand strongly, especially as he was not asked formally to assent to the acts but only to publish them, the assumption being that his assent was not necessary.[8] Surprisingly the king quickly agreed on 3 December to publish the acts (though he at first tried to get some of them omitted). This, reported Robert Baillie exuberantly, had been the demand expected to cause most difficulty (obviously he had no idea of how the Scots were to interpret the final demand), 'the rest are but corolaries and appendices to it', and it was rumoured in London that the Scottish treaty was nearly at an end.[9] The second and third demands—that royal castles in Scotland should be used only for defence of the realm (and that with the advice of parliament), and that Scots subjects in England and Ireland should not be forced to take oaths or be censured for signing the covenant—were also soon accepted by the king.[10]

The fourth demand, that any found guilty of being authors of the troubles should be liable to sentence by the parliament of England or Scotland (depending on their nationality), caused more trouble. The king was naturally unwilling to abandon his most loyal and trusted supporters to the vengeance of the covenanters. Some of the Scots commissioners were evidently willing to compromise on this point, for Wariston, fearing their weakness, wrote urgently to the committee of estates begging it to write insisting that the incendiaries be sent to Scotland for trial.[11] Eventually on 30 December the Scots accepted as a satisfactory answer to their demand a statement by the king that he would not employ such persons as were judged incapable by parliament, nor allow such persons access to him,[12] though the Scots later renewed their demands that incendiaries should be punished when an act of oblivion was discussed.

Demands five, for the return of all Scots ships and goods captured, and six, that the Scots should be paid for their expenses incurred in resisting the king, were settled by early February 1641. The English parliament would grant only £300,000 sterling to the Scots (as a brotherly or friendly assistance), far less than they had asked but probably as much as they had expected. The seventh demand was also quickly settled; the king agreed that all declarations, proclamations and books published against the covenanters would be withdrawn and suppressed. He insisted that this should be reciprocal, all publications in Scotland prejudicial to his honour also being withdrawn, but as he conceded that the Scottish parliament should be the judge of these works this meant little.[13]

So far the treaty had proceeded fairly smoothly. Though it had taken nearly three months to get seven articles agreed, the king had shown himself willing to give way on most points after argument, and many of the delays had been caused by the need for the English commissioners to consult king and parliament, and for the Scots to consult the committee of estates. Delays were also caused by the growing quarrel between the king and the English parliament as it inevitably distracted their attention from the treaty; by the end of December 1640 Laud and Strafford were prisoners in the Tower awaiting trial on a variety of charges (some of them made by the Scottish commissioners),[14] and several of the king's ministers had fled abroad. Indeed, the speed at which the king made concessions to the Scots was no doubt partly dictated by his desire to get rid of them so that he could concentrate on his struggle with parliament. The Scots offered to mediate between king and parliament but the king refused to allow this, not surprisingly as the Scots interpretation of the situation in England was that papists, prelates and their adherents, having failed with their plots in Scotland, were now troubling England and Ireland, and that the king should join with parliament to defeat them.[15] The Scots had had much support and encouragement during the negotiations from the English commissioners and parliament. To their surprise they also found a friend in Hamilton, who was active throughout the treaty in urging the king to make concessions.[16] He justified his conduct on the ground that only by making concessions would the king regain the loyalty of the Scots, but there is a strong suspicion that he had concluded that it was likely that in future the covenanters would be the real rulers of Scotland, and that he therefore decided to ingratiate himself with them. He might dislike Scotland and prefer to live in England, but most of his income came from his Scottish estates. He may (as Clarendon claimed) have got the king to agree that he should pretend friendship with the covenanters, so that he could save himself and his property from the enmity of the covenanters while at the same time serving the king by trying to influence them in his favour and discovering their secret plans.[17] But in February 1641 he supported a proposal that his son should marry Argyll's daughter,[18] which was surely going further than a feigned friendship with the covenanters to safeguard his interests required. Hamilton was followed throughout his career by gossip that he thought that the Hamiltons had a better claim to the throne than the Stewarts, and while this was probably completely untrue it does seem that in 1641 he saw no reason why he should not be one of those who benefited from the king's loss of power.

The progress that the treaty had made by February 1641 led many of the English who were trying to use the presence of the Scots army to force concessions from the king to fear that they would soon be deserted by their Scots allies. There were rumours that the Scots were no longer interested in prosecuting Laud and Strafford or in attacking episcopacy in England,[19] and fears of a compromise settlement (with moderate episcopacy) being accepted. Alexander Henderson therefore wrote a declaration that was issued by the Scots commissioners on 24 February, refuting the charges that they lacked zeal in attacking prelacy and the two 'firebrands'; they longed to see justice done, especially on Strafford —'Better that One perish than Unity', 'Mercy to the bad is cruelty against the good'.[20] This paper was meant to be distributed privately to members of parliament only, but somehow a printer got hold of a copy and printed it. The king was furious, 'inflamed as he never was before',[21] or, as Wariston put it, 'the King has run stark mad at it'. The bitterness of the paper, so unlike Henderson's usual moderate style, led to its being called 'Johnston's paper' on the assumption that Wariston was the author—he seems to have regarded this as a compliment. Charles threatened to denounce the declaration by proclamation and to make the Scots commissioners pay for having issued it, as their action had forfeited their safe conduct and they were guilty of sedition.[22] The Scots, embarrassed by the publication of what had been intended to be a private paper, agreed to issue an explanation stating that they had no wish to interfere in English affairs.[23] The king agreed to be satisfied with this,[24] and in fact the publication of the 24 February declaration had probably been to his advantage, as many members of parliament were indignant that the Scots should so far interfere in English affairs as to attack episcopacy. Even among those who opposed episcopacy many were coming to think it discreditable that England's reformation should be dependent on Scotland's army.[25] The English parliament was becoming increasingly confident of its ability to achieve its ends without the help of the Scots.

With the king still angry and suspicious over the declaration, the time was hardly ideal for proceeding to the concessions demanded from him under the eighth demand. There were divisions among the Scots as to what they should ask. Two of the Scots commissioners, Riccarton and Cavers, opposed a demand that officers of state and councillors should in future be chosen with advice of parliament, while Rothes, Loudoun and Wariston argued that this was essential.[26] In addition the committee of estates kept sending new instructions to the commissioners while the treaty was in progress. The most important of these afterthoughts was contained in a letter of 8 March 1641: 'We know that the Noblemen and gentilmen will desyre that they may be

warranted be act of parliament to have ther seuerall meittings
yeirlie as the burrowis have'. This suggestion that there should
be conventions of nobles and lairds as well as of burghs had
previously been put forward by the lairds in 1639 but had never
been mentioned in the negotiations with the king, and he would
obviously resist such an innovation. Consequently the Scots commissioners in London refused to introduce such a controversial
new proposal in the middle of the treaty and the idea was abandoned;[27] the commissioners already had enough on their hands in
trying to persuade the king to accept the proposals they had already presented under the eighth demand as necessary 'for ane
happie and durable peace which is the cheefest of all our desyres
And wnto which all the former sevine articles being now agried
wpon are as many preparations'.[28] The proposals were given in
in February, March and April, but none were answered satis-
factorily by the king until June.

First the Scots commissioners asked that the king and the Prince
of Wales should undertake to reside in Scotland for some part
of each year. In fact they never expected the king to agree to this
but made the request to emphasise that they regarded the absence
of their king as a grievance, so that they could use it as a reason
for demanding constitutional changes.[29] This being so, they eventually declared themselves content with a very vague reply from
the king to the effect that he would come to Scotland whenever it
was convenient to do so and affairs required it.[30]

In religion the Scots demanded unity, and uniformity in church
government, between England and Scotland, as a means to preserve peace. By this the Scots really meant that episcopacy must
be abolished in England and forms of government, worship and
theology similar to Scotland's substituted. Partly this demand was
the result of missionary zeal and the arrogance instilled by success.
Having revolted against the king's attempt to impose England's
religion on Scotland, the covenanters now embarked on the futile
policy of trying to reverse the process. But in desiring union in
religion the reasons put forward by the Scots commissioners were
not entirely, or even primarily, religious. Time and again they
emphasised that they saw religious unity as a means of preserving

peace. Religious disputes were a common cause of wars between nations; episcopacy in England therefore posed a threat not just to Scotland's presbyterian kirk but to the nation as a whole. The covenanters wanted not only a 'cessation of armes for a time, but peace for ever; and not peace onely, but a perfect amity and a more neere union than before'. Religious unity was essential if this was to be achieved.[31] It was such non-religious considerations that led most lay covenanters to support the demand for religious union, not mere bigotry and clerical domination as has often been alleged. In opposing the Scots demand for unity and uniformity the king was joined by a majority in parliament, for few English puritans wanted Scots presbyterianism established in England, though they did not openly admit this for fear of losing the support of their Scots allies in other matters. Consequently king and parliament would only state that they approved the desire for conformity (not uniformity) of church government and that parliament would proceed with this 'in due tyme', while unity of religion was not mentioned. The Scots had thus to be content with being fobbed off until some indefinite future date.[32]

It was not only in religion that the covenanters sought union. In civil affairs they demanded regular meetings every three years of the parliaments of the two countries to try disputes between the kingdoms and appoint commissioners to negotiate about them. Standing commissions of each parliament, the conservators of the peace, were to meet between parliamentary sessions to keep the peace between the countries, the conservators of both meeting jointly to discuss matters of mutual interest. Neither country was, without the consent of its parliament, to raise forces against the other or make war on it. Citizens of each country were to have the full rights of natives in the other. Free trade and commercial co-operation were to be established.[33]

To the covenanters it seemed obvious that such closer union would be mutually beneficial, but they found no more enthusiasm in England for civil than for religious unity. The English parliament showed little interest in their demands, and the king naturally opposed them. But some concessions were made. The king at first rejected the proposal to establish conservators, claiming that they

14

would merely be the continuation of the Tables under another name, but eventually he agreed to their appointment.[34] He and parliament also agreed that neither kingdom would make war (without consent of its parliament) on the other. Each country would assist the other against common enemies.[35] All the other Scots demands for closer civil union were, however, left to be discussed after the main peace treaty was concluded.[36] The English parliament and the king, intent on their quarrel with each other, simply were not interested in such matters.

The Scots had also to accept for the time being an unsatisfactory answer from the king in the matter of his choosing officers of state, councillors and lords of session with parliamentary approval. Charles would promise only that he would listen to the information of parliament before making appointments, and would allow parliament to state whether it had any just objections to those appointed. He did however concede that if this answer did not satisfy the Scots he would settle the matter later with the Scottish parliament.[37]

The most bitter and prolonged of the disputes between the Scots commissioners and the king concerned an act of oblivion which was to be passed by the Scottish parliament for all acts committed during the troubles. The covenanters were determined to exclude the main 'incendiaries' from benefiting under the act. The king replied that if the covenanters excepted any royalists from the act, then he should be allowed to except an equal number of covenanters. He had received information (through Montrose) of the report that leading covenanters had discussed appointing dictators and deposing him in June 1640, and he hoped to try them for this treason if they tried the incendiaries. But the covenanters refused any such compromise, and though Charles 'raged at it, and called us Jesuitical . . . cried and swore, that if they accepted any, he would except some also; and this he declared over and over again', he gave way in the end.[38]

The treaty had reached what was to be its final form by the end of June 1641. It omitted many matters that the Scots had hoped to get settled (such as free trade between Scotland and England)[39] and many of the concessions made by the king were not so comprehensive as the covenanters would have liked, but they were anxious to bring the treaty to a close and have it ready for ratification by the time Charles arrived in Scotland. He had announced in April his intention of coming to Scotland (to the dismay of some covenanters, who feared that he intended to cause trouble there)[40] but he delayed his visit mainly through the opposition of the English parliament which feared (rightly) that he hoped to gain support against it in Scotland. On 24 July the Scots parliament approved the draft of the treaty and sent it back to London, where it was ratified by the king on 10 August. Only six of the eleven Scots commissioners who had been negotiating the treaty were empowered to sign it—Rothes, Loudoun, Wauchton, Cavers, John Smith and Hew Kennedy.[41] Of the other five commissioners Alexander Henderson and Wariston were presumably excluded since they represented none of the three estates, while the conduct of the other three had aroused suspicions; Dunfermline was suspected of favouring the king[42] (so for that matter were Loudoun and Rothes, but not so seriously), letters from Riccarton to the royalist laird of Keir had been intercepted,[43] while Alexander Wedderburne was believed to have dissuaded two burgesses who were members of the committee of estates from attending meetings at Newcastle, though it is not clear whether this was why it was decided that he should not sign the treaty; his motives are obscure.[44]

GROWING DISUNITY: THE PLOTTERS AND THE TREATY

The king's decision to visit Scotland was looked on with suspicion by the covenanters as well as by the English parliament. His hopes of getting sufficient help there to overthrow the English parliament were absurd—he had, after all, just spent several years demonstrating that he was incapable of invading Scotland with the vastly greater resources of England at his disposal—but there had been some small signs which encouraged him to think that it might be possible to get help from Scotland. First, there were growing divisions among the covenanters during 1641 as to how far royal power should be limited. Several of the Scottish commissioners in London earned themselves the disfavour of the committee of estates by appearing to have been partly won over by the king's arguments and promises. It was rumoured in February 1641 that Rothes and Loudoun were to be made gentlemen of the bed-chamber and members of the English privy council—six English opposition peers were admitted to the council at this time, which gave the story credibility.[45] Rothes certainly was offered and wished to accept the position of gentleman of the bedchamber. He argued that he could use such a position at court to influence the king in favour of the Scots,[46] but he was evidently strongly opposed by Argyll and most of the other leading nobles among the covenanters. Though one of the Scots demands in the treaty had been that the king should employ Scotsmen about his person,[47] the other covenanters were too suspicious and jealous to let Rothes accept such a position. He was reported by June 1641 to be much in favour at court and about to marry a rich English noble-woman 'and be little more a Scottish man'.[48] He died suddenly in August 1641 before his actions could prove whether or not he had agreed to support the king, but the rumours that he had come to such an agreement[49] may have had some truth in them; though a sincere covenanter he was no fanatic and he may well have disliked the prospect of Scotland being dominated by Argyll.

More important in persuading the king that he might win sup-port in Scotland than any success he may have had in winning over some of the Scottish commissioners in London was the encouragement he got from Montrose and his friends. The exist-ence of the Cumbernauld Band had become known to the com-mittee of estates in November 1640.[50] It had been bitterly denounced by many of the leading ministers and in January 1641 the committee of estates persuaded twelve of those who had signed it (including Montrose) to subscribe a declaration that they had not intended by the Band to cause divisions or break the covenant, while the original Band was burnt.[51] It had in fact proved a failure even before it was discovered; it had not created an effective party among the nobility willing to work together against Argyll and the more extreme covenanters. Consequently Montrose had turned again to corresponding with the king, this time with the support of a small group of his relatives and friends, later to be known as 'the Plotters'—Lord Napier (his brother-in-law and former tutor), Sir George Stirling of Keir (his nephew) and Sir Archibald Stewart of Blackhall (Keir's brother-in-law). They met in Edinburgh at about Christmas 1640 and agreed that there was a grave danger that the king's power in Scotland would be so limited that the land would be subjected to the worst of all forms of tyranny, the oppression of weaker subjects by the stronger. They therefore decided to send their advice to the king with Lieutenant-Colonel Walter Stewart, who was to communicate with Lennox (whose friendship he falsely claimed to possess) and perhaps Traquair. The king was to be urged to come to Scotland to settle affairs there. The Plotters later claimed that this was the only advice they sent with Walter Stewart, but they admitted that other matters were discussed and there seems little doubt that either at Christmas 1640 or on a later journey to court Walter Stewart was instructed to declare that if Charles would secure the religion and just liberties of Scotland this would win him powerful support, and Montrose and his followers would stand for him against all men. They also asked that the king should not appoint any new officers of state until he had come to Scotland and seen who best deserved them—an obvious hint that they hoped for the offices for themselves—and gave Walter Stewart a copy of John Stewart younger of Ladywell's account of the treason spoken by Argyll at the Ford of Lyon to be communicated to the king.[52]

If Montrose was the man of action among the Plotters, Lord Napier was the theorist, providing political ideas with which to justify their actions in his letter on sovereign power, usually attributed to Montrose.[53] Napier was not always in agreement with Montrose; Montrose had opposed parliament's sitting against the king's wishes in June 1640, while Napier had aided the fiction that the king had not ordered a prorogation (by refusing to act as a commissioner to prorogue parliament). Napier had not signed Montrose's Cumbernauld Band. In general, however, they were in agreement that the king's power had been too great before 1637 but was now in danger of being too much weakened. Napier distinguished two opposite tendencies which could damage sovereign power; it could be extended or restrained. It was extended when the prince tried to increase his power unduly (as most princes did), and this weakened sovereign power because subjects would not long endure such tyranny. But the results of the opposite tendency, restrained power, were even worse; the prince was unable to control his subjects and some of them oppressed others, 'the most fierce, insatiable, and insupportable tyranny in the worlde'. Rather than risk bringing the evils of restrained power on their country, subjects would be wise to put up with the extended power of the prince. Napier's fear was that unless royal power was at least partially restored there would be a prolonged period of disorder and anarchy in Scotland. Chaos and collapse of the social order would ensue. The people, who had helped the nobles overthrow the king, would soon turn against the aristocracy and try to destroy it. But the people were incapable of ruling themselves and would become the tools of great men ambitious for power, as the 'seditious preachers' already unconsciously were. Napier was now evidently prepared to argue that armed resistance to the prince was in no circumstances justifiable. Subjects could legitimately try to limit the extended power of the prince by peaceful means, but if these failed they must submit and tolerate his vices.[54]

Napier's ideas had some appeal to moderate men who feared anarchy, that the covenanters' cure for the king's irresponsibility before 1637 was worse than the disease, but his advocacy of what amounted to passive obedience was unlikely to prove attractive to the majority of covenanters, convinced that their duty to God obliged them to resist. At a time when both the king and his opponents based their political theories closely on religion, Napier made no attempt to provide a religious justification for his ideas. Scotland's troubles were mainly religious in origin, yet he never mentions the kirk in his essay—and the only clergy he refers to are 'seditious preachers'. Admittedly he mentions God's law as something in accordance with which the prince should rule (along with fundamental law and the law of the country) but otherwise religious considerations have no part in his essay. He seems to have made no attempt to spread his ideas beyond the narrow circle of the Plotters; the essay on sovereignty was not intended as a party manifesto. Indeed Montrose and the other Plotters seem to have done little to gain support for their policies. Discouraged by the failure of the Cumbernauld Band they resolved to limit their activities to secret negotiations with the king until he came to Scotland.

The Scottish parliament had met on 19 November 1640 (as had been agreed in June), and though many royalists had been cited to appear to answer charges against them[55] it was decided to delay the meeting until 14 January 1641. Until the treaty at London was completed there was little point in parliament sitting, and therefore on 14 January parliament was again continued, to 13 April. This continuation was in accordance with a letter from the king, but as the letter mentioned the king's commissioner to parliament a protest was made by one member of each estate that this should not be taken to refer to Traquair (the last holder of that office) since he was one of those cited to parliament as an incendiary. Parliament therefore would not recognise him as commissioner. Interestingly, Montrose and Stirling of Keir were two of the three who protested; it seems likely that they were chosen to protest as a test of their loyalty as they were suspected of favouring the king.[56] On 13 April parliament again continued itself, with a similar protest, to 25 May, when the continuation was repeated (Montrose and Keir again being among those who protested) to 15 July.[57] These continuations were decided on in advance by the committee of estates,[58] though all members of parliament assembled since it was now held that any act of continuation had to be passed by the full parliament.

When in April Charles announced his intention of coming to Scotland the covenanters could hardly object. But they were deeply suspicious of his motives, fearing that he hoped to win support in Scotland and that his journey was part of some plot by Traquair. It was feared that when he came to Scotland he would accuse those supposed to have discussed deposing him of treason, basing the charges on information sent to him by Montrose.[59] Evidence that Montrose was mainly responsible for spreading the now widespread rumours about plans to depose the king was soon forthcoming. One of those questioned about the rumour gave him as its source. Montrose in turn gave John Stewart younger of Ladywell as his authority, and brought him to Edinburgh in May to prove it. Stewart duly swore that at the Ford of Lyon in June 1640 Argyll had said the king was to be deposed and had offered treasonable bands to be signed. Argyll hotly denied this and John Stewart was imprisoned while the matter was examined. When re-examined a few days later, Stewart partly withdrew his allegations against Argyll, now claiming that he had talked only of deposition of kings in general, not specifically of deposing King Charles. Moreover, he revealed that Montrose, Napier, Keir and Blackhall had been negotiating with the king through Walter Stewart.[60] This was confirmed when Walter Stewart was intercepted and searched on returning from a visit to court. Hidden in his saddle was found a letter from the king to Montrose. On examination Walter Stewart gave a very full account of his and the Plotters' activities—probably adding to the truth such embellishments and exaggerations as he thought would please his captors. The king's letter to Montrose proved to be innocuous; it simply stated his intention of coming to Scotland to satisfy his people in religion and just liberties and that he expected Montrose's concurrence in this.[61] But the evidence that covenanters got from John Stewart and Walter Stewart was alarming enough for the committee of estates to order the imprisonment of the Plotters on 11 June,[62] to prevent further contacts between them and the king and hinder the formation of a moderate royalist party by removing its potential leaders.

Charles gave orders that parliament should again be prorogued on 15 July, as he could not be in Scotland by that time, but the covenanters decided not to delay any longer. They wanted parliament to have time to prepare the acts which were to be passed in Charles' presence, and to begin proceedings against the Incendiaries and the Plotters.[63] After electing Lord Burleigh president, parliament considered the king's letter ordering a prorogation. It had been brought from court by Dunfermline and Loudoun, and the latter announced some promises made by the king; he would maintain religion and church government as established by the late assemblies and would govern according to the fundamental laws of the kingdom, all matters civil being judged by parliament and the inferior judicatories. But 'becaus kyndness cannot stand one the one syd alone His Majestie expects mutuall retributione of thankfullnes from his parliament'. He therefore asked for some reciprocal concessions; that parliament should accept the answer he had given in the treaty concerning the appointment of officers of state, councillors and lords of session as satisfactory, that proceedings against Traquair and the other Incendiaries should be dropped, and that nothing should be done derogating from his honour. Dunfermline and Loudoun argued in favour of making these concessions and proroguing parliament, but it was decided that 'the present necessitie of the kingdome requyrit that they should sit still' and the king's desires were ignored, though it was conceded that parliament would only prepare business and not pass any acts until 17 August, by which time they expected the king to be present.[64]

Now that most business was conducted by the full parliament there was a need for rules to be agreed to regulate debate, procedure and discipline, and therefore articles for ordering the house were compiled and accepted on 19 July.[65] The clerk of the general assembly and the agent of the kirk were (among others) permitted to be present during debates. Wariston argued that some commissioners appointed by the general assembly should be allowed to be present, but 'that motion was rejected by Argyle with storme, as makeing way for Churchmens voyces in Parliament'.[66] It was at first ruled that there should normally be two three-hour sessions of parliament daily, but it was later agreed that committees (a wide variety of which were soon appointed to consider and prepare various matters for presentation to parliament) should meet in the afternoon instead of the second session, and that the three estates should meet separately in the early morning.[67] When any proposal or overture was given in to parliament each estate was to be given a copy of it to consider for twenty-four hours before voting on it.[68] Later, arrangements were made for the payment of the expenses of the shire commissioners.[69]

Early in August parliament approved an oath for signature by all members by which they bound themselves to speak freely on everything discussed in parliament, 'as wee think in our conscience may conduce to the glorie of god the good and peace of this church and kingdome'. They swore to maintain the king's person, honour and estate 'as is exprest in our nationall covenant', the power and privileges of parliament, the lawful rights and liberties of subjects, and to do their best to preserve the peace between England and Scotland.[70] The fact that an oath of parliament, equivalent to the oath *de fideli administratione* taken by officials and councillors, was thought necessary was an indication of the increasing confidence and self-consciousness of parliament as it emerged from domination by the king and the lords of the articles. As a number of royalist nobles were expected to accompany the king to Scotland it was ordered that none should sit in parliament who had been cited to appear before it to answer charges or who had not signed the national covenant, the band to maintain the acts of the June 1640 parliament, and the new oath of parliament.[71]

The most important matters dealt with by parliament in July-August 1641, before the king arrived in Scotland, were preparing the cases against the Incendiaries and Plotters and considering the draft of the treaty of London. Though many royalists had been cited to appear before parliament, only five principal Incendiaries were proceeded against with any vigour—Traquair (treasurer), Sir John Hay (clerk register), Sir Robert Spottiswood (president of the court of session), Walter Balcanquhal (author of the *Large Declaration* of 1639) and the Bishop of Ross. A committee was elected to prepare the process against them. Craighall (on the king's orders) refused to take part in any action against them, so four procurators of state appointed by the covenanters acted in his place.[72] They were also entrusted with raising summonses against the four Plotters (Montrose, Napier, Keir and Blackhall) and Walter Stewart.[73] The Incendiaries and Plotters were not to be tried until after the king's arrival, but it was decided to make an example of John Stewart younger of Ladywell, as being the main source of the stories that the Banders and Plotters had used to justify their activities. On 20 July Argyll and Craighall asked parliament to allow the justice general or his deputies to sit in judgement on Stewart though parliament was sitting (which normally debarred other courts from meeting). Parliament granted the request, appointed four assessors to sit in the court, and ordered the procurators of state to aid Craighall in the pursuit of Stewart[74]—Craighall was willing to lead the prosecution against Stewart as the king had not specifically ordered him not to do so.

The case was heard on 21, 22 and 23 July in the justiciary court before Alexander Colville of Blair (one of the two justices depute and the auditor general of the covenanters' army).[75] Stewart had the unhappy distinction of being the first man to be tried for lease-making under the new enlarged definition of that crime introduced by the covenanters in the June 1640 parliament. As he had already been declared guilty by the committee of estates after his confession the result of the trial was a foregone conclusion; the justiciary court was used to give a semblance of legality to the proceedings. Stewart was sentenced to death and executed by the 'Maiden' (the Scots beheading machine) on 28 July.[76] Royalists claimed that he had been promised that his life would be spared if he withdrew his allegations against Argyll, and that this accounted for his recantation, but that he was then treacherously executed lest he should later renew the charges.[77] However, there is no evidence for this, and if Stewart's recantation was false it was remarkable that he did not withdraw all his charges against Argyll; he continued to allege that Argyll had spoken of deposition of kings in general, which Argyll denied. This suggests that his recantations are at least approximately true, with the additions he had invented to stir up feeling against Argyll removed. The sentence against him was harsh, but he had after all given the king grounds for proceeding against Argyll and other leading covenanters for treason; Robert Baillie was worried by the execution but was willing to justify it on the grounds of expediency and necessity—John Stewart had been aiming at the destruction of Argyll and others 'and by consequence at the overthrow of our Treatie of the peace, and welfare of the whole Isle', so it was necessary to make an example of him.[78] But it was also undeniable that his execution removed the main witness on whom the Plotters relied to justify their activities.

The general assembly sat concurrently with parliament from 20 July to 9 August. It first met at St Andrews (as had been arranged the previous year), but this was inconvenient as many members of the assembly were also members of parliament, and therefore it moved to Edinburgh after a few days. The Earl of Wemyss, vaguely royalist but inoffensive, sat as king's commissioner; 'the modestie and simplicitie of the man made him displeasing to none'.[79] As in 1640 much time was taken up with arguments concerning conventicles, for many radicals continued to hold private prayer meetings and Henry Guthry and other moderates remained determined to stamp them out. Many came to the assembly 'as it had been a place of combat', and tension was increased when the previous year's moderator, Andrew Ramsay, tactlessly opened the assembly by preaching a sermon 'as if our Kirk were presentlie burning with schisme' against conventicles. David Dickson replied with a passionate speech in which he denounced those who unjustly slandered religious people.[80] Many private meetings were held before and during the assembly by leading ministers and lay covenanters to try to settle the quarrel. All the ministers of Edinburgh wanted private prayer meetings banned, while Dickson, Robert Blair and others argued that such meetings were legitimate and not innovations. Eventually an act drafted by Alexander Henderson (who had been elected moderator) was agreed on and presented to the assembly.[81]

This act 'against Impiety and Schisme' was passed on 4 August. It extolled the public worship of congregations and the private worship of families, and even recognised the value of mutual edification by instruction, admonition, and comforting one another, by which was meant the private prayer meetings. But 'the best means have been, and may still be despised or abused, and particularly the duetie of mutuall edification, which hath been so little in use, and so few know how to practice in the right manner' and it was therefore open to error and abuse. The godly might be drawn into 'Error, Heresie, Schisme, Scandall, selfconceit, and despising of others, pressing above the common calling of Christians, etc and usurping that which is proper to the Pastoral Vocation . . . idle and unprofitable questions which edifie not, uncharitable censurings' and other failings 'which have dolefully rent the bowels of other Kirks'. Therefore all ministers and other members of the kirk were ordered to avoid all meetings which were apt to breed error and schism, though at the same time they were to suppress all 'mocking of religious exercises, especially of such as put foule aspersions, and factious or odious names upon the godly'.[82] Thus prayer meetings were to be banned as potentially dangerous rather than as intrinsically evil, while those who had abused the godly for taking part in such meetings were rebuked for doing so. Not surprisingly some found the act too general and vague,[83] but it represented a reasonable compromise aimed at restoring unity in the kirk, though certainly it was rather illogical to condemn prayer meetings but not those who had taken part in them. Moreover a loop-hole remained for the radicals; could not conventicles be held to be no more than legitimate 'mutual edification'?[84] The next assembly was appointed to meet at St Andrews on 27 July 1642, and a commission of ministers and elders was appointed to meet while parliament was sitting to advise it on religious matters.[85] It sat regularly from 10 August to 18 November 1641, making proposals to parliament as to what acts were necessary concerning religious matters and being consulted by parliament on such subjects.[86]

THE KING IN PARLIAMENT

King Charles reached Edinburgh on 14 August and ceremonially entered parliament on 17 August. He declared that his intentions in coming to Scotland were to end the unhappy mistakings between him and his subjects, and to get to know (and be known in) his native country. He had come to settle religion and the just liberties of the country.[87] As a sign of his willingness to perform what he had promised he offered to touch with the sceptre the acts passed by the June 1640 parliament, but parliament asked him to delay doing this, ostensibly because the Scots commissioners had not yet returned from London, but really because it was feared that if the acts were touched with the sceptre it would imply that they had not been legal and binding until they were thus touched. The king reluctantly agreed to the delay,[88] and a few days later allowed the acts to be published in his name without touching them,[89] thus implicitly conceding that acts of parliament did not require his assent.

On the first day that the king attended parliament most of the royalist nobles who accompanied him were refused admission as they had not subscribed the covenant, band and oath. In the following days most of them, including Lennox, Hamilton, Perth, Roxburgh, Lanark and Annandale, signed and took their seats, but others, who had been cited to appear before parliament to answer charges, were denied the right to sit—among them Linlithgow, Carnwath and Tullibardine.[90] The royalists who took the covenant, band and oath presumably did so with the king's approval, but they could do little to help their master as the great majority of members of parliament were staunch covenanters, suspicious of the king and willing to follow the lead given by the noble covenanters. None the less, he still hoped to regain the loyalty of his Scottish subjects and break the covenanters' alliance with the English parliament. He even accepted Lord Balmerino as president of parliament[91] (Lord Burleigh being ill) though a few years before he had had him sentenced to death for opposing his policies after the 1633 parliament. With the king so compliant and the treaty ratified by him and the English parliament, the covenanters agreed to withdraw their army from England, and this was done as soon as the army had been paid all that was due to it from the English parliament. It left Newcastle on 21 August and most of it was disbanded at Leith six days later, though three regiments were kept in arms.[92]

Meanwhile the Scots commissioners had returned from London with the treaty, and the king signed it on 25 August before parliament, which ratified it the next day. The act of oblivion and pacification annexed to the treaty contained exemptions so sweeping as to include (or be capable of being interpreted as including) all who had been active royalists in the troubles of the past four years. All the Scottish bishops, Traquair, Sir Robert Spottiswood, Sir John Hay and Walter Balcanquhal were specifically excluded, as were all persons who had been cited to parliament and were found guilty of being incendiaries or of other crimes, and all thieves, robbers, broken men and outlaws. In the part of the act dealing with the pacification the king agreed that in future the consent of the English parliament would be necessary before England or Ireland made war on Scotland, and vice versa. In addition the king and the parliaments of England and Scotland would appoint commissioners or conservators for each kingdom to meet between sessions of parliament to preserve peace between the kingdoms.[93]

Once the treaty of London had been ratified there was only one major claim of the covenanters that remained unsettled—the demand that officers of state, councillors and lords of session should be appointed by advice of parliament. It was to take another two-and-a-half months before king and parliament agreed on how they should be chosen and on who should be chosen. In this period all possibility that the king might win support in Scotland against the English parliament vanished.

The arguments over choosing officers of state began immediately after the treaty was ratified. The king refused to consent to parliamentary control over appointments, complaining that however much he granted the covenanters, they always asked for more, so there seemed no limit to their demands. Quite apart from the effects such a concession as he was now asked to make would have in Scotland, he feared that similar demands would be made in England if he gave way. Parliament insisted that its demand was based on the ancient laws and customs of the kingdom, adding that in spite of this they would not insist on the demand if the king resided continually in Scotland.[94] When, on 16 September, the king at last agreed to appoint officers of state, councillors and lords of session with the advice and approbation of parliament, he made use of this last point as his reason for making the concession; being normally resident in England he might not always know the qualifications of Scotsmen for office, and he would therefore in future choose with parliament's approval. Between sessions of parliament he would obtain the privy council's approval, though the ensuing parliament was to have power to disallow appointments thus made.[95] Nominally the king still retained the initiative in making appointments; parliament only advised him and approved those he nominated. But in fact if parliament was strong enough to defy the king there was nothing to stop it simply refusing to approve any nomination by the king unless he nominated the person it wished. The opposition the king made before agreeing to the act shows that he was well aware of the importance of the concession he had made, that he would no longer be free to choose his own councillors, judges and officers. Coupled with all the religious and constitutional concessions he had already made, it left him with very little power in Scotland. 'If this be that you call Liberty, God send me the old slavery againe' grumbled the royalist Earl of Perth.[96] On the other hand, many of the commissioners for burghs thought the act was too vague; among other changes they wanted a definition of what the advice and approbation of parliament consisted of inserted in the act.[97]

A new chancellor, treasurer and clerk register were immediately needed—the first office was vacant and the other two held by Incendiaries whose removal was demanded. The covenanters proposed that Argyll should be chancellor and Loudoun treasurer (thus giving the two highest offices in the kingdom to Campbells), while the king proposed the Earl of Morton (a former treasurer) as chancellor, and conceded that Loudoun should be treasurer. He was determined not to accept Argyll as chancellor and may have chosen Morton instead in the hope that Argyll would not oppose him since he was his father-in-law and former tutor. If this was Charles' hope he had miscalculated; Argyll vigorously denounced the royalist Morton as unsuitable for office through being practically bankrupt, a deserter of his country in her greatest need, and old and decrepit. At length the king reluctantly proposed that instead Loudoun should be chancellor and Lord Almond treasurer, but this too was opposed; it was argued that Loudoun had been already accepted as treasurer, and the covenanters had no wish to see Almond advanced even if he had been their lieu-tenant general, for his zeal was suspect—he had signed the Cum-bernauld Band. Charles denounced the covenanters' ingratitude and refused to suggest any more names for the chancellorship. Further complications arose in the form of disputes over what exactly was meant by parliament's 'advice and approbation' and over how the voting on approbation should be conducted; the shire commissioners proposed that the voting should be by secret ballot, lest any should vote against their conscience out of fear. Charles opposed secret voting, stating that he would never be displeased with any man for voting freely (a sentiment which was hardly in accord with his conduct in the 1633 parliament when he had tried to influence the voting by openly noting the names of those who voted against him), and that any man who was afraid to vote publicly was unworthy to sit in parliament. In the end it was decided to leave aside these complications for the time being; the covenanters agreed to accept Loudoun as chancellor and he was duly elected on 30 September.[98]

The long dispute over the chancellorship had greatly increased the tension and bitterness between the king's supporters and the covenanters, and Charles began to despair of winning the covenanters' trust no matter what he conceded; 'It would pity any man's heart to see how he looks; for he is never at quiet amongst them, and glad he is, when he sees any man that he thinks loves him.'[99] The first open sign of the growing tension came when Lord Ker (son of the Earl of Roxburgh and a former covenanter) denounced Hamilton as a traitor and 'a juglar with the King', and sent his 'no less furious and drunken second' the Earl of Crawford (an ardent but indiscreet royalist who had served in the Spanish army) to challenge Hamilton to a duel. The belief that Hamilton had betrayed the king was now all but universal among royalists and certainly since he had come to Scotland with the king he had associated much with Argyll, but whether he did this to further his own ends or to try to help the king is not clear. To some extent he was probably being driven into the hands of the covenanters by the distrust and hatred of the royalists. Parliament was greatly indignant at Ker's insult to one of its most prominent members (especially one who seemed to be about to join the covenanters) and eventually Ker was forced to apologise. But he came to parliament accompanied by several hundred armed royalists, the first royalist show of strength Edinburgh had seen since the troubles began.[100]

15

Many royalists more loyal than wise (of whom the Earl of Crawford was most prominent) now determined to use violence to help the king, planning to seize Argyll, Hamilton and Lanark and either carry them off by ship or murder them. The details of the plot are obscure, as is how far the king was implicated in it, but he seems at least to have known that some sort of intrigue for helping him by violent action was afoot, and weakly to have done nothing either to stop it or to help ensure that it succeeded. With the disbanding of the covenanters' army there were many unemployed mercenary officers in Edinburgh and some of them were drawn into the plot. Colonel Cochrane (who commanded one of the three regiments which had not been disbanded) and Colonel Alexander Stewart were deeply involved, and attempts to persuade others to join the plot soon led to its discovery; Robert Home (Cochrane's lieutenant colonel), Colonel John Hurry or Urry and Captain William Stewart reported what they had learnt of the plot (through attempts to recruit them, and the indiscreet boasts and drunken threats of royalists) to General Alexander Leslie on 11 October, and he warned Argyll, Hamilton and Lanark. By the next day wild rumours were circulating about royalist plots. The king came to parliament to declare his innocence of any such plottings, but stupidly let himself be accompanied by some hundreds of armed and aggressive royalists. Not unnaturally it was feared that he was coming to try to seize the three nobles, and they fled from Edinburgh to Hamilton's house at Kinneil, claiming they did so to prevent fighting between their supporters and the king's. Charles furiously insisted that they had been in no danger and the whole 'Incident', as the affair became known, was a plot by his enemies to discredit him, the blame for which he put on Hamilton.[101] Certainly this was the main result of the Incident; any covenanters who had decided that Charles could be trusted and was perhaps being asked to concede too much were shocked back into uncompromising attitudes by the plottings soon revealed by the depositions of those involved in the Incident.

The covenanters did not, as the king implied, invent the Incident, but they made the most of it. The king demanded that

there be a public investigation to clear his honour, but the covenanters had no interest in stilling the rumours of royalist plots and
insisted on a private inquiry, on the grounds that witnesses would
not reveal all they knew in public. On 21 October the king gave
way and accepted a secret investigation by a committee; a committee of four of each estate (Lennox being the only royalist) was
elected and began examining those involved.[102]

Before the distrust and suspicion of the king raised by the
Incident had had time to subside, news arrived of a Catholic
rebellion in Ireland, and it was immediately suspected that the
king had encouraged or even organised the rising. The rebels
claimed to be acting on his orders and produced a forged commission (under the great seal of Scotland) to prove it. In fact they
had no orders from the king, but they had undoubtedly been
encouraged by the fact that Charles had been negotiating for the
help of an Irish Catholic army under the Earl of Antrim for use
against the English parliament.[103] Immediately on hearing of the
Irish rebellion the king asked for Scottish help in crushing it if it
should prove serious (28 October). Parliament was anxious to see
the rebellion suppressed; there were many thousands of Scottish
settlers in Ulster, the centre of the rebellion, who were in danger.
On the other hand, the covenanters were suspicious of the king's
motives in asking them to send help to Ireland, and insisted on
obtaining the consent of the English parliament before intervening.[104]

It was not until the beginning of November that Argyll, Hamilton and Lanark returned to Edinburgh and parliament again
turned its attention to the choice of officers of state and councillors. By this time Charles was anxious to get back to London;
he had been away for nearly three months and it was clear he was
not going to get any help in Scotland against the English parliament. In September he had given in a list of privy councillors
which included many royalist nobles (though it also, at the request
of the covenanters, included eight lairds),[105] but he now (13
November) agreed to remove most of the royalists; Huntly, Airth,
Linlithgow, Home, Tullibardine, Galloway, Dumfries and Carnwath were replaced by covenanters. The only well-known royalists

left on the council were Lennox (who usually lived in England), Hamilton (if he can still be called a royalist), Morton and Perth, and a few of the officers of state such as Roxburgh and Sir James Galloway.[106] Four new ordinary lords of session were appointed (including Wariston) to replace royalists.[107] The extraordinary lords of session included two Incendiaries, the Bishop of Ross and Traquair, and they were replaced by Lords Lindsay and Balmerino.[108]

Charles had formally nominated Lord Almond as treasurer on 30 September, immediately after Loudoun had been elected chancellor,[109] but he was now even less acceptable to the covenanters than he had been at first, as he had been implicated in some of the depositions concerning the Incident. Therefore the king agreed to the appointment of five treasury commissioners instead of a single treasurer.[110] The office of clerk register went to Sir Alexander Gibson of Durie; many had expected Wariston to be appointed, but the king probably refused to consider his appointment and Argyll supported Durie's claims.[111] All the other officers of state were confirmed in their offices,[112] though the covenanters refused to recognise the royalist Sir James Galloway as joint secretary of state (with Lanark) as well as master of requests.[113]

Parliament appointed four commissions to sit after it had dissolved. The committee for common burdens was entrusted with clearing up the financial confusion left by the two bishops' wars, by seeing that the taxes that had been imposed were paid and that all debts and loans were repaid.[114] The commission for receiving the brotherly assistance had exactly the same membership as the committee for common burdens and was empowered to receive the £220,000 sterling which had not yet been paid of the £300,000 brotherly assistance granted by the English parliament; the money was to be devoted to paying the expenses of the wars.[115] The commission for conserving the treaty named eighteen conservators of the peace of each estate who were, by themselves or together with commissioners appointed by the English parliament, to use all lawful means for preserving the articles of the treaty and preventing divisions between the kingdoms.[116] Finally, in the commission anent the articles referred to consideration by the treaty,

Loudoun, Argyll and three members of each estate were appointed to negotiate with the parliament of England about a variety of matters that had not been settled in the treaty at London. These included mutual consent by the parliaments of both kingdoms before either kingdom made war with foreign states, free trade between the kingdoms, and agreement on what forces Scotland should send to Ireland against the rebels.[117]

In addition to accepting the establishment of these commissions —composed almost entirely of staunch covenanters—the king heaped rewards on his recent enemies, hoping at least to buy their neutrality since he could not win their support in his quarrel with the English parliament. Most of the leading covenanters were given pensions. Argyll was created a marquis, General Leslie Earl of Leven and Lord Almond Earl of Callander. Lords Loudoun and Lindsay were allowed to assume the earldoms which they had been granted in 1633 but which had been suspended because of their opposition to the king in parliament in that year, while Johnston of Wariston was knighted. On the other hand, royalists who had risked their lives and squandered their fortunes for the king got no reward or thanks; the Earl of Carnwath remarked bitterly that he could see that he would have to go to Ireland and join the rebels there if he wanted the king's favour.[118] In return for all his concessions the king gained very little except vague promises of future loyalty. Parliament agreed not to prosecute any of the royalists who had been cited to appear before parliament except the five chief Incendiaries and the four Plotters, who were to be tried by a committee before 1 March 1642, and sentence of those found guilty was to be left to the king. Meanwhile those of the Incendiaries who were in prison, the Plotters, and those who had been arrested for their parts in the Incident were released.[119] On 17 November parliament dissolved after appointing (according to the 1640 triennial act) the next parliament to meet on 4 June 1644, and the king returned to London.

During his stay in Scotland Charles had practically surrendered the country to the covenanters. But they still did not feel secure in the concessions they had extorted from him. They had as yet little to fear from within Scotland, for the royalist minority was demoralised by defeat, but few could doubt that if the king over-came the English parliament and established absolute power in England all the concessions he had made in Scotland would be in jeopardy. For the past few years English attention had been focused on Scotland, as the leaders of opposition to the king in England hoped that if the covenanters could overcome the king this would give them the chance to do the same in England. Now, for the next two years, Scottish attention was to be concentrated on England and the contest between king and parliament there. Victory for parliament would effectively ratify the revolution in Scotland; if the king was victorious he would soon try to over-throw the covenanters in Scotland. Events were to continue to prove what the covenanters always claimed in arguing in favour of closer union: that the kingdoms were interdependent, and that events in one inevitably affected the other.

CHAPTER EIGHT

The Rule of the Covenanters in Scotland, November 1641–June 1643

THE SCOTTISH ARMY IN IRELAND

The first and most urgent matter requiring attention once the king had left Scotland was the Irish rebellion. The covenanters had a number of good reasons for wanting to send troops to Ireland. They had 'a very great part of the province of Ulster planted by their own nation',[1] whom they wished to protect, and they feared that 'if the Rebellione of Irland be prevalent' the Highlands and Islands 'who speak the same language the Irishe doe' would also rebel and receive help from Ireland.[2] Scotland had been threatened with invasion by armies from Ireland in 1639 and 1640 and it was hoped by sending a Scots army there to prevent any such danger in future. Finally, sending an army to Ireland gave the covenanters an excuse to keep an army on foot (at English expense), which was felt to be desirable to deal with any danger of a royalist rising in Scotland or invasion from England.

The king also had several motives for urging the sending of Scots forces to Ireland. He wanted the rebellion crushed and to demonstrate that he in no way countenanced the rebels, and it was surmised that he was nothing loth to send those he regarded as Scottish rebels to fight Irish rebels; he would have less need to fear Scottish intervention in England in favour of parliament if a Scottish army was involved in Ireland.[3] But he was soon to regret having encouraged the Scots to intervene in Ireland. In the years ahead when he was trying to negotiate an alliance with the Irish Catholics whereby they would send troops to help him in England, one of the main reasons for their reluctance to do so was their fear of the Scottish army in Ulster.

As for the English parliament, it too favoured Scottish intervention in Ireland. It wished to see the rebels defeated as soon as possible but feared that if it allowed the king control of an army sent against the Irish he might use it against parliament instead. On the other hand if they refused the king control of such forces and ensured that they were composed of men loyal to parliament this would weaken their position in England if the quarrel with the king led to civil war. By sending a Scottish army to Ireland they could avoid both these alternatives. From the point of view of the Protestants of Ireland the main advantage of sending them Scots help at first seemed to be that it could be sent quickly. The crossing from Scotland to Ulster was short and there were three regiments on foot in Scotland. But in the event nearly six months were to pass after the outbreak of the rebellion on 23 October 1641 before the Scots army began to arrive in Ireland. The main reason for the long delay was that most of the time of the English parliament was spent in debates connected with its quarrel with the king, and the terms under which the Scots were to go to Ireland were only considered in intervals between more urgent business. Moreover many peers were opposed to Scots intervention on the grounds that it would be dishonourable and taken as a sign of weakness if England appeared only able to reduce her dependency to obedience by calling for Scottish help.[4] In many cases this expressed fear of dishonour disguised dislike of the covenanters and fears that the Scots had ambitions in Ireland—what if they refused to leave once they had crushed the Irish?[5]

The English parliament first heard of the Scottish offer to send help to Ireland on 3 November, and after nearly two weeks of argument the Lords and the Commons agreed to ask for 5,000 Scots soldiers.[6] In Scotland the new privy council first met on 18 November and a few days later it ordered the Earls of Lothian and Lindsay (two of the commissioners appointed by parliament for concluding the articles of the treaty) to repair to the king and English parliament at once. They were told to treat for sending 10,000 Scots to Ulster and given detailed instructions as to the terms on which they were to be sent; these formed the basis of the eventual treaty.[7] The negotiations began in London on 10

December, but it took much argument to persuade the Lords to agree to 10,000 Scots going to Ireland.[8] The Scots offered to pay for the levy of the army and for transporting it to Ireland, to show how concerned they were to get help to the Irish Protestants quickly.[9] Loudoun wrote from Edinburgh that he believed that if 5,000 Scots had been sent promptly to Ireland many thousands of lives could have been saved. 'Ingland hes bein so slow as all Ireland wil be in the Rebells hands befoir any armie can be sent over. I pray god gife the parliament wisdome'.[10] On 24 January 1642 parliament agreed to a Scottish proposal that the 2,500 Scots already in arms should be sent to Ireland at once,[11] but it refused to promise that the Scots army would be rewarded for its services by grants of forfeited rebel estates in Ireland since many Englishmen feared the ambitions of the Scots in Ireland—Loudoun had urged that they be given 'Londonderrie and the plantationes of Irland in recompence of or services'.[12]

The treaty was not completed until July 1642. By that time England was on the verge of civil war and the king refused to ratify it, having had second thoughts as to the advisability of agreeing to the covenanters' raising an army at the expense of his English enemies. He had been little consulted about the treaty and though his assent to it was sought it made no practical difference that this was not forthcoming. Scotland undertook to levy and transport 10,000 men (plus officers) to Ireland. These men would be paid by England at English rates of pay (which were considerably higher than Scottish rates).[13] The Earl of Leven was chosen as general with the Earl of Lothian as lieutenant-general and Robert Monro as major-general.[14] Leven spent only a few weeks in Ireland and it is doubtful if Lothian ever set foot in the country, so the effective commander of the army was Monro, who landed in Ulster with the first 2,500 men in April.[15] The privy council organised the levying of the other 7,500 men[16] and these crossed to Ireland piecemeal during the summer and autumn; by November the army mustered over 11,000 men and officers.[17]

By June Monro's army had secured the counties of Down and Antrim. Using Carrickfergus as his base he had led one expedition south to Newry and another north through Antrim, during which the Earl of Antrim was captured.[18] Little organised opposition was encountered, most of the rebels withdrawing without being defeated. Leven arrived in Ireland in August and, joining the Scots army with local forces, marched against a rebel army, but after some indecisive skirmishing both sides withdrew[19] and Leven returned to Scotland. He had evidently quarrelled with Monro and was on bad terms with many of the officers of the army. Angry that most of the pay and supplies promised by the English parliament had not materialised, these officers had sworn an oath of mutual assurance not to disband until they had gained satisfaction of their just demands. Leven had denounced this as treason but they had refused to submit and blamed him for not protecting their interests. Unable to restore his authority, he left the army and took little further interest in it.[20] Lack of pay and supplies had seriously restricted the activities of the army, and as the English civil war was now beginning there seemed little possibility that parliament would be able to fulfill its promises to pay it in the near future. However, there was no question of withdrawing the army. Though promised English pay, it was not merely a mercenary army; it was fighting to protect Scotland and the Protestant settlers in Ulster. In August 1642 the Scottish privy council therefore decided that Scotland would do its best to provide for the army if the troubles in England prevented parliament from carrying out its promises.[21]

The commissioners whom the king and Scottish parliament had agreed to send to London in November 1641 had been originally intended to concern themselves mainly with concluding the articles not settled in the 1641 treaty. But the urgency of the need to send forces to Ireland had led to the commissioners' devoting most of their attention to that subject. In December 1641 the Scottish council had placed on the commissioners the additional onerous task of labouring to maintain a right understanding between the king and his English subjects. This led the commissioners in January 1642 to offer to mediate in the quarrel between the king and the parliament of England; parliament thanked the Scots for their offer but the king angrily ordered the commissioners not to act without consulting him—it was not their business to meddle in matters of this sort.[22]

In Scotland the main internal matter occupying the attention of the leading covenanters at the beginning of 1642 was the trial of the Incendiaries and Plotters. Traquair was ordered to appear before the committee appointed by the king and parliament on 4 January for trial, but difficulties soon arose. Though the king had agreed to the trial the lord advocate, Craighall, refused to take part in the prosecution, though he was willing to draw up papers and give advice privately. Three of the four procurators of state went further and refused to take any part in the prosecution, in spite of orders from the privy council to do so. Their motives are unknown but their conduct suggests that there were divisions among the covenanters as to the wisdom of holding the trials. In the end only one trial, that of Traquair, seems to have been completed by 1 March when the powers of the commissioners appointed by parliament to hold the trials expired.[23] He was found guilty on several charges but it appears that no report on his trial or those of the other Incendiaries and Plotters was sent to the king,[24] so he escaped without punishment. The evident reluctance of many covenanters to proceed with the trials was probably based on the feeling that it was best to forget the past now that agreement with the king had been reached; continued pursuit of the accused would seem vindictive and might provoke royalist demonstrations. In retrospect the power of the covenanters seems firmly established, but this was not clear at the time. It was feared that the Irish rebellion was having an unsettling effect in the Highlands and Islands, and that advantage might be taken by 'turbulent spirits' of the sending of all Scottish troops to Ireland to make disturbances in Scotland. It was therefore proposed that England should pay 1,000 men to remain in Scotland to deal with any such trouble, since the country would otherwise be left defenceless,[25] but nothing came of this plan and it was soon found that it was unnecessary to keep men in arms in Scotland. The strength and aggressiveness of the royalists had been over-estimated.

ATTEMPTS TO MEDIATE IN ENGLAND AND THE CROSS PETITION

The weakness of the royalists was partly the king's fault, since at first he did little to help or encourage them, as he still hoped that he could eventually persuade the covenanters to support him against the English parliament. The royalists were thus left divided, demoralised and leaderless. Charles' attitude is seen in his treatment of Montrose; he thanked him for his loyalty and asked for his support, but refused to allow him or the Earl of Airlie to come to his court at York,[26] presumably for fear that by associating with them he would offend the covenanters. Hamilton had managed to regain the king's confidence since the Incident without antagonising the covenanters, but he was still too much hated by most Scots royalists to rally support for the king in Scotland. Yet in spite of lack of leadership and encouragement from the king, some royalists had the resolution to appear publicly on his behalf in May 1642.

The privy council had in April sent Loudoun to the king to ask him to allow the Scots to mediate between him and parliament, and clearly indicated that it held him to be mainly at fault in the dispute.[27] Charles refused to allow this and sent Loudoun back to Scotland with orders to summon the council to meet on 25 May and to persuade it to condemn parliament's proceedings. In a letter to the council he informed it that 'We desyre not that you sould intermedle so farre as to take upon yow to decyde the differences betuix us and our Parliament', while in a declaration he repeated that the Scots were not to sit in judgement on the affairs of another kingdom. Royalist councillors who were with the king at York were sent to Edinburgh to attend the meeting. When the English parliament heard of the council meeting it too sent down a declaration justifying its conduct. A group of royalist nobles and lairds met in the Canongate together with a large number of their followers and prepared to petition the council in the king's favour. These 'banders', as they soon became called, alarmed the covenanters, who doubtless feared that they intended to terrorise and overawe the council as the covenanting mobs had done in 1637–8. The covenanters therefore hurriedly summoned their supporters to Edinburgh. Lairds and ministers from Fife and their followers came 'running over in thousands', while many more assembled from the Lothians. They greatly outnumbered the 'banders', most of whom dispersed quietly. But some of them refused to be frightened into submission and, led by Lord Montgomery (formerly a covenanter), gave in a petition to the council on 25 May[28] proposing that it should take the king's side against parliament.

The council ignored the petition[29] and it probably had the opposite effect to that intended; many moderate covenanters on the council had some sympathy with the king over his troubles in England but were alarmed by the attempted royalist demonstration into fearing that to support the king in England would encourage also the Scottish royalists, perhaps endangering the domination of the covenanters. On 31 May the covenanters who had assembled in Edinburgh, led by the Earl of Haddington and Lord Elcho, handed in a rival petition to the council, begging it not to offer to help the king or in any way endanger peace, but to mediate between king and parliament. The council assured the petitioners that it had no intention of jeopardising peace, but it showed some irritation at the attempts to influence its proceedings by stating that there was no need for petitions like the one given in by the covenanters and that it hoped it would not be troubled with the like in future.[30] In answer to the king the council indicated that it was sorry at the condition of affairs in England and would do its best to help bring about a settlement there conducive to his honour and authority and the good of both kingdoms.[31]

The king's hopes of receiving some declaration of support from the council were thus disappointed. Probably as a result of this he decided that Hamilton should return to Scotland to rally the royalists. As usual Hamilton was full of confidence in his own political ability, and he assured the king that 'he would at least keep that people from doing any thing that might seem to countenance the carriage of the parliament'.[32] He arrived in Scotland early in July and advocated an extraordinary scheme whereby the Scots would invite the queen, Henrietta Maria, to come to Scotland to mediate between king and parliament. As it was widely believed that the Catholic queen was one of the most important of the evil influences that were leading the king astray, there was no possibility of parliament accepting her as a mediator, so Hamilton's plan came to nothing.[33]

One covenanter who had been partly won over to the king by the concessions he had made in 1641 was the Earl of Dunfermline, and consequently Charles appointed him king's commissioner to the general assembly which sat at St Andrews from 27 July to 6 August 1642 with Robert Douglas as moderator. Many more covenanting nobles attended as elders than in 1640 and 1641 since it was rumoured that the royalist 'banders' intended to gather at St Andrews and 'extort from the Assemblie ane exposition of our Covenant, favourable to ane expedition to England' on behalf of the king. In the event no royalist demonstration took place.[34] As had become usual, the matters to be debated and acts to be passed in the assembly were discussed and decided on in private meetings of the moderator and leading covenanters (in which Argyll was especially active), though there was some resentment in the assembly at such control of business by a small committee. It refused to appoint assessors to the moderator to make up the committee, so he and his advisers had to meet secretly and unofficially.[35] Predictably, the assembly was presented with rival declarations from the king and the English parliament. Charles promised to govern his kingdoms by their laws and their kirks by their constitutions, and to endeavour the reformation of anything found amiss in a fair and orderly way. He ordered Dunfermline to tell the assembly that he would never try to withdraw concessions that he had made in Scotland and would do all he could to avoid civil war; but the assembly was also to be told not to interfere in things that did not concern it.[36] Parliament similarly stressed its wish to avoid civil war, to advance the work of the reformation and settle a stable union between the two kingdoms.[37] Dunfermline urged the assembly not to answer parliament's declaration without permission of the king, but 'his weeping could not obtain this'[38] and parliament was thanked for its message, though it was chided for not proceeding faster in the work of bringing about unity of religion and uniformity of church government. A similar rebuke was sent to the king.[39]

As in 1640 and 1641 most heat was generated, in the assembly itself and in the moderator's committee, by disputes between radicals and moderates over the 'novations' in worship proposed by the former. Conventicle holding continued, and some moderates continued to protest at it, but in this matter the radical minority had largely got their own way by their persistence. Prayer meetings were increasingly accepted as compatible with presbyterianism, but the moderates continued to defend traditional forms of worship from attack. 'At last, for feare of scandall' it was decided not to pass an act in the assembly against novations but to write to the moderators of all presbyteries troubled by them (all of which were in the South West) condemning them.[40] The main motives for this forbearance were to prevent open division in the kirk and to avoid offending their English allies. Thus later in the year when complaints were sent to the commission of the assembly of increasing 'Brownist' activities, the commission recommended that such matters should be treated carefully 'for eschewing offence to the good people of England that favoured those ways'.[41]

Before dissolving (the next assembly having been appointed to meet at Edinburgh on 2 August 1643)[42] the assembly appointed a commission for public affairs of the kirk, consisting of forty-eight ministers and twenty-five elders. It was given wide general powers to supervise the kirk's affairs until the next assembly met, to concern itself with 'presenting of overtures and prosecuting the other desires of the Kirk' with the king, Scottish privy council and English parliament. It was to do all it found necessary, by preparing drafts of a confession of faith, catechism and directory of public worship (tasks which had been laid on Alexander Henderson in 1641 but on which he had made little progress),[43] and by all lawful means, to advance the great work of religious unity and uniformity of church government with England.[44] This commission of the kirk was the more powerful successor of earlier, limited commissions established by previous assemblies; the 1638 commission to represent articles to parliament, the 1639 commission to the presbytery of Edinburgh, and the commissions to attend parliament appointed in 1640 and 1641.[45] Such commissions were now 'lyke to become almost a constant judicatorie, and verie profitable; bot of so high a straine, that to some it is terrible allreadie'.[46] Some ministers opposed the establishment of the 1642 commission 'out of a fear that it would encroach upon the affairs belonging to the ordinary judicatures of the church, and so prove prejudicial to them'.[47] Those who had such fears of the growing powers of the commission of the kirk, of its development into a constant central executive committee with power to interfere in the activities of kirk sessions, presbyteries and synods, were to have their fears realised in the years to come.

In September 1642 Mungo Murray, whom the king had sent into Scotland to inform royalists there of the state of affairs in England, reported to Charles that opinion was turning increasingly in favour of the English parliament, and suggested that to counter this the king should issue a declaration clearly in favour of religious unity between England and Scotland. He also reported that the covenanters had decided to summon a meeting of the conservators of the peace. The initiative for this came from the commission of the kirk, on whose petition the council had agreed on 20 August that the conservators should meet,[48] though the English parliament had failed to appoint English conservators to meet with them. The council also decided that though most of the Scottish commissioners in London should return home (the treaty for sending the Scottish army to Ireland being completed) two should remain behind. The king protested at this on the grounds that the quorum fixed for the commissioners was five, though his real objection was that the commissioners in London were becoming in effect ambassadors of the covenanters to the English parliament. The council ignored his protests, stating that it was necessary to keep commissioners in London to see that parliament paid the Scots army in Ireland. In spite of this rebuff and the report that opinion in Scotland was moving against him, the king agreed to the meeting of the conservators and wrote to them emphasising his wish for peace.[49] He can hardly have failed to realise that the actions of the conservators would almost certainly be against his interests, since most of them were convinced covenanters, but he

Page 253 A CONTRAST IN POLITICAL THEORISTS: (*left*) Alexander Henderson, *c.* 1585–1646, author of the 'Instructions for Defensive Arms; (*below*) Archibald, 1st Lord Napier, 1576–1645, author of the 'Letter on Sovereign Power'

Page 254 (*left*) THE MAIDEN, the Scottish beheading machine made in the 1560s. Used to execute John Stewart younger of Ladywell in 1640; (*below*) BRONZE CANNON cast in Edinburgh in 1642 by James Monteith, a pewterer employed by the covenanters on several occasions to cast musket balls. Found in a Sikh fortress stormed in 1826. Length 29½″; bore 3″

may have reasoned that they would meet whether he liked it or not so that he might as well try to preserve the fiction that he had some control over them by giving his approval to their decision to meet.

The conservators met on 23 September and three days later decided that their commission authorised them to endeavour to remove the distractions between king and parliament since their quarrel might endanger peace between England and Scotland. They wrote informing them of their decision and asking them to send safe conducts for some of the conservators to come and negotiate with them, for if, the conservators explained, their quarrel 'shall come, by Force of Arms, and by the effusion of blood, to be decided' (the first skirmishes of the English civil war had already been fought), Scotland 'cannot but in the end be involved in that common calamity'; they would be betraying their trust if they remained 'silent at this time and sit still as idle beholders'.[50] Parliament sent a safe conduct, but the king replied that the conservators had no need of one from him and it was noted that in his letters he carefully avoided saying whether or not he approved their offer to mediate;[51] was he reverting to his old time-wasting tactics when in difficulty, hoping that by a quick military victory he could end the civil war before they could begin to mediate? The conservators suspected as much, and re-affirmed on 14 November their determination to do their duty by trying to remove the differences between king and parliament.[52]

Both soon renewed their efforts to secure Scots help, or at least to prevent the Scots helping their opponents. The king wrote to the privy council promising to do all he could to promote unity of religion and uniformity of church government, though he weakened the effect of this by adding that he would do it only 'in such a way as we in our conscience conceave to be best for the floorishing estat of the true protestant religion'. He added with some justice that the English parliament, with which the covenanters urged him to join in this work, had never made any proposals to him on the subject and in fact had no desire to introduce presbyterian government, whatever it might pretend. Parliament in turn declared that it was always ready to advance the work of unity and uniformity,[53] and at the beginning of November sent the first

16

open request for military aid to the Scottish council, relating that under the 1641 treaty each kingdom was obliged to help the other in suppressing 'the common enemy of the Religion and Liberty of both nations'.[54] A few weeks before this John Pym and other parliamentarians had contemplated replacing senior officers in their army by 'Scotch commanders',[55] in the hope presumably of thus improving their military fortunes, a striking indication of the esteem in which Scottish soldiers were held and of parliament's doubts as to the competence of its officers. Perhaps also it was hoped that such an action, flattering to the Scots, would help to persuade them to intervene in England. Nothing further was heard of this plan, but later in November parliament followed up its declaration by sending John Pickering to Scotland with secret instructions to negotiate business of importance concerning the good of England and Ireland and the peace between England and Scotland, business of which the most important item was probably discussion of Scottish intervention in England. Pickering was not authorised to negotiate with the privy council but only privately with leading covenanters.[56]

When Charles heard of parliament's declaration to the Scots he immediately, as an 'antidote to that poison',[57] sent his secretary, Lanark, to Edinburgh with a letter denouncing parliament's misrepresentation of events in England. He claimed that parliament had ignored all his offers and proposals for peace, that he had taken up arms only to defend his person, maintain the Protestant religion, and preserve the liberties of England. The Scottish council was to do its utmost to see that all subjects were informed of this, the true state of affairs.[58] The king's letter and parliament's declaration were considered by the council on 20 December and, for once, Hamilton's efforts on behalf of the king met with some success. He asked that the king's letter be printed, but Balmerino argued that, since parliament had not asked for its declaration to be printed and it would be unjust to print the letter but not the declaration, neither should be printed. Hamilton protested that such an attitude suggested that the council 'owed as much to the Parliament of England as to the King'. Lanark now revealed that he had an order from the king for printing the letter, whereupon

Argyll sarcastically remarked that 'they sate there to good purpose, if every Message to them was a Command', and Lanark and Argyll 'let fly at one another for a while with much eagerness'. Hamilton stated that the point now at issue was whether to 'Obey or Not Obey' a direct order from the king, but Lord Balcarres spoke in support of Argyll's attitude—'that was the Bishops way of Proceeding, to procure Orders from the King without Advice, and then charge all who offered better Counsel with Disobedience'. Was the council to revert to being a rubber stamp for orders from the king about which it had not been consulted?

Hamilton brought back the argument from the general to the particular; did the covenanters mean to reduce the king's authority so much that he might not defend himself and his government in print? Were the covenanters afraid that the king's explanation of events would make him more popular than they wished? Further confused argument and votes revealed advocates for four different courses of action. Glencairn and Lauderdale argued in favour of printing both the king's letter and parliament's declaration. Argyll, Loudoun and Balmerino argued that neither should be printed immediately, decision being deferred until a later meeting of the council, by which time they doubtless hoped to have assembled enough covenanting councillors to outvote the royalists. Only one councillor, Balcarres, voted in favour of the third alternative, to print parliament's declaration but not the king's letter; other covenanters probably favoured this policy but saw no possibility of the council accepting it, and so voted instead for the more moderate proposal supported by Argyll. The fourth possibility, to print only the king's letter as Lanark, Hamilton and Southesk urged, was the one eventually adopted by the council, by eleven votes to nine. However, the covenanters did manage to carry a motion delaying consideration of the contents of the king's letter and parliament's declaration until a 'more frequent meeting' of the council.[59]

None the less the vote of the council caused great alarm among covenanters; it 'was a trumpet that awakened us all out of our deep sleep'.[60] It marked the beginning of the end of the covenanters' attempt to rule Scotland through the privy council; they came increasingly to govern through committees which had been appointed by parliament, whose membership was confined almost exclusively to covenanters and which had not the embarrassing tradition of obedience to the king possessed by the council.

As soon as he heard of the vote in the council on 20 December John Pickering complained to Argyll that the English parliament, which had willingly suppressed all papers published in England against the covenanters, would be indignant to hear that presses in Scotland were thus being encouraged to issue propaganda against parliament.[61] The covenanters did not need Pickering's promptings to organise opposition to the council's vote, for they feared that unless they took action quickly the council would next vote in favour of allowing men to be levied in Scotland to fight for the king in England—and that such forces might take part in 'the knocking downe our best patriots'[62] before they left for England. As had happened the previous May when it had been feared that the royalists might have a majority on the council, many ministers and lairds with their friends and followers flocked to Edinburgh, mainly from Fife, and met in the Tailors' Hall in the Cowgate to decide what should be done. The conservators of the peace and the commission of the kirk also considered the situation. With the approval of the commission the meeting in the Tailors' Hall drew up a petition to the conservators complaining that the English parliament would be offended by the council's order to print the king's letter, taking it as implying approval of the letter's contents. They therefore asked that parliament's declaration should also be printed, and that other papers Lanark was having printed should be suppressed.[63] The pretext for directing this petition to the conservators instead of to the council was convenience—the council was not meeting at the time—but the real reason was to give the conservators an excuse for intervening in the affair. The petition was presented to the conservators on 3 January 1643, and they agreed to recommend it to the council and to stop Lanark having papers printed for the king for the present.[64]

Meanwhile the royalists had not been idle. On hearing of the covenanters' petition to the conservators they met in Holyroodhouse and drew up a rival petition 'crossing' it, soon known as the Cross Petition, directed to the council. This was compiled mainly by Hamilton and Traquair but neither signed it; the petition was carefully worded in the hope of making it acceptable to many covenanters, and the signatures of Hamilton and Traquair would have clearly revealed its royalist origins. The Cross Petition appeared superficially to contain little offensive to the covenanters; it urged the need for peace and unity of religion with England, and quoted the national covenant with approval. But its emphasis was very different from that of the covenanters, putting the maintenance of peace above the achievement of religious unity; it favoured unity but 'without presuming or usurping to prescribe Rules, or Laws of Reformation to our Neighbour-kingdom', and the council was asked in answering parliament's declaration not to make any promises that might trouble the peace of Scotland.[65] The Cross Petition was signed by eight nobles and eldest sons of nobles and many lairds, though its supporters failed to find a single minister willing to sign.[66] It was considered by the council, together with the conservators' recommendation of the covenanters' petition, on 10 January. This time the covenanters had a majority on the council; several who had not been present on 20 December attended, and some of those who had then voted for printing the king's letter only had probably thought better of such a decision. When it became clear that the council would vote to print parliament's declaration, Lanark produced a letter which he had procured from the king for use in such an emergency, in which Charles authorised the printing of the declaration, expressing his confidence that his subjects would see through its malice. Thus though the council ordered the printing of parliament's declaration, and moreover declared that the orders by the council for printing papers (such as, by implication, the king's previous letter) did not imply approbation of their contents, the king's face was saved.[67]

This reversal of the council's decision of 20 December was a victory for the covenanters, but they decided that they could no longer trust the council and that the Scottish parliament should meet to consider the dangers facing the kingdom. The covenanters' meeting in the Tailors' Hall had already given in a second petition to the conservators urging them to supplicate the king to summon parliament, as the dangers from the Irish rebels, English civil war and divisions in Scotland required consideration by it as soon as possible—the next triennial parliament was not due to meet until June 1644.[68] The conservators considered this petition early on 10 January, before the council met, and resolved to ask the king to indict a meeting of parliament. Hamilton, Lanark, Glencairn, Callander and three lairds opposed this, declaring rather oddly that they were not opposed to calling a parliament but only to supplicating for one at that time;[69] Hamilton always preferred to oppose decisions of the covenanters of which he disapproved by some such oblique and ambiguous statement rather than to denounce their actions outright. No doubt he hoped thus to avoid an open break with them and to retain the support of moderates among them, but to many royalists his conduct seemed cowardly and damaging to the king's interests; instead of clearly protesting on behalf of the king against actions detrimental to him, he seemed to be content to quibble at details.

The conservators had at the beginning of January at last received from the king the safe conduct for which they had asked the previous September,[70] though Charles still avoided stating that he approved their offers to mediate in England. They again resolved that it was their duty to do so, and on 18 January commissioned Loudoun, Lindsay, Wariston and Robert Barclay to go to the king and the English parliament to work for the abolition of episcopacy in England and the summoning of a meeting of divines of both kingdoms to discuss religious matters. They were to try by their mediation to bring the civil war to an end and were to beseech the king to call a parliament to meet in Scotland to help in this work.[71]

Earlier in January the commission of the kirk had petitioned the conservators and the council to advance the work of religious unity. It had indicated (when protesting against the Cross Petition) the extent of the powers which it claimed by stating that the council should not accept any petitions concerning religious matters which had not been approved by the commission. Rather surprisingly, the council agreed to this.[72] The commission was very concerned about the influence of the Cross Petition, fearing that its talk of the need for religious unity and quotations from the national covenant would mislead covenanters into signing it, and therefore drew up a declaration denouncing it as 'nothing else but a secret plot and subtle undermining of all the present designes of this Kirk and Kingdome, for Unitie of Religion, and of all the work of God in this Land'. The petitioners professed to desire religious unity but in fact hindered it and did 'very much wrest and mis-apply' the national covenant. The commission admitted that 'to judge charitably' not all the petitioners were malignants; some had been taken in by the petition's specious pretences, 'not considering the bad intentions of the contrivers'.

The cross petitioners sent delegates to the commission expressing their surprise and sorrow at the imputations made against them, protesting the sincerity of their intentions, but the commission refused to accept their explanations and its declaration against the Cross Petition was printed by order of the conservators.[73] Orders were sent to all ministers to read it from their pulpits together with a 'necessary warning' from the commission against the enemies of religion. Ministers were to see that the Cross Petition was not signed in their parishes and to denounce secret malignants as enemies of religion, so that none would be deceived by them. But the warning showed some moderation in stressing that all 'who hope the best of the Kings Majestie' should not be regarded as malignants and enemies.[74] The commission's order to ministers to read the warning and declaration met with some opposition, not because of the contents of these papers but as the result of the widespread dislike among ministers of the commission as a new body usurping and undermining the powers of the traditional ecclesiastical judicatories. Many claimed that only a general assembly could order ministers to read such papers to their congregations. However, in the end nearly all the ministers complied with the orders.[75]

TOWARDS INTERVENTION IN ENGLAND

To the four commissioners whom the conservators had appointed to go to England the commission of the kirk added Alexander

Henderson, who was to join with them in supplicating the king in favour of religious unity and the holding of a synod of divines in England. The privy council also gave its support to their mission.[76] The commissioners went first to Oxford—all except Wariston, who remained in Scotland as the king had refused to include him in his safe conduct—but received a very cold welcome, being largely ignored by the king and insulted by his supporters.[77] On 23 February they asked Charles to accept their offer of mediation, but he replied that he could find nothing in the commission granted to the conservators (by him and the Scottish parliament in 1641) which gave them any right to interpose in English affairs. He therefore refused to accept them as mediators or to allow them to negotiate with parliament until they showed him by what authority they meddled in such matters.[78] The talks with the king dragged on until 19 April, when he finally told the commissioners that he was still not satisfied that the conservators had any right to interfere in the English civil war, and that in any case they had no power to delegate their authority to commissioners. He therefore refused to let them go to London and rejected their supplication that a parliament should be summoned in Scotland.[79]

In Edinburgh the conservators had already realised that the negotiations with the king had no hope of success and abandoned their attempt at mediation in England by recalling their commissioners.[80] They left Oxford after receiving the king's uncompromising reply of 19 April, Loudoun, Robert Barclay and Alexander Henderson returning home while Lindsay went back to London to continue efforts to get money and supplies for the Scottish army in Ireland.[81] Charles had never had any intention of accepting the mediation of the conservators, since it was obvious that they favoured the English parliament, but by keeping them talking he had succeeded in delaying the negotiation of a treaty between the covenanters and the English parliament for some months, giving him time, he was confident, to triumph in England before the Scots could intervene. The covenanters rightly concluded that if they had not recalled their commissioners from Oxford the king would have been content to have continued desultory and inconclusive talks with them indefinitely,[82] and they now turned to negotiating with parliament. But the Scots commissioners were recalled to Scotland, not sent immediately to London to negotiate an alliance, as the Commons had evidently expected.[83] The covenanters apparently felt that opinion in Scotland had not yet been adequately prepared for a clear declaration in favour of parliament. It may also have been felt that if an alliance was to be negotiated this should be done in Edinburgh, English commissioners being sent there, since it was the English who were asking for help.

It was obvious that the report that the commissioners made to the conservators on their fruitless weeks in Oxford would be very unfavourable to the king. To try to counteract this Charles sent his secretary, Lanark, to Scotland with a declaration denouncing the English parliament and its invitation to the Scots to intervene in England. He emphasised his hatred of popery, denying parliament's charges that his forces were composed largely of papists; the parliamentarians who opposed him were Brownists, Anabaptists and Independents who had no intention of introducing presbyterian church government in England, while their malicious suggestions that if the king was victorious in England, he would no longer observe the new laws concerning church and state that he had approved in Scotland in 1641 were completely false.[84] Charles also gave Lanark letters to be dispatched to many nobles and burghs asking for the support of them and their friends and followers and solemnly promising to maintain inviolably the laws he had accepted in 1641;[85] obviously he realised how damaging to his cause were the fears that he would go back on his word at the first opportunity. All royalist councillors and conservators at court—Morton, Roxburgh, Kinnoull, Annandale, Carnwath— were ordered back to Scotland with Lanark to use their votes on behalf of the king.[86] In addition some of the royalist nobles— Hamilton, Morton, Glencairn, Roxburgh, Kinnoull, Southesk, and Lanark—were given detailed instructions by the king. Those to whom the instructions were imparted were probably selected as being men who could be trusted to follow Hamilton's lead, for they formed the nucleus of his party or faction of what might be called 'royalist covenanters'; moderate covenanters who believed that the king should be allowed more power than he had been since the 1641 settlement, and moderate royalists who were prepared to accept the covenant and most of the ecclesiastical and constitutional changes agreed in 1641. Since the middle of 1642 the covenanters had been splitting into two factions. The more extreme, led by Argyll, so distrusted the king and were so militant in religion as to demand intervention in England to prevent his triumphing there and to establish presbyterianism. The moderate covenanters who came to follow Hamilton on the other hand believed that the king's promises could be trusted, and argued (as the Cross Petition had done) that England should be left to settle her own religion without Scottish interference.

As well as being opposed by the extreme covenanters, the moderates who supported Hamilton were faced with the enmity of the extreme royalists, who believed that he had betrayed the king. Some, like the Marquis of Huntly and the Earl of Airlie, did little at this time to oppose the covenanters actively, but they rejected the idea of any compromise with them. Others, including the Earls of Montrose and Nithsdale and Lord Aboyne, were ready to rise in arms in Scotland for the king if he would agree to this—or perhaps even if he would not. They believed that the sooner a royalist rising took place the more chance of success it would have, for given time the covenanters would raise forces of their own. In February 1643 when Queen Henrietta Maria was at York Montrose had tried to win her support for a royalist rising but Hamilton had persuaded her not to agree.[87] Nor would the king listen to Montrose's advice. The facile optimism which had led Charles to believe when he left Scotland in November 1641 that out of gratitude to him the covenanters would never help the English parliament against him had long since departed. He now accepted that the covenanters would intervene in England unless the civil war was quickly ended, but like Hamilton he thought it best to try to delay intervention by negotiation and moderation rather than by a royalist rising perhaps to precipitate it. He told Lanark at this time (April 1643) that it was his 'positive Pleasure that the first Breach should not come from his Party; but they should draw things out as long as was possible before they

hazarded on a Rupture' with the covenanters. He showed his confidence in Hamilton's judgement and advice by creating him a
duke on 12 April.[88]

The instructions sent to Hamilton and his supporters by the
king directed them to do all they could to prevent divisions in
Scotland, and to give in his name all necessary assurances that he
would preserve government by parliament and assembly as then
established in Scotland without alteration. They were to do what
they could to get declarations and papers sent by the king printed
in Scotland and to prevent the English parliament sending agents
or commissioners to Scotland—Charles knew by intercepted
letters of John Pickering's mission. They were to forbid in the
king's name the council or the general (Leven) to remove the
Scottish army from Ireland and were even, if necessary, to declare
that the king would do all in his power to maintain and supply
that army, provided it remained in Ireland.[89]

Considering that the king had never given his consent to the
treaty which had sent the army to Ireland, his sudden concern for
its wellbeing was incongruous, but he feared that if the covenanters decided to intervene in England on behalf of parliament
they would transport the army in Ireland to England. If he could
ensure that it remained in Ireland, then the covenanters would
need to raise, train and equip a new army in Scotland before invading England, which would delay their intervention for several
months. In spite of numerous complaints[90] the English parliament
had proved unable to pay or supply the army and it had been on
the verge of starvation during the winter. The council, the conservators and the commissioners for common burdens had met
jointly in March 1643 and agreed to raise a loan to help the army
in Ireland,[91] but the amount raised was totally inadequate for its
needs and a decision either to withdraw it or to agree on some way
of paying it would have to be taken soon. Hamilton told the king
that it would be very difficult to keep it in Ireland, though Leven
had promised him that it would not be used against the king.[92]

Lanark received the declaration, instructions and letters from
the king on 21 April, but before he and the other royalists from
Oxford could reach Edinburgh the covenanters acted on the news

brought by their commissioners; indeed it seems likely that they acted hurriedly since they knew that the royalists were coming. The conservators heard the report of Loudoun and Robert Barclay on 9 May,[93] and the next day the privy council resolved, on a proposal by Argyll, that a joint meeting of the council, conservators and the commissioners for common burdens should be held on 11 May. The reason given for the joint meeting was so 'that by joynt advyce some course may be tane concerning the Scottish armie in Ireland';[94] there were precedents for joint meetings for such a purpose in that the council and the commissioners for common burdens had met jointly in March 1642, and all three bodies had met in March 1643, to discuss raising money for that army, though certainly on the first occasion and probably on the second the bodies had voted separately.[95] But the needs of the army in Ireland were now only a pretext for a joint meeting in which the more extreme covenanters led by Argyll, who formed a majority of the conservators and commissioners for common burdens, could out-vote the potential royalist and moderate majority on the council.

The conservators met alone on the morning of 11 May and formally approved the conduct of their commissioners at Oxford.[96] The moderates among them tried to delay a vote on this point for twenty-four hours, hoping that Lanark would have arrived by then to give the conservators the king's version of the negotiations at Oxford, but the motion for a delay was defeated by sixteen votes to seven.[97]

At the joint meeting of the three bodies in the afternoon the necessities of the army in Ireland were first considered, and it was decided to continue borrowing money for use of the army. Next it was debated at length whether a convention of estates should be summoned, a decision being delayed until the following day.[98] The reason for wishing to summon a convention was given as the state of the army in Ireland; a convention was needed to decide on its future and to provide money to pay it. But in fact the decision to hold a convention, without the king's consent if necessary, was simply the covenanters' answer to the king's refusal to call a parliament to discuss the dangers to Scotland presented by the

English civil war. On 12 May the joint meeting began with another long debate, on the condition of Scotland, the army in Ireland, and the failure of the English parliament to pay much of the Brotherly Assistance promised in 1641. The first question voted on was whether the three bodies could vote together; first the council and then the conservators and the commissioners for common burdens together voted that they could and should. Next all three bodies jointly voted that it was necessary that a convention of estates should be summoned, after Argyll and Wariston had 'made clear by law and sundrie palpable practices' that they had power to do this. Two more votes resolved that a date for the meeting of the convention should be fixed immediately, without consulting the king, and that that date should be 22 June. A proclamation in the king's name announced the holding of the convention, while those entitled to attend or to elect commissioners to attend were summoned by letters signed by Chancellor Loudoun and two members of each of the three bodies.[99]

Opposition to calling a convention was led by Hamilton, though as usual his methods seem to have been oblique; he protested that the council could not vote jointly with or in the presence of the conservators and commissioners for common burdens, hoping no doubt to get the matter referred to the council alone, as he might there be able to muster a royalist majority to oppose a convention. Craighall joined Hamilton in objecting to the three bodies voting jointly, but though he protested as king's advocate that to summon a convention without the king's consent was to infringe the royal prerogative he was believed to have privately advised the covenanters to call a convention since the king had refused them a parliament.[100]

By comparing the list in the council register of those present on 12 May with those who signed the letter from the meeting to the king announcing the calling of the convention, the extent of the opposition to the summons can be estimated, since those who opposed it refused to sign the letter.[101] Of sixteen nobles present six did not sign the letter (Hamilton, Glencairn, Southesk, Callander, Morton and Dunfermline). The treasurer depute and justice clerk joined the advocate in refusing to sign, but the clerk register did. Only one laird out of ten present and one or two burgesses out of ten did not sign. Thus, of about forty members of the three bodies present at the meeting, twenty-eight signed the letter and about twelve refused—and judging by some of the votes of the councillors alone which have survived, considerably less than twelve had actually voted against the majority.[102] The figures show the strong support for summoning the convention among the lairds and burgesses, and that the nobles and officers of state were almost evenly divided, even though most of the royalists from Oxford were not present.

Lanark did not reach Edinburgh until 15 May 'when he seemed to be in a great rage' at the decision to hold a convention. He found that the chancellor, whose authority was necessary to summon an extraordinary meeting of the council, had left Edinburgh, so the council could not be called to hear what the king had to say and publish his declaration, though Lanark was able to dispatch the letters from the king to the nobles and burghs asking for their support.[103] Charles wrote to the council denying its power to summon a convention and forbidding the convention to meet. He had some hopes that when the council next met alone, reinforced by the royalist councillors from Oxford, it would reverse the decision of 12 May; he pointed out to Lanark that only a minority of councillors then present had signed the letter telling him of the convention.[104] Charles' hope that Hamilton could gain a majority for him on the council was realised on 1 June. It agreed to publish the declaration the king had given to Lanark in April[105] and it wrote to him the most friendly letter that he had received from his Scottish council since it had been reconstituted in November 1641. It expressed itself 'fully satisfied with the Expressions of Your gratious intentions towards us, and desire of preserving Peace among ws' and promised to 'endeavoure to prevent all jealouseis which may arise upon anie groundles report of levying of armes or mainteaning of forces within this kingdom without speciall warrant from your Majestie and Estats of Parliament'. Loudoun and others strongly opposed the inclusion of this promise in the letter, claiming that it contradicted the letter writ-

ten to the king on 12 May by the joint meeting; the point at issue
was that the earlier letter had left it to the convention to decide
what action should be taken to meet the dangers and difficulties
facing Scotland, and such action might include raising and maintaining forces, but now the council was promising that this would
not be done without the consent of the king and the parliament
of Scotland. The council voted by fifteen votes to eleven to retain
the promise in the letter, and Loudoun signed it as president of
the council though declaring that he had 'reasouned, voiced and
protested aganis that claus in it'.[106]

Though Hamilton and his supporters formed a majority of the
council on 1 June they made no attempt to reverse the decision
to summon the convention, and the king's letter of 22 May forbidding the meeting of the convention was not produced.[107] The
reasons for this failure were explained in a verbal message which
the royalists sent to the king on 5 June. They advised him not to
forbid the convention to meet, since the covenanters would
ignore his orders and this would bring his authority into contempt.
If it proved necessary he could declare at some later date that the
convention had been illegal. He should agree to the convention
meeting but order it to confine its activities to securing the kirk
from any dangers and raising money for the Scottish army in
Ireland (so that the covenanters would have no excuse for recalling
it). Provided the convention did not levy forces or recall the army
in Ireland, its meeting would not damage the king's interests.[108]

This advice was based on Hamilton's confidence, strengthened
by his success in the council on 1 June, that he could manage the
convention so that it would stay within these bounds. Charles
accepted his advice and on 10 June wrote a letter to be presented
to the convention. In this he protested at the convention having
been summoned without his consent, but related that in spite of
this he had decided to allow it to meet to settle matters concerning
providing for the army in Ireland, getting the Brotherly Assistance
paid and guarding against any innovations in religion, but forbade it to raise any forces or to withdraw the army from Ireland.[109]
On the day that the king wrote this letter Hamilton told the queen
that though the situation in Scotland was not as he would have

liked it, 'yet I was never so hopeful as at this present, that no Forces will come from hence this Summer into England'.[110] His policy of avoiding an open break with the covenanters for as long as possible had so far had much success in delaying their intervention in England, but by this time the king must have begun to wonder when, if ever, Hamilton would decide that the time to break with them had arrived. Was Hamilton's policy perhaps after all negative, the result of weakness and fear of the consequences of breaking with the covenanters, rather than a positive policy protecting the king's interests? In the months ahead Charles was to come slowly to the conclusion that Hamilton had betrayed him, but his failure was probably simply the result of political ineptitude and weakness that prevented his making a stand against the covenanters.

Whatever chance Hamilton might have had of preventing the convention making an alliance with the English parliament was destroyed by the revelation of royalist plots against Scotland. The ever-intriguing Earl of Antrim had escaped from Carrickfergus castle some months after his capture in May 1642 by the Scots army in Ireland, but was recaptured in May 1643 as he landed in Ulster from England. Letters found on him showed that he was in correspondence with the Earl of Nithsdale and Lord Aboyne, and referred to various military preparations by them in which Huntly, Montrose and the queen were all to some degree involved.[111] When questioned, Antrim claimed that he and the Scots royalists named had only been planning to raise forces in Scotland to join the royalist army of the Earl of Newcastle in the north of England to oppose the English parliament. Aboyne had agreed to levy a regiment in the Highlands and Isles, though Montrose had refused to help Antrim except 'in a legal way'. But one of Antrim's servants gave details of more far-reaching plots before he was executed for corresponding with the Irish rebels and having helped Antrim escape from Carrickfergus the previous year. It is hard to know how much of his testimony referred to plans actually being put into practice, and how much was based only on the enthusiastic and indiscreet talk of the ambitious Antrim about what he would like to do at some future date. It seems most likely that

Page 271   A CONTRAST
IN COVENANTERS:
(*left*) the Fanatic. Sir Archi-
bald Johnston of Wariston,
c. 1610–63. By George
Jamesone. From
Johnston, *Diary, 1639*;
(*below*) the Financier.
Sir William Dick of
Braid, *c.* 1580–1655. By
George Jamesone. From
M.A.H. Forbes, *Curiosities
of a Scots Charta Chest*
(Edinburgh 1897)

Page 272 PRINTS FROM JOHN SLEZER, *THEATRUM SCOTIAE*
(1693): (*above*) Linlithgow Palace; (*below*) Stirling Castle

when Antrim was captured he was actively engaged in trying to levy Irish Catholic troops to join the king in England, and to provoke royalist risings in Scotland by Aboyne and Nithsdale to prevent the covenanters intervening in England, while his talk of destroying the Scottish army in Ireland and leading an Irish army to Scotland referred to more long-term plans to regain Kintyre and other former Macdonald lands in Scotland from the Campbells.[112]

The plans of Antrim and his confederates were certainly known to the queen at York, but the king at Oxford probably knew only that he was trying to bring Irish troops to his aid in England, a plan which he had approved. Yet it was inevitably the reputation of the king which suffered when Antrim's plottings were revealed, for it was hard to believe that the king's supporters would take part in such plots without his knowledge. Many Scots who had been influenced by Hamilton's arguments that the king could be trusted not to try to overthrow the 1641 settlement in Scotland were now faced with evidence which suggested that while making promises to that effect he had been secretly planning royalist risings in Scotland. Argyll and his supporters could not have asked for better propaganda on the eve of the meeting of the convention.

Montrose's refusal to take an active part in Antrim's schemes may have been based on unwillingness to act without the king's approval,[113] as well as on the practical consideration that the plots of such garrulous intriguers as the queen and Antrim would be unlikely to stay secret for long or have much hope of success. Montrose had left York by this time and returned to Scotland, probably to try to reach agreement with Huntly for a combined royalist rising (though the covenanters believed that he had deserted the king's cause and made overtures to try to win him back to the covenant), but failed and returned to England at the end of June, probably for fear of arrest in connection with Antrim's revelations.[114]

The privy council first considered the news of Antrim's plots on 6 June, and immediately ordered the trial of Aboyne and Nithsdale for treason before the justice general. Three days later the council and conservators met jointly and issued a declaration summarising the treacherous and damnable plots by papists in England, Ireland and Scotland. The queen's part in these plots was tactfully not mentioned, and knowledge of them was not attributed to the king. But it was observed that 'whill his Majestie is making a publict declaration of his intentions to defend and maintain the religioun, rights and liberteis of this kingdome . . . the papists ar conspiring, plotting and practising aganis the lyves of his Majesties good subjects'; the moral to be drawn from this was obviously that even if the king could be trusted the papist supporters on whom he was dependent could not.[115]

The same joint meeting of council and conservators was presented by Michael Welden (an agent sent by the parliament of England) with a letter to the queen which had been intercepted. In it the Earls of Roxburgh, Morton, Annandale, Kinnoull, Lanark and Carnwath gave her advice on how the war against the English parliament should be conducted. Parliament claimed that this made them incendiaries causing trouble between the king and his subjects, and demanded that they be arrested while charges against them were prepared.[116] As the complaint of parliament concerned a breach of the 1641 peace treaty, the council and the conservators resolved that the matter should be dealt with by the latter.[117] Four of the six earls accused were conservators and were present at their meetings on 19 and 20 June.[118] The covenanters demanded that they withdraw while parliament's allegation against them was discussed, but they angrily refused to leave. Kinnoull, being especially vehement, swore 'with oathes and curses, he would abyde and voyce' but after his rage brought on a heart attack which nearly killed him the other three earls agreed to consult their lawyers on 21 June instead of attending the conservators' meeting. The noble conservators proposed that the six earls should write to the English parliament apologising for their letter to the queen and promising not to meddle in anything concerning England until they had been tried on the charges parliament was preparing against them. The earls seemed willing to accept this but Wariston demanded that a promise that 'in the mean tyme they should not intermedle' should be substituted for the promise not to interfere in English affairs. The point of this change was presumably that it could be interpreted as an undertaking not to take part in any political activities, and could thus be used to deprive the six royalist earls of their votes in the convention. The lairds and burgesses among the conservators supported Wariston's amendment and out-voted the nobles, but the six earls refused to sign the new promise and appealed to the convention for justice.[119]

CHAPTER NINE

The Solemn League and Covenant, June 1643–January 1644

THE CONVENTION OF ESTATES

After a long and complicated evolution the convention of estates had become by the reign of Charles I a body with a membership similar to that of parliament, and it was generally regarded as being a less formal meeting of the estates than parliament, with limited powers. The powers of conventions were traditionally restricted; they were often summoned primarily to grant taxes, they could take executive action and could pass temporary legislation, but they could not pass permanent laws and it was usual for even their temporary laws to be ratified by a subsequent parliament.[1] The word 'convention' was of course often used non-technically to describe any meeting and, as we have seen, the covenanters had called several of their meetings in 1639–40 'conventions' or even 'conventions of estates'. But they did not subsequently claim that these had been formal conventions of estates nor demand that the king ratify their proceedings, in the same way as they had insisted that he ratify the actions of the June 1640 session of parliament.

In summoning a convention of estates in May 1643 instead of a parliament the covenanters may have hoped that the meeting of the less formal and powerful of the two bodies without royal consent would less offend the consciences of royalists and moderate covenanters who were unhappy at the undermining of royal authority. In the event the covenanters were spared the necessity of holding a convention in defiance of the king by his letter of 10 June giving permission for it to meet.

The first few days of the convention were spent mainly in

arguments over its powers. Hamilton and the royalists claimed that as it was meeting in accordance with the king's letter it was bound to accept the limitations on its powers laid down in that letter, while Argyll and his supporters asserted that on the contrary the convention had met on the authority of the council, conservators and commissioners for common burdens, and that these bodies had placed no limitation on it. Though there were no organised parties in the convention, members soon found that they had to choose between the opposing arguments of Hamilton and Argyll on all the main issues being considered, though the exact membership of the two loose parties or factions thus formed was ill-defined and variable. It soon became clear that a majority of the nobles generally supported Hamilton while the lairds and burgesses were almost unanimous in their support for Argyll. The fact that most nobles would support Hamilton was first demonstrated on 24 June. A committee of nine of each estate was chosen to draft an act of constitution which would formally constitute the convention and define its powers. Each estate elected its own representatives; those chosen by the lairds and burgesses were almost entirely supporters of Argyll, but the nobles elected only two of the more extreme covenanters, Argyll and Balmerino. Two of the seven other nobles chosen were waverers whose allegiance was doubtful—Callander and Lauderdale—but the other five could all be relied on to support the king —Hamilton, Morton, Roxburgh, Southesk and Lanark.[2] Thus Hamilton's confidence that he could manage the convention would have been justified if he had had to deal only with the nobles. But the lairds and burgesses refused to follow the lead given by the nobles, and the act of constitution which the committee presented to the convention on 26 June was a triumph for Argyll. It stated that it was a 'Lawfull free and full convention . . . And hath power to treate Consult and determine in all matters that shall be proposed vnto thame als freelie and amplie as any Convention quhilk hes beene within this kingdome at any time bygane'.[3] Nineteen nobles voted against the act, but only one laird and no burgess.[4] The seeming unanimity of the burgesses in this and other votes may be misleading in that it was an established habit among the burgesses that once a majority of the estate had decided how to vote on an issue, the minority who had opposed the decision reached should vote with the majority when the vote was taken publicly in the full parliament or convention, so that outwardly the unity of the estate of burgesses would be preserved.

Nonetheless, the vote on the act of constitution represented a resounding defeat for Hamilton. He and Lanark had previously resolved that if the convention thus voted to ignore the limits set on its powers by the king they would protest and leave. But Craighall suggested that to protest at a convention that had declared itself legally constituted would be treason. On his advice they therefore confined themselves to declaring that in spite of the act of constitution the convention was not free. Lanark demanded that the king's letter of 10 June to the convention should be recorded in its register, but this was refused. Hamilton and Lanark withdrew baffled, but Hamilton refused to advise royalist nobles as to whether they too should leave the convention, probably for fear that to order them to leave would be held to be treason. Thus the royalists and moderates in the convention were left leaderless. Some continued to attend its meetings in the hope of delaying the implementation of Argyll's policies, while others withdrew.[5]

Argyll and his supporters were now ready to begin negotiations to send help to the parliament of England, and the convention was urged on in this work by remonstrances from the commission of the kirk. These confined themselves to emphasising the dangers to religion of the revolts and other activities of papists. Nothing was said directly as to the need for military intervention in England since that was adjudged to be a civil matter outwith the sphere of the kirk, but clear hints as to the kirk's opinions in the matter were given. It was related that the dangers to true religion in England inevitably also threatened the kirk, that papists were now in arms under pretext of serving the king, and that 'great things are expected from this Kingdome for the benefit of all the Reformed Kirks, especially the Kirk of England'. Many of the commissioners of the kirk had opposed sending the remonstrances to the convention as they could be taken as interfering in civil affairs, but the ubiquitous Wariston persuaded them that it was their duty to send them.[6]

In reply the convention promised to work to remedy the dangers to religion,[7] but it was in fact embarrassed by the fact that no commissioners from the English parliament had appeared to negotiate the military alliance which it was believed was necessary to safeguard religion. 'Some did conjecture one cause, some another' for the delay in sending English commissioners; the civil war had been going badly for parliament since the beginning of the 1643 campaigns, and it was thought that it might be the emergencies caused by military defeats which were preventing parliament from sending commissioners—though on the other hand these very emergencies made parliament's need for an alliance with the Scots all the more urgent. The real reason for the delay, as many Scots suspected, was divisions among the English parliamentarians. 'The House of Lords was said to be opposite to the Commons conclusion of craveing our help', and many members of the Commons as well had serious doubts as to the wisdom of calling in a Scottish army.[8] The Commons had resolved at the beginning of May to send commissioners to Scotland to ask for aid, but in spite of repeated urgings the Lords were reluctant to agree to this. But they did agree to appoint commissioners of the peace to meet with their Scots counterparts, the conservators, and to appoint commissioners to complete the 1641 treaty by negotiating with the Scots on the articles which had then been referred to further consideration.[9] The appointments were, in a sense, irrelevant; the Scots conservators had virtually ceased to sit, and no joint meeting ever took place; what was needed was commissioners to negotiate with the convention of estates. But they were probably intended as a gesture of goodwill to the Scots. The conservators had been intended to provide links between the parliaments. The articles referred to further consideration mainly concerned various aspects of closer union. Thus the English parliament, now that it needed Scots help, was indicating that it was willing to proceed to closer union between the kingdoms, as the Scots had desired in 1641.

At length the Lords agreed to send an agent, John Corbett, to

Scotland with a declaration of both houses (dated 27 June) apologising for the delay in sending commissioners and inviting the Scots to send ministers to attend the 'Westminster assembly' which parliament had just established (as the kirk had advised) to make recommendations on the reformation of religion.[10] Thus in religion as well as civil affairs the bait of closer union was held out to the Scots.

While awaiting news from England the convention had occupied itself by instituting proceedings against several of the more extreme royalists, though it took no action against Hamilton and his friends since there seemed to be little to fear from them. Thus proceedings against five of the six earls denounced by the English parliament for writing to the queen were dropped (since they were all followers of Hamilton) after they had signed a rather vague submission stating that they had not tried to incite the king against parliament.[11] But the sixth of the earls, Carnwath, 'that monster of profanitie',[12] was well known to be a bitter hater of the covenant and charges were prepared against him. He fled rather than be tried and was ordered to forfeit £10,000 Scots for his failure to appear before the convention.[13]

A committee was set up to try Carnwath and Traquair; the latter was believed to have helped to draft the Cross Petition. In examining witnesses about the petition the committee gave an undertaking that evidence given would be used against no one except Traquair.[14] Hamilton had probably taken part in drafting it but the covenanters believed that it would benefit them more to leave him alone than to take action against him which might stir him out of his indecision and inactivity. Thus the royalists proceeded against those who, it was feared, might lead active opposition to the covenanters. The Earl of Nithsdale and Lord Aboyne were declared outlaws and fugitives by the justiciary court for failing to appear to be tried for treason for their part in Antrim's plotting, while Huntly and Lords Ogilvie, Herries and Banff were ordered by the convention to find caution to keep the peace.[15]

Hamilton tried to rouse feeling against the English parliament by inciting those of his friends who still attended the meetings of the convention to point out that the English parliament still had not paid half the Brotherly Assistance promised in 1641.[16] Another reminder that parliament had proved an unsatisfactory paymaster came from Ireland. The officers of the Scots army there sent commissioners to the convention, who related how the army had been neglected; its necessities were such that it was unable to take the field against the Irish rebels and could not continue any longer in its present condition. The army demanded that its arrears be paid, food and other necessities provided for it, and guarantees given for its future payment. Once these demands had been met the army would agree to send part of itself back to Scotland[17]—which seems to indicate that the army suspected that the convention would wish to transfer all or part of it to England. In reply the convention announced on 17 July that it had resolved to raise money for the army and would negotiate with parliament for payment of its arrears and future pay.[18]

Meanwhile the House of Lords had at last agreed to send commissioners to Scotland; they named two peers to go, but one refused and the other was (or at least claimed to be) too ill to travel. The Lords therefore suggested on 19 July that the Commons should send their commissioners to Scotland at once while the Lords' representatives followed later,[19] and this was agreed. In the event no peers were appointed to follow the commoners to Scotland, probably because none willing to help negotiate an alliance with the Scots could be found, even though the Lords acquiesced in the Commons undertaking such negotiations. The four commissioners appointed by the Commons (Sir William Armyne, Sir Henry Vane junior, Thomas Hatcher and Henry Darley) were instructed to make known to the Scots the calamities that were preventing parliament from paying the army in Ireland and the remainder of the Brotherly Assistance. They were to negotiate agreements on how these debts were eventually to be paid; the army in Ireland could be paid by grants of lands formerly belonging to the Irish rebels, and the army could then be withdrawn, though it could leave garrisons there until the debts due to it were paid.

There seems little doubt that in asking for the removal of the

Scots army from Ireland parliament hoped that that army would
be sent straight to England, for the instructions to the English
commissioners next ordered them to ask the Scots for military
help in the common cause of all Protestants. The Scots were to
be requested to send at least 10,000 foot and 1,000 horse to England on English pay under the Earl of Leven. In return for this
parliament would undertake to send a similar army to the help of
the Scots if they were troubled by civil war or invasion, and to
send ships to guard Scotland against invasion from Ireland.
Parliament would make no peace with the king without provisions
for the peace and security of Scotland being included. The English
commissioners were also empowered to negotiate articles for the
security and defence of the religion and liberties of both kingdoms
if this proved convenient, but their most important task was to
get prompt military help from Scotland.[20]

On 14 July, after hearing the declaration of parliament brought
by John Corbett, the convention of estates sent Robert Meldrum
to London to complain that the arrival of parliamentary commissioners had long been expected, to ask that the remainder of the
Brotherly Assistance be paid, and to represent the necessities of
the army in Ireland.[21] In preparation for negotiating a treaty with
parliament and raising an army the convention at the end of July
ordered the levy of three troops of horse and 600 foot to guard
against any danger caused by the papists in arms in England and
disaffection in Scotland.[22] Thus if an alliance with parliament was
made and aroused opposition from royalists, there would be men
ready in arms to overawe them. This was exactly what Montrose
had feared earlier in the year when he had advocated an immediate
royalist rising before the covenanters had time to raise troops.

The general assembly met in Edinburgh on 2 August; a few
days earlier leading covenanters who were members of it had met
in Wariston's chamber and decided that Alexander Henderson
should be moderator. The king had shown his continuing trust in
the Hamiltons by not naming a royal commissioner to the assembly but sending a blank commission to Lanark to appoint whom-
ever he thought fit. Not unnaturally, none of the royalist nobles
wished to be king's commissioner at such a difficult time, and

eventually they and Hamilton agreed to appoint lord advocate Craighall 'of whom they had small care, whether he lost himself or not'.[23] They doubtless thought it a suitable revenge for the harm Craighall had done the king's cause by his advice to and support for the covenanters to put him in a position where it would be impossible to avoid alienating either king or covenanters, or both. But the appointment was a shirking of responsibility by the royalist nobles, who were afraid to appear as the king's representatives. They might have reflected that as Craighall had shown so little fear of earning the king's displeasure in the past, he was unlikely now to fear to offend him. Charles instructed Craighall to assure the assembly of his unalterable adherence to religion as established in Scotland and to oppose any treaty with parliament or the appointment of a new commission of the kirk,[24] but there is no sign that he made any serious attempt to carry out these orders. Like the convention the assembly 'did greatlie long for the English Commissioners, of whose comeing we were all well near out of hope, manie thinking their stay to be from the Lords denying them a commission'.[25]

CIVIL LEAGUE AND RELIGIOUS COVENANT

The commissioners from the English parliament at last arrived in Edinburgh on 7 August, accompanied by two well-known English ministers, Stephen Marshall and Philip Nye. The former was known to be much in favour of the presbyterian system, but Nye was a leading Independent, as was Sir Henry Vane who soon emerged as the spokesman and leader of the lay commissioners. At this time there existed what amounted to a truce in religious controversy among English parliamentarians, a tacit abandonment of religious strife so that attention could be concentrated on winning the war; discussion of what form of church government was to be established in England was to be delayed, as far as possible, until the war was won.[26] What parliament wanted to negotiate with the Scots was a military alliance, but it was obvious from the stream of exhortations and declarations that the covenanters had directed to it in the past few years that they would insist on some promise by parliament to bring about closer union,

and more specifically to reform the Church of England into conformity with the kirk as a *sine qua non* of any treaty. Parliament was
therefore ready to sign some sort of agreement on religion with
the Scots, but wished to keep this as vague and inexplicit as possible. This difference in attitude between the English and the Scots
was common knowledge—'the English pressed chiefly a Civil
League, and the Scots a Religious one';[27] 'The English were for
a civill League, we for a religious Covenant'.[28] But for both
covenanters and parliamentarians the need for an alliance was so
urgent that they were willing to make concessions.

The English commissioners soon found that the Scots would
not discuss in detail the sending of an army to England until they had
first accepted a general band stating the ultimate religious goals at
which the two kingdoms would aim. The general assembly, on its
best behaviour to impress the English—'We were exhorted to be
more grave than ordinare; and so indeed all was carried to the
end with much more awe and gravitie than usual'—allowed them
to be present at its meetings, though they were not allowed to
address the assembly directly, commissioners being appointed to
negotiate with them. The convention of estates made similar
arrangements.[29] On 10 August the English presented a declaration
from parliament to the assembly, relating that the Westminster
assembly had been summoned to help reform religion and asking
that some Scots ministers should be sent to attend its meetings.
The English parliament also desired the general assembly to 'stir
up' Scotland to send forces to England to oppose the papists,[30]
an invitation to the assembly to interfere in civil affairs. A letter
signed by more than seventy English ministers also begged for
Scots help, outlining the miseries of England so graphically as
to reduce many members of the assembly to tears.[31]

To the convention the English commissioners gave papers
based on their instructions from parliament, requesting Scots
help, and these were considered jointly by commissioners appointed by the convention and the general assembly.[32] After
several meetings the Scots and English commissioners assented
unanimously to a draft league and covenant prepared mainly by
Alexander Henderson, the solemn league and covenant. Unfor-

tunately details of the debates over this new covenant have not survived, but it is well known that the English, led by Vane, 'were, more nor we could assent to, for keeping of a doore open in England to Independencie. Against this we were peremptor'.[33] It was approved, again unanimously, by the general assembly and the convention on 17 August,[34] and two days later the assembly appointed five ministers (Alexander Henderson, Robert Douglas, Samuel Rutherford, Robert Baillie and George Gillespie) and three elders (the Earl of Cassillis, Lord Maitland and Wariston) to attend the Westminster assembly. They were to consult and conclude with that assembly on the furtherance of unity of church government and in drafting a confession of faith, catechism and directory of worship for both kingdoms.[35] After appointing a new commission of the kirk, with powers similar to that appointed the previous year, the assembly dissolved; the next assembly was to meet in Edinburgh on 29 May 1644.[36] Craighall as king's commissioner had taken very little part in the assembly's proceedings; he had made a few half-hearted objections to the solemn league and covenant, but in general Argyll and Alexander Henderson 'did so alwayes overawe' him and he gave no trouble.[37]

The draft of the solemn league and covenant, as approved by convention, assembly and English commissioners, was in the form of a declaration by the inhabitants of England and Scotland. They, 'liveing in on Iland wnder on King and of on true protestant reformed religione', having before them the glory of God, the honour and happiness of the king, and the liberty, peace and safety of the two kingdoms, and calling to mind the bloody plots of the enemies of God, had resolved to enter into a league and covenant whereby they bound themselves to six articles. First, they promised to strive to preserve 'the true protestant reformed religion in the church of Scotland in doctrine worship discipline and government according to the word of God and the reformation of religione in the church of England according to the same holy word and the example of the best reformed churches'. Secondly, they undertook to do all they could to extirpate popery, prelacy, superstition, heresy, schism, profaneness and whatever else was found contrary to God's will in both nations. Thirdly, they swore to do their best to preserve the rights and privileges of the parliaments and the liberties of both kingdoms, and to preserve the king's person and authority in the defence of true religion and the liberties of both kingdoms. They had, they declared, no intention of diminishing the king's just powers and greatness—phrases too vague to bring any comfort to the king. Fourthly, they swore to seek out and bring to trial all incendiaries, malignants and evil instruments who hindered the reformation of religion, or divided the king from his people or one kingdom from another. They undertook to observe inviolably the 1641 peace treaty, and finally swore to assist and defend all who entered this league and covenant with them, and that they would not withdraw from it or fall into 'detestable indifference or newtralitie'.[38]

The solemn league and covenant has often been assumed to be an entirely religious document, the insistence of the covenanters on its acceptance as the price of military aid being a symptom of the backward-looking religious mania of the Scots. In fact it was a 'civil league' as well as a 'religious covenant'. Only two of its six articles are concerned exclusively with religion (admittedly the first two, and in the event the most important). The aims of the two kingdoms are defined as including not only religious reform and unity, but also the preservation of peace and the 1641 treaty (with its provisions for closer union), and the securing of constitutional liberties.

Once the new covenant had been agreed and sent to London for ratification by parliament, the Scottish and English commissioners turned immediately to negotiating the details of a treaty to send an army to England. On 17 August, the same day that it approved the covenant, the convention made arrangements to raise money to pay for military preparations. An act provided for the raising of a tax of £120,000 Scots to pay the small force already being levied, and of a compulsory loan of £800,000 Scots.[39] The loan was ostensibly to be used to pay and supply the army in Ireland, and was to be repaid when the English parliament sent money to pay its debts to that army, but there seems little doubt that the reason that the convention voted such a large sum for that army was that it was assumed it would be withdrawn from Ireland to form the nucleus of the army which would invade England, so the loan was really intended to finance that invasion. Thus when, in the event, the army in Ireland remained there, most of the loan was diverted to pay for the raising of a new army in Scotland. On 18 August the convention issued a proclamation ordering all men between sixteen and sixty to be ready to join together to form regiments on forty-eight hours' notice; the next day the English commissioners gave details of their request for 11,000 or more Scots troops.[40]

The treaty for sending an army to England was approved by the convention on 26 August. It laid down that the solemn league and covenant should be sworn in both England and Scotland, and that an army should be levied in Scotland to advance the ends of the new covenant. The size of the army was not specified in the draft treaty but was later fixed at 18,000 foot, 2,000 horse and 1,000 dragoons, plus a train of artillery.[41] Scotland was to pay for levying and arming the army but was to be repaid by England when peace was restored. The parliament of England would pay the army £30,000 sterling monthly and, since this would not amount to full pay, the arrears would be paid by England after the war. Each kingdom undertook not to make peace or any truce without the advice and consent of the other. Scotland gave the public faith of the kingdom that while in England the Scots army would only be used to advance the ends expressed in the covenant and England undertook to assist Scotland on the same conditions as Scotland now agreed to help England, if Scotland was troubled by rebellion or invasion. Parliament also promised to send ships to the west coast of Scotland to guard it against any invasion from Ireland.[42] Once completed the treaty was sent, like the covenant, to London to be approved by parliament.

The English commissioners had reached Edinburgh on 7 August. Within ten days of their arrival the solemn league and covenant had been agreed, and within twenty days the treaty for sending an army to England had also been completed.[43] This remarkable expedition is an indication of how anxious both parties were to reach agreement as news of royalist successes in the English civil war continued. 'Wise observers wondered to see a matter of that Importance, carried through upon so little Deliberation or Debate',[44] but in the circumstances it seemed that an alliance of the covenanters and the English parliament must be made as soon as possible if it was to save parliament from defeat. As it was, the long delays in sending English commissioners to Scotland prevented a Scots army coming to the aid of parliament in 1643.

The Westminster assembly and parliament also showed a sense of urgency over the new covenant, and approved it within two weeks of receiving it at the end of August. But urgency did not prevent them from making some important alterations. The solemn league and covenant was extended to include Ireland as well as England and Scotland, and changes were made in the wording of the first article of the covenant, designed to avoid committing parliament too explicitly to following the Scottish model in reforming the Church of England, while not going so far as to risk rejection of the alterations by the Scots. Thus the draft covenant had talked of the need to preserve 'the true protestant reformed religion in the church of Scotland . . . according to the word of God' and of reforming the Church of England 'according to the same holy word'.[45] After revision by the Westminster assembly and parliament the words 'true protestant' were omitted, and for 'according to the word of God' was substituted a neutral phrase, 'against our common enemies', while the Church of England was now to be reformed 'according to the word of God' instead of 'according to the same holy word'. The only other major alteration was the substitution of a vaguely worded promise to preserve the peace and union between the two kingdoms, in place of the undertaking to preserve inviolably the 1641 peace treaty.[46] Many members of both houses of parliament would have liked to make further changes to make it clear that parliament was not obliging itself to set up a presbyterian church in England. Opposition to the covenant came from all religious groups, for many feared that Scots military intervention in England would lead to the Scots trying to dictate to parliament in political as well as religious matters. But the need for the help of a Scots army was so great that such misgivings were over-ridden. The treaty detailing the terms on which the Scots army would enter England was accepted by parliament without any significant alterations or additions, except the fixing of the size of the army at 21,000 men.[47]

On 26 August the convention, continuing its preparations for the invasion of England, wrote to the officers of the army in Ireland announcing that the English parliament wished to recall them from Ireland and asking for their advice as to whether the whole army should leave Ireland or whether garrisons should be left behind.[48] Leven was re-appointed general and the convention appointed shire colonels and committees of war, similar to those set up in the Bishops' Wars, to see that men were trained, armed and supplied. They were given responsibility for keeping order in the shires and implementing orders sent by the convention.[49] The convention then adjourned until 3 January 1644 (the first occasion on which a convention of estates had ever been adjourned to a second session)[50] after appointing a committee of estates to govern Scotland in the interim and see the solemn league and covenant and the treaty implemented. When an army was levied the committee was to divide into two parts, one to sit at Edinburgh or elsewhere in Scotland while the other accompanied the army. The convention did not so far humour Hamilton as to appoint him or any of his supporters members of the committee of estates, though some nobles who had at one time been covenanters but who had shown royalist sympathies in the past few years—like the Earl of Dunfermline—were elected, probably in the hope of persuading them to abandon their royalism.[51]

When the committee of estates heard that the English parliament had approved the solemn league and covenant and the treaty it summoned a frequent (well frequented) meeting of the committee on 12 October to consider them.[52] On 11 October the commission of the kirk accepted the covenant, as amended by parliament, 'As agrieing with the Draught wnanimouslie and cheerfully approvine and imbraced by the late Generall Assembly and Conventions of estates', and ordered it to be sworn and subscribed by all ministers; refusers were to be regarded as enemies of religion.[53] The next day the committee of estates joined the commission in heartily approving the covenant 'as not materiallie

18

differing from the forme read in the [general] Assemblie',[54] and
ordered it to be sworn and signed by all subjects. Any who refused
would have their goods and rents confiscated and would not be
allowed to hold public offices.[55]

Did the covenanters really regard the changes made in the new
covenant by the English parliament as insignificant? Probably
they realised well enough that some of the alterations were designed
to leave a door open in England for Independency, but their
interests were much more seriously threatened by what seemed
the prospect of an inevitable royalist victory in England if they
did not quickly send an army there than by a few alterations in
the covenant. They therefore decided to ignore the changes; after
all, parliament had still bound itself to reform religion in England
according to the word of God, and the covenanters were confident
not only that they could demonstrate convincingly that this implied presbyterianism, but also that the Scots army would quickly
win the civil war for parliament, and that this would put them in
such a strong position in England that they could ensure that their
interpretation of the covenant was accepted. In such circumstances
verbal changes in the covenant would have little importance.

The commissioners of the kirk, the committee of estates and
the English commissioners had signed the covenant on 13 October.[56] The privy council soon added what authority it had left to
the order for all subjects to sign, and on 2 November those councillors who were willing to do so signed; the names of those who
refused were sent to the committee of estates.[57] The king had
written to the council and to the conservators protesting plain-
tively at the convention's alliance with the English parliament—
'we believe they have forgot they have a King'—but they refused
to register his letters and copies of them were sent to parliament.[58]
Thus the covenanters finally committed themselves to intervention
in England in alliance with parliament. To many the new war was,
partly at least, a crusade, designed to spread true reformed church
government, worship and discipline to England and Ireland. But
the covenanters were careful to stress that the war, like the 1640
invasion of England, was defensive and not offensive. They were
fighting to preserve the religious and constitutional liberties they

had won from the king, for these would be endangered if he triumphed in England. Samuel Rutherford wrote at length on the subject; wars might be defensive in essence though 'offensive by accident'. The two did not differ physically, in outward form, but only in intention. Thus an invasion of England against the king could be defensive. 'Better the King weep for the childish trifle of a prerogative than Popery be erected and three Kingdoms be destroyed'.[59]

Proceedings were soon begun against prominent refusers of the covenant. On 6 November the Duke of Hamilton and the Earls of Morton, Roxburgh, Kinnoull, Southesk and Lanark were ordered to appear within ten days and sign. Other Scots who were in England—the Duke of Lennox, the Earls of Crawford, Montrose, Tullibardine, Traquair, Dumfries, Carnwath and Forth, Lords Ogilvy, Eythin and Reay, Sir James Galloway (master of requests) and William Murray (gentleman of the king's bedchamber)—were given until 12 January to appear. Later they were all forbidden to dispose of any of their property (including offices) in Scotland, to prevent them trying to evade the penalties for not signing. By 16 November only one of the six nobles ordered to sign by then—Southesk—had done so; the other five were declared enemies to religion and arrangements were made to devote their incomes to public uses.[60] Action was also taken against the Earl of Winton and Lords Seton and Sempill. Roxburgh signed the new covenant in December rather than lose his estates, but none of the Scots nobles in England had signed by 12 January and their incomes were confiscated, while orders were given for the imprisonment in Edinburgh castle of the Earl of Morton, Lord Seton and several lesser refusers of the covenant.[61] When the convention had first met in June the covenanters had tolerated the opposition of moderate royalists, but now that their position had been strengthened by the raising of an army in Scotland and the alliance with parliament they showed themselves determined to crush all sign of opposition. Except for isolated incidents there was little public and open opposition at first to the solemn league and covenant. Some of the royalist nobles refused it, but most signed to save themselves from trouble and persecution.[62] The new covenant was greeted with far less enthusiasm than the national covenant had been, but it was generally accepted.

This marked the complete failure of Hamilton's attempt to prevent the covenanters making an alliance with the English parliament. Yet at first the king still retained confidence in him, and when in August Montrose again advocated a royalist rising in Scotland Charles refused to sanction it.[63] The fact that Hamilton had no longer any useful advice or positive policy to offer was demonstrated when he and his supporters sent Traquair to the king with a message. They congratulated themselves on the fact that no Scots forces had entered England in the summer of 1643; this was all that Hamilton had undertaken to achieve. Unfortunately this policy had been based on the assumption that the king would completely defeat parliament in 1643 provided the Scots did not intervene and, in spite of many successes, the king had failed to do this. In these circumstances Hamilton had no idea what to do next. He assured Charles (through Traquair) that he and his friends were ready to fight and die for him, but, since Charles had previously ordered that the covenanters were to be left to be the first to break the peace, they had decided to do nothing; in any case there was not the least hope of a royalist rising having any success—unless arms, ammunition, men and money were sent from England. He therefore unhelpfully advised the king to prepare for the worst.[64]

The following month he and other royalists met at Kelso with about 1,000 men, using Lady Roxburgh's funeral as a pretext for the gathering, but, gloomily deciding that there was no hope of a successful royalist rising, dispersed peacefully.[65] Hamilton and Lanark fled to England—their mother had begun raising men for the covenanters' army from Hamilton's lands[66]—but when they reached Oxford in mid-December the king denounced Hamilton for betraying him, and had him imprisoned. He was not released until the end of the English civil war in 1646. Lanark was left free and retained the office of secretary, but his movements were restricted. He fled to London after a few weeks, and parliament sent him back to Scotland where, not surprisingly considering

the way the king had treated him and his brother, he swore the
solemn league and covenant.[67] The charges which were soon
made against Hamilton by his enemies among the royalists at
Oxford were mainly unjust. He had not betrayed the king, but as
usual he had been over-confident and sure of his own ability, and
had led the king to expect far more from his activities in Scotland
than he could achieve. He was certainly incompetent, but not a
traitor.

THE ARMY OF THE COVENANT

As soon as the convention had risen (at the end of August 1643)
the committee of estates had got down to the work of raising an
army. Detailed orders were sent on 1 September to the shire
colonels and committees of war for training men and appointing
officers. The numbers of horse and foot to be raised in each shire
were set down, a total of about 32,000 foot and 2,720 horse.[68]
This was far more than the 21,000 men called for in the treaty as
ratified by the English parliament, which may indicate that the
Scots, in the hope of bringing about a quick victory in England,
were willing to send more men there than parliament was willing
to employ; on the other hand the committee of estates may merely
have been allowing for the probable inefficiency of the levy by
calling for far more men than were required to ensure that sufficient men actually appeared, or it may have intended the surplus
to remain in Scotland to guard against invasion or rebellion. The
committee agreed to delays in paying the remainder of the Brotherly Assistance and the arrears of the army in Ireland, though insisting that £60,000 sterling should be provided immediately for the
latter. The English commissioners offered to pay the arrears in
a variety of ways, but the most the army's officers would agree
was that if parliament paid the army £60,000 sterling and gave
it confiscated lands, then 5,000 men, half the army, would come
to Scotland to join in the invasion of England.[69]

A further complication in the position of the army in Ireland
was now emerging. In September 1643 the king agreed to a
cessation of arms or truce with the Irish rebels, and the royalist
government in Dublin (under whose orders came, in theory, the

Scots army in Ireland), ordered the army to observe the truce. But the English parliament was not a party to the cessation; indeed it was largely designed to allow the king to transfer troops from Ireland to England for use against parliament, so if the Scots army adhered to the cessation parliament might refuse to continue paying it. If, on the other hand, it continued hostilities against the Irish rebels, the rebels could now concentrate all their forces against them. Lacking money and supplies of all kinds as they did, the Scots would have difficulty in opposing the Irish, especially if weakened by sending 5,000 men to Scotland. The committee of estates instructed Major General Monro not to accept or reject the cessation until the English parliament had been consulted.[70] As for the king, he was anxious that the Scots army should remain in Ireland, so that it could not take part in the invasion of England.

The evident desire of most of the officers of the Scottish army in Ireland to remain there (though there were divisions among them on this point)[71] and the news of the cessation soon led the English parliament and the committee of estates to accept that it should stay—parliament voted a denunciation of the cessation on 30 October.[72] But the army officers, who seem to have been of the opinion that the best way to get their demands satisfied was to refuse to do whatever they were asked, now professed great reluctance to remain in Ireland. However, after much further negotiating, the army, the English commissioners in Edinburgh and the committee of estates reached agreement. On clothes and £10,000 sterling being sent to the army at once it would remain in Ireland. £50,000 sterling more would be sent by 1 February 1644, and if it had not arrived by then the army would be transported to England to join the Scottish army there. While the Scots army remained in Ireland the English conceded that its commander should command all parliament's forces in Ireland.[73]

By the 1641 peace treaty it had been agreed that the town of Berwick should not be garrisoned, but there were now rumours that royalist forces in the north of England would try to seize the town to hinder the invasion of England by the Scots—Carlisle had already been seized by royalists. Therefore parliamentary

forces occupied the town and the English commissioners negotiated a new treaty with the committee of estates whereby the
Scots would provide a garrison for Berwick, and parliament
would add £1,000 sterling monthly to the £30,000 monthly it had
already undertaken to pay for the Scots army, to help pay the
garrison.[74] The three troops of horse and 600 foot that the convention had ordered to be levied in July marched into Berwick
at the end of September;[75] these were the first Scots troops to cross
the border on behalf of parliament. 'So the play is begun: the
good Lord give it a happie end'.[76]

The committee of estates gave orders on 28 September for the
mustering of all men between sixteen and sixty in the shires between 4 and 20 October. The shire colonels were to choose from
them the number of men already laid down to come from the
shires. Those chosen were then to march to rendezvous appointed
by the general.[77] Needless to say, all did not go as smoothly as
intended and a constant stream of supplementary orders concerning the levies had to be issued.[78] The treaty for sending the army
to England was returned to Scotland after being ratified by
parliament, and was signed by the committee of estates on 28
November. Four days before this a joint meeting of the committee
and the privy council had granted commissions to Leven as
general, Sir Alexander Hamilton as general of the artillery and
Sir Adam Hepburn of Humbie as treasurer of the army and
commissary general. Later David Leslie and William Baillie were
appointed major-general of the horse and lieutenant-general of
the foot respectively. Instructions were sent for 25,740 men to
rendezvous near Berwick on 29 December; money from the loan
ordered by the convention for the army in Ireland was to be used
to pay the soldiers their levy and transport money.[79]

The reduction of the number of men to assemble compared
with previous orders was mainly the result of omitting the
northern shires from those sending out men, probably partly
because of the difficulty of getting men levied in the Highlands
and partly because it was thought wise to retain troops in the
North East where royalist sympathies were strongest. In addition,
Argyll, Bute and Dunbarton were freed from sending men to the

rendezvous as 600 men were to be levied there to oppose Alexander Macdonald, who had appeared in the Isles with about 300 Irish papists and was rumoured to be expecting reinforcements from Ireland. Argyll was given by the committee of estates a commission to act as the king's lieutenant in suppressing these rebels[80]—who also claimed to be acting for the king.[81] This Alexander or Alaster Macdonald, Macdonnell or MacColla was the son of Col Macgillispeck or Macdonald (whose nickname, Col Keitach, is sometimes misleadingly given to his son). Col Keitach had made himself master of Colonsay after 1615, though Argyll's father had been granted the island by a royal charter. Argyll (or Lord Lorne as he then was) had legalised Col's position in the 1630s by giving him a lease of Colonsay; doubtless he had wished from the first to drive out the Macdonalds as the Campbells had recently driven them from Kintyre and Islay, but he delayed acting against Col until his father's death had put him in possession of his estates indisputably. On the first favourable opportunity after his father died, the First Bishops' War, Campbells from Islay had seized Colonsay for Argyll, capturing Col and two of his sons. Alexander had raided Islay with about eighty men in November 1640 and had joined the Irish rebels in 1641. Now, at the end of 1643, he had returned to the Isles to revenge himself on the Campbells, and perhaps in the hope of freeing his father and two brothers.[82]

On 4 December the committee of estates divided itself into two parts, appointing Argyll president of that part which was to accompany the army[83]—presumably it was understood that he would appoint a deputy lieutenant to suppress the rebels in the Isles. There had been many delays in raising and assembling the levies which were to form the army, for even though there was almost no open opposition to the solemn league and covenant many objected to paying the loan and tax imposed by the convention and to serving as soldiers. In spite of all difficulties, however, by the end of the year about the full number of troops with which the covenanters had undertaken to enter England—21,000 men— had assembled on the Borders.[84] But this was still less than the committee of estates had ordered to assemble, so the convention

of estates (which met from 3 to 11 January 1644) renewed orders
to the shires to send out the full number. Moreover the troops
which had reached the Borders were not nearly so well equipped
as had been ordered, and there was great difficulty in finding
sufficient provisions to feed them. On 8 January the convention
ordered the general and the committee of estates with the army
to go to the Borders and do what they thought fit for the good
of the army, and, in imitation of an expedient of the English
parliament, excise duties were imposed to raise money urgently
needed by the army.[85]

When the committee of estates with the army reached the
Borders it found the army in a sorry state. Very few horses to
carry baggage or ammunition had appeared, and many officers
had not arrived to take command of their men. Most of the supplies which the shires had been ordered to provide had not
arrived; the officers blamed the shires while the shires claimed
that they had given what was due from them to the officers. The
army was clearly in no fit condition to enter England with any
confidence, but it was fast consuming the provisions gathered to
feed it in the early stages of the invasion. Without money and
food it could not long subsist in the 'Barren wilderness' of the
Borders in winter. Therefore on 17 January the general and the
committee of estates with the army, meeting at Berwick, resolved
to march into England in two days' time; it was considered less
dangerous to invade England with an army in such poor condition than inactively to wait for reinforcements and supplies, for
while waiting the army might well become demoralised and begin to
disintegrate, while its continued quartering on the Eastern Borders
would place great burdens on the inhabitants of the area.[86]

The army of the covenant duly crossed the Tweed on 19 January
1644, with high hopes that it would soon win the war for the
English parliament. This, the covenanters dreamed, would put
them in a position to dictate a peace settlement in England.
Establishment of presbyterianism there would follow, pleasing
to God and securing the kirk's position. Limits on royal power
in England and closer union would protect Scotland's constitutional gains. Peace, prosperity, unity and Godly reformation

would be established in Britain. Effective action could then be taken to help Protestants on the Continent; ultimately covenanting armies might march on Rome itself.[87] Such was the dream at its most extreme. Doubtless many covenanters were less ambitious, more realistic, seeing intervention in England as primarily defensive, necessary to preserve their revolution in Scotland. Nevertheless the general mood was one of facile optimism. Many obvious questions as to the future remained unanswered, indeed virtually unasked. The achievements predicted for the army in England were immense; could it possibly live up to expectations? The fact that what precipitated the army into England on 19 January was not offensive zeal but necessity hardly seemed a good omen. Scotland already had an army in Ireland, and intervention in England might be expected to provoke royalist reaction within Scotland; could she then sustain a war on three fronts? Again, even if successful in England, was it realistic to expect the English to accept a peace on Scots terms? Would not such interference provoke resentment? The failure of the covenanters to achieve their goals in England in 1640–1 was a discouraging precedent.

So far the covenanters had moved on from success to success, which had convinced them of their own invincibility. Overconfidence and the logic of events now led them to attempt more than they could achieve.

CHAPTER TEN

Conclusion: The Triumph of the Covenanters

THE KIRK

The years after 1637 saw a religious revolution in Scotland. The Jacobean compromise in church polity was destroyed; presbyterian elements triumphed over episcopalian. Innovations in worship were abolished. In theology Arminian influences were rooted out in the name of pure Calvinist predestinarianism, though the federal theology which won general acceptance in its place tended to undermine predestination in other ways. In church-state relations the supremacy of parliament in civil matters and of the general assembly in ecclesiastical matters was asserted. The clerical estate disappeared from parliament, and in theory at least the general assembly became less a meeting of the estates than previously.

On the one hand this revolution went much further than any but a tiny minority had contemplated in 1637; on the other it did not go nearly as far as this minority and those who were converted to their doctrinaire Melvillian outlook wished. From one point of view the reform of the kirk marked the triumph of the extremists; from another it was a compromise. Most ministers agreed in the end not only to accept but to support actively all the changes that had been made as necessary and justifiable, but whereas the majority saw these reforms as final and were reluctant to contemplate going any further, many of the minority who had pushed through these reforms saw them as only the first steps towards a pure kirk. Much tension therefore remained in the kirk between moderate and radical ministers.

The success of the minority of more extreme ministers—above

all in securing the abolition of episcopacy (and its abolition as wrong in principle, not just as inexpedient)—is fairly easy to account for. With their years of opposition to royal religious policies, their zeal and organisation through conventicles and personal links, they were in a position to dominate the leadership of the opposition to the king by the ministers which they had helped to spark off. Aided by the lack of any constructive response from the king they gradually managed to widen the scope of resistance to his religious policies. At first opposition was limited to the latest innovations in worship represented by the new liturgy. Quickly this was extended to include, in turn, the Five Articles of Perth, royal domination of the kirk and the conduct of the bishops; and finally to the existence of any degree of royal influence in church matters, and the existence of bishops. Even when the Glasgow assembly deposed the bishops many ministers who accepted the necessity of this (to protect the kirk from corruption and royal control) were unhappy at condemning episcopacy in principle. Yet this was done, and soon such condemnation, on presbyterian principles of the parity of ministers, became one of the hallmarks of the kirk. Robert Baillie, so reluctant to denounce episcopacy in Scotland in 1637–8, within a few years became well known as an advocate of its abolition in England. Once such moderates had accepted that episcopacy was inexpedient it was hard to avoid the further step pressed by the radicals of strengthening the argument for its abolition by declaring it wrong in principle. The king's refusal to make concessions—or to make sincere ones—drove moderates to accept radical arguments.

So the zeal and leadership provided by the radicals were helped in winning acceptance for their ideas by the conduct of the king. But the successes of the doctrinaire presbyterian or Melvillian minority over the moderate majority of the ministers would have been impossible without one further aid: the support of the leading lay covenanters. The most radical of the reforms of the kirk in these years had far more united support from laymen than from ministers.

From the first this alliance was based on expediency rather than on agreement in principle. Lay covenanters on the one hand and radical ministers on the other were agreed that certain changes were needed in the kirk; but their reasons for desiring such changes were often entirely different. That they none the less worked together is not, however, simply a sign of cynicism; they did share some ambitions, and in their zeal to achieve them, faced by the obvious need to unite if the king was to be overcome, it was easy for them to overlook each other's differing motives and ultimate ambitions.

Such differing motives can be seen clearly over the abolition of the bishops. Radical ministers desired this on principle, to achieve parity of ministers and destroy the main instrument of royal control of the kirk. Nobles and to a lesser extent lairds and even burgesses wanted rid of bishops as they were rivalling their status in society, and because of their influence with the king and their power in government. Here the motives of lay covenanters and radical ministers were different but not directly incompatible. This was also true of their agreement over the fate of the clerical estate in parliament. Laymen wanted it abolished, no church commissioners being admitted in place of the bishops, in order to prevent the king again using the clerical estate to control elections to the lords of the articles and thus dominate parliament, as well as more generally to deprive clerics of any place in politics and government. For radicals, on the other hand, abolition of the clerical estate was simply, as with the removal of bishops, a matter of principle. It was a step towards separating church and state, ecclesiastical and civil power, in accordance with the theory of the two kingdoms, each supreme in its own sphere. Many moderate ministers would probably have liked to see representatives of the kirk continue to sit in parliament, but radicals and laymen combined to force on the kirk belief that for churchmen to hold civil office was wrong in principle.

The differing motives of these allies are perhaps most clearly seen over the matter of elders. Doctrinaire presbyterians saw their introduction into presbyteries as completing the membership of these courts as envisaged by Melville, and therefore supported the move. But instead of being men set apart from the laity for life, semi-clerical in status, the elders thus introduced were simply lay covenanters elected for short periods, many of whom were not even parish elders. Laymen insisted on entry into the presbyteries in this way in order to control them and dominate elections to the general assembly. Presbyterians accepted this since they needed this reinforcement of church courts by their lay allies if they were to overcome the moderate majority among their ministerial colleagues. They could square this conniving at lay power in the kirk with their principles by arguing that at least it was a step towards establishing a proper eldership. Similarly the domination of the general assembly by laymen was accepted by presbyterians since these laymen were necessary to push through radical reforms in church government, so long as a gesture towards Melvillian principles was made by calling these laymen elders.

Thus the 'second reformation' in Scotland was based on an unnatural alliance. The tensions inherent in this alliance began to emerge when it became clear that one of the allies, the lay covenanters, thought that reform had gone far enough while the other, the radical ministers, believed that much remained to be achieved. Lay interests had gained most from the alliance. They had gone along with the theory of the two kingdoms to the extent of excluding ministers from all civil courts and offices, from any direct part in civil affairs. But when it came to excluding laymen from ecclesiastical courts they succeeded in distorting the theory in order to gain increased power in the kirk. By defining themselves as elders they pushed their way into presbyteries and dominated the general assembly. The upholders of presbyterian principles were forced to accept this through their need for lay support. Thus in these years some of the Melvillian programme was achieved in form, but little in substance. The kirk had freed itself from royal control, but lay control was substituted.

Once the reforms of the general assemblies of 1638 and 1639 had been achieved the radical presbyterians found that they no longer had the lay support necessary to get further reforms accepted. And once the more moderate majority of ministers proved to have accepted the reforms already made (as most quickly did) it was they who increasingly became the allies of the laity; they were agreed that reform had gone far enough. They saw as the ultimate destination what radicals saw as only the first steps of the journey. The radicals found, indeed, that in achieving some of their ambitions they had made achievement of their ultimate ambitions harder than ever. They had achieved parity of ministers and moves towards the separation of church and state, but in doing so had greatly increased the hold of nobles and lairds on the kirk. This blocked further implementation of their programme. Making a reality of the two kingdoms by introducing a true Melvillian eldership would involve surrender by the laity of their new hold on the kirk, which would obviously not be done voluntarily. Regaining former church revenues for the kirk and abolishing lay patronage would naturally be opposed by lay vested interests. The changes in worship advocated by the radicals were no more palatable to most laymen than the innovations of Charles I.

Thus after 1641 the radical ministers in Scotland found themselves isolated so far as further reform was concerned. But they retained their conviction of their own righteousness, and could draw some consolation and hope for the future from two developments. Firstly, though they might be losing the support of most nobles and lairds they had won considerable popular support in some parts of the country. While nobles and lairds were taking a firm hold on the polity of the kirk radical ministers were securing the primary loyalty of many lesser lay covenanters, though it was not to be until the late 1640s that the importance of this compensation emerged. Secondly, radicals had great hopes of events in England. They found their progress in Scotland blocked by moderate ministers and lay covenanters, but would not their position be strengthened if the covenanting regime felt it necessary, in the interests of security, to make an alliance with English puritans? Such hopes may have been unrealistic, based on a facile equation of English puritanism with Scottish presbyterianism, but they combined with missionary enthusiasm and the need to defend the reformation already achieved in Scotland in winning the support of radical ministers for intervention in England. For most ministers adequate reform had been secured, but for a minority the hardest tasks still lay ahead.

How is this picture, of ministers manipulated by lay interests, compatible with the royalist accounts of the dictatorial power of covenanting ministers, of ministers free to persecute their social superiors, and powerful enough to do this effectively? Surely this suggests that the ministers were successful in asserting their power and independence in spiritual matters, and even that (as Melville had approved in practice if not in theory) the spiritual kingdom was dominating the temporal. Yet in fact the undoubted power of ministers in many areas to persecute anti-covenanters of all ranks was not so much a sign of their independence of lay control as of how sure the covenanting laity were of their grip on the ministers. An interesting analogy is provided by J. R. Tanner's interpretation of the place of parliament in Tudor England; its development and the growth of its privileges are to be explained not by its strength but by its weakness. 'It was the Tudor policy to rule by means of Parliament because the Tudor sovereigns were not afraid of Parliament'.[1] The covenanting laity used the kirk because they were not afraid of it. Ecclesiastical courts were useful to police the land just as pulpits were useful to spread propaganda, and the estates were willing to support their use for these purposes since they remained ultimately under lay control. Samuel Rutherford later recognised that this had been the case, that the kirk had allowed itself to be used as the state's police force, suppressing and punishing opposition, instead of concentrating on spiritual functions.[2] The need for lay support, and the irresistible temptation to accept such a role when the regime offered it, had led the kirk to compromise and allow itself to be used for secular purposes.

THE THREE ESTATES

In 1637 and the following years those politically active in Scottish (or at least in Lowland) society had united against its head, the king. In England a few years later revolt was to come through a split in the political nation; what is remarkable in Scotland is how united those who had a share of power in the community were in opposing the king. Of course there were royalists, a few of them active on the king's behalf, and many men remained passive, anxious to avoid trouble, but even after discounting covenanting propaganda it is the unity of the country behind the covenanting movement which is striking. The cause was taken up by many prominent men of all three estates as well as by great numbers of those of no estate. It is hard to see that tensions between the main elements in society contributed significantly to the revolt unless the narrow circle of the bishops and the king's other advisers be counted as such an element.

Admittedly this impression of unity may be caused partly by our ignorance of this society resulting from lack of research into it. It could also be argued that the semblance of unity was an illusion, or at least that it was artificial, in that it was achieved only in reaction to the errors and follies of Charles I. It is true that different groups in society had different (sometimes incompatible) grievances and ambitions, but these differences were easily overlooked since the king was held responsible for virtually all the various grievances, for thwarting the various ambitions. The unity of Scots society might thus be said to be a negative unity thrust on it by the existence of a common enemy and the need for common action if he was to be overcome, not the positive unity of completely shared interests. As in any society there were social tensions in Scotland, but these were partly disguised by shared hostility to the king, partly overcome by the bond between ranks in society provided by religion. But though negative in this sense the unity was none the less real, and that a large measure of positive unity underlay it is suggested by the fact that once victory was won the latent tensions which then emerged were relatively weak and incoherent. They proved controllable without tearing the covenanting movement apart. The vertical ties of kinship and feudalism, holding together men from the top to the bottom of society, on the whole proved more powerful than the horizontal bonds uniting men at each level of society— 'the ordering of society in Early Modern Europe tended to militate against class solidarity'.[3] Nobles might wish to increase their power, ideally to share it with no one, lesser landholders might hope for freedom from domination by nobles, but such conflicting interests were weakened by vertical ties and restrained by the need

19

for unity. Only when new tensions were produced by the disasters of the mid and late 1640s did the essential unity which had brought victory dissolve.

The unity of Scottish society in opposition to the king reached its peak in 1639–40, when his untrustworthiness was most evident and his attempts to subdue Scotland with an English army roused even men normally of royalist sympathies to action against him. After this there are signs of some decline in the extent of unity, with disputes over how much could justly be demanded of the king in 1640–1, and over attitudes to events in England in 1642–3. The solemn league and covenant drove some to break finally with the covenanters, but on the other hand the new crisis that engendered it helped to reunite the majority. The disunity which had appeared, however, showed little correlation with the various ranks of Scottish society. The bonds of society remained unbroken. The fears of Lord Napier and others that resistance to the king would lead to anarchy, a collapse of the social order, proved unjustified in the short term. The estates had gained a victory over the king without losing control of those of no estate, the commons. The Edinburgh mob had been raised to demonstrate when required but had never become a force in its own right. The grievances of the commons and the poor had not become articulate. Events had pushed the covenanters on from demanding moderate religious reform to carrying out religious revolution. To protect this—and themselves—from the king's vengeance and to satisfy other grievances they had moved on to constitutional revolution. There had been changes in the relative positions of the estates, but no social revolution, unless the redefining of the society's relationship with its head be held to constitute one. What is perhaps most surprising about the changes in the relationships of the estates to each other is not that they took place at all, but that they were so limited.

Political and religious divisions are most obvious among the nobility, but in many cases this seems rather an indication of the central part they played in Scottish society than of any particular factiousness among them. They form the smallest estate, and the one about which most is known, so the divisions that existed among them are more obvious than divisions elsewhere. More-over, for any faction to receive attention and win support it needed noble leadership to give it respectability. Lairds, burgesses and lesser men might disagree with aspects of the policies of the covenanters, or with the covenanting movement altogether, but without noble spokesmen their viewpoints were likely to have little influence and to go unrecorded.

Throughout these years the noble leadership of the covenanting movement was accepted without question; the nobility were the natural leaders of the community. The fact that a considerable proportion of nobles had royalist or Catholic sympathies (or both), and that many nobles were reluctant to make an alliance with the English parliament in 1643 led to action being taken against individual nobles with the support of the other estates. But this led to no discernible suspicion of the nobility as such. Only a minority of nobles might whole-heartedly support the solemn league and covenant, but the right of this minority to dominate the movement was taken for granted. None the less it may be that even some covenanting nobles had doubts as to the future. They had led opposition to the king, and retained control of it. But might not justifying resistance to the head of a hierarchical society eventually stir up questions as to their own place in the hierarchy, especially as a hierarchy in the church had been declared ungodly? The longer a final settlement was delayed the more likely such questions were to arise. The extreme ministers with their dan-gerous ideas had been controlled, but they had not abandoned their ambitions. Again, the powers of lairds and burgesses in parliament had been increased, and the principle that each estate should be equally represented in parliamentary committees had been accepted. Admittedly the lairds and burgesses had not made full use of this improvement in their constitutional position, being mainly content to follow the lead of the nobles. Thus in commis-sions to negotiate with the king or the English parliament each estate had equal representation; but usually the nobles did virtu-ally all the talking. The burgesses especially often seemed little more than observers. But would this always be so? The lairds and burgesses had on several occasions been prepared to go further than the majority of nobles; the more extreme covenanting nobles had been ready to use this support of the other estates against their more moderate peers, and had sanctioned their constitutional advances for this purpose. (The parallel with the way radical ministers had called in lay support against their moderate colleagues is obvious.) This had involved removing any formal constitutional privileges from the nobility. It was only the traditions of deference of a hierarchic society—and of course their positions as great landlords and feudal superiors—which now gave the nobles pre-eminence in the regime. Any future challenge to their position in the regime need involve no change in the constitution of parliament or its committees. The 1641 settlement with the king had temporarily regained the nobility some formal recognition of their pre-eminence; the government of the country reverted to the privy council, and as was traditional the majority of the councillors were nobles. But the question of intervention in the English civil war so divided the council that the more extreme covenanting nobles had to call in parliamentary committees (with equal representation of all estates) to maintain their policies. That they could not rule through a largely noble council and had to rely on the support of the other estates was clearly demonstrated.

In formal constitutional terms the lairds had gained most in the struggle against the king. They had made good their claim to be recognised as a separate estate of the realm in place of the clergy (another example of laymen taking advantage of those parts of the theory of the two kingdoms that suited them). Their effective strength in parliament had been almost doubled by their gaining the right for each commissioner to have one vote instead of each shire. In local government they dominated the shire committees of war and the collecting of taxes. Together with the nobles their places in presbyteries and the general assembly gave them a large say in ecclesiastical matters. The lairds formed the backbone of the covenanting movement, and the increase in their status which resulted was reflected in both church and state.

The burgesses had been the last of the estates to join wholeheartedly in opposing the king. Recognising that they were no great power in the land, they awaited the example of the other estates and the leadership of Edinburgh. Yet once they had declared themselves they soon proved the most united and the most radical of the estates. Partly this unity may be an illusion arising from their tradition of all publicly supporting whatever policy a majority had agreed in private. None the less the fact that this tradition could survive (with minor exceptions) the events of these years in itself suggests that the estate really was basically united. Explaining why the burgesses became the most zealously covenanting of the three estates is not altogether easy. They had some specific grievances against the crown; high taxes which fell most heavily on them, royal interference in burgh government, and so on. As they had gained the least from the plundering of former church property, they had the least in ill-gotten gains to need protecting from the claims of a powerful and independent kirk. It might be suggested that as the estate with the least political power (and perhaps the least political ambitions) the burgesses had least reason to fear the kirk's claims to a dominating position in society. Kirk sessions and burgh councils had long co-operated amicably in local government in many burghs, and they tended not to see each other's ambitions as conflicting. Indeed since the reformation there had been ample evidence that the kirk's ideal had a strong appeal in the burghs—even if these ideals failed to stimulate capitalism and economic prosperity and thus provide a link between Calvinism and the rise of capitalism. Discipline, frugality, hard work and intense earnestness as urged by the more extreme ministers were more likely to find an echo in the hearts of merchants and craftsmen than in those of feudal landlords. It is perhaps no coincidence but a sign that this alliance was recognised that the burgh commissioners were the only laymen allowed to remain in the general assembly without accepting redefinition as elders.

In secular matters also the burgesses tended to be more ready for radical change than the other estates. They had a smaller stake in the *status quo*; less need, for example, to fear that strict curbs on the king might undermine their own social position. But their radicalism at this time should not be exaggerated—it is only really evident when compared with the conservatism of the other estates.

Burgesses might demand their say in parliament and equal representation on committees, but they knew their place; though prepared on occasion to argue for their point of view, they still accepted the role of the nobility as spokesmen for the regime.

THE KING AND THE UNION

In his visit to Scotland in 1641 King Charles had agreed to limitations on his power which left him as what a few years before he had said he would rather die than be, a Doge of Venice, a figurehead. To the mistake of ignoring the grumbling discontent which underlay his Scottish subjects' obedience to his policies before 1637, he had added error after error in dealing with resistance to his orders. He had wasted long months in trying to pretend that the situation in Scotland was not serious. By the time he had at last resolved on decisive action and openly denounced the activities of his opponents, forbidding them to hold further meetings on pain of treason, the opposition had been strong enough and well organised enough to defy him and to reply by compiling and signing the national covenant. After this Charles had embarked on the disastrous policy of negotiating and making concessions while at the same time preparing armies to crush the covenanters. To have had any hope of success this policy required that the king's forces should be raised quickly and defeat his enemies promptly. But he had failed to assemble an army in 1638 and the forces he had gathered in 1639 and 1640 had been totally inadequate. Meanwhile the duplicity of his attempts to placate the covenanters by concessions while preparing for war had become obvious, leading them to the conclusion that in no circumstances could his word be trusted. This led them to enlarge their demands gradually in order to provide guarantees for the changes they had originally sought, the withdrawal of religious innovations. In addition advantage was taken of the king's weakness to demand redress of a wide variety of non-religious grievances and satisfaction of many personal and sectional ambitions. What had begun as a revolt with very limited aims broadened into the achievement of religious and constitutional revolutions in Scotland and attempts to provoke and inspire similar revolutions in England in the interests of Scotland's security.

In the 1641 settlement the king admitted defeat, in the vain hope that this would win him support, or at least neutrality, from the covenanters with regard to events in England. Deposition of the bishops deprived him of the instruments through which he had controlled the kirk and parliament, of some of his most trusted advisers and councillors. His right to appoint a royal commissioner to the general assembly was not questioned, but in practice his representative was defied if he was present, and his absence was ignored if he was not. Similarly his right to attend parliament personally or through a commissioner proved an empty privilege. With no bishops and no lords of the articles he had no way of imposing his will on rebellious estates. Triennial parliaments and the need for parliamentary approval of appointments of officers of state, councillors and judges meant that he would have to rule with the consent of the estates.

Few other specific limitations were placed on his power; he had agreed in general terms that ecclesiastical matters should be settled by the general assembly, civil ones by parliament, and this could be used to justify depriving him of virtually any power. In any case the political realities of the situation made formal constitutional restraints superfluous for the time being. Thus the militia question, so central to the 1642 crisis in England, did not arise in the 1641 settlement in Scotland. With the country firmly in the hands of the covenanters and the examples of 1639 and 1640 to show that the king was incapable of raising strong forces in Scotland, there was no need to risk a deadlock in the negotiations by insisting on a formal concession from the king on this point. In any case, as Charles himself was to remark in 1646, 'If the pulpits teach not obedience . . . the king will have but small comfort of the militia'.[4] In Scotland both pulpits and parliament were in the hands of his enemies.

As it worked in practice, the 1641 settlement deprived the king of all power in Scotland. Even in minor matters he was obeyed only if it suited the covenanters. Yet they probably had not really wanted this. It was the justifiable fear that Charles did not fully

accept their triumph, and that he would try to overthrow them
once he overcame his enemies in England, that forced the covenanters to rule Scotland without him after 1641. Perhaps this comes
close to saying that the covenanters would not allow any power
to a king unless he agreed not to exercise it; that they would allow
power to a godly magistrate but that no magistrate would ever
be godly enough for them. Having tasted power the covenanters
were reluctant to surrender any of it. Yet on the other hand it was
natural that they should seek security for their revolution, and
under the union of the crowns and the consequent absentee
monarchy the 1641 settlement did not provide this. The king still
had a potential power base beyond their control, in England. If
the Scottish revolution was to be secure it would have to be exported. Without the complication (which of course underlay the
whole crisis) provided by the union, some attempt might have
been made to work a mixed constitution with power shared by
king and estates; with that complication, it became inevitable that
the estates would monopolise power.

The history of Scotland throughout the seventeenth century
was dominated by the question of relations with England. Geographical neighbours with many common interests, linked by the
union of the crowns, the complete separation of England and
Scotland, a return to mutual independence, seemed inconceivable.
Yet the two kingdoms differed too much in history and traditions,
in customs and manners, in society, constitution, law and religion
for complete amalgamation. What type of union, how close an
association would best serve the interests of both kingdoms? The
union of the crowns was of course merely personal, a dynastic acci-
dent(though one widely greeted as a happy dispensation). Early
efforts by James I and VI to bring about a closer union had failed,
neither country being ready for it and mutual suspicion still being
strong. However, as James and Charles I became increasingly anglicised they began to try to unite the kingdoms more closely by
anglicising Scotland. Seeing the differences between kingdoms
which now had a common ruler as anachronistic, they worked to
lessen them. But inevitably they chose England as the model into
which Scotland should be brought into conformity, rather than vice

versa. Not only was England by far the richer and more powerful of the two kingdoms but it had much else to lead a monarch to prefer it to Scotland. The rule of law and order was more firmly established, the nobility was more subservient, more respect was paid to the crown, the established religion was more genteel and obsequious. Needless to say, such less attractive features of English life as the power of parliament were not to be exported to Scotland.

Scotland gained in security by the union of the crowns, and was flattered to see a Scottish king on the English throne. The union did not at first seem to threaten Scotland's identity with absorption by her great neighbour. But as James VI and Charles I became English in manner, outlook and policy, satisfaction with the union, or rather with the form of the union, turned to bitterness and suspicion. It seemed now that the union undermined rather than strengthened the security of Scotland. Instead of helping to protect Scotland the union was enabling absentee kings to introduce foreign influences and institutions, destroying in particular her religion. It was anglicising policies that were mainly responsible for driving Scotland to rebellion in 1637. Charles, intent on reforming and dominating the kirk so that it could not rebel or oppose him, overlooked the possibility that he might instead be driving it (and indeed the whole country) into rebellion. His father had routed the supporters of Andrew Melville, and in the early years of Charles' reign the ministers who looked back to the good old days when the kirk had been free from royal control and hoped that it would one day again be free were a small minority. But Charles' attempts to reform the kirk on anglican and (so it seemed to many Scots) popish lines roused a general atmosphere of fear, distrust and suspicion in Scotland which led many laymen and ministers to recall the days when the kirk had been freer and more aggressive. The plight of the kirk came to be taken as symbolic of Scotland's position under the union of the crowns.

At first those opposing the king thought they could cure Scotland's ills by persuading him to change his policies. His intransigence led them on to new demands which resulted in the transformation of the kirk and the constitution. But even this proved inadequate. It was impossible to control the king while his freedom of action in England remained. The covenanters were driven on to the conclusion that Scotland could not be safe under the existing terms of union. It was not feasible to end the union; Charles' position as legitimate king of Scotland was virtually unquestioned, and obviously he would not relinquish his English crown. In any case any attempt to break the union would be interpreted in England as a hostile move, and the covenanters were realistic enough to know that to alienate opinion in England would be fatal to their cause. Moreover the covenanters were not anti-English. They did not try to unite Scotland by stirring up traditional hatreds. They accepted that Scotland's future lay in union, that the kingdoms sharing the British Isles were inevitably interdependent.

It was the form of union which was damaging Scotland. The covenanters' cure for this was not less union but more. Personal union had increased effective royal power. To counter this, union at other levels was needed. Religious unity, so that English bishops could not threaten the kirk. Links between parliaments to discuss matters of mutual interest and prevent the king using the resources of one country against the other. Provision for Scots interests to be taken into account in foreign policy and wars. Free trade, commercial co-operation and mutual naturalisation to bring prosperity and closer links between the people of the two kingdoms. Thus Scotland would gain security. But the English parliament showed little interest in such schemes. Alliance with the Scots might be valuable, but closer union on the covenanters' terms seemed suspiciously like replacing English domination of Scotland under what was supposed to be an equal union with Scottish domination of England. There was some truth in such fears. Missionary zeal, self-righteousness and confidence instilled by success, greed for power and the search for security led many covenanters to mean by closer union a Scots-dominated one. In 1640–1 they failed to make the English parliament make more than vague gestures in favour of closer union; the opportunity seemed to have been lost. But parliament's need for Scots help in 1643 offered a second chance, and this time the covenanters were determined not to be satisfied with any settlement that did not provide for closer union as they understood it. Robert Baillie's hopes that the Scots commissioners then sent to London 'would get the guiding of all the affairs both of this [English] State and Church'[5] was widely shared. The naivety and impracticability of such hopes were soon to become apparent.

THE SCOTTISH REVOLUTION

The study of revolutions in general, and of other early modern European revolutions in particular, can help us see the Scottish revolution in a wider context, throwing light on it by the contrasts as well as by the similarities which emerge. But perhaps first some justification of the use of the word in connection with Scotland in the mid-seventeenth century is necessary.

Strict Marxists can be excused for complaining that in recent seventeenth-century studies 'the very concept of "revolution" is being used in an unscientific spirit',[6] but common usage permits a wider definition of the word than this implies. It is, none the less, worth noting J. H. Elliott's doubts as to its usefulness in the context of early modern Europe, on the grounds that its use tends to lead to connotations derived from later revolutions being read back into the earlier period. As he says, connotations of major economic, social and political developments, of 'violent, irresistible and permanent change in the political and constitutional structure', the urge to break with the past and construct a new order are often contained in the word. Class conflict and the revolutionary organisation of later revolutions are assumed to have existed in earlier ones.[7] Use of the words tends to make historians look for innovation when in fact renovation was being sought.[8] Revolutions are assumed to imply structural weaknesses in a society, though in reality 'Political disagreements may, after all, be no more and no less than political disagreement—a dispute about the control and exercise of power'.[9] These points clearly need consideration before using the term 'Scottish revolution'. If the word does always imply new 'progressive' ideas emerging and basic changes in the structure of society resulting almost irresistibly

from its earlier weaknesses and contradictions, then it is mislead
ing in this context. Ministers looked back to the (partly mythical)
pristine glory of the kirk. Nobles sought to retain and restore
their position in society and their political power. The ideology
(Elliott also questions the value of this term) by which the
covenanters justified their actions was old-fashioned. Little of what
they did or said was new.

However, provided the dangers of the words are borne in
mind, there can be no real objection to its use in the Scottish
context; it may have limitations, but then so does any alternative
available. Events in Scotland in and after 1637 amounted to more
than a mere *coup d'état*. The structure of society may have changed
little, but the removal of any real power from the king put vastly
more power than before into the hands of the estates. This was a
major change in the character of the government of the country
brought about by violence. To look ahead, the continuing crisis
caused by the inability of the covenanters to reach a final settlement without involving England, and the disasters which followed
from the consequent intervention in England, were to bring some
questioning of the social structure, demands for social change,
and a shift of power within society. That these later developments
had not yet emerged by 1644 highlights the artificiality of trying
to draw a clear line between rebellion and revolution, since, as in
Scotland, many 'revolutions' begin as limited rebellions. Apart
from anything else, such a distinction inevitably leads in many
cases to the judging of the character of an upheaval by its success;
obviously a rebellion quickly suppressed cannot develop into a
wide-ranging revolution. More attention should perhaps be paid
to the way in which rebellions or revolutions evolve after the first
outbreak. By showing how revolts often change in character as
they develop this would emphasise the danger of deducing causes
not from the immediate revolt but from its ultimate results. As
in Scotland, weaknesses in the structure of society may be more
caused by revolution or rebellion than responsible for causing
them. The real revolutionary element in such upheavals may
sometimes lie not in bringing political structure into line with
developments in society but in causing—through political change

—changes in society which then require further, more radical, political change. In interactions between politics and society it is not always the latter which takes the initiative. Of course it is true that social tensions which appear long after a revolt has begun can often be seen to have their roots in long-term social changes which preceded the revolt; but to claim them for this reason as the real, if unconscious, causes of the revolt is not always legitimate. Such latent tensions may develop and become serious only through the events of the revolt itself. There need be nothing inevitable about them.

A convenient introduction to modern theories of revolution is provided by Lawrence Stone's discussion (and development) of such theories in connection with the English revolution.[10] Serious lack of harmony between the social system and the political system is seen as fundamental to revolutions. To use an ugly but convenient term, this is multiple dysfunction, and is caused by some development in society or in its ruling élite which controls its political system, or in both. (Of course in practice the social and political systems cannot be completely separated, but the distinction is none the less useful.) Tension of some sort between society and political system is of course universal. If change is slow, and adjustments are made in the political system to keep in step with society (or vice versa) such dysfunction may not be dangerous. But if change is rapid and profound a sense of deprivation and alienation may spread to many sectors of society at once. Such multiple dysfunction 'may be all but incurable within the existing political system'.[11] Stone concentrates on multiple dysfunction caused by developments in society, but when we try to apply this analysis to Scotland it is clear that dysfunction there was caused mainly by a swift and drastic change in the political system resulting from the union of the crowns. Absentee monarchy made former methods—constitutional as well as unconstitutional—of controlling or influencing the king irrelevant at a time when the monarchy was exerting and extending its power vigorously.

Multiple dysfunction creates a potentially revolutionary situation; much then depends on the condition and attitude of the ruling élite. It may make errors in dealing with the situation while failures, whether arising from incompetence or from misfortune, may discredit it. 'What is ultimately fatal, however, is the compounding of its errors by intransigence'—by failing to anticipate the need for reform, by blocking peaceful, constitutional adjustment. This 'unites the various deprived elements in single-minded opposition to it, and drives them down the narrow road to violence'. Opinion polarises, what are 'naturally and normally a series of fractional and shifting tensions and conflicts within a society' become coherent. Revolution thus becomes possible 'when a condition of dysfunction meets an intransigent élite'.[12] Clearly there is much here of relevance to Scotland, though the regime of Charles I had suffered no sudden disaster which discredited it by 1637. Charles' intransigence had exactly the effect suggested. It drove peaceful protest into revolt and revolt into revolution. It helped to unite in one movement the holders of a variety of grievances which had little in common except that the king was held responsible for them.

Such are the preconditions making revolution possible; new elements, precipitants or accelerators, make it probable. The most common of these are the emergence of an inspired leader, the formation of a secret military and revolutionary organisation, and the defeat of the regime in foreign war.[13] None of these has any obvious relevance to Scotland. Nor has the way in which action taken to cure dysfunction by reform can sometimes precipitate revolution.[14] Indeed it was more the case that the main precipitant in Scotland was political action (in imposing further religious innovations) by the king, who failed to recognise or to attempt to cure dysfunction but blindly increased it. The part ideas played as a precipitant in Scotland is hard to assess, but the role of the developing federal theology was certainly central in providing justification of resistance and confidence of success, in providing ideological bonds giving coherence to the movement and uniting all ranks of society.[15] It also helped to prevent the revolutionary movement from becoming narrowly nationalist; religious ideology gave it claims to universal relevance.

Another way discussed by Stone of looking at potentially revolutionary situations is to see them not in terms of the objective social situation but in terms of expectation and satisfaction. Revolutionary potential is often created when expectations outstrip satisfaction. Thus reforms may create new expectations which are not satisfied by the reforms. This (as already mentioned) has no relevance to Scotland, but the same principle applied to economic progress probably has. The revolutions of the 1640s, it has been pointed out, came twenty years after the end of a sustained period of economic growth in Europe.[16] Definite evidence that Scotland followed this pattern must await further research, but the presumption that it did so is strong, and is supported by some of the fragmentary evidence available. Certainly harvest failures in the 1630s were more frequent and severe than usual.

In both economic and other matters the idea of potentially revolutionary discontent arising from unsatisfied expectations is especially interesting in relation to the union of the crowns. The union had raised very high hopes in Scotland which were disappointed. Free trade (and the prosperity it was supposed to bring) had not materialised. Early favour shown to Scots in England soon disappeared. The dynasty became anglicised. In religion and in society generally union was found to bring Scotland not security but alien influences. No doubt the benefits expected from union had been unrealistically great, but this did not make their failure to appear any the less bitter, or the resultant dissatisfaction any the less serious.

Linked with analysis based on expectation and satisfaction is reference group theory, in that both are based on the realisation that men act not only in reaction to objective conditions, but also to subjective standards. They are also associated in their relevance to Scotland in that the union of 1603 is central to their application. Reference group theory holds that 'Human satisfaction is related not to existing conditions but to the condition of a social group against which the individual measures his situation'. Stone adds that in an age of mass communications 'knowledge of high consumption standards elsewhere spreads rapidly, and, as a result the reference group may be in another, more highly developed country'.[17]

Such a situation need not await the arrival of mass communications; it existed in Scotland in the early seventeenth century. The

1603 union destroyed the Scottish court as the main reference group against which the nobles measured themselves. In its place was the essentially English court of Great Britain. With a few exceptions the Scots nobility could not compete with the English nobility in the new court. Apart from the differences of manners and customs which made them feel foreigners, they could seldom afford to stay long at court or make much show there which would establish for them the status (of equality with the English) which they felt to be their due. The Scottish nobility had suddenly been transformed, in their own eyes, from the proud leaders of the society of an independent nation into a poor and provincial nobility. Their old reference group had been disbanded and they had not the resources to compete with the new one. They reacted with mixed envy and resentment. Closer contact with a richer nobility made them more aware than before of their own poverty, while at the same time the union which brought this closer contact also lowered their status. To a lesser extent the same probably also applies to lairds and burgesses; closer contact with richer counterparts emphasised their relative poverty. Perhaps only the ministers could look at their English equivalents without envy. The tendency for reference groups to shift through the union, with the resulting reassessments and adjustments, inevitably gave rise to dissatisfaction with the *status quo* in Scotland. Union had shown the Scots new horizons, but did not seem to provide them with opportunities to reach them.

The gaps between expectation and satisfaction, between the high claims of federal theology and the reality of everyday life, and between the nobility and others and their new reference groups all gave rise to a sense of 'relative deprivation', a sense which tends to lead through frustration to aggression.[18]

Clearly the fact of union was of great importance in bringing about revolution in Scotland, and it is therefore not surprising that the closest parallels with events in Scotland in other sixteenth- and seventeenth-century revolutions are to be found in revolutions which had their origins in the discontent of weaker partners in unions of formerly separate countries brought about by dynastic accident.[19] Unions between disparate countries inevitably caused great strains in an age when monarchs tended to take it for granted that all areas under their rule should be as alike as possible in religion, society and government. In trying to bind their countries together by imposing homogeneity they sometimes brought about disaster. The most obvious of such parallels is with the revolt of the Netherlands against Spain. The Netherlands gave Spain a king just as Scotland gave England one. At first this established Netherlandish and Scots influence and personnel in the courts of Spain and England respectively, but in the long run the influence of the larger, richer country naturally predominated.[20] Many contemporary Scots must have been very well aware of these similarities; Scotland had closer links with the United Provinces both in trade and religion than with any other country.

Except as regards the smaller kingdom providing a monarch for the larger member of the union, and the religious issues involved, the closest of all such parallels are to be found between Scotland and the Catalan revolt of 1640.[21] Much of what J. H. Elliott has written of the grievances of Catalonia can be applied word for word to Scotland. In Spain a union of the crowns worked, in theory, on the principle that 'the kingdoms must be ruled and governed as if the king who holds them all together were king only of each one of them', the false assumption being that nothing had really changed. In fact the prince no longer lived among his people in the smaller partners in these unions. 'The fact of absentee kingship was of incalculable importance as a source of discontent'; complaints stressed this absence and the infrequency of royal visits, though in Spain a substitute (though a poor one) was provided by viceroys and vice-regal courts.[22] Interestingly, James VI had suggested establishing such a viceroy or deputy in Scotland, citing the Spanish example (and after all one already existed in Ireland), but the Scottish parliament denounced the idea in 1607 as turning 'a trew and friendlie Unioun, into a conquered and slavishe province . . . lyke suche of the King of Spaynes provinceis as your Majestie . . . made mentioun of'.[23]

The way in which the permanent absence of the king from Catalonia prompted a search for a compensating focus for loyalty also has relevance to Scotland. In Catalonia compensation tended to be found in the *patria* or fatherland, a rather uncertain concept based on memories of the country's earlier achievements. In Portugal (which revolted a few months after Catalonia) there was also a hint at the country's mission as an agent of providence, interrupted by union.[24] In Scotland a strikingly similar role was played not by the idea of the nation but by the idea of the kirk, accompanied by an idealised picture of the past when it had been the best reformed church in the world, and by the concept of the kirk having a unique role to play in implementing God's will. The fact that in Scotland the emphasis was on the kirk rather than the nation was probably bound up with the fact that secular nationalism had previously been so closely connected with the dynasty and Scotland's long, unbroken (though mythical) line of kings; as it was now the action of the dynasty which was giving rise to discontent, this was obviously inappropriate.

In Catalonia as well, however, the church was closely bound up with the national consciousness, even though there was no religious dispute with the crown. The parish clergy acted as guardians of the memories of liberty, independence and past achievement, while being 'close enough to the people to enjoy authority among them, and sufficiently educated in the national traditions to be able to transmit them to the populace and to urge from the pulpits that they should be defended to the last drop of blood'.[25] This description may be applied to many of the ministers of the kirk without alteration.

The fact that Catalonia and Portugal retained their own laws, institutions and forms of government meant that they had a large degree of autonomy and agencies 'which might be used as vehicles for collective protest'.[26] This also recalls the situation in Scotland. The lesser kingdoms in these unions retained their own institutions and social structure, and this made it easier for them to act and organise as a single unit when rebellion came. That the unions should mainly affect the dominant social groups, above all the nobility, was predictable, but nonetheless here too the parallels are notable. Catalan nobles felt themselves excluded from patronage and opportunities for employment in the king's service. Burgesses thought their social and economic interests neglected.

The political nation as a whole resented absentee government as heavy-handed and inefficient. Some degree of tension between local communities and central government might be universal, but it was most serious when the local community concerned was a formerly independent one with its own traditions, laws and institutions.[27] Again, one could say much the same of Scotland.

Of course, these parallels cannot be taken too far; a warning against doing so is provided by the contrast between events once revolt had begun. Catalonia saw in 1640 a spontaneous peasant uprising against the oppressions of the army temporarily quartered there. This revolt was then joined by the upper ranks of society, and hatred of Castile for a time allowed united action. Portugal in the same year experienced a nationalist *coup d'état*, asserting independence of Castile and setting up a new king.[28] Events in Scotland had little in common with these patterns. Perhaps the most noteworthy contrast lies in the fact that the Iberian revolts were (or, in the case of Catalonia, became) secessionist movements accompanied by hatred of the dominant partner in the union, Castile. The covenanters, on the other hand, sought alliance with the people of England against the crown, and urged the need for closer union. Anti-English feeling and discontent at the existence of union was restrained by realisation that grievances related to those of Scotland were widespread in England, by the need for English support if success was to be achieved, and by the fact that rule by Scotland's native Stewart dynasty was unquestioned, making a complete breaking of the union impossible.

How does Scotland fit into H. R. Trevor-Roper's explanation of the mid-seventeenth-century revolutions? In essence, he sees most of these revolutions as arising not out of conflict between classes in society, but in a breakdown of relations between state and society, court and country. In sixteenth- and early seventeenth-century Europe centralised and absolute monarchies were emerging, creating increasingly large bureaucracies in their courts. These were at first necessary to deal with the expanding functions of the central government, but in time expanded out of all proportion to their functions and became parasitic on society. The vast cost of supporting inflated and extravagant courts causes rising discontent, and eventually 'country' rises to purge 'court' and the administration of their excesses.[29] Rather surprisingly, Trevor-Roper dismisses Scotland as 'largely irrelevant' to his analysis, since the revolt in Scotland (like those of Portugal and Catalonia) was of a different type from those he discusses.[30] Yet (as he himself appears to realise in his next paragraph) these revolts are very relevant to parts of his thesis. For Scotland's court to be absorbed in that of England was simply the carrying of the centralising of royal authority beyond former international boundaries. Scotland was virtually all country and no court. This made the alienation of the court from those it was supposed to serve in what had formerly been an independent nation all the more obvious. It may be objected that Scotland did not have the main grievance usually made against the court, the cost of its upkeep—just as Catalonia did not contribute to the court of Castile.[31] This is true, but one might despise the court for more than purely financial reasons and Scotland did have a growing bureaucracy, extending royal power and increasing taxation—even if one can offer only the rather uninspiring figure of Traquair to stand alongside Strafford, Olivares and Richelieu as a powerful first minister dedicated to *raison d'état* and abolutism.[32] The ambivalent attitude of Catalans to the court of Castile—half envy, half hatred[33]—was very similar to that of many Scots to the essentially English court.

Trevor-Roper's general points as to a conflict between court and country are of interest in a Scottish context. Successful revolt was comparatively easy in Scotland because there was no resident court; on the other hand, this complicated the reaching of any final settlement, for seizure of control of the land did not include seizure of the centre of power revolted against, the king and the court. None the less J. H. Elliott's criticism that Trevor-Roper's interpretation does little more than state the obvious has much truth in it; any revolution involves a crisis in the relations of state and society, and a court versus country split is simply an example of this;[34] to put it in other terms, it is a type of multiple dysfunction. Elliott concludes that 'The essential clue to the revolutionary situation of the 1640s is, I suspect, to be found in the determination of governments to exercise fuller control over their states without yet having the administrative means or fiscal resources to ensure obedience to their will', this determination springing mainly from the demands of war.[35] Charles I clearly had such a determination even though it was not war that led him to it. In taxes, in control of parliament and local government as well as in religion, he demanded more than ever before of his Scots subjects.

Here Stone's criticism of Trevor-Roper is pertinent: that so far as England was concerned the trouble was not too large a government machine but too small a one. There was no standing army, no paid local officials in the shires, only a small and badly paid bureaucracy.[36] The king's position in Scotland was even weaker; the governmental machinery was rudimentary compared with England's. Yet the king combined his increased demands on the Scots not only with inadequate resources and bureaucracy but with a lack of attention to and supervision of what machinery there was, which led to growing inefficiency in it. The combination was fatal in Scotland, though it is worth noting H. G. Koenigsberger's denial that absence or presence of a standing army, and of a strong bureaucracy (the absence of which was almost universal), need be significant in bringing about revolt. A standing army did not prevent revolt in the Netherlands in the late sixteenth century, and one actually provoked revolt in Catalonia in 1640. Whether a standing army existed or not bears no relation to the incidence of revolts in Germany.[37]

Koenigsberger further makes the point that in studying early modern revolutions it is necessary to examine societies in which they did not occur as well as those in which they did, if we are to fully understand what caused these upheavals.[38] The criticism is analogous to that of psychiatrists who try to explain the causes of mental illness without ever studying the mind of any person who is not mentally ill, and is perhaps equally pertinent.

Whether one accepts the existence of a 'general crisis' of the seventeenth century, or concludes that 'The only basis for comparing them is their simultaneity (which is also more apparent than real)',[39] clearly the study of the revolutions of the 1640s can throw light on events in Scotland. But just as much light can be shed by consideration of other early modern revolutions, such as that of the Netherlands in the sixteenth century. Indeed it could be argued that the Scottish revolution had more in common with the revolutions of the 1560s, when the quarrel between state and society was primarily religious in form (including, of course, Scotland's first reformation), than with those of the 1640s which Elliott sees as arising mainly from the fiscal demands of the state,[40] though obviously there was a financial element in the Scottish crisis. Perhaps the old term 'the second reformation' is worth reviving as it emphasises the religious form of the revolt in Scotland.

Comparisons of the Scottish revolution with other early modern European revolutions are intriguing and stimulating, raising many questions. But before the questions can be answered, and the comparisons carried any further, we need to know much more about Scotland's society and political system. Knowledge of other major early modern revolutions may be very incomplete, but probably less is known about Scotland's revolution than about any of the others.

Conventions and Abbreviations

Dates. Old Style dates (as used in contemporary Britain) are used throughout, New Style dates as used on the Continent (ten days ahead of the Old Style) being adjusted where necessary. The new year is taken to begin on 1 January (the Scottish usage), not 25 March (English usage).

Quotations. All abbreviations are extended, but otherwise the original spelling and punctuation are retained.

Money. The £ sterling was worth £12 Scots in the seventeenth century. All sums cited without the addition of 'sterling' or 'Scots' are in £ Scots. The 'merk' is the Scots merk worth 13*s* 4*d* Scots, not the English mark worth 13*s* 4*d* sterling.

References. Full details of a work are usually given the first time it is cited, with short-title references thereafter. All MSS cited without any location being given are in the Scottish Record Office. All printed works are published in London unless otherwise stated.

Abbreviations. The following abbreviations have been used.

Aber Recs	*Extracts from the Council Register of the Burgh of Aberdeen, 1625–42* and *1634–1747*, ed J. Stuart (SBRS, 1871–2)
APS	*The Acts of the Parliaments of Scotland*, ed T. Thomson & C. Innes (12 vols, 1814–75). The new edition (1870–2) of vols v and vi has been used
BM	British Museum
BUK	*Booke of the Universall Kirk of Scotland*, ed T. Thomson (Bannatyne & Maitland Clubs, 1839–45)
CJ	*Journals of the House of Commons* (1803)
CSPD	*Calendar of State Papers, Domestic*

CSP Ven   *Calendar of State Papers and Manuscripts, relating to English Affairs, existing in the Archives and Collections of Venice*

Econ HR   *Economic History Review*

Edin Recs   *Extracts from the Records of the Burgh of Edinburgh, 1626–1641* and *1642–1655*, ed M. Wood (Edinburgh, 1936–8)

EHR   *English Historical Review*

EUL   Edinburgh University Library

Gordon, *History*   Gordon J. *History of Scots Affairs* (3 vols, Spalding Club, 1841)

HMC   Historical Manuscripts Commission. References to HMC publications take the form of serial number followed by the report and appendix numbers or the collection title, as recommended in *Government Publications, Sectional List* No. 17

IHS   *Irish Historical Studies*

LJ   *Journals of the House of Lords*

NLS   National Library of Scotland

NRA(S)   National Register of Archives (Scotland)

PEBS   *Papers of the Edinburgh Bibliographical Society*

PRO   Public Record Office, London

PSAS   *Proceedings of the Society of Antiquaries of Scotland*

RGBS   *Records of the Glasgow Bibliographical Society*

RMS   *Registrum Magni Sigilli Regum Scotorum, 1634–51*, ed J. M. Thomson (Edinburgh, 1897)

RPCS   *Register of the Privy Council of Scotland*, 2nd ser, ed P. H. Brown (Edinburgh, 1899–1908)

RSCHS   *Records of the Scottish Church History Society*

SBRS   Scottish Burgh Record Society

SHR   Scottish Historical Review

SHS   Scottish History Society

SNPG   Scottish National Portrait Gallery

Stirling Recs   *Extracts from the Records of the Royal Burgh of Stirling, 1519–1666*, ed R. Renwick (Glasgow, 1887)

TRHS   *Transactions of the Royal Historical Society*

Notes and References

PREFACE

1 Elton, G. R. *Political History. Principles and Practice* (1970), 67.
2 Burnet, G. *The Memoires of the Lives and Actions of James and William Dukes of Hamilton* (1677), preface, a.2.
3 Mousnier, R. *Peasant Uprisings in Seventeenth Century France, Russia and China* (1971), xvii–xix, 305–6.
4 Buckle, H. T. *On Scotland and the Scotch Intellect*, ed H. J. Hanham (Chicago and London, 1970), xxx.

CHAPTER 1: *The Rule of Charles I in Scotland and the Causes of Discontent, 1625–1637*

1 There are several good modern introductions to early seventeenth-century Scotland: Donaldson, G. *Scotland: James V to James VII* (Edinburgh & London, 1965); Lythe, S. G. E. *The Economy of Scotland in its European Setting, 1550–1625* (Edinburgh, 1960); Smout, T. C. *A History of the Scottish People, 1560–1830* (1969). See also Mathew, D. *Scotland under Charles I* (1955).
2 Quoted in Wedgwood, C. V. 'Anglo-Scottish Relations, 1603–40', *TRHS*, 4th series, xxxii (1950), 31.
3 Hyde, E., Earl of Clarendon. *The History of the Rebellion*, ed W. D. Macray (Oxford, 1888), i.109.
4 Donaldson. *Scotland: James V to James VII*, 290.
5 Hyde. *History of the Rebellion*, i.108.
6 For details of the Scottish parliament, see pp 166–9 below.
7 Rogers, C. (ed). *Estimate of the Scots Nobility* (Grampian Club,

1873), 63–80; Stone, L. *The Crisis of the Aristocracy, 1558–1641* (Oxford, 1965), 758; PA.7/2/139, Supplementary Parliamentary Papers.

8 Donaldson. *Scotland: James V to James VII*, 217–21.

9 Mayes, C. R. 'The Early Stuarts and the Irish Peerage', *EHR*, lxxiii (1958), 236n, 246n, 248n. Some at least of the Englishmen granted Scots titles were naturalised at the same time, Balfour, J. *Historical Works* (Edinburgh, 1824–5), ii.81.

10 Gordon, P. of Ruthven. *A Short Abridgement of Britane's Distemper* (Spalding Club, 1844), 76–7.

11 See Dunlop, A. I. 'The Polity of the Scottish Church, 1600–1637', *RSCHS*, xii (1958), 161–84. For puritan proposals at the Hampton Court conference for similar mixed government in England, see Collinson, P. *The Elizabethan Puritan Movement* (1967), 458.

12 Foster, W. R. 'The Operation of Presbyteries in Scotland, 1600–38', *RSCHS*, xv (1964–6), 29; Donaldson, G. *Scotland: Church and Nation through Sixteen Centuries* (1960), 78–9.

13 McMahon, G. I. R. 'The Scottish Courts of High Commission, 1610–38', *RSCHS*, xv (1964–6), 193–209.

14 Cowan, I. B. 'The Five Articles of Perth', *Reformation and Revolution*, ed D. Shaw (Edinburgh, 1967), 160, 176; Donaldson. *Scotland: James V to James VII*, 208–11.

15 Ibid, 211.

16 Cowan. 'The Five Articles of Perth', 177.

17 Smout. *A History of the Scottish People*, 65.

18 McMahon. 'Courts of High Commission', 200–1.

19 Stevenson, D. 'Conventicles and the Kirk, 1619–37. The Emergence of a Radical Party', *RSCHS* (forthcoming).

20 Rutherford, S. *Letters*, ed A. A. Bonar (1894), 136, 204, 213, 216, 290.

21 Donaldson, G. 'Scotland's Conservative North in the Sixteenth and Seventeenth Centuries', *TRHS*, 5th series, xvi (1966), 65, 79.

22 Balfour. *Historical Works*, ii.134, 141–2.

23 Row, J. *The History of the Kirk of Scotland* (Wodrow Society, 1842), 385.

24 *RPCS, 1633–5,* 228.

25 E 4/5, Exchequer Act Book, 1634–9, ff 142–3.

26 *RPCS, 1625–7,* 265.

27 Donaldson. *Scotland, James V to James VII,* 299, n 6.

28 Trevor-Roper, H. R. 'Scotland and the Puritan Revolution', *Religion the Reformation and Social Change* (1967), 396.

29 Zagorin, P. *The Court and the Country* (1969), 131.

30 Smout. *History of the Scottish People,* 44–7.

31 MacNeill, P. G. B. 'The Jurisdiction of the Scottish Privy Council, 1532–1708' (Glasgow PhD thesis, 1961), 42.

32 Ibid, 37.

33 See Turner, E. R. *The Privy Council of England, 1603–1784* (Baltimore, 1927), i.137–8.

34 Donaldson. *Scotland: James V to James VII,* 290.

35 Ibid, 300.

36 *RPCS, 1625–7,* vi–viii, xliv–xlv; *RPCS, 1630–2,* 188.

37 Donaldson. *Scotland, James V to James VII,* 291.

38 Wedgwood, C. V. 'Anglo-Scottish Relations, 1603–40', *TRHS,* 4th series, xxxii.40.

39 Aylmer, G. E. *The King's Servants* (1961), 20.

40 Collins, A. *Letters and Memorials of State . . .* (1746), ii.646.

41 Roots, I. *The Great Rebellion* (1966), 22.

42 Knowler, W. (ed). *The Earl of Strafford's Letters and Dispatches* (Dublin, 1740), ii.190, 325.

43 Hyde. *History of the Rebellion,* i.145.

44 Balfour. *Historical Works,* ii.128–31; Scot, J. of Scotstarvet. 'Trew Relation of the Principall Affaires concerning the State', ed G. Neilson, *SHR,* xi (1913–14), 168–91.

45 Carlyle, E. H. 'Committees of Council under the Earlier Stuarts', *EHR,* xxi (1906), 679–81.

46 *RPCS, 1625–7,* lxiii–lxiv, 338.

47 *RPCS, 1625–7,* lxv, 365–8, 378–9, 380–1; *RPCS, 1627–8,* 57, 146; Balfour. *Historical Works,* ii.133.

48 *RPCS, 1625–7,* 263–5.

49 Balfour. *Historical Works,* ii.131, 133.

50 *RPCS, 1622–5,* xv–xvi, xix–xxvii.

51 Scot. 'Trew Relation', *SHR,* xi.171; *RPCS, 1633–5,* 139–41.

52 *RPCS*, *1625-7*, 265-7.

53 For the revocation see *RPCS*, *1625-7*, xix–ccii; *APS*, v. 23–8, 31–9, 189–207; Dickinson, W. C. & Donaldson, G. (eds). *A Source Book of Scottish History* (1961), iii.66–77; Connell, J. *A Treatise on the Law of Scotland respecting Tithes* (Edinburgh, 1830).

54 Foster, W. R. 'A Constant Platt Achieved: Provision for the Ministry, 1600–38', *Reformation and Revolution*, ed D. Shaw (Edinburgh, 1967), 124–40; Hill, C. *Economic Problems of the Church* (Oxford, 1956), 205, 251; HMC 24: *Rutland*, i.511.

55 Donaldson. *Scotland, James V to James VII*, 298.

56 Balfour. *Historical Works*, ii.128, 134.

57 Scot. 'Trew Relation', *SHR*, xi.169.

58 Malcolm, C. A. 'The Office of Sheriff in Scotland', *SHR*, xx (1922–3), 304–6; Malcolm, C. A. (ed). *The Minutes of the Justices of the Peace of Lanarkshire, 1707–23* (SHS, 1931), ix–xx.

59 Donaldson. *Scotland: James V to James VII*, 302.

60 Rait, R. S. *The Parliaments of Scotland* (Glasgow, 1924), 495.

61 Row. *History*, 365–6.

62 See Stevenson, D. 'The King's Scottish Revenues and the Covenanters, 1625–51', *Historical Journal*, xvii (forthcoming).

63 Hill. *Economic Problems of the Church*, 224–7.

64 Balfour. *Historical Works*, ii.142.

65 [Rogers, C. (ed)]. *The Earl of Stirling's Register of Royal Letters* (Edinburgh, 1885), i. lvii–lviii.

66 *APS*, v.20–1.

67 Balfour. *Historical Works*, ii.207–16.

68 Ibid, ii.216–20; Cobbett, W. (ed). *State Trials*, iii.591–712; Hay, R. A. *Genealogie of the Hayes of Tweeddale* (Edinburgh, 1835), 86–100; *RPCS*, *1635-7*, 43–4, 47, 54, 334. One is reminded of Wentworth's action as lord deputy of Ireland in having the vice-treasurer of Ireland sentenced to death on a trumped-up charge and then pardoned in 1635, Wedgwood, C. V. *Thomas Wentworth, First Earl of Strafford, 1593–1641. A Revaluation* (1961), 200.

69 Masson, D. *Drummond of Hawthornden* (1873), 233–41.

70 Brown, P. H. (ed). *Early Travellers in Scotland* (Edinburgh, 1891), 138.

71 McMahon. 'Courts of High Commission', 198, 208.

72 Kitshoff, M. C. 'Aspects of Arminianism in Scotland' (St Andrews M. Th. Thesis, 1968), 63–9, 76–110.

73 Lamont, W. M. *Godly Rule. Politics and Religion 1603–60* (1969), 64–6.

74 Henderson, G. D. 'The Idea of the Covenant in Scotland', *The Burning Bush* (Edinburgh, 1957), 61–74; Burrell, S. A. 'The Covenant Idea as a Revolutionary Symbol: Scotland 1596–1637', *Church History*, xxvii (1958), 338–50; Torrance, J. B. 'Covenant or Contract? A Study of the Theological Background of Worship in Seventeenth Century Scotland', *Journal of Scottish Theology*, xxiii (1970), 51–75.

75 Leith, W. F. (ed). *Memoirs of Scottish Catholics during the XVIIth and XVIIIth Centuries* (1909), i.196–8.

76 Rutherford. *Letters*, 301.

77 Laud, W. *Works*, ed J. Bliss & W. Scott (Oxford, 1847–60), v.597.

78 Mathieson, W. L. *Politics and Religion*, i.368.

79 Laud. *Works*, v.589.

80 Row. *History*, 392.

81 Ibid, 369.

82 Leslie, J., Earl of Rothes. *A Relation of Proceedings concerning the affairs of the Kirk of Scotland*, ed D. Laing (Bannatyne Club, 1830), 4.

83 Donaldson, G. *The Making of the Scottish Prayer Book* (Edinburgh, 1954), 71.

84 Masson. *Drummond of Hawthornden*, 250.

85 Trevor-Roper. *Religion the Reformation and Social Change*, 398.

86 Baillie, R. *Letters*, ed D. Laing (Bannatyne Club, 1841–2), i.2.

87 Donaldson. *Scotland: James V to James VII*, 300.

88 Thirsk, J. (ed). *The Agrarian History of England and Wales*, iv (Cambridge, 1967), 621.

89 Figures of grain prices in Fife and the Lothians support this. They are very high for the crops of 1621–3, 1628–30, 1633–5 and 1637 in Fife, *Fife Fiars, from 1619 to 1845* (Cupar, 1846). East Lothian grain prices reached peaks for the crops of 1628–31 and 1635–6, *Archaeologia Scotica: Transactions of the Society of Antiquaries of Scotland*, i (1792), 91. The prices of these years suggest severe

shortages, Mitchison, R. 'The Movement of Scottish Corn Prices in the Seventeenth and Eighteenth Centuries', *Econ. HR*, 2nd series, xviii (1965), 283,286. For some evidence against there being an end to the growth of trade before 1637 see Devine, T. M. & Lythe, S. G. E. 'The Economy of Scotland under James VI. A Revision Article', *SHR*, 1 (1971), 102.

90 Donaldson. *Scotland: James V to James VII*, 303–4; Hannay, R. K. & Watson, G. P. H. 'The Building of the Parliament House', *Book of the Old Edinburgh Club*, xiii (1924), 1–78.

91 *Edin. Recs, 1626–41*, xiv, 149–50, 152. In 1635 Charles refused to allow a man who had opposed him in the 1633 parliament to be provost of Aberdeen, insisting that he be replaced, *Aber. Recs, 1625–42*, 71–3.

92 *Edin. Recs, 1626–41*, xv, 179.

93 Stevenson, R. B. K. 'The "Stirling" Turners of Charles I, 1632–9', *British Numismatic Journal*, xxix (1958–9), 128–37.

94 Mathieson. *Politics and Religion*, i.368.

95 Quoted in Wedgwood, C. V. *The King's Peace* (1955), 151.

96 Donaldson. *Scotland: James V to James VII*, 219.

97 Hill. *Economic Problems of the Church*, 332.

98 Zagorin. *The Court and the Country*, 31, 91.

99 Baillie. *Letters,* i.6, 8.

100 Stevenson. 'The King's Revenues and the Covenanters'.

101 Baillie. *Letters,* i.7–8, 11, 17.

102 Burnet, G. *Memoires of the Lives and Actions of James and William Dukes of Hamilton* (1677), 52.

103 Wedgwood. *The King's Peace*, 150–1.

104 Malcolm. 'The Office of Sheriff in Scotland', *SHR*, xx.306.

105 Malcolm. *Minutes of the Justices of the Peace of Lanarkshire*, xxi.

106 Connell. *A Treatise on the Law of Scotland relating to Tithes*, i.152–3; Baillie. *Letters,* i.7–8, 17.

107 *RPCS, 1635–7*, xxx–xxxiv; Wedgwood. 'Anglo-Scottish Relations, 1603–40', *TRHS*, 4th series, xxxii.36–9.

CHAPTER 2: *The Prayer Book and the National Covenant, 1636–February 1638*

1 Spalding, J. *Memorialls of the Trubles in Scotland . . .*, ed J. Stuart (Spalding Club, 1850–1), i.77. Spalding's story (ibid, i.78–9) of a meeting of nobles (including the Marquis of Hamilton and the Earl of Traquair!) and ministers to plot changes in religion is also absurd.

2 Guthry, H. *Memoirs of Henry Guthry, late Bishop of Dunkeld . . .* (2nd ed, Glasgow, 1747), 15.

3 McCrie, T. (ed). *The Life of Mr Robert Blair . . .* (Wodrow Soc., 1848), 53–61, 140–8; Barcley, J. M. 'Some Scottish Bishops and Ministers in the Irish Church, 1605–35', *Reformation and Revolution*, ed D. Shaw, 141–59.

4 Rogers, C. (ed). *Historical Notices of St Anthony's Monastery, Leith, and Rehearsal of Events . . . 1635 to 1645 . . .* (Grampian Club, 1877), 41.

5 *RPCS, 1635–7*, 336.

6 Ibid, 343; Baillie. *Letters,* i.4, 16, 31, 441; Donaldson. *The Making of the Scottish Prayer Book*, 58–9.

7 *RPCS, 1635–7*, 252–3; HMC 72: *Laing*, i.197.

8 In [Balcanquhal, W.]. *A Large Declaration concerning the Late Tumults in Scotland* (1639), 21–2, issued in the king's name, it is said that the council ordered use of the prayer book in all churches at Easter 1637.

9 Baillie. *Letters*, i.16–17; Gordon, J. *History of Scots Affairs* (Spalding Club, 1841), i.4.

10 Gardiner, S. R. (ed). *The Hamilton Papers . . . 1638–50* (Camden Soc, 1880), 2.

11 Gordon. *History*, i.6.

12 BM, MS Add 23,112, Register of the Secretary of State of Scotland, f.51; *RPCS, 1635–7*, 409–10.

13 Wodrow, R. *Selections from Wodrow's Biographical Collections: Divines of the North East of Scotland*, ed R. Lippe (New Spalding Club, 1890), 171.

14 McCrie. *Life of Blair*, 150.

15 Guthry. *Memoirs*, 23–4.

16 Wodrow. *Biographical Collections,* 171–2.

17 Baillie. *Letters,* i.17; Leslie. *Relation,* 198; Gordon. *History,* i.5.

18 Henderson, J. M. (ed). 'An "Advertistment" about the Service Book, 1637', *SHR,* xxiii (1925–6), 199–204.

19 Johnston, A. *Diary, 1632–9,* ed G. M. Paul (SHS, 1911), 259, 262.

20 Ie letters enjoining obedience on pain of denunciation as rebels.

21 *RPCS, 1635–7,* 448–9.

22 [Balcanquhal]. *Large Declaration,* 22.

23 Gordon. *History,* i.5.

24 [Balcanquhal]. *Large Declaration,* 22; Baillie. *Letters,* i.18; Row. *History,* 408; Wodrow. *Biographical Collections,* 173.

25 Rushworth, J. *Historical Collections . . .* (1659–1701), I.ii. 389–90.

26 Baillie. *Letters,* i.18.

27 This account of the events of 23 July is taken from [Balcanquhal]. *Large Declaration,* 22–5; 'A breefe and true Relatione of the Broyle' in Leslie. *Relation,* appendix, 198–200; Row. *History,* 408–9; Gordon. *History,* i.7–11; Wodrow. *Biographical Collections,* 173–4.

28 Row. *History,* 409; Johnston. *Diary, 1632–9,* 265.

29 [Balcanquhal]. *Large Declaration,* 24.

30 Ibid, 24; Johnston. *Diary, 1632–9,* 265; Wodrow. *Biographical Collections,* 174.

31 Baillie. *Letters,* i.17; [Balcanquhal]. *Large Declaration,* 24–5.

32 Johnston. *Diary, 1632–9,* 265.

33 Spalding. *Memorialls,* i.79; [Balcanquhal]. *Large Declaration,* 23; Baillie. *Letters,* i.18.

34 Wodrow. *Biographical Collections,* 173.

35 Wodrow, R. *Analecta* (Maitland Club, 1842–3), i.64. As to the 'Jenny Geddes' credited by tradition with having begun the riot in St Giles, she is first mentioned in a continuation added to the 1670 edition of Baker, Sir Richard. *A Chronicle of the Kings of England,* 478. Doubt is thrown on the authenticity of this account by the fact that it combines two separate incidents described in a

strictly contemporary account of the riots, Leslie. *Relation,* 198–200, and attributes them to this otherwise unknown 'Jenny Geddes'.

36 Gordon. *History,* i.7n; Wodrow. *Analecta,* i.64.

37 Gordon. *History,* i.13–14; Row. *History,* 409; Baillie. *Letters,* i.18–19; Hope, Sir Thomas. *Diary . . . 1633–45* (Bannatyne Club, 1843), 64.

38 Rushworth. *Historical Collections,* II.i.390.

39 *RPCS, 1635–7,* 483–4.

40 *RPCS, 1635–7,* 486–7, 489.

41 Leslie. *Relation,* 3–4.

42 *RPCS, 1635–7,* 490; Johnston. *Diary, 1632–9,* 267; Gordon. *History,* i.14.

43 *RPCS, 1635–7,* 509; BM, MS Add 23,112, f 73v.

44 *RPCS, 1635–7,* 510–11.

45 Leslie. *Relation,* 4–5.

46 Baillie. *Letters,* i.19; Gordon. *History,* i.14–16.

47 Baillie. *Letters,* i.19,32; Leslie. *Relation,* 5–6, 203.

48 Balfour. *Historical Works,* ii.226–9; Leslie. *Relation,* 17–18, 45–6; Baillie. *Letters,* i.449–50.

49 Balfour. *Historical Works,* ii.227.

50 *RPCS, 1635–7,* 521; Leslie. *Relation,* 7; Baillie. *Letters,* i.20.

51 *RPCS, 1635–7,* 521, 694; Guthry. *Memoirs,* 16–17; NLS, MS Adv 33.2.32, Miscellaneous Collections by Sir James Balfour, 39, 42.

52 Balfour. *Historical Works,* ii.229–31.

53 Burnet. *Hamilton,* 31.

54 Guthry. *Memoirs,* 25.

55 For the activities of Robert Baillie, minister of Kilwinning, in urging ministers to draw up supplications against the book and organising the sending of ministers and lairds to Edinburgh, see Baillie. *Letters,* i.13–15.

56 Ibid, i.14.

57 Rushworth. *Historical Collections,* II.i.393–4, 399–400; Leslie. *Relation,* 11–12.

58 *Edin Recs, 1626–41,* 192, 194.

59 Leslie. *Relation,* 8–9, 18.

21

60 BM, MS Add 23,112, f 74; Balfour. *Historical Works*, ii.232–3.

61 Leslie. *Relation*, 9; Burnet, G. *History of his Own Times*, ed O. Airy (Oxford, 1897–1900), i.40–1; Mathieson. *Politics and Religion*, i.408, dismisses charges of double dealing against Traquair in 1637–8 as 'idle gossip' but they are far more than this and impossible to explain away.

62 Guthry. *Memoirs*, 26.

63 Leslie. *Relation*, 8–10; Baillie. *Letters*, i.22; *RPCS, 1635–7*, 699.

64 Hyde. *History of the Rebellion*, i.161.

65 Baillie. *Letters*, i.23.

66 Forty-six local petitions are printed in *RPCS, 1635–7*, 700–16. Only one is dated (17 Sept) but with one exception (that of Kirkcudbright presbytery) they all date from September or early October. Of 41 from 35 parishes and 6 burghs, 25 are from the sheriffdom of Ayr, 2 each from Dunbarton and Lanark, 11 from Fife and 1 from Stirling. The other 4 petitions are from presbyteries—Haddington, Coupar, Perth and Stirling.

67 Guthry. *Memoirs*, 27.

68 *Edin Recs, 1626–41*, 194–5.

69 *RPCS, 1635–7*, 534.

70 Guthry. *Memoirs*, 29.

71 Baillie. *Letters*, i.33–4.

72 Guthry. *Memoirs*, 27–8; Leslie. *Relation*, 13, 18–19; Gordon. *History*, i.19; Johnston. *Diary, 1632–9*, 270.

73 *RPCS, 1635–7*, 536–8, 541.

74 Baillie. *Letters*, i.35; Leslie. *Relation*, 19.

75 Baillie. *Letters*, i.37–8; Leslie. *Relation*, 14–15, 19–22; Gordon. *History*, i.21–5; *Edin. Recs, 1626–41*, 197; Laing, D. (ed). *Correspondence of . . . Earl of Ancrum and . . . Earl of Lothian* (Edinburgh, 1875), i.95–7.

76 *RPCS, 1635–7*, 541–2.

77 Baillie. *Letters*, i.38.

78 Leslie. *Relation*, 49–50; Fleming, D. H. *Scotland's Supplication and Complaint . . . 18th October 1637* (Edinburgh, 1927), 60–2.

79 Guthry. *Memoirs*, 30; Baillie. *Letters*, i.35–6.

80 Fleming. *Scotland's Supplication*, 62–6. It is necessary to note that a few of the signatures were not written on 18 October but

were added later. In particular, the Earl of Montrose probably did not sign until November: all sources agree that it was not until then that he joined the opposition (ibid, 68) and his signature is crowded between those of two nobles who were certainly present on 18 October. Wedgwood. *King's Peace*, 184, soon, took his signature as proof that he had joined earlier than was previously realised.

81 Guthry. *Memoirs*, 30–1; Ogilvie, J. D. 'The Kirkcudbright Petition, 1637' *PEBS*, xiv (1926–30), 47–8.

82 [Yorke, P., Earl of Hardwicke (ed)]. *Miscellaneous State Papers, from 1501 to 1726* (1778), ii.95–7.

83 Baillie. *Letters*, i.43; Hope. *Diary, 1633–45*, 66; GD 112/39/700, Breadalbane Muniments.

84 *RPCS, 1635–7*, 544–5; Row. *History*, 485–6.

85 Baillie. *Letters*, i.39; Leslie. *Relation*, 17, 30.

86 Leslie. *Relation*, 23–6; Baillie. *Letters*, i.40.

87 This and later discussions between the supplicants and privy councillors are often mentioned by contemporaries as being between supplicants and the council itself, thus transforming concessions or promises made by a few councillors into official acts of the council. The council did not sit in Edinburgh (or Holyroodhouse) between 19 October 1637 and July 1638 except briefly on 4 February.

88 Baillie. *Letters*, i.40–1; Leslie. *Relation*, 26–8, 32; Johnston. *Diary, 1632–9*, 272.

89 Baillie. *Letters*, i.42.

90 Several of the local petitions against the prayer book refer to the privy council as a 'Table', Fleming. *Scotland's Supplication*, 67n.

91 Eg, Gordon. *History*, i.28.

92 Leslie. *Relation*, 33.

93 *Stirling Recs, 1519–1666*, 178–9; BM, MS. Sloane 650, ff22v–23v.

94 Leslie. *Relation*, 33; Baillie. *Letters*, i.25.

95 HMC 8: 9th R. ii, *Traquair*, 248.

96 *RPCS, 1635–7*, 545–8.

97 Leslie. *Relation*, 43; Johnston. *Diary, 1632–9*, 282.

98 Leslie. *Relation*, 34–6, 44; Baillie. *Letters*, i.44–5.

99 Leslie. *Relation*, 36–8; *RPCS*, *1635–7*, 553–4.

100 Balfour. *Historical Works*, ii.241–4.

101 Leslie. *Relation*, 38–41, 45, 50–2; HMC 8: 9th R. ii, *Traquair*, 253–4; Row. *History*, 487–8; *RPCS*, *1635–7*, 554; Johnston. *Diary*, *1632–9*, 285.

102 HMC 8: 9th R. ii, *Traquair*, 248.

103 Leslie. *Relation*, 53; Johnston. *Diary*, *1632–9*, 289–90; Baillie. *Letters*, i.48.

104 Gordon. *History*, i.31.

105 Baillie. *Letters*, i.50–1.

106 [Yorke]. *State Papers*, ii.99–100.

107 Johnston. *Diary*, *1632–9*, 316; Baillie. *Letters*, i.50.

108 Leslie. *Relation*, 59–60; Johnston. *Diary*, *1632–9*, 317.

109 [Yorke]. *State Papers*, ii.97–9.

110 Leslie. *Relation*, 32, 52, 54–60, 63; Baillie. *Letters*, i.50; Johnston. *Diary*, *1632–9*, 317.

111 *RPCS*, *1638–43*, 3–4.

112 [Balcanquhal]. *Large Declaration*, 50.

113 *RPCS*, *1638–43*, 5; Leslie. *Relation*, 63–6; Baillie. *Letters*, i.50–1, 59–60; GD 45/1/35, Dalhousie Muniments.

114 *RPCS*, *1638–43*, 15–16.

115 Leslie. *Relation*, 66; Baillie. *Letters*, i.61; NLS, CH 903, Protestation, 22 February 1638.

116 Leslie. *Relation*, 67–8. Another common advertisement was sent to the burghs by the commissioners of burghs meeting in Edinburgh, Taylor, L. B. (ed). *Aberdeen Council Letters* (Oxford, 1950), ii.85–6.

117 Leslie. *Relation*, 69; Baillie. *Letters*, i.52.

118 Dickinson & Donaldson. *A Source Book of Scottish History*, ii.32–5.

119 Johnston. *Diary*, *1632–9*, 269.

120 Baillie. *Letters*, i.52.

121 Leslie. *Relation*, 71; Johnston. *Diary*, *1632–9*, 318–20.

122 Baillie. *Letters*, i.52–4; Johnston. *Diary*, *1632–9*, 321–2; Leslie. *Relation*, 72–8.

123 Ibid, 78–9; Johnston. *Diary, 1632–9*, 322–5; Fleming, D. H. *The Subscribing of the National Covenant* (Edinburgh, 1912).

124 Leslie. *Relation*, 79–80.

125 Tweedie, W. K. (ed). *Select Biographies* (Wodrow Society, 1845), i.159.

126 Leslie. *Relation*, 80–3.

127 Dickinson & Donaldson. *Source Book of Scottish History*, iii.95–104.

128 Ibid, iii.104.

129 Donaldson. *Scotland: Church and Nation through Sixteen Centuries*, 84.

130 Leslie. *Relation*, 90, 211.

131 Baillie. *Letters*, i.62–4.

132 [Yorke]. *State Papers*, ii.99–100.

133 *RPCS, 1638–43*, 7–11. The council's instructions to the justice clerk were later signed by five of the bishops who were councillors, Burnet. *Hamilton*, 34–6.

CHAPTER 3: *The Glasgow Assembly, March–December 1638*

1 *RPCS, 1638–43*, 17–18.

2 [Yorke]. *State Papers*, ii.106; Johnston. *Diary, 1632–9*, 329.

3 Hume, D. *The History of Great Britain: The Reigns of James I and Charles I*, ed D. Forbes (1970), 371.

4 Baillie. *Letters*, i.16.

5 Johnston. *Diary, 1632–9*, 332.

6 Ibid, 330.

7 Leslie. *Relation*, 96–8, 100–3; Balfour. *Historical Works*, ii.252–7; Burnet. *Hamilton*, 38–41.

8 Baillie. *Letters*, i.73, 75, 464–5.

9 Guthry. *Memoirs*, 36.

10 *RPCS, 1638–43*, 19; Hope. *Diary, 1633–45*, 72; *RMS, 1634–51*, no 814.

11 Taylor. *Aberdeen Council Letters*, ii.86–9; Baillie. *Letters*, i.64; Row. *History*, 490.

12 Henderson, A. *Sermons, Prayers and Pulpit Addresses, 1638*, ed
R. T. Wishaw (Edinburgh, 1866), 20–1, 23, 29–30; Baillie. *Letters,*
i.62, 64, 463–4.

13 Burnet. *Hamilton,* 41–2; [Yorke]. *State Papers,* ii.107.

14 Foster. 'The Operation of Presbyteries in Scotland', *RSCHS,*
xv.32–3 & n.

15 Leslie. *Relation,* 98, 104–7; Rose, H. & Shaw, L. *A Genealogical
Deduction of the Family of Rose of Kilravock* (Spalding Club, 1848),
321–2.

16 HMC 5: 6th R. *Ross of Pitcalnie,* 718; Fraser, W. (ed). *The
Sutherland Book* (Edinburgh, 1892), ii.169–70.

17 Leslie. *Relation,* 107–10.

18 Spalding. *Memorialls,* i.87–8.

19 Dalrymple, D., Lord Hailes (ed). *Memorials and Letters relating
to the History of Britain in the Reign of Charles the First* (Glasgow,
1766), 24–5.

20 Leslie. *Relation,* 110–12; [Balcanquhal]. *Large Declaration,*
79–81.

21 Baillie. *Letters,* i.75.

22 Ibid, i.75, 78; Leslie. *Relation,* 110.

23 Baillie. *Letters,* i.79; Burnet. *Hamilton,* 43, 52.

24 Leslie. *Relation,* 130–1.

25 Ibid, 113, 131–2, 133–4; Baillie. *Letters,* i.80.

26 Ibid, i.81; Leslie. *Relation,* 113–15; *RPCS, 1638–43,* 20–1.

27 Burnet. *Hamilton,* 27, 38. Since at least 1631 (Ibid, 11–12)
Hamilton had known Eleazar Borthwick, who in 1637 acted as his
agent in negotiations with Sweden (HMC 21: *Hamilton,* ii.39–41).
As we have seen, Borthwick is alleged by that time to have been
working for the king's enemies in Scotland. In 1639 Borthwick
denounced Hamilton for fighting against God (Ibid, i.106–7).

28 Baillie. *Letters,* i.74–5; Burnet. *Hamilton,* 38.

29 Burnet. *Hamilton,* 43–51.

30 Ibid, 52; Gardiner. *Hamilton Papers,* 6–7.

31 Baillie. *Letters,* i.82; *RPCS, 1638–43,* 21.

32 Leslie. *Relation,* 115; Balfour. *Historical Works,* ii.264; Baillie.
Letters, i.83. Hamilton himself put the number of people at 60,000,
Gardiner. *Hamilton Papers,* 7.

33 Leslie. *Relation*, 115–20, 135–40; Baillie. *Letters*, i.84; Gardiner. *Hamilton Papers*, 8–11.

34 Leslie. *Relation*, 120, 143–9; Johnston. *Diary, 1632–9*, 351–2; Baillie. *Letters*, i.85.

35 Burnet. *Hamilton*, 55–6, 59–61.

36 Leslie. *Relation*, 121–3, 149–73; Baillie. *Letters*, i.85–8; Balfour. *Historical Works*, ii.266–73; HMC 21: *Hamilton*, i.95–6.

37 *RPCS, 1638–43*, 32–4; [Balcanquhal]. *Large Declaration*, 96–8.

38 Ibid, 98–106; Johnston. *Diary, 1632–9*, 360; Ogilvie, J. D. 'A Bibliography of the Glasgow Assembly, 1638', *RGBS*, vii (1918–1920), 4; Leslie. *Relation*, 173–5; Baillie. *Letters*, i.91–2; Balfour. *Historical Works*, ii.275–7. Guthry. *Memoirs*, 40–1, states that on the same day (5 July) Hamilton had a private talk with some of the leading covenanters in which he said he spoke to them 'as a kindly Scotsman' and not as a king's commissioner, and encouraged them to 'go on with courage and resolution' in their quarrel with the king. Mathieson. *Politics and Religion*, i.407, inclined to believe this story of Hamilton's treachery (though not the far stronger evidence against Traquair), but though Hamilton later became well known for political intrigue there is no evidence of his disloyalty to the king in 1638 except for Guthry's story, and Guthry admits that reports of what Hamilton said varied greatly.

39 Leslie. *Relation*, 135.

40 Ibid, 142, 182.

41 Ibid, 141–77.

42 Ibid, 164, 169.

43 HMC 21: *Hamilton*, ii.50.

44 Gardiner. *Hamilton Papers*, 11.

45 Baillie. *Letters*, i.82–3.

46 Clarke, A. 'The Earl of Antrim and the First Bishops' War', *Irish Sword*, vi (1963–4), 108–9; Gardiner. *Hamilton Papers*, 12–13; Baillie. *Letters*, i.93.

47 Monson, W. *Naval Tracts*, ed M. Oppenheim (Navy Record Society, 1913), iii.318–22.

48 Wedgwood. *Thomas Wentworth*, 250–2; Knowler. *The Earl of Strafford's Letters and Dispatches*, ii.190–2.

49 Dalrymple. *Memorials*, 43.

50 *CSPD, 1637–8*, 574–5.

51 [Yorke]. *State Papers,* ii.109.

52 Innes, C. (ed). *The Black Book of Taymouth* (Bannatyne Club, 1855), 391–404; Murray, J., 7th Duke of Atholl (ed). *Chronicles of the Atholl and Tullibardine Families* (Edinburgh, 1908), i, app., x–xx.

53 *Aber. Recs, 1625–42,* 128–30.

54 Spalding. *Memorialls,* i.93. The dean of faculty and two professors of Glasgow University made similar reservations when signing the covenant, NLS, MS Acc 3142, Fleming of Wigtown Papers, Box XVIII, no B5/1, 3.

55 Spalding. *Memorialls,* i.94.

56 HMC 21: *Hamilton,* ii.47–8; Spalding. *Memorialls,* i.91–7; Gordon. *History,* i.82–96; Row. *History,* 495–6; Rogers. *Historical Notices of St Anthony's Monastery,* 42–4; Ogilvie, J. D. 'The Aberdeen Doctors and the National Covenant', *PEBS,* xi (1912–20), 73–86.

57 HMC 21: *Hamilton,* i.96; Burnet. *Hamilton,* 69; Spalding. *Memorialls,* i.106; HMC 8: 9th R. ii, *Traquair,* 254.

58 Gordon. *History,* i.97 & n.

59 In HMC 21: *Hamilton,* i.96 Hamilton is said to refer to his difficulties in getting the 1560 confession signed but it is clear from Gardiner. *Hamilton Papers,* 32, that it is the king's covenant (for which see below) to which he refers.

60 Burnet. *Hamilton,* 65–8.

61 [Balcanquhal]. *Large Declaration,* 116–17; Balfour. *Historical Works,* ii.272–9; Baillie. *Letters,* i.99.

62 [Balcanquhal]. *Large Declaration,* 117–21; Balfour. *Historical Works,* ii.279–86.

63 Baillie. *Letters,* i.99–100; Johnston. *Diary, 1632–9,* 374–5.

64 [Balcanquhal]. *Large Declaration,* 123.

65 Baillie. *Letters,* i.100–1; Johnston. *Diary, 1632–9,* 375–7; Gordon. *History,* i.98–103.

66 Burnet. *Hamilton,* 70–1.

67 Ibid, 72–4.

68 Johnston. *Diary, 1632–9,* 377.

69 [Balcanquhal]. *Large Declaration,* 129–31; Baillie. *Letters,* i.469, 471–2; Gordon. *History,* i.103–6.

70 Baillie. *Letters,* i.469–70.

71 *BUK*, ii.549, 601; Foster. 'Operation of Presbyteries in Scotland', *RSCHS*, xv.23.

72 *BUK*, ii.567.

73 Foster. 'Operation of Presbyteries in Scotland', 22–3.

74 Smout. *A History of the Scottish People,* 64–5; Donaldson. *Scotland: James V to James VII,* 199–200.

75 *BUK*, ii.947–8.

76 Makey, W. H. 'The Elders of Stow, Liberton, Canongate and St Cuthberts in the Mid-Seventeenth Century', *RSCHS*, xvii (1969–72), 155–67. For the role of the laity in the kirk see Cowan, I. B. 'Church and Society in Post-Reformation Scotland', *RSCHS*, xvii, 185–201.

77 Rutherford, S. *Lex Rex* (1644), preface. In 1648 the general assembly ruled that no burgh commissioners would be admitted who had not got the consent of the burghs' ministers and kirk sessions, Peterkin, A. (ed). *Records of the Kirk of Scotland* (Edinburgh, 1843), 496.

78 *BUK*, iii.974–9, 1022, 1085–91, 1116, 1143; Calderwood. *History of the Kirk of Scotland,* vi.752, vii.223, 304, 308, 316–17.

79 *RPCS, 1638–43,* 64–78; Balfour. *Historical Works,* ii.287–92; Gardiner. *Hamilton Papers,* 26–32.

80 Johnston. *Diary, 1632–9,* 391.

81. Burnet. *Hamilton,* 79.

82 [Balcanquhal]. *Large Declaration,* 157–73.

83 Johnston. *Diary, 1632–9,* 392; Balfour. *Historical Works,* ii. 292–3.

84 Gordon. *History,* i.118–19.

85 Ibid, i.119; [Balcanquhal]. *Large Declaration,* 186–8; Baillie. *Letters,* i.106.

86 Gardiner. *Hamilton Papers,* 43–4; HMC 21: *Hamilton,* i.97; Burnet. *Hamilton,* 84–5.

87 Ibid, 84, 86; Row. *History,* 500; Spalding. *Memorialls,* i.112–14; NLS, MS Adv 34.5.15, The King's Covenant, 1638; HMC 21: *Hamilton,* i.100.

88 *Aber. Recs, 1625–42,* 136–9; Burnet. *Hamilton,* 86–7.

89 Scot. 'Trew Relation', *SHR*, xiv.62–4; Balfour. *Historical*

Works, ii.294; Gardiner. *Hamilton Papers,* 49–55; [Balcanquhal]. *Large Declaration,* 193; Hope. *Diary, 1633–45,* 79.

90 Baillie. *Letters,* i.474.

91 Hope. *Diary, 1633–45,* 78, 79.

92 *RPCS, 1638–43,* 71–2; [Balcanquhal]. *Large Declaration,* 152; Baillie. *Letters,* i.107–8.

93 Ibid, i.115–16; Spalding. *Memorialls,* i.120–1.

94 HMC 21: *Hamilton,* i.97.

95 Gardiner. *Hamilton Papers,* 40–1.

96 Ibid, 22–5.

97 Gordon. *History,* i.103.

98 NLS, MS 3430, Lee Papers, f 7.

99 Baillie. *Letters,* i.104–5; Gardiner. *Hamilton Papers,* 36. Of 34 commissions to the assembly in NLS, MS 3430, Lee Papers, ff 7–66, 11 date from before the end of September, 10 from October and 13 from 1–17 November.

100 Register of the Presbytery of Glasgow, 1628–47 (in custody of Glasgow Town Clerk), 129–35.

101 [Balcanquhal]. *Large Declaration,* 188–92; Burnet. *Hamilton,* 85–6.

102 Out of the fourteen commissions from presbyteries in NLS, MS 3430 and Baillie. *Letters,* i.473 only two or three are signed by more elders than ministers. For a protest by nine ministers of the presbytery of Haddington against elders voting in the elections, see NLS, MS Wodrow, Fol LXII, f 36.

103 [Balcanquhal]. *Large Declaration,* 198–200.

104 Gardiner. *Hamilton Papers,* 38.

105 Dalrymple. *Memorials,* 46. The original letter is in NLS, MS Wodrow, Fol LXVI, no 58.

106 [Balcanquhal]. *Large Declaration,* 230–1.

107 Gardiner. *Hamilton Papers,* 46–55.

108 [Balcanquhal]. *Large Declaration,* 209–20; Balfour. *Historical Works,* ii.297–300; Baillie. *Letters,* i.108; Johnston. *Diary, 1632–9,* 395.

109 Burnet. *Hamilton,* 92; Gardiner. *Hamilton Papers,* 48–55; Hope. *Diary, 1633–45,* 80.

110 *RPCS, 1638–43,* 82–3.

111 Johnston. *Diary, 1632–9*, 399–400; Guthry. *Memoirs*, 46–7; Baillie. *Letters*, i.122.

112 Gardiner. *Hamilton Papers*, 46–9; Baillie. *Letters*, i.121.

113 Ibid, i.121–2; Johnston. *Diary, 1632–9*, 400, 401.

114 Baillie. *Letters*, i.124.

115 Burnet. *Hamilton*, 74, 79, 89; *RPCS, 1638–43*, 81–2; Gordon. *History*, i.140; [Balcanquhal]. *Large Declaration*, 235–6; Baillie. *Letters*, i.124.

116 Gardiner. *Hamilton Papers*, 59–60.

117 Baillie, *Letters*, i.123–5; Peterkin. *Records*, 129–31; Gordon. *History*, i.139–40; [Balcanquhal]. *Large Declaration*, 134–6.

118 Baillie. *Letters*, i.125.

119 Ibid, i.125–8; Hamilton's assessors were Traquair, Roxburgh, Argyll (the former Lord Lorne), Lauderdale, Southesk and Sir Lewis Stewart. [Balcanquhal]. *Large Declaration*, 236–7; Gordon. *History*, i.141–5.

120 Johnston. *Diary, 1632–9*, 401–2; Donaldson. *Scotland: James V to James VII*, 321–2.

121 Dickinson & Donaldson. *Source Book of Scottish History*, iii. 105.

122 Baillie. *Letters*, i.128–31; Gordon. *History*, i.145–9; [Balcanquhal]. *Large Declaration*, 237–9; Peterkin. *Records*, 131–5.

123 Baillie. *Letters*, i.131–6; Gordon. *History*, i.149–58; [Balcanquhal]. *Large Declaration*, 239–45; Peterkin. *Records*, 135–8; NLS, MS Wodrow, Fol LXII, ff 34, 56.

124 Baillie. *Letters*, i.136.

125 *BUK*, i.383, ii.646–7, iii.979–80, 1046, 1092, 1116, 1152; Calderwood. *History of the Kirk of Scotland*, vi.161, 752, vii.95, 223, 317–21.

126 Gordon. *History*, i.159.

127 Baillie. *Letters*, i.136–8; Gordon. *History*, i.158–71; [Balcanquhal]. *Large Declaration*, 247–68; Peterkin. *Records*, 138–40; *Edin. Recs, 1626–41*, 321.

128 [Balcanquhal]. *Large Declaration*, 268–9.

129 [Yorke]. *State Papers*, ii.113–21.

130 Peterkin. *Records*, 146.

131 Baillie. *Letters*, i.138–45; Gordon. *History*, i.171–93, ii.3–6;

Peterkin. *Records,* 22–4, 140–7; [Balcanquhal]. *Large Declaration,* 269–88; *Edin. Recs, 1626–41,* 321–2.

132 [Balcanquhal]. *Large Declaration,* 289–94; *RPCS, 1638–43,* 91–4; Baillie. *Letters,* i.145; Balfour. *Historical Works,* ii.305.

133 As with the 4 July protestation, that of 29 November was rewritten by Wariston before being printed, [Balcanquhal]. *Large Declaration,* 294–303; Stewart, W. 'On "The Protestation of the General Assemblie of the Church of Scotland" made at Glasgow in November, 1638', *RGBS,* i (1912–13), 106–17.

134 Gardiner. *Hamilton Papers,* 62–4; Gordon. *History,* ii.27.

135 Baillie. *Letters,* i.145–6.

136 Ibid, i.145–52; Gordon. *History,* ii.27–31, 39–54; Peterkin. *Records,* 24–6, 147–62.

137 Ibid, 26, 163–4; Baillie. *Letters,* i.153–4; Gordon. *History,* ii.58–95.

138 Johnston. *Diary, 1632–9,* 403.

139 This recalls the ruling in the 1618 assembly that any member who voted against one of the Five Articles of Perth would be marked as having voted against all five, Calderwood. *The History of the Church of Scotland,* vii.331.

140 Peterkin. *Records,* 28–32; Baillie. *Letters,* i.156–7, 158–9; Johnston. *Diary, 1632–9,* 403, shows little regard for truth when he says that while recording the vote he 'heard no word bot "Abjured and Removed"'.

141 Peterkin. *Records,* 32–3.

142 Baillie. *Letters,* i.154–6, 160–9; Gordon. *History,* ii.95–102, 131–52; Peterkin. *Records,* 26–8, 46, 164–80.

143 Ibid, 34–9.

144 Ibid, 46, 47. Wariston appointed Andrew Kerr to be his depute in both offices of clerk and procurator, CH 1/1/9, Acts and Proceedings of the General Assemblies, 1642–6, 1642, 100–2; CH 8/108.

145 Peterkin. *Records,* 39–42, 47; Balfour. *Historical Works,* ii.313–14; Ogilvie, J. D. 'A Bibliography of the Glasgow Assembly', *RGBS,* vii.1–12.

146 Baillie. *Letters,* i.158–9, 177–9, 181–4; [Balcanquhal]. *Large Declaration,* 324–6.

147 Donaldson. *Scotland: James V to James VII*, 321; NLS, MS Wodrow, Fol LXII, f 231; Peterkin. *Records*, 109–11. NLS, MS 7032, Yester Papers, ff 32–35v gives the names of many of those whose commissions were rejected by the assembly.

148 *RPCS, 1638–43*, 95–102; [Balcanquhal]. *Large Declaration*, 366–401.

149 Burnet. *Hamilton*, 107–8, 111.

150 Hope. *Diary, 1633–45*, 83.

CHAPTER 4: *The First Bishops' War and the Treaty of Berwick, January–July 1639*

1 GD 112/39/762, Breadalbane Muniments, cited in Wedgwood. *The King's Peace*, 240, 244.

2 Argyll MSS, Inverary Castle, Vaults, papers in vol. V.39; SRO, GD 112/39/763, 781, Breadalbane Muniments.

3 GD 16/52/19, Airlie Muniments; PA 7/2/52, Supplementary Parliamentary Papers; *CSPD, 1638–9*, 405–10; HMC 21: *Hamilton*, i.105. See Stevenson, D. 'The Financing of the Cause of the Covenants, 1638–51', *SHR*, li. (1972), 89–123, for the valuations and taxes of the covenanters.

4 [Yorke]. *State Papers*, ii.124; Knowler. *The Earl of Strafford's Letters and Dispatches*, ii.271–2.

5 Masson. *Drummond of Hawthornden*, 301.

6 Fischer, T. A. *The Scots in Sweden* (Edinburgh, 1907), 114–15.

7 Terry, C. S. 'Charles I and Alexander Leslie', *EHR*, xvi (1901), 115–20.

8 Turner, J. *Memoirs* (Bannatyne Club, 1829), 11, 14–15, 16.

9 HMC 23: *Cowper*, ii.227–8; HMC 21: *Hamilton*, i.105; Burnet. *Hamilton*, 132.

10 Gordon. *Britane's Distemper*, 12–13.

11 [Yorke]. *State Papers*, ii.123; Johnston. *Diary, 1632–9*, 405; Baillie. *Letters*, i.188.

12 Rushworth. *Historical Collections*, II.i.791–2, 818; HMC 8: 9th R. ii, *Traquair*, 249.

13 Rushworth. *Historical Collections,* II.i.798–802; Ogilvie, J. D.
'A Bibliography of the Bishops' Wars', *RGBS,* xii (1936), 21–2.

14 Gordon. *History,* ii.191–3; Baillie. *Letters,* i.188–9.

15 Baillie. *Letters,* i.189; Gordon. *History,* ii.198–202; Ogilvie.
'Bishops' Wars', 22–3.

16 Gordon. *History,* ii.240–6; *The Remonstrance of the Nobility,
Barrones, Burgesses, Ministers and Commons within the Kingdome of
Scotland, Vindicating them and their Proceedings* . . . (Edinburgh,
1639).

17 Johnston. *Diary, 1632–9,* 408, 410.

18 Baillie. *Letters,* i. 189–90.

19 *Some Speciall Arguments which warranted the Scottish Subjects lawfully to take up Armes in Defence of their Religion and Liberty when
they were in Danger. Extracted out of the Manuscripts of one of their
chiefe Reformers* . . . [1642]; Henderson's paper is also printed in
Stevenson, A. *History of the Church of Scotland* (Edinburgh, 1840)
356–60.

20 This is very similar to the question Knox began to ask in 1553
—'is obedience to be given to a Magistrate who commands
idolatry and condemns true religion?', Allen, J. W. *A History of
Political Thought in the Sixteenth Century* (3rd ed, 1951), 108; Burns,
J. H. 'The Political Ideas of the Scottish Reformation', *Aberdeen
University Review,* xxxvi (1955–6), 254.

21 Allen. *History of Political Thought in the Sixteenth Century,* 114.

22 Guthry. *Memoirs,* 51; Gordon. *History,* ii.204–5; Baillie. *Letters,*
i.191–2; GD 112/39/753, Breadalbane Muniments.

23 Baillie. *Letters,* i.190–1.

24 Gordon. *History,* iii.7–9; Dalrymple. *Memorials,* 57–65.

25 Baillie. *Letters,* i.191.

26 Ranke, L. *History of England* (Oxford, 1875), ii.156; Robertson,
A. *Sir Robert Moray* (1922), 6; Gardiner, S. R. *History of England*
(1883–4), viii.382. For rumours and allegations of Scots-French
contacts see Ranke, op cit, v.457–63; HMC 23; *Cowper,* ii.219;
Gordon. *Britane's Distemper,* 5–6.

27 *RPCS, 1638–43,* 104–16; Burnet. *Hamilton,* 115.

28 Peterkin. *Records,* 211–12; Hope. *Diary, 1633–45,* 89; Baillie.
Letters, i.198.

29 Hope. *Diary, 1633–45*, 89–92; *RPCS, 1638–43*, 116–19.

30 *Aber Recs, 1625–42*, 145–8; Spalding. *Memorialls*, i.125, 128–9, 132–3.

31 Spalding. *Memorialls*, i.131.

32 Macgill, W. *Old Ross-shire and Scotland* (Inverness, 1910–11), Supp vol, 9–10.

33 Row. *History*, 507; Spalding. *Memorialls*, i.133.

34 Spalding. *Memorialls*, i.135–6.

35 Ibid, i.136–8; Row. *History*, 507; Gordon. *History*, ii.210–14; HMC 10: 10th R. i, *Eglinton*, 48.

36 Gordon. *History*, ii.213; Spalding. *Memorialls*, i.138; Gardiner. *History of England*, ix.3 wrongly states that Huntly 'was ordered to take the aggressive' by the king. Huntly's commission as lieutenant did not reach Aberdeen until 9 March, Spalding. *Memorialls*, i. 144–6.

37 Ibid, i.143–4; Gordon. *History*, ii.219–22; *Aber Recs, 1625–42*, 151–4.

38 Spalding. *Memorialls*, i.149–56.

39 Baillie. *Letters*, i.196; Johnston. *Diary, 1639*, 92.

40 Burnet. *Hamilton*, 90, 114; Macray, W. D. (ed). *Ruthven Correspondence* (Roxburghe Club, 1868), 9–12; PS 1/109, Register of the Privy Seal, ff 108–108v.

41 Balfour. *Historical Works*, ii.321; Gordon. *History*, ii.209–10; Baillie. *Letters*, i.195.

42 Guthry. *Memoirs*, 52–3; Balfour. *Historical Works*, ii.321–2; Rushworth. *Historical Collections*, II.ii.906–8.

43 GD 112/39/755; Gardiner. *Hamilton Papers*, 68–70; Burnet. *Hamilton*, 64, 117.

44 Baillie. *Letters*, i.196; Burnet. *Hamilton*, 115–16.

45 Burnet. *Hamilton*, 113.

46 Clarke, A. 'The Earl of Antrim and the First Bishops' War', *Irish Sword*, vi (1963–4), 111–15.

47 Burnet. *Hamilton*, 120; Rushworth. *Historical Collections*, II.ii. 903–5.

48 *CSPD, 1639*, 79–81.

49 Burnet. *Hamilton*, 119–20, 123; *Calendar of Clarendon State Papers* (Oxford, 1872), i.175.

50 *CSPD, 1639,* 77–9; Gordon. *History,* ii.246–8.

51 HMC 24: *Rutland,* i.504.

52 HMC 21: *Hamilton,* i.47.

53 Gardiner. *Hamilton Papers,* 72–6.

54 Burnet. *Hamilton,* 123.

55 Gardiner. *Hamilton Papers,* 77.

56 Burnet. *Hamilton,* 124; *Edin. Recs, 1626–41,* 217–19; *CSPD, 1639,* 126–8, 166–7.

57 GD 112/39/768, Breadalbane Muniments; Gordon. *History,* ii.249–50.

58 Gardiner. *Hamilton Papers,* 79–84; Burnet. *Hamilton,* 131, 133–5.

59 Gardiner. *Hamilton Papers,* 86–7; Burnet. *Hamilton,* 133, 138, 139.

60 Gardiner. *History of England,* ix.10–11.

61 Peterkin. *Records,* 214–15, 218–19, 222–3; HMC 23: *Cowper,* ii.225, 226; *CSPD, 1639,* 58–61; Johnston. *Diary, 1639,* 37–41.

62 HMC 24: *Rutland,* i.508.

63 *CSPD, 1639,* 189; Johnston. *Diary, 1639,* 38–9.

64 Gardiner. *History of England,* ix.22–3; Baillie. *Letters,* i.209–10.

65 Gardiner. *History of England,* ix.23–31, 35–6.

66 Spalding. *Memorialls,* i.156–7; Gordon. *History,* ii.229–32.

67 Spalding. *Memorialls,* i.168–72, 176–80; Gordon. *History,* ii.234–40.

68 Ibid, ii.225–9; Spalding. *Memorialls,* i.156–68, 171–3; *Aber Recs, 1625–42,* 155–8.

69 Spalding. *Memorialls,* i.173–6, 181–2, 185–6; Gordon. *History,* ii.254–9.

70 *Aber Recs, 1626–42,* 164–5; Spalding. *Memorialls,* i.186–94, 198–9; Gordon. *History,* ii.261–5.

71 Spalding. *Memorialls,* i.198–213; Gordon. *History,* ii.265–82.

72 HMC 8: 9th R. ii, *Traquair,* 255; McKechnie, H. *The Lamont Clan* (Edinburgh, 1938), 155–6, 158; Baillie. *Letters,* i.193, 206.

73. Innes, C. (ed). *The Book of the Thanes of Cawdor* (Spalding Club, 1859), 299; GD 112/39/776, Breadalbane Muniments.

74 For the orders of a meeting of the sheriffdom of Perth on 3 May for implementing these instructions see GD 112/43/1, bundle

marked 'State Papers, c 1545–1639'; *Aber Recs, 1625–42*, 161; Baillie. *Letters,* i.200–1.

75 Baillie. *Letters,* i.200, 203; *RPCS, 1678–43*, 118–19; Hope. *Diary, 1633–45*, 95; Gordon. *History,* ii.250–1; *APS,* v.247.

76 Fraser, W. (ed). *The Melvilles earls of Melville, and the Leslies earls of Leven* (Edinburgh, 1890), iii.162–4.

77 Baillie. *Letters,* i.213–14.

78 Johnston. *Diary, 1639*, 35–6.

79 Ibid, 44; Baillie. *Letters,* ii.438–9; Terry, C. S. *Alexander Leslie* (1899), 61. The letter is undated in Baillie and misdated 18 May by Terry.

80 Johnston. *Diary, 1639*, 44–5, 46–7, 50–1, 52–3, 55–7; Baillie. *Letters,* ii.440.

81 Johnston. *Diary, 1639*, 58, 61–2.

82 Baillie. *Letters,* i.213.

83 Hill, G. *An Historical Account of the Macdonnells of Antrim* (Belfast, 1873), 444–6; NLS, MS 3784, Miscellaneous Documents, ff 36–40.

84 Johnston. *Diary, 1639*, 63–6; Baillie. *Letters,* i.215; Gordon. *History,* iii.9–10.

85 Ibid, iii.10–11; Johnston. *Diary, 1639*, 66n, 68; Baillie. *Letters,* i.215–16.

86 Baillie. *Letters,* i.216; Johnston. *Diary, 1639*, 68–70.

87 [Yorke]. *State Papers,* ii.131–9; Johnston. *Diary, 1639*, 70–6.

88 [Yorke]. *State Papers,* ii.139–41; Johnston. *Diary, 1639*, 77–80.

89 Ibid, 82–4.

90 Ibid, 84–5.

91 Wedgwood. *The King's Peace,* 276.

92 Johnston. *Diary, 1639*, 85, 87–8.

93 Baillie. *Letters,* i.218.

94 Balfour. *Historical Works,* ii.327–8.

95 Ibid, ii.329–32.

96 Johnston. *Diary, 1639*, 93–5; Gordon. *History,* iii.18–19, 20–2.

97 *A True Representation of the Proceedings of the Kingdome of Scotland since the late pacification . . .* (1640), 15–16.

98 Balfour. *Historical Works,* ii.329, 332; Johnston. *Diary, 1639*, 92–3, 95.

99 Ibid, 95.

100 Hope. *Diary, 1633–45*, 99; Burnet. *Hamilton*, 144.

101 Ogilvie. 'A Bibliography of the Bishops' Wars', *RGBS*, xii. 34–5.

102 HMC 55: *Various Collections*, v.234–5; Johnston. *Diary, 1639*, 96–7; Balfour. *Historical Works*, ii.333.

103 *RPCS, 1638–43*, 122–3.

104 Peterkin. *Records*, 231–2.

105 Baillie. *Letters*, i.220; Burnet. *Hamilton*, 144; Gardiner. *Hamilton Papers*, 94–5; Guthry. *Memoirs*, 60.

106 Balfour. *Historical Works*, ii.334; Guthry. *Memoirs*, 60–1.

107 Gardiner. *Hamilton Papers*, 92–3, 94, 96.

108 Ibid, 92, 94, 96, 97–9; Guthry. *Memoirs*, 61.

109 *CSPD, 1639*, 407–9; Guthry. *Memoirs*, 61–2; Spalding. *Memorialls*, i.221–3.

110 Ibid, i.219–21, 223; Balfour. *Historical Works*, ii.334–40, 344–5.

111 Rushworth. *Historical Collections*, II.ii.965–6; *CSPD, 1639*, 432–4.

112 Burnet. *Hamilton*, 149.

113 Gardiner. *Hamilton Papers*, 99–100.

114 [Yorke]. *State Papers*, ii.141–2.

115 Burnet. *Hamilton*, 144–8.

116 *RMS, 1634–51*, no 916; *RPCS, 1638–43*, 128–9.

117 Gardiner. *History of England*, ix.7.

CHAPTER 5: *The Failure of the Treaty of Berwick, July 1639–March 1640*

1 Burnet. *Hamilton*, 149–51, 156–7.

2 Ibid, 154.

3 Gordon. *History*, iii.39–43; Peterkin. *Records*, 238–51.

4 Ibid, 204–5; Gordon. *History*, iii.45–7.

5 Peterkin. *Records*, 251–2.

6 Ibid, 254. The agreement was presumably contained in the unpublished 'Act anent the Assembly of Glasgow', ibid, 209; Balfour. *Historical Works*, ii.353.

7 Burnet. *Hamilton,* 156–7. The king had debated the difference between unconstitutional and unlawful at Berwick with Rothes in July, Gardiner. *Hamilton Papers,* 99.

8 Peterkin. *Records,* 208.

9 Ibid, 207; *RPCS, 1638–43,* 131–2; Gordon. *History,* iii.55–60.

10 Peterkin. *Records,* 207–8, 268–9.

11 Burnet. *Hamilton,* 156–7.

12 Ibid, 150.

13 Peterkin. *Records,* 270–2.

14 *RPCS, 1638–43,* 132–3. In August 1641 parliament (at the request of the general assembly) ordered Traquair's declarations to be deleted from the council records, *APS,* v.328; Baillie. *Letters,* i.374, 384.

15 Burnet. *Hamilton,* 158–9.

16 *RPCS, 1638–43,* 124; *APS,* v.247–50; HMC 8: 9th R. ii, *Traquair,* 249.

17 Rait. *Parliaments of Scotland,* 166–75.

18 Ibid, 165–6, 178–9, 195–200, 203–4, 206–7; *APS,* iii.509–10. As the old extent was a fixed traditional valuation the size of the electorate did not increase with inflation as in England.

19 Rait. *Parliaments of Scotland,* 249–58, 265–9, 271–3; Mackie, J. D. & Pryde, G. S. *The Estate of the Burgesses in the Scots Parliament* (St Andrews, 1923), 6–8.

20 Rait. *Parliaments of Scotland,* 13–15; Mackie & Pryde. *The Estate of the Burgesses in the Scots Parliament,* 9–10, 12–27.

21 Rait. *Parliaments of Scotland,* 279–80, 370–1.

22 Ibid, 410; Sir Robert Gordon, 'Anent the Government of Scotland as it was before the late troubles', in Macfarlane, W. *Geographical Collections* (SHS, 1907), ii.393.

23 Ibid, ii.400–1.

24 Rait. *Parliaments of Scotland,* 408–9; Row. *History,* 366.

25 *APS,* v.351–2; Balfour. *Historical Works,* ii.354–8.

26 HMC 8: 9th R. ii, *Traquair,* 261.

27 Ibid, 249.

28 Balfour. *Historical Works,* ii.353–60; Gordon. *History,* iii.63–4.

29 GD 112/39/786, Breadalbane Muniments; *APS,* v.252–4; Gordon. *History,* iii.64.

30 *APS,* v.253.

31 Taylor. *Aberdeen Council Letters,* ii.145-8.

32 Ibid, ii.140-5; NLS, MS Wodrow, Fol LXIV, no 26; Gardiner. *History of England,* ix.53-4n.

33 GD 112/39/786, Breadalbane Muniments; Taylor. *Aberdeen Council Letters,* ii.134-5.

34 GD 112/39/786.

35 *APS,* v.593, 601.

36 Ibid, v.598, 601, 602.

37 BM, MS Add 11,045, f 57; Gordon. *History,* iii.66-8.

38 *APS,* v.614; BM, MS Add 11,045, f 70.

39 Gordon. *History,* iii.74.

40 Burnet. *Hamilton,* 158-9.

41 Gardiner. *History of England,* ix.51-2n.

42 Balfour. *Historical Works,* ii.361.

43 GD 112/39/789, Breadalbane Muniments.

44 GD 112/39/791; *APS,* v.608.

45 Balfour. *Historical Works,* ii.361-2.

46 *APS,* v.616.

47 Burnet. *Hamilton,* 159-60; Guthry. *Memoirs,* 65-6; Gordon. *History,* iii.76-8; Gardiner. *History of England,* ix.73-4.

48 Gordon. *History,* iii.74-5.

49 Gardiner. *History of England,* ix.74.

50 *APS,* v. 255-8.

51 Eg, HMC 77: *De L'Isle,* vi. 201.

52 *RPCS, 1638-43,* 141-2.

53 Balfour. *Historical Works,* ii.364-9; HMC 21: *Hamilton,* i.109; Guthry. *Memoirs,* 66.

54 *RPCS, 1638-43,* 131.

55 Burnet. *Hamilton,* 160; Dalrymple. *Memorials,* 76-7.

56 Burnet. *Hamilton,* 160; Gardiner. *History of England,* ix.76.

57 Ibid, ix.75-6; Gordon. *History,* iii.107.

58 Mackie, J. D. & Dunbar J. G. (eds)., *Accounts of the Master of Works,* ii.399-430 (not yet published; seen in proof at Scottish Record Office).

59 Gordon. *History,* iii.86-7.

60 Gordon. *History,* iii.78-80; Spalding. *Memorialls,* i.244.

61 Gordon. *History,* iii.111–13.

62 Ibid, iii. 93–8; Spalding. *Memorialls,* i.247–51.

63 Gordon. *History,* iii.99–100; Spalding. *Memorialls.* i.245–6; *Edin. Recs, 1626–41,* 231–2; Macray. *Ruthven Correspondence,* 21–9, 31–2.

64 Rose & Shaw. *A Genealogical Deduction of the Family of Rose of Kilravock,* 326–7; Taylor. *Aberdeen Council Letters,* ii.176.

65 Macray. *Ruthven Correspondence,* 59.

66 Spalding. *Memorialls,* i.260; Gordon. *History,* iii.125–8; Taylor. *Aberdeen Council Letters,* ii.89–90.

67 Macray. *Ruthven Correspondence,* 43–4, 58, 61.

68 Gardiner. *History of England,* ix.91–2; PRO.31/3/71, Transcripts of Dispatches by Bellièvre, ff 86–86v, 139v–140v.

69 Gardiner. *History of England,* ix.92.

70 The letter cannot have been signed on 19 February as Loudoun was in London at the time.

71 *CSPD, 1640,* 103–4.

72 Mazure, F. A. J. *Historie de la Revolution de 1688 en Angleterre* (Paris,1825), iii.405–10; *CSPD, 1640,* 103–4; Gardiner. *History of England,* ix.92–3.

73 Balfour. *Historical Works,* ii.76; *APS,* v.432, 670, 711–12; Guthry. *Memoirs,* 69.

74 *CSPD, 1639–40,* 496.

75 Spalding. *Memorialls,* i.257–8.

76 Gordon. *History,* iii.114–15.

77 Ibid, iii.106–25; Rushworth. *Historical Collections,* II.ii.992–1018; *CSPD, 1639–40,* 534–5, 543, 553; *A True Representation of the Proceedings of the Kingdome of Scotland since the late pacification. By the Estates of the Kingdome Against mistakings in the late Declaration* (1640), Part 2.

CHAPTER 6: *The Second Bishops' War and the Treaty of Ripon, March–November 1640*

1 *CSPD, 1639–40,* 610–11.

2 Spalding. *Memorialls,* i.262.

3 Rushworth. *Historical Works*, II.ii.1103–4; *CSPD, 1640*, 32; HMC 77: *De L'Isle*, vi.244.

4 Collins. *Letters and Memorials of State*, ii.644–5.

5 *CSPD, 1640*, 29–30; Burnet, *Hamilton*, 161; Dalrymple. *Memorials*, 57–8.

6 Rushworth. *Historical Collections*, II.ii.1117–20; *CJ*, ii.5; *LJ*, iv. 46–8.

7 Gardiner. *History of England*, ix.98–118.

8 *A True Representation of the Proceedings of the Kingdome of Scotland since the late pacification* . . . (1640), Pt 2, 88–9; *A Remonstrance concerning the Present Troubles* . . . (1640), 33–6.

9 Ibid, 37–8; Dalrymple. *Memorials*, 62–5; *CSPD, 1640*, 29–30; *LJ*, iv.55; NLS, MS.3368, Scottish Historical Letters, ff 16–16v.

10 Avenal, D. (ed). *Lettres, Instructions Diplomatiques et Papiers D'Etat du Cardinal de Richelieu* (7 vols, Paris, 1853–67), vi.688n, 689n.

11 Ibid, v.1094; Hay, M. V. *The Blairs Papers* (1929), 122–3, 126, 251, 252–3; Blakhal, G. *A Breiff Narration of the Services done to Three Noble Ladyes* (Spalding Club, 1844), 114, 121; Collins. *Letters and Memorials of State*, ii.562, 596, 599.

12 Collins. *Letters and Memorials of State*, ii.646; *CSPD, 1640*, 100–1.

13 Gardiner. *History of England*, ix.97.

14 Collins. *Letters and Memorials of State*, ii.647–8.

15 *A Remonstrance concerning the Present Troubles*, 1, 2–3, 4–5, 22, 25–6.

16 Baker, R. *Chronicle of the Kings of England* (1670), 492.

17 Burnet. *A History of My Own Times*, i.42.

18 [Denniston, J. (ed)]. *Coltness Collections* (Maitland Club, 1842), 20–1. Stewart noted in his diary (now lost) on 6 February 'Mr Frost and I came from London in ten days. What have I to doe in the quarel, Earl Strafford and Lord Savill? . . . What if Traquare is at the back of the halland', ie, what if Savile was an *agent provocateur* incited by Traquair?, ibid, 19n.

19 *CSPD, 1640*, 140–1, 144–5, 156; HMC 77: *De L'Isle*. vi.272, 276; Guthry. *Memoirs*, 71; Whitelocke, B. *Memorials of the English Affairs* (Oxford, 1853), i.94.

20 Gardiner. *History of England,* ix.120, 122, 136, 140, 154, 163.

21 *Aber. Recs, 1625–42,* 193–5.

22 *CSPD, 1639–40,* 577.

23 Cuningham, T. *Journal* (SHS, 1928), 37–8.

24 Gordon. *History,* iii.148–53.

25 Fraser. *The Leslies earls of Leven and the Melvilles earls of Melville,* iii.164–7.

26 Gordon. *History,* iii.159.

27 *Spalding. Memorialls,* i.266–8, 272–9; Gordon. *History,* iii.160, 166–9.

28 *Aber. Recs, 1625–42,* 219–20.

29 Napier, M. *Montrose and the Covenanters* (1838), i.362.

30 Ibid, i.330, 380–2; Napier, M. *Memorials of Montrose* (Maitland Club, 1848–50), i.227, 266–7.

31 Napier. *Montrose and the Covenanters,* i.373–4, 380, 382–3, 387, 389–90; Napier. *Memorials of Montrose,* i.276, 278, 279–81.

32 Gardiner. *History of England,* ix.136; Fraser, W. (ed), *The Elphinstone Family Book* (Edinburgh, 1897), ii.162.

33 Hope. *Diary, 1633–45,* 116.

34 To fence a court was to make a declaration formally constituting it.

35 Burnet. *Hamilton,* 166–7 states that the commission that the king intended Craighall to use was a blank one which he sent for the purpose, but the king himself refers to that of 20 August as the one to be used, Fraser. *The Elphinstone Book,* ii.162; *APS,* v. 249.

36 *APS,* v.259–62.

37 Balfour. *Historical Works,* ii.379.

38 *APS,* v.262.

39 Ibid, v.268.

40 Ibid, v.270.

41 *Edin. Recs, 1626–41,* 241–2; GD.112/40/2, Breadalbane Muniments, bundle 'Letters 1640–1649', 8 June 1640, Glencarradale to Glenorchy.

42 Warner, G. F. (ed). *The Nicholas Papers* (Camden Society, 1886), i.24.

43 *APS,* v.296–7.

44 Ibid, v.282–4.

45 Ibid, v.270–8.

46 Ibid, v.269, 290–2. For a copy of the band signed by nobles and many of the leading covenanters of Caithness, see J. A. Fairley, 'Lord Sinclair, Covenanter and Royalist', *Trans. Buchan Field Club*, viii (1904–5), 161–6, 168.

47 *APS*, v.280–2.

48 Ibid, v.262, 264, 292–4.

49 Ibid, v.286–7, 289–90.

50 Ibid, v.299–300.

51 Lanark, the younger brother of the Marquis of Hamilton, had been appointed joint secretary of state with the master of requests in February 1640 on the death of the Earl of Stirling, though he had no experience of public affairs—'The Choice is much wondered att, for till now, no Man that I have mett with, did euer know whether he could write or not' wrote Northumberland, Collins. *Letters and Memorials of State*, ii.640; HMC 8: 9th R. ii, *Traquair*, 250.

52 Burnet. *Hamilton*, 170–3.

53 Spalding, *Memorialls*, i.280–90; Gordon. *History*, iii.197–200; Taylor. *Aberdeen Council Letters*, ii.169–72.

54 Spalding. *Memorialls*. i.297–306, 314–15; Gordon. *History*, iii. 201–3, 210–14, 251–5.

55 HMC 3: 4th R. *Argyll*, 491–2.

56 Fairley. 'Lord Sinclair', *Trans. Buchan Field Club*, viii.153.

57 GD.112/40/2, Breadalbane Muniments, bundle 'Letters 1640–1649', 25 May 1640, Glencarradale to Glenorchy.

58 Terry. *Alexander Leslie*, 93–5; HMC 26: *Atholl & Home*, 25.

59 GD.44/9/13/1,2,3, Gordon Castle Muniments; Gordon. *History*, iii.163; Spalding. *Memorialls*, i.240, ii.87.

60 GD.112/39/801, 802, 803, 804.

61 GD.112/39/809.

62 Napier. *Memorials of Montrose*, i.259.

63 Baillie. *Letters*, i.247; GD.112/39/806, 807, 808, 809.

64 Napier. *Memorials of Montrose*, i.264–6, 328–30; Gordon. *History*, iii.164–5; Spalding. *Memorialls*, i.290–2.

65 Napier. *Memorials of Montrose*, i.298, 477.

66 In June 1641 Argyll produced six bands which he had offered for subscription in July 1640, Napier. *Montrose and the Covenanters*, i.502, 503n.

67 Napier. *Memorials of Montrose*, i.266–7, 279–81, ii.46–7; Guthry. *Memoirs*, 94–5.

68 Spalding. *Memorialls*, i.271; Gordon. *History*, iii.164; Balfour. *Historical Works*, ii.380–1.

69 GD.112/43/1, Breadalbanes Muniment, commission dated 5 October 1640 in bundle 'State Papers, 1640–9'.

70 Peterkin. *Records*, 278, 279.

71 Sprott, G. W. *The Worship of the Church of Scotland during the Covenanting Period, 1638–61* (Edinburgh, 1893), 10.

72 Baillie. *Letters*, i.252.

73 Guthry. *Memoirs*, 78–82; Gordon. *History*, iii.221–3; Baillie. *Letters*, i.248–55; Stevenson, D. 'The Radical Party in the Kirk, 1637–45', *Journal of Ecclesiastical History* (1973—forthcoming).

74 Ibid.

75 Peterkin. *Records*, 279.

76 Terry. *Alexander Leslie*, 99.

77 Spalding. *Memorialls*, i.314, 316–18, 320; Steele, R. *A Bibliography of Royal Proclamations of the Tudor and Stuart Sovereigns* (Oxford, 1910), ii.314; *Minute Book kept by the War Committee of the Covenanters in the Stewartry of Kirkcudbright in 1640 and 1641* (Kirkcudbright, 1855), 1–26.

78 An English account of doubtful authority asserts that late in 1639 Lord Saye and Sele sent a message to Loudoun and Rothes urging the Scots to invade England, or the king's English opponents would be forced to fight for him, and that in 1640 a similar message was sent to the covenanters, Gardiner. *Hamilton Papers*, 264–7; Zagorin. *The Court and the Country*, 103–4.

79 Oldmixon, J. *The History of England during the Reign of the Royal House of Stuart* (1730), 141–2. Oldmixon is not in general reliable, but the letters quoted by him and cited in this and following notes seem to be genuine. See Gardiner. *History of England*, ix.179–81n.

80 Oldmixon. *History of England*, 142–4.

81 Gardiner. *History of England*, ix.178–9 & n; Welwood, J. *Memoirs of the Most Material Transactions in England . . .* (1820), 85–7;

Burnet. *History of his Own Times,* i.44n. The text of the Savile Letter has not survived but there seems no doubt as to its contents.

82 Johnston. *Diary, 1639,* 97; Edinburgh University Library, MS.Dc.4.16, The Transactions of the Committee of Estates, ff 1–iv.

83 Spalding. *Memorialls,* i.321–9.

84 Rushworth. *Historical Collections,* II.ii.1223–7.

85 Guthry. *Memoirs,* 88; Napier. *Montrose and the Covenanters,* i.373–5, 380.

86 Napier. *Memorials of Montrose,* i.254–5; Guthry. *Memoirs,* 89.

87 Dalrymple. *Memorials,* 81–106; Terry. *Alexander Leslie,* 95–100, 103–6.

88 Ibid, 107; Rushworth. *Historical Collections,* II.ii.1221.

89 Johnston. *Diary, 1639,* 97–8; Baillie. *Letters,* i.255.

90 Steele. *Tudor and Stuart Proclamations,* ii.314.

91 EUL.MS.Dc.4.16, f iv.

92 Baillie. *Letters,* i.256–9; Terry. *Alexander Leslie,* 107–38; Balfour. *Historical Works,* ii.383–91.

93 Spalding. *Memorialls,* i.336.

94 Baillie. *Letters,* i.620; Fraser, W. (ed). *The Book of Carlaverock* (Edinburgh, 1873), ii.15–17, 134–7.

95 Macray. *Ruthven Correspondence,* 12–69; Somerville, J. *Memorie of the Somervilles* (1815), ii.223–70; NLS, MS.2618, ff 2–20; Spalding. *Memorialls,* i.340.

96 Ibid, i.336.

97 Terry. *Alexander Leslie,* 128–9; Gordon. *History,* iii.255.

98 For efforts to supply the army see Taylor. *Aberdeen Council Letters,* ii.236–9; *Minute-book . . . of Kirkcudbright,* 48–55, 63–4, 68–70, 71–2, 76–8.

99 [Yorke]. *State Papers,* ii. 180; Gardiner. *History of England,* ix.189; Terry. *Alexander Leslie,* 144–6.

100 Baillie. *Letters,* i.258.

101 Collins. *Letters and Memorials of State,* ii.658–9.

102 Gardiner. *History of England,* ix.198–9, 200.

103 Burnet. *Hamilton,* 174–6.

104 Rushworth. *Historical Collections,* II.ii.1258–9; *CSPD, 1640–1,* 59–60.

105 Napier. *Montrose and the Covenanters*, i.376.

106 Burnet. *Hamilton*, 179; Hope. *Diary, 1633–45*, 120; Baillie. *Letters*, i.262.

107 Rushworth. *Historical Collections*, II.1276–7; [Yorke]. *State Papers*, ii.186–8, 208.

108 Ibid, ii.217–26, 235–41; Rushworth. *Historical Collections*, II.ii.1282–4.

109 Balfour. *Historical Works*, ii.408–11.

110 [Yorke]. *State Papers*, ii. 192,227–34.

111 Rushworth. *Historical Collections*, II.ii.1285; Balfour. *Historical Works*, ii.407–8.

112 Borough, J. *Notes of the Treaty carried on at Ripon* . . . (Camden Society, 1869), 2–69; Rushworth. *Historical Collections*, II.ii.1286–96, 1305–10; [Yorke]. *State Papers*, ii.193–208.

113 Oldmixon. *History of England*, 152; Welwood. *Memoirs*, 88; Nalson, J. *Impartial Collection* (1682–3), ii.428.

114 [Yorke]. *State Papers*, ii.292–6; Gardiner. *History of England*, ix.215–16.

CHAPTER 7: *The Treaty of London and the 1641 Parliament, November 1640–November 1641*

1 *APS*, v.336–7; *CSPD, 1640–1*, 244–6.

2 NLS, MS.Adv.33.4.6., Treaties at Newcastle and London, 1640–1, 109–10.

3 Balfour. *Historical Works*, ii.421–2, 424–5; Gardiner. *History of England*, ix.220.

4 Baillie. *Letters*, i.275–6.

5 Balfour. *Historical Works*, ii.419–20.

6 BM, MS.Harl.457, 'Minutes of the Treaty . . .', ff 3–6; BM, MS. Stowe 187, 'Proceedings of the Parliaments of England and Scotland . . .', ff 2–3.

7 Burnet. *Hamilton*, 177.

8 *CSPD, 1640–1*, 244–5.

9 *APS*, v.337; Baillie. *Letters*, i.276, 277.

10 *APS*, v.337–8; Baillie. *Letters*, i.278.

11 Napier. *Montrose and the Covenanters*, i. 350–1.

12 *APS*, v.338; Baillie. *Letters*, i.279, 284, 285.

13 *APS*, v.338–40; Baillie. *Letters*, i.297, 300.

14 Ibid, i.280; Spalding. *Memorialls*, i.363–74.

15 Steele. *Tudor and Stuart Proclamations*, i.224.

16 Burnet. *Hamilton*, 184, 185–6; Baillie. *Letters*, i.304, 305, 310; HMC 5: 6th R. *Argyll*, 622.

17 Hyde. *History of the Rebellion*, i.200–2.

18 NRA(S), Survey /0006, Argyll MSS (1967), 122; GD.112/40/2 Breadalbane Muniments, Glencarradale to Glenorchy, 9 March 1641.

19 Baillie. *Letters*, i.305; Dalrymple. *Memorials*, 107.

20 Steele. *Tudor and Stuart Proclamations*, i.224; Spalding. *Memorialls*, ii.9–10.

21 Baillie. *Letters*, i.305–6.

22 EUL, MS.Dc.4.16, Transactions of the Committee of Estates, ff 74v–75; Dalrymple. *Memorials*, 107–9.

23 Steele. *Tudor and Stuart Proclamations*, i.224; Ogilvie, J. D. 'A Broadside of 1641', *PEBS*, xii (1921–5), 78–83.

24 Dalrymple. *Memorials*, 110; Baillie. *Letters*, i.306–7.

25 Gardiner. *History of England*, ix.297.

26 Napier. *Montrose and the Covenanters*, i.507.

27 EUL, MS.Dc.4.16, Transactions of the Committee of Estates, ff 78, 82.

28 *APS*, v.340.

29 Baillie. *Letters*, i.301.

30 *APS*, v.340.

31 Hetherington, W. M. *History of the Westminster Assembly of Divines* (Edinburgh, 1843), 376–84.

32 *APS*, v.340; See Ogilvie, J. D. 'Church Union in 1641', *RSCHS*, i. (1926), 143–60, and Hamilton, C. L. 'The Basis for Scottish Efforts to create a Reformed Church in England, 1640–1', *Church History*, xxx (1961), 171–8.

33 *CSPD, 1640–1*, 513–14.

34 Dalrymple. *Memorials*, 115; EUL, MS.Dc.4.16, ff 82, 95; *APS*, v.343.

35 Ibid, v.340, 341, 342–3.

36 Ibid, v.344–5; Hamilton, C. L. 'The Anglo-Scottish Negotiations of 1640–1', *SHR*, xli (1962), 84–6.

37 *APS*, v.340–1; EUL, MS.Dc.4.16, ff 86v–88.

38 Dalrymple. *Memorials*, 123–6, 129–33; Napier. *Montrose and the Covenanters*, i.354–5, 357, 359–62, 367–8; EUL, MS.Dc.4.16, f 95; NLS, MS.Wodrow, Fol. LXXIII, ff 102v–103, 104v–105; *CSPD, 1641–3*, 10.

39 NLS, MS.Wodrow, Fol. LXXIII, f 105. For restrictions on Anglo-Scottish trade in the early seventeenth century, see Lythe. *The Economy of Scotland in its European setting*, 199–215.

40 The king had told the Scots commissioners on 21 April that he would come to Scotland if parliament there was prorogued, Napier. *Montrose and the Covenanters*, i.354, 357, 367.

41 *APS*, v.316–17, 629–30, 641–2; *LJ*, iv.356–7.

42 Baillie. *Letters*, i.380.

43 Balfour. *Historical Works*, iii.27–30.

44 Ibid, iii.30.

45 Baillie. *Letters*, i.305.

46 HMC 5: 6th R. *Argyll*, 622; Leslie. *Relation*, 225–6.

47 *APS*, v.341.

48 Baillie. *Letters*, i.354.

49 Hyde. *History of the Rebellion*, i.252, 368–9, 396; PRO, SP.16/483/96.

50 Guthry. *Memoirs*, 90.

51 Baillie. *Letters*, ii.468–9; Guthry. *Memoirs*, 89–91; HMC 26: *Atholl & Home*, 26–7.

52 Napier. *Montrose and the Covenanters*, i.440–52, 464–5; Napier. *Memorials of Montrose*, i.266–7, 279, 286–7.

53 The letter survives only in a late seventeenth or early eighteenth century copy (NLS, MS.Wodrow, Quarto XL, no 2), where it takes the form of a letter signed by Montrose. But though it may have circulated under his name, in style, substance and even wording it is based on works by Lord Napier. Mark Napier first printed the letter (*Montrose and the Covenanters*, i.397–409), and though at one point he suggested that it was a joint work by Montrose and Lord Napier (*Life and Times of Montrose* (Edinburgh, 1840), 157) elsewhere he insisted, doggedly and inconsistently to the point

of absurdity, on Montrose's authorship, even claiming that Montrose was joint author with Lord Napier (or even sole author) of Napier's works which closely resemble the letter, though there is not the least evidence for this. Eg, *Montrose and the Covenanters*, i.409–10; *Memorials of Montrose*, i.79, 268–71, ii.34, 54–5; *Memoirs of Montrose*, i.289–90n, 311n, 314. Yet Napier's attribution of the essay to Montrose never seems to have been questioned. When exactly the letter was written is not clear; it may date from some years after 1641, when Napier (died 1645) adopted a more clearly royalist position.

54 Napier. *Memorials of Montrose*, ii.43–53.

55 Balfour. *Historical Works*, ii.403–4; *CSPD, 1640–1*, 77–8.

56 *APS*, v. 301–3, 620–1; Balfour. *Historical Works*, ii.424–6, iii.1–2; Hope. *Diary, 1633–45*, 122, 124.

57 *APS*, v.304–7, 621–3; Balfour. *Historical Works*, iii.2–3; Spalding. *Memorialls*, ii.7.

58 *APS*, v.621, 622–3.

59 Dalrymple. *Memorials*, 120–1, 123, 129–33; Napier. *Montrose and the Covenanters*, i.354, 359–62, 446, 453–4.

60 Guthry. *Memoirs*, 92–4; Napier. *Montrose and the Covenanters*, i.371–84, 386–90; Napier. *Memorials of Montrose*, i.273–9, 283–5, 296–301.

61 Guthry. *Memoirs*, 94; Napier. *Memorials of Montrose*, i.272–3, 279–80; Napier. *Montrose and the Covenanters*, i.440–58.

62 Guthry. *Memoirs*, 94.

63 NLS, MS Wodrow, Fol LXXIII, f 106.

64 *APS*, v.309–11, 312, 313, 637; Balfour. *Historical Works*, iii. 4–9; Baillie. *Letters*, i.377–8.

65 *APS*, v.313–14.

66 The king's advocate, Craighall, tried to sit in parliament as an officer of state but was removed. Later it was decided that he might be present since he was employed by the state as well as being advocate, Balfour. *Historical Works*, iii.15, 31–2; *APS*, v.324, 332; Hope. *Diary, 1633–45*, 150, 152.

67 *APS*, v.333.

68 *APS*, v.312, 313–14, 625–6; Baillie. *Letters*, i.378–9; Balfour. *Historical Works*, iii.27.

69 *APS*, v.384. It was already usual for burgh commissioners to be paid their expenses by their burgh.

70 *APS*, v.328, 332, 623; Balfour. *Historical Works*, iii.32–4. The copy of the oath signed by most (if not all) members who sat in parliament in 1641–51 is at GD.37/319, Airth Papers.

71 *APS*, v.329.

72 *APS*, v.311–13, 319, 320–2, 624; Baillie. *Letters*, i.380, 383; Balfour. *Historical Works*, iii.2–3; Hope. *Diary, 1633–45*, 126–7, 129, 131, 137.

73 *APS*, v.312, 315–16, 317–19, 326, 328, 637–9; Balfour. *Historical Works*, iii.14, 16, 19–21, 23.

74 *APS*, v.314, 315.

75 PA.14/1, Register of the Commission for the Common Burdens, f 91.

76 Gillon, S. A. & Smith J. I. (eds). *Selected Justiciary Cases, 1624–50* (2 vols, Stair Society, 1953–72), ii.423–42.

77 Guthry. *Memoirs*, 93–5.

78 Baillie. *Letters*, i.381.

79 *APS*, v.313; Baillie. *Letters*, i.359–61; Peterkin. *Records*, 292–3.

80 Baillie. *Letters*, i.358–60.

81 Ibid, i.358–9, 362–3.

82 Peterkin. *Records*, 294.

83 Baillie. *Letters*, i.369.

84 Stevenson. 'The Radical Party in the Kirk', *Journal of Ecclesiastical History* (1973—forthcoming).

85 Peterkin. *Records*, 297; Baillie. *Letters*, i.376–7.

86 The minutes of the commission are in NLS, MS Wodrow, Fol LXV, ff 4–23. *APS*, v.348–9, 351–2, 645–6.

87 Balfour. *Historical Works*, iii. 40–1.

88 Ibid, iii.42, 45–6; Baillie. *Letters*, i.386.

89 *APS*, v.347, 363–4.

90 Balfour. *Historical Works*, iii.44–6; Baillie. *Letters*, i.386; Warner. *Nicholas Papers*, i.24.

91 *APS*, v.333; Balfour. *Historical Works*, iii.45.

92 Ibid, iii.46, 51; *APS*, v.333, 335, 643–4; Terry. *Alexander Leslie*, 155–7.

93 *APS*, v.334–45; Balfour. *Historical Works*, iii.51, 52–3.

94 *APS*, v.653–4.

95 Ibid, v.354–5, 663; Balfour. *Historical Works*, iii. 64–6. For fears that the English parliament would demand concessions similar to those granted in Scotland see Evelyn, J. *Diary and Correspondence*, ed W. Bray (1852), iv.74, 76, 79, 80.

96 Warner. *Nicholas Papers*, i.39.

97 Ibid, i.41–2; *APS*, v.655–6.

98 BM, MS Eg.2,533, Nicholas Papers, vol i., ff 222, 233; Warner, *Nicholas Papers*, i.50–1; Carte, T. *A Collection of Original Letters and Papers* . . . (1739), i.2–3; Balfour. *Historical Works*, iii. 68–73, 77–81, 84–5; *APS*, v.356–7, 366–8. Baillie. *Letters*, i.390 wrongly states that Argyll and Morton were rivals for the treasurership, not the chancellorship.

99 Carte. *Original Letters*, i.4.

100 Baillie. *Letters*, i.391; Balfour. *Historical Works*, iii.82–4; Carte. *Original Letters*, i.6–7; *APS*, v.366.

101 [Yorke]. *State Papers*, ii.299–302; *CSPD, 1641–3*, 137–9; Gardiner. *Hamilton Papers*, 104–6; Balfour. *Historical Works*, iii. 94–7; HMC 3: 4th R. *House of Lords*, 102, 163–70; Wedgwood, *King's Peace*, 461–3, 485–6.

102 Balfour. *Historical Works*, iii.97–118; *APS*, v.374–5; Wedgwood. *King's Peace*, 463–5.

103 Dunlop, R. 'The Forged Commission of 1641', *EHR*, ii. (1887), 527–33.

104 *APS*, v.376–8; Balfour. *Historical Works*, iii.119–21, 125, 128–30.

105 Carte. *Original Letters*, i.3.

106 *APS*, v.388–9, 405–7, 666; Balfour. *Historical Works*, iii.66–8, 148–52.

107 No president of the court of session was appointed to replace Spottiswood, and in 1642–50 the lords of session elected their own president each term, Brunton, G. & Haig, D. *An Historical Account of the Senators of the College of Justice* (1832), xxxv. The king appointed Sir Thomas Hope of Kerse to replace Sir William Elphinstone as justice general, but this appointment was evidently not regarded as requiring parliamentary approval, *RMS, 1634–51*, nos 1032, 1037.

108 *APS*, v.389; Balfour. *Historical Works*, iii.152–3.

109 Ibid, iii.85.

110 *APS*, v.388, 428.

111 Ibid, v.388; Baillie. *Letters*, i.396.

112 *APS*, v.387–8, 407.

113 Ibid, v.721; *RPCS, 1638–43*, 156, 269–71, 274–6, 482, 484–5. For the development of the office of master of requests after 1603 into a second secretaryship, see McNeill, P. G. B. 'The Office of Master of Requests', *Juridical Review*, New Series, iv (1959), 211–12.

114 *APS*, v.391–5.

115 *APS*, v.395–6.

116 *APS*, v.404. Cassilis' name is omitted in the list of commissioners in *APS* but is given in Thurloe, J. *A Collection of State Papers . . .*, ed T. Birch (1742), i.15.

117 *APS*, v.404–5, 721.

118 Guthry, *Memoirs*, 108–9.

119 *APS*, v.407, 408–9, 709; Balfour. *Historical Works*, iii. 158–9.

CHAPTER 8: *The Rule of the Covenanters in Scotland, November 1641–June 1643*

1 Hyde. *History of the Rebellion*, ii.382.

2 NLS, MS Wodrow Fol LXVI, Original Letters, 1606–42, ff 199–200.

3 Burnet. *Hamilton*, 191.

4 Warner, F. *History of the Rebellion and Civil War in Ireland* (1768), i.145.

5 *CSPD, 1641–3*, 167–8; *CSP Ven, 1640–2*, 265, 267.

6 *CJ*, ii.304, 306, 312–15; *LJ*, iv.422, 435, 438.

7 *RPCS, 1638–43*, 142, 155, 485, 506–10.

8 *CJ*, ii.331, 339–40, 349; *LJ*, iv.459–61, 471, 472, 482, 483, 486.

9 *CJ*, ii.341; *LJ*, iv.472.

10 NLS, MS Wodrow, Fol LXVI, no 98.

11 *CJ*, ii.392, 393, 399; *LJ*, iv.534, 545–6; *His Majesties message to both houses of Parliament, January 20 . . .* (1641/2), 22–4.

12 *CJ*, ii.429–30; NLS, MS Wodrow, Fol LXVI, ff 204–5.

13 Hazlett, H. 'The Recruitment and Organisation of the Scottish Army in Ulster', Cronne, H. A., Moody, T. W. & Quinn, D. B. (eds). *Essays in British and Irish History in Honour of J. E. Todd* (1949), 115–16.

14 *RPCS*, *1638–43*, 202, 208–9, 211.

15 Ibid, 209; Turner. *Memoirs*, 18.

16 *RPCS*, *1638–43*, 197, 221, 222; Hazlett. 'Scottish Army in Ulster', 109–17.

17 PRO, SP.28/120, SP.16/492/58, SP.16/539/1/105.

18 Turner. *Memoirs*, 19–22; *A true and exact relation of divers principall actions . . .* (1642), 1–5.

19 Terry. *Alexander Leslie*, 166–7; Warner. *History of the Rebellion*, 226–7.

20 Turner. *Memoirs*, 24–5; Spalding. *Memorialls*, ii.140–1; Fraser. *The Melvilles Earls of Melville . . .*, ii.94–5.

21 *RPCS*, *1638–43*, 315.

22 Rushworth. *Historical Collections*, III.i.498–501; Burnet. *Hamilton*, 189–91; *RPCS*, *1638–43*, 163, 198.

23 Ibid, 162–3, 199; NLS, MS Wodrow, Fol LXVI, nos 98, 100, 102; HMC 1: 2nd R. *Montrose*, 168–9.

24 *RPCS*, *1638–43*, 233–4, 235, 246; Spalding. *Memorialls*, ii.99, 137–8; HMC 8: 9th. R. *Traquair*, 251, 262.

25 NLS, MS Wodrow, Fol LXVI, nos 100, 104.

26 Napier. *Memorials of Montrose*, ii.56; Spalding. *Memorialls*, ii.141.

27 *RPCS*, *1638–43*, 245, 248–51, 256.

28 Napier. *Memorials of Montrose*, ii.60–1 prints (from a draft in Lord Napier's handwriting which lacks date or title) what he calls the petition of Montrose and his friends to the council on 25 May, but there is no evidence that this was the royalist petition presented on 25 May, or that Montrose and his circle had anything to do with the petition that was presented.

29 Baillie. *Letters*, ii.34–7, 43–4; Guthry, *Memoirs*, 115–16; Spalding. *Memorialls*, ii.143–9; *RPCS*, *1638–43*, 256–8.

30 Guthry, *Memoirs*, 116; *RPCS*, *1638–43*, 260–4; *Edin. Recs*, *1642–1655*, 8; Spalding. *Memorialls*, ii.148–51.

31 *RPCS, 1638–43,* 264–5.

32 Hyde. *History of the Rebellion,* ii.383–4.

33 Burnet. *Hamilton,* 195, 201; Spalding, *Memorialls,* ii.158–60.

34 CH.1/1/9, Acts and Proceedings of the General Assemblies, 1642–6; Baillie. *Letters,* ii.45, 46.

35 Ibid, ii. 46, 47.

36 Peterkin. *Records,* 320; Napier. *Memorials of Montrose,* ii.64–7.

37 Peterkin. *Records,* 323–4.

38 Baillie. *Letters,* ii.48; Spalding. *Memorialls,* ii.172–3.

39 Baillie. *Letters,* ii.50, 53; Peterkin. *Records,* 323, 324–6, 330; Napier. *Memorials of Montrose,* ii.67–8.

40 Baillie. *Letters,* ii.51, 52–3; Stevenson. 'The Radical Party in the Kirk', *Journal of Ecclesiastical History* (1973—forthcoming).

41 Ibid; Baillie. *Letters,* ii.54.

42 Peterkin. *Records,* 333.

43 Baillie. *Letters,* i.365, 376, ii.1–2; Peterkin. *Records,* 297.

44 Ibid, 330–1.

45 Ibid, 47, 209, 279, 297.

46 Baillie. *Letters,* ii.55.

47 Guthry. *Memoirs,* 120.

48 Burnet. *Hamilton,* 198–9; *RPCS, 1638–43,* 316.

49 Ibid, 318–19; Burnet. *Hamilton,* 195, 197–8, 200–1.

50 PA.14/2, Proceedings of the Scots Commissioners appointed . . . for Conserving the Articles of the Treaty . . ., 1–6; *The Proceedings of the Commissioners appointed by the Kings Majestie and Parliament of Scotland, for Conserving the Articles of the Treaty and Peace . . .* ([Edinburgh], 1643), 5–10; Rushworth. *Historical Collections,* III.ii.398.

51 PA.14/2, pp 7, 8, 12–13; *Proceedings of the Conservators,* 10–18; Rushworth. *Historical Collections,* III.ii.397–9.

52 PA.14/2, pp 10–11.

53 *RPCS, 1638–43,* 331–2, 341.

54 Gardiner, S. R. *History of the Great Civil War* (1893–4), i.54; Ogilvie, J. D. 'The Cross Petition, 1643', *PEBS,* xv (1930–5) 56; Rushworth. *Historical Collections,* III.ii.393–4; *LJ,* v.430–1.

55 HMC 15: 10th R. vi, *Bouverie,* 87.

56 Guthry. *Memoirs,* 124; *LJ,* v.469; HMC 21: *Hamilton,* ii.63, 64.

57 Hyde. *History of the Rebellion*, ii.405.

58 *RPCS*, *1638–43*, 361–3; Ogilvie. 'Cross Petition', 56–7; Guthry. *Memoirs*, 124.

59 Ie, a meeting at which more councillors were present (letters having been sent summoning them to attend), a better frequented meeting; *RPCS*, *1638–43*, 359–63; Burnet. *Hamilton*, 204–5; HMC 21: *Hamilton*, ii.63; Ogilvie. 'Cross Petition', 57–8.

60 Baillie. *Letters*, ii.58.

61 HMC 21: *Hamilton*, ii.63.

62 Baillie. *Letters*, ii.58.

63 Spalding. *Memorialls*, ii.219–21; Baillie. *Letters*, ii.58–9; Guthry. *Memoirs*, 124–5.

64 Spalding. *Memorialls*, ii.221; PA.14/2, pp 16–19.

65 Burnet. *Hamilton*, 206–9; Spalding. *Memorialls*, ii.221–2; Guthry. *Memoirs*, 125; Ogilvie. 'Cross Petition', 59–60.

66 *RPCS*, *1638–43*, 597; Burnet. *Hamilton*, 209.

67 *RPCS*, *1638–43*, 372–4.

68 *Two Petitions Lately presented by Noblemen, Barons, Gentlemen, Burgesses and Ministers . . . To the . . . Commissioners for the Conservation of the Peace . . .* [1643], 6–8.

69 PA.14/2, p 21; Burnet. *Hamilton*, 209.

70 PA.14/2, pp 13–15.

71 PA.14/2, pp 20, 26–36; *Proceedings of the Conservators*, 20–8.

72 Rushworth. *Historical Collections*, III.ii.406–10; Spalding. *Memorialls*, ii.222–3; *RPCS*, *1638–43*, 374–6.

73 *A Declaration Against the Cross Petition . . . By the Commissioners of the Generall Assembly* (Edinburgh, 1643); Spalding. *Memorialls*, ii.222–4; Ogilvie. 'Cross Petition', 60–2.

74 *A Necessary Warning to the Ministers of the Kirk of Scotland from the Commissioners of the Generall Assembly* (Edinburgh, 1643).

75 Baillie. *Letters*, ii.63, 69, 76, 91–2; Spalding. *Memorialls*, ii.228. See Masson, *Drummond of Hawthornden*, 368–74 for Drummond's denunciation of the action of the commission of the kirk.

76 Baillie. *Letters*, ii. 60, 69; *RPCS*, *1638–43*, 375–6, 378–80, 384; Ogilvie. 'Cross Petition', 62–5.

77 Baillie. *Letters*, ii.66–7.

78 Rushworth. *Historical Collections*, III.ii.399–400.

79 Ibid, III.ii.400–6; Burnet. *Hamilton*, 213–17; Hyde. *History of the Rebellion*, ii.504–5, 509–20; Ogilvie. 'Cross Petition', 65–7.

80 PA.14/2, pp 41–3; Baillie. *Letters*, ii.65–7.

81 PA.14/2, p 44; Burnet. *Hamilton*, 216–17.

82 Baillie. *Letters*, ii.66.

83 *CJ*, iii.90.

84 Burnet. *Hamilton*, 221–4.

85 Eg, Spalding. *Memorialls*, ii.251; Napier. *Memorials of Montrose*, ii.75–6; *Edin. Recs, 1642–55*, 28–9.

86 Burnet. *Hamilton*, 216–17.

87 Guthry. *Memoirs*, 126–8; Wishart, G. *Memoirs of James Marquis of Montrose*, ed A. D. Murdoch & H. F. M. Simpson (1893), 25–8.

88 Burnet. *Hamilton*, 220, 224.

89 Ibid, 219–20.

90 Eg, *LJ*, v.524, vi.45–6.

91 *RPCS, 1638–43*, 407–9, 412; PA.14/1, Register of the Committee for the Common Burdens, ff 209v–211v; PA.14/2, Proceedings of the Conservators, 37–9.

92 Burnet. *Hamilton*, 215, 217.

93 PA.14/2, pp 45–9.

94 Baillie. *Letters*, ii.68; *RPCS, 1638–43*, 425.

95 Ibid, 232–3, 407–9; PA.14/1, ff 69–70v, 209v–211v; PA.14/2, pp 37–9.

96 PA.14/2, p 59.

97 PA.13/1, Papers relating to Negotiations with the King and the English Parliament, 139.

98 *RPCS, 1638–43*, 425–6; PA.14/2, pp 59–61; PA.14/1, ff 223–4.

99 *RPCS, 1638–43*, 426–8; PA.14/2, pp 61–4; PA.14/1, ff 224–6; Baillie. *Letters*, ii.68; NLS, MS 80, Morton Papers, f 31.

100 Guthry. *Memoirs*, 129–30; Burnet. *Hamilton*, 218–19; *RPCS, 1638–43*, 428; *RPCS, 1544–1660*, 93–4.

101 *RPCS, 1638–43*, 425, 426, 428. Slightly different lists are given in PA.14/1, ff 224–224v and Burnet. *Hamilton*. 218–19.

102 *RPCS, 1544–1660*, 93.

103 Baillie. *Letters*, ii.68–9; Burnet. *Hamilton*, 225–6.

104 Ibid, 230.

105 *RPCS, 1638–43*, 429–34.

106 *The King's Majesties Declaration to all his loving Subjects of His Kingdome of Scotland* . . . (Oxford, 1643), 9–10. The letter to the king was not inserted in the privy council register, presumably because the covenanters objected to it and the clerk of the council (Archibald Primrose) was a good covenanter. *RPCS, 1638–43*, 434, 643; Baillie. *Letters*, ii.72–3.

107 Burnet. *Hamilton*, 231.

108 Ibid, 226–7.

109 Ibid, 231–2.

110 Ibid, 229–30.

111 Spalding. *Memorialls*, ii.243–7.

112 HMC 29: *Portland*, i.120–3.

113 Wedgwood, *King's Peace*, 213.

114 Ibid, 240; Guthry, *Memoirs*, 128–9, 131; Spalding. *Memorialls*, ii.252; Baillie. *Letters*, ii.73–4; Wishart. *Memoirs of Montrose*, 29–33.

115 *RPCS, 1638–43*, 436, 442–4; PA.14/2, pp 64–7; Spalding. *Memorialls*, ii.248–50.

116 *CJ*, iii.79; *LJ*, vi.37, 43, 49.

117 PA.14/2, pp 67–8; *RPCS, 1638–43*, 444.

118 PA.13/1, p 131; PA.14/2, p 68.

119 PA.13/1, pp 131–2; PA.14/2, pp 68–70; Baillie. *Letters*, ii. 77–8.

CHAPTER 9: *The Solemn League and Covenant, June 1643–January 1644*

1 Rait. *Parliaments of Scotland*, 146–7, 150–1, 156–7.

2 *APS*, VI.i.6.

3 Ibid, VI.i.6.

4 Burnet. *Hamilton*, 234.

5 Ibid, 233–4; *APS*, VI.i.6; Hyde. *History of the Rebellion*, iii.219–20.

6 *The Remonstrance of the Commissioners of the General Assembly to the Convention of Estates at Edinburgh, June 1643* (Edinburgh, 1643); *APS*, VI.i.7; Baillie, *Letters*, ii.75.

7 *APS*, VI.i.8–9.

8 Baillie, *Letters*, ii.79; See L. Kaplan, 'Steps to War: the Scots and Parliament, 1642–3', *Journal of British Studies*, ix (1970), 60–1.

9 *CJ*, iii.66, 92, 110, 113, 121, 132; *LJ*, vi.25, 32, 38, 55–6, 60, 97, 99.

10 *LJ*, vi.106, 111; *APS*, VI.i.13–14.

11 *LJ*, vi.151, 152; PA.14/2, Proceedings of the Conservators, pp. 72–6.

12 Baillie. *Letters*, ii.78.

13 *APS*, VI.i.5–6, 44; *RPCS, 1544–1660*, 63; PA.14/2, pp. 77–8.

14 *APS*, VI.i.7–8; PA.7/24, Parliamentary and State Papers, ff 250–1.

15 Court of Justiciary, Books of Adjournal, Old Series, viii. 312–13, 322–3; *APS*, VI.i.14, 22–3, 24.

16 Burnet. *Hamilton*, 234–5.

17 NLS, Adv. MS 33.4.8, Transactions of the Scots Army in Ireland, 9–15.

18 *APS*, VI.i.17–18.

19 *LJ*, vi.121, 122, 128, 136; *CJ*, iii.174.

20 *LJ*, vi.140–2; Notestein, W. 'The Establishment of the Committee of Both Kingdoms', *American Hist. Rev.*, xvii (1912) 479–80.

21 *APS*, VI.i.15–17.

22 Ibid, VI.i.13, 20, 47; Baillie. *Letters*, ii.80.

23 Hope. *Diary, 1633–45*, 192; *RPCS, 1544–1660*, 4; Baillie. *Letters*, ii.83.

24 Burnet. *Hamilton*, 235.

25 Baillie. *Letters*, ii.85.

26 Kaplan, L. 'Presbyterians and Independents in 1643', *EHR*, lxxxiv (1969), 246–50.

27 Burnet. *Hamilton*, 237.

28 Baillie. *Letters*, ii.90; See Notestein. 'Committee of Both Kingdoms', 481n.

29 Baillie. *Letters*, ii.88–9; *APS*, VI.i.23, 24.

30 Peterkin. *Records*, 347–8.

31 Ibid, 348–9; Baillie. *Letters*, ii.89.

32 *APS*, VI.i.36–8.

33 Baillie. *Letters*, ii.90.

34 Peterkin. *Records*, 353; *APS*, VI.i.41–3.

35 Baillie. *Letters*, ii.96; Peterkin. *Records*, 355–9; *APS*, VI.i.59.

36 Peterkin. *Records*, 359–60.

37 Baillie. *Letters*, ii.95–6.

38 *APS*, VI.i.41–3.

39 Ibid, VI.i.26–36.

40 Ibid, VI.i.43–4, 46–7.

41 Mulligan, L. 'The Scottish Alliance and the Committee of Both Kingdoms, 1644–6', *Historical Studies*, xiv (1970), 175, claims that the English parliament was horrified when the Scots sent 21,000 men to England (since a much smaller army had been expected) and therefore diverted most of them to Ireland; this is completely untrue.

42 *APS*, VI.i.47–9.

43 Kaplan. 'Steps to War', *Journal of British Studies*, ix.66–7, wrongly asserts that it took two months of hard bargaining in Scotland after the new covenant had been agreed to reach agreement on the military treaty.

44 Burnet. *Hamilton*, 239.

45 *APS*, VI.i.42.

46 Ibid, VI.i.150; Gardiner. *Civil War*, i.232–5.

47 Pearl, V. 'Oliver St John and the "Middle Group" in the Long Parliament', *EHR*, lxxxi (1966), 495–500; *APS*, VI.i.152–4.

48 Ibid, VI.i.49–50.

49 Ibid, VI.i.51–7, 59.

50 Rait. *Parliaments of Scotland*, 157.

51 *APS*, VI.i.57–9.

52 PA.11/1, Register of the Committee of Estates, ff 29–29v.

53 *APS*, VI.i.152.

54 Baillie. *Letters*, ii.102.

55 PA.11/1, ff 36v–39.

56 Baillie. *Letters*, ii.102; Fleming, D. H. 'Some Subscribed Copies of the Solemn League and Covenant', *PEBS*, xi (1912–20), 5–7.

57 *RPCS*, *1544–1660*, 6–7, 10, 11.

58 Burnet. *Hamilton*, 244–7; *LJ*, vi.277, 312.

59 Rutherford. *Lex Rex*, 324, 338; Campbell, W. M. 'Lex Rex and its Author', *RSCHS*, vii.204–10, 224.

60 PA.11/1, ff 52v–54, 55–57v, 60, 61v–62, 87v, 91–91v, 94, 94v–95.

61 Ibid, ff 92v–93, 98–99, 102–102v, 106–107.

62 'The Straloch Papers', in J. Stuart (ed), *Spalding Miscellany* (1841), i. 29–30.

63 Wishart. *Memoirs of Montrose*, 34–6; Burnet. *Hamilton*, 240–1.

64 Ibid, 248–9.

65 Baillie. *Letters*, ii.105; Burnet. *Hamilton*, 250.

66 Spalding. *Memorialls*, ii.295.

67 Burnet. *Hamilton*, 250–70; Hyde. *History of the Rebellion*, iii. 320; Baillie. *Letters*, ii.124–5, 138; *APS*, VI.i.88.

68 PA.11/1, ff 9–11.

69 Ibid, ff 6–7; NLS, MS Adv.33.4.8, Transactions of the Scots Army in Ireland, 28–9, 30–6.

70 PA.11/1, ff 12–13, 13v, 14v–15v.

71 HMC 36: *Ormonde*, N.S., i.67.

72 *CJ*, iii.294.

73 PA.11/1, ff 62v–64, 81–2, 85v; NLS, MS Adv.33.4.8, pp 36–42.

74 PA.11/1, ff 16–19v; *APS*, VI.i.154–5.

75 PA.11/1, ff 19v, 20v–21, 22.

76 Baillie. *Letters*, ii.100.

77 PA.11/1, ff 25–7.

78 Eg, Ibid, ff 39v, 42–3, 43v, 45v–46, 48–48v, 50–52v.

79 Ibid, ff 54v, 58v, 66v–72, 75v–79, 91v–92.

80 Ibid, ff 64–6; HMC 3: 4th R. *Argyll*, 490; *APS*, VI.i.61.

81 McNeill, C. (ed), *The Tanner Letters* (Dublin, 1943), 168–9.

82 Loder, J. de V. *Colonsay and Oronsay* (Edinburgh, 1935), 131–8, 219–20, 228–9; *RPCS, 1638–43*, 185; Hill. *Macdonnells of Antrim*, 55–8, 61–72, 74–6; GD.112/39/823, Breadalbane Muniments.

83 PA.11/1, ff 86v–87, 100–100v.

84 Terry. *Alexander Leslie*, 176–7.

85 *APS*, VI.i.60–2, 69; Stevenson, 'The Financing of the Cause of the Covenants', *SHR*, li.103–5.

86 PA.11/2, Register of the Committee of Estates, Army, 1643–4, ff 7–9v.

87 Fotheringham, J. G. (ed). *The Diplomatic Correspondence of Jean de Montereul* (SHS, 1898–9), ii.555–6.

CHAPTER 10. *Conclusion: The Triumph of the Covenanters*

1 Tanner, J. R. *Tudor Constitutional Documents* (Cambridge, 1930), 550, quoted in Carsten, F. L. *Princes and Parliaments in Germany* (Oxford, 1959), 442.

2 Rutherford, S. *A Testimony . . . to the Work of Reformation in Britain and Ireland* (Glasgow, 1719), 6.

3 Elliott, J. H. 'Revolution and Continuity in Early Modern Europe', *Past and Present*, 42 (1969), 42.

4 Quoted Underdown, D. *Pride's Purge. Politics in the Puritan Revolution* (Oxford, 1971), 9–10.

5 Baillie. *Letters*, ii.106.

6 Lublinskaya, A. D. *French Absolutism: The Crucial Phase, 1620–1629* (Cambridge, 1968), 101.

7 Elliott. 'Revolution and Continuity', 39–42.

8 Ibid, 44.

9 Ibid, 45.

10 Stone, L. *The Causes of the English Revolution, 1529–1642* (1972), 3–22. Stone bases much of his discussion on Johnson, C. *Revolutionary Change* (1968). Koenigsberger, H. G. 'Revolutionary Conclusions', *History*, lvii (1972), 398, argues that the models of social scientists have 'so far, not proved to be very illuminating for the problems of early modern history'; if historians want models they should build their own. I sympathise with this point of view; but none the less tentative discussion of the relevance of the work of social scientists can be stimulating; even if the validity of a model as a whole is doubted there is no need to disregard every detail of it, for some aspects may remain useful.

11 Stone. *Causes of the English Revolution*, 9.

12 Ibid, 9–10.

13 Ibid, 10.

14 Ibid, 11.

15 Koenigsberger, H. G. 'The Organisation of Revolutionary Parties in France and the Netherlands during the Sixteenth Century', in *Estates and Revolutions* (Ithaca and London, 1971), 225–6, 250–1.

16 Stone. *Causes of the English Revolution*, 15–16, citing Hobsbawm,

E. J. 'The Crisis of the Seventeenth Century', in Aston, T. H. (ed). *Crisis in Europe, 1560–1660* (1965), 5–58.

17 Stone. *Causes of the English Revolution*, 18.

18 Ibid, 18.

19 Mitchison, R. *A History of Scotland* (1970), 163–4.

20 Wedgwood, C. V. 'Anglo-Scottish Relations, 1603–40', *TRHS*, 4th series (1950), 35.

21 The parallel between the Catalan and Portuguese revolts on the one hand and the Scottish on the other was made in Elliott, J.H. 'The King and the Catalans, 1621-1640', *Cambridge Historical Journal*, xi (1953–5), 253, 259, 260, 270, though not elaborated.

22 Elliott, J. H. 'Revolts in the Spanish Monarchy', in Forster, R. & Greene, J. P. (eds), *Preconditions of Revolution in Early Modern Europe* (Baltimore and London, 1970), 113–14.

23 Wedgwood. 'Anglo-Scottish Relations', 34.

24 Elliott. 'Revolts in the Spanish Monarchy', 114–15.

25 Ibid, 115–16.

26 Ibid, 115.

27 Ibid, 116.

28 Ibid, 122, 128.

29 Trevor-Roper, H. R. 'The General Crisis of the Seventeenth Century' in Aston. *Crisis in Europe*, 59–95.

30 Ibid, 116.

31 Elliott, J. H. 'Trevor-Roper's "General Crisis": Symposium' in Aston. *Crisis in Europe*, 107.

32 Forster & Greene. *Preconditions of Revolution*, 6.

33 Elliott. 'Trevor-Roper's "General Crisis" ', 107.

34 Ibid, 104.

35 Ibid, 110.

36 Stone, L. 'Trevor-Roper's "General Crisis": Symposium', *Past and Present* (1960), 31–3, cited in Lublinskaya. *French Absolutism*, 96.

37 Koenigsberger. 'Revolutionary Conclusions', 395–6.

38 Ibid, 395, 398.

39 Lublinskaya. *French Absolutism*, 101. Elliott. 'Revolution and Continuity', 37–9, makes the same point.

40 Ibid, 54.

Select Bibliography

I Sources
  i Manuscripts
  ii General printed
  iii Pamphlets

II Secondary
  i Bibliographies and catalogues
  ii Theses
  iii General printed

I SOURCES: i MANUSCRIPTS

Scottish Record Office

CH. CHURCH RECORDS
CH.1/1/9, Acts and Proceedings of the General Assemblies, 1642–6.

CS. COURT OF SESSION RECORDS
Books of Sederunt, 1626–49.

GD. GIFTS AND DEPOSITS
GD.37/319, Airth Papers, Oath signed by Members of Parliament.
GD.44, Gordon Castle Muniments.
GD.112/39, Breadalbane Muniments, Mounted Letters (Typescript calendar for 1600–69 in SRO).
GD.112/40/2, Breadalbane Muniments, Letters, 1636–59.
GD.112/43/1, Breadalbane Muniments, State Papers, 1545–1690.

JC. JUSTICIARY COURT RECORDS
Books of Adjournal, Old Series, vols vii–viii, 1631–50.

PA. RECORDS OF PARLIAMENT

PA.6, Warrants of Parliament.

PA.7/2–3, Supplementary Parliamentary Papers, 1606–45.

PA.7/23/1–2, Additional Parliamentary Papers.

PA.7/24, Parliamentary and State Papers, 1581–1651.

PA.7/25/1, Commissions to Commissioners to Parliament, 1567–1651.

PA.11/1, Register of the Committee of Estates, 1643–4.

PA.11/2, Register of the Committee of Estates, 1643–4 (Army).

PA.12/1, Warrants of the Committee of Estates, 1640–6.

PA.13/1, Papers relating to negotiations with the King and English Parliament, 1641–6.

PA.13/2, Proceedings of the Scots Commissioners sent to England, 1641–2.

PA.13/3, Register of Letters to and from the Scots Commissioners in London, 1642, 1644–5.

PA.13/5, Register of Negotiations, 1643–7.

PA.14/1, Register of the Committee for Common Burdens, 1641–5.

PA.14/2, Proceedings of the Scots Commissioners for conserving the articles of the Treaty, 1642–3.

National Library of Scotland

ADV. ADVOCATES' MANUSCRIPTS

Adv.33.4.6, Treaties at Newcastle and London, 1640–1.

Adv.33.4.8, Transactions of the Scots Army in Ireland, 1643–8.

WODROW MANUSCRIPTS

Folio xxxi, Church and State Papers, 1618–85.

Folio lxii, Church Papers, mainly concerning Glasgow Assembly, 1638.

Folio lxiv, Church and State Papers, 1638–41.

Folio lxv, Church and State Papers, 1639–50.

Folio lxvi, Original Letters, 1606–42.

Folio lxvii, Letters, 1641–53.

Folio lxxiii, Collection of Papers, 1640–1.

Quarto xl, Miscellaneous.

Quarto lxxii, part 1, includes account of Glasgow assembly by Robert Douglas, 1638.

Quarto lxxvii, Church and State Papers, 1584–1648.

Edinburgh University Library

Dc.4.16, Transactions of the Committee of Estates in Scotland, 1640–1.

Public Record Office

SP.16, State Papers, Domestic, Charles I.

SP.28/120, State Papers, Domestic, Commonwealth Exchequer Papers, Muster Rolls of Scottish and other Protestant Forces in Ireland, 1642–3.

SP.46/106, State Papers, Domestic, Supplementary.

SP.46/129, State Papers, Domestic, Supplementary, Documents relate to Scotland, 1546–1653.

PRO.31/3/71, Transcripts of Dispatches of de Bellièvre, 1639.

British Museum

MS. Egerton 2533, Nicholas Papers, vol i, 1560–1649.

MS. Harleian 457, Minutes of the Treaty between the English and Scots held at London, 1640–1.

MS. Sloane 650, Relation of Passages in Scotland touching Church Worship.

MS. Stowe 187, Proceedings of the Parliaments of England and Scotland in 1640 and 1641 relating to the affairs of Scotland.

MS. Add. 11,045, Scudamore Papers, vol v, Newsletters, 1638–41.

MSS. Add. 23,110–12, Registers of the Secretaries of State of Scotland, 1626–40.

MS. Add. 24,984, Copies of Papers Relating to the Scotch invasion of England in 1640.

I SOURCES: ii GENERAL PRINTED

The Acts of Parliament of Scotland, eds T. Thomson & C. Innes (12 vols, 1814–75).

The Acts of Sederunt of the Lords of Council and Session, from the 15th January 1553, to the 11th of July 1790 (Edinburgh, 1790).

Airy, O. (ed). *The Lauderdale Papers* (3 vols, Camden Society, 1884–5).

Baillie, R. *The Letters and Journals*, ed D. Laing (3 vols, Bannatyne Club, 1841–2).

[Balcanquhal, W.]. *A Large Declaration concerning the Late Tumults in Scotland . . .* (1639).

Balfour, Sir J. *Historical Works* (4 vols, Edinburgh, 1824–5).

Birch, T. (ed). *A Collection of State Papers of John Thurloe*, vol i (1742).

Bruce, J. (ed). *Notes on the Treaty carried on at Ripon between King Charles I and the Covenanters of Scotland, A.D. 1640, taken by Sir John Borough* (Camden Society, 1869).

Burnet, G. *History of My Own Times*, ed O. Airy (2 vols, Oxford, 1897–1900).

Burns, J. 'Memoirs by James Burns, Bailie of the City of Glasgow,

1644–1661', in Maidment J. (ed). *Historical Fragments* (Edinburgh, 1833).

Calderwood, D. *The History of the Kirk of Scotland*, ed T. Thomson (7 vols, Wodrow Society, 1842–9).

Calendar of Clarendon State Papers in the Bodleian Library (4 vols, Oxford, 1872–1932).

Calendar of State Papers, Domestic, Charles I, vols x–xix (1867–88).

Calendar of State Papers and Manuscripts, relating to English Affairs, existing in the Archives and Collections of Venice, and in other Libraries of Northern Italy, vols xxiv–xxvii (1923–6).

Carte, T. (ed). *A Collection of Original Letters and Papers, concerning the affairs of England* (2 vols, 1739).

Clarendon, Earl of, see Hyde, E.

Cobbett, W. (ed). *State Trials*, vols iii–v (1809).

Collins, A. (ed). *Letters and Memorials of State* (2 vols, 1746).

Craighall, see Hope, T.

Cuningham, T. *Journal*, ed E. J. Courthope (SHS, 1928).

Dalrymple, D., Lord Hailes (ed). *Memorials and Letters relating to the History of Britain in the Reign of Charles the First* (Glasgow, 1766).

Dickinson, W. C. & Donaldson, G. (eds). *A Source Book of Scottish History*, vol iii (1961).

Evelyn, J. *Diary and Correspondence*, ed W. Bray (4 vols, 1852).

Fairley, J. A. (ed). 'Lord Sinclair, Covenanter and Royalist', *Trans. Buchan Field Club*, viii (1904–5), 129–84.

Gardiner, S. R. (ed). *The Hamilton Papers* (Camden Society, 1880).

Gardiner, S. R. (ed), 'Hamilton Papers. Addenda', *Camden Miscellany*, ix (1895).

Gillespie, G. *Works*, ed W. M. Hetherington (2 vols, Edinburgh, 1846).

Gillon, S. A. & Smith, J. I. (eds). *Selected Justiciary Cases, 1624–50* (2 vols, Stair Society, 1953–73; 3rd volume forthcoming).

Gordon, J. *History of Scots Affairs, from MDCXXXVII to MDCXLI*, eds J. Robertson & G. Grub (3 vols, Spalding Club, 1841).

Gordon, P., of Ruthven. *A Short Abridgement of Britane's Distemper*, ed J. Dunn (Spalding Club, 1844).

Gordon, Sir R., of Gordonstoun & Gordon, G., of Sallach. *A Genealogical History of the Earldom of Sutherland* (Edinburgh, 1813).

Guthry, H. *Memoirs* (2nd ed, Glasgow, 1747).

Hailes, Lord, see Dalrymple, D.

Henderson, J. M. (ed). 'An "Advertistment" about the Service Book, 1637', *SHR*, xxiii (1925–6), 199–204.

Historical Manuscripts Commission:
  HMC 1: 2nd Report, *Montrose* (1871).
  HMC 3: 4th Report, *Argyll* (1874).

HMC 5: 6th Report, *Argyll* (1877).

HMC 8: 9th Report, ii, *Traquair* (1884).

HMC 21: *Hamilton*, i, ii (1887, 1932).

HMC 72: *Laing*, i (1914).

Hope, Sir T., of Craighall. *A Diary of the Public Correspondence* . . . *1633–1645*, ed T. Thomson (Bannatyne Club, 1843).

Hyde, E., Earl of Clarendon. *The History of the Rebellion and Civil Wars in England begun in the year 1641*, ed W. D. Macray (6 vols, Oxford, 1888).

Jaffray, A. *Diary*, ed J. Barclay (Aberdeen, 1856)

Johnston, A., of Wariston, *Diary* . . . *1632–9*, ed G. M. Paul (SHS, 1911).

Johnston, A., of Wariston, *Diary* . . . *1639 and other Papers*, ed G. M. Paul (SHS, 1896).

Journals of the House of Commons, vols ii–iii.

Journals of the House of Lords, vols iv–vi.

Knowler, W. (ed). *The Earl of Strafford's Letters and Dispatches* (2 vols, Dublin, 1740).

Laing, D. (ed). *Correspondence of Sir Robert Kerr, first Earl of Ancrum, and his son William, third Earl of Lothian* (2 vols, Edinburgh, 1875).

Leith, W. F. (ed). *Memoirs of Scottish Catholics during the XVIIth and XVIIIth Centuries* (2 vols, 1909).

Leslie, J., Earl of Rothes. *A Relation of Proceedings concerning the Affairs of the Kirk of Scotland, from August 1637 to July 1638*, ed D. Laing (Bannatyne Club, 1830).

Livingstone, J. *A Brief Historical Relation* . . ., ed T. Houston (Edinburgh, 1848).

McCrie, T. (ed). *The Life of Mr. Robert Blair, minister of St Andrews, containing his Autobiography* (Wodrow Society, 1848).

Mackenzie, C. F. (ed). *Antiquarian Notes* (Stirling, 1913).

McNeill, C. (ed). *The Tanner Letters* (Dublin, 1943).

Macray, W. D. (ed). *Ruthven Correspondence* (Roxburghe Club, 1868).

Maidment, J. (ed). 'Collections by a Private Hand at Edinburgh', in *Historical Fragments* (Edinburgh, 1833).

Marwick, J. D. (ed). *Extracts from the Records of the Burgh of Glasgow*, vols i–ii (SBRS, 1876–81).

Marwick, J. D. (ed). *Extracts from the Records of the Convention of Royal Burghs of Scotland*, vols iii–iv (Edinburgh, 1870–80).

Minute Book kept by the War Committee of the Covenanters in the Stewartry of Kirkcudbright in 1640 and 1641 (Kirkcudbright, 1855).

Nalson, J. (ed). *An Impartial Collection of the Great Affairs of State* (2 vols, 1682–3).

Napier, M. (ed). *Memorials of Montrose and his Times* (2 vols, Maitland Club, 1848–50).

24

Peterkin, A. (ed). *Records of the Kirk of Scotland, containing the Acts and Proceedings of the General Assemblies* (Edinburgh, 1838).

The Register of the Privy Council of Scotland, 2nd ser, i–viii, 1625–60 (1899–1908).

Registrum Magni Sigilli Regum Scotorum: *The Register of the Great Seal of Scotland, 1634–1651*, ed J. M. Thomson (Edinburgh, 1897).

Renwick, R. *Extracts from the Records of the Royal Burgh of Stirling*, vol i (Glasgow, 1887).

[Rogers, C. (ed)]. *The Earl of Stirling's Register of Royal Letters relative to the affairs of Scotland* (2 vols, Edinburgh, 1885).

Rothes, Earl of, see Leslie, J.

Row, J. *The History of the Kirk of Scotland from the year 1558 to August 1637, with a continuation to July 1639 by his son* (Wodrow Society, 1842).

Rushworth, J. (ed). *Historical Collections* (8 vols, 1659–1701).

Rutherford, S. *Letters*, ed A. A. Bonar (1894).

Rutherford, S. *Lex Rex: The Law and the Prince . . .* (1644).

Scot, Sir J., of Scotstarvet, *The Staggering State of Scottish Statesmen from 1550 to 1650*, ed C. Rogers (Edinburgh, 1872).

Scot, Sir J., of Scotstarvet. 'Trew Relation of the Principall Affaires concerning the State', ed G. Neilson, *SHR*, xi.164–91, 284–96, 395–403, xii.76–83, 174–83, 408–12, xiii.380–92, xiv.60–8.

Scrope, R. & Monkhouse, T. (eds). *State Papers collected by Edward, Earl of Clarendon* (3 vols, Oxford, 1767–86).

Spalding, J. *Memorialls of the Trubles in Scotland and in England, A.D. 1624–A.D. 1645*, ed J. Stuart (2 vols, Spalding Club, 1850–1).

Spreul, J. 'Some Remarkable Passages of the Lord's Providence towards Mr. John Spreul, Town Clerk of Glasgow, 1635–1664', in J. Maidment (ed). *Historical Fragments* (Edinburgh, 1833).

Stewart, W. (ed). 'The Protestation of the General Assemblie of the Church of Scotland made at Glasgow in November, 1638', *RGBS*, i (1912–13), 106–17.

Stuart, J. (ed). *Extracts from the Council Register of the Burgh of Aberdeen, 1625–1747* (2 vols, SBRS, 1871–2).

Stuart, J. (ed). 'The Straloch Papers, 1585–1665, chiefly of Robert Gordon of Straloch, on public affairs', *Spalding Club Miscellany*, i (1841), 1–58.

Taylor, L. B. (ed). *Aberdeen Council Letters* (vols ii–iii, Oxford, 1950–2).

Terry, C. S. (ed). *Papers Relating to the Army of the Solemn League and Covenant, 1643–1647* (2 vols, SHS, 1917).

Turner, J. *Memoirs of his own Life and Times*, ed T. Thomson (Bannatyne Club, 1829).

Tweedie, W. K. (ed). *Select Biographies* (2 vols, Wodrow Society, 1845).

Wariston, Lord, see Johnston, A.

Warner, G. F. (ed). *The Nicholas Papers. Correspondence of Sir Edward Nicholas, Secretary of State,* vol i (Camden Society, 1886).

Wishart, G. *The Memoirs of James Marquis of Montrose, 1639–1650,* eds A. D. Murdoch & H. F. M. Simpson (1893).

Wood, M. (ed). *Extracts from the Records of Edinburgh, 1626–55* (2 vols, Edinburgh, 1936–8).

[Yorke, P., Earl of Hardwicke (ed)]. *Miscellaneous State Papers, from 1501 to 1726* (2 vols, 1778).

I SOURCES: iii PAMPHLETS

A Declaration against the Crosse Petition . . . By the Commissioners of the Generall Assembly (Edinburgh, 1643).

[Henderson, A.]. *Some Speciall Arguments which warranted the Scottish Subjects lawfully to take up Armes in Defence of their Religion and Liberty when they were in Danger . . .* ([1642]).

Information from the Estaits of the Kingdome of Scotland, to the Kingdome of England ([Edinburgh], 1640).

The King's Majesties Declaration to all his loving Subjects of his Kingdome of Scotland . . . (Oxford, 1643).

A Necessary Warning to the Ministers of the Kirk of Scotland from the Meeting of the Commissioners of the Generall Assembly at Edinburgh 4 Jan. 1643 (Edinburgh, 1643).

Pike, R. *A True Relation of the Proceedings of the Scots and English forces in the North of Ireland . . .* (1642).

The Proceedings of the Commissioners appointed by the Kings Majestie and Parliament of Scotland, for Conserving the Articles of the Treaty and Peace betwixt the Kingdomes . . . ([Edinburgh], 1643).

A Remonstrance concerning the present Troubles, from the meeting of the Estates of the Kingdome of Scotland, Aprill 16 unto the Parliament of England (1640).

The Remonstrance of the Commissioners of the General Assembly to the Convention of Estates at Edinburgh, June 1643 (Edinburgh, 1643).

The Remonstrance of the Nobility, Barrones, Burgesses, Ministers and Commons . . . (Edinburgh, 1639).

A True and Exact Relation of divers principall actions of a late Expedition in the north of Ireland, by the English and Scottish Forces (1642).

A True Representation of the Proceedings of the Kingdome of Scotland since the late Pacification By the Estates of the Kingdome against mistakings in the late Declaration ([Edinburgh], 1640).

Two Petitions Lately presented by Noblemen, Barons, Gentlemen, Burgesses and Ministers, of the Kingdome of Scotland. To the Right Honourable the Commissioners for the Conservation of Peace between the two Kingdoms . . . ([1643]).

II SECONDARY: i BIBLIOGRAPHIES AND CATALOGUES

Aldis, H. G. *A List of Books Printed in Scotland before 1700* (revised ed, Edinburgh, 1970).

Catalogue of Prints and Drawings in the British Museum: Political and Personal Satires, vol i, 1320–1689 (1870).

Davies, G. & Keeler, M. F. *Bibliography of British History, Stuart Period* (2nd ed, Oxford, 1970).

Edinburgh University Library, *Index of Manuscripts* (2 vols, Boston, Mass, 1964).

Ferguson, J. P. S. *Scottish Family Histories held in Scottish Libraries* (Edinburgh, 1960).

Gouldesbrough, P., Kup, A. P. & Lewis, I. *Handlist of Scottish and Welsh Record Publications* (British Records Association, 1954).

Hancock, P. D. *A Bibliography of Works relating to Scotland, 1916–1950* (2 vols, Edinburgh, 1959–60).

Livingstone, M. *Guide to the Public Records of Scotland* (Edinburgh, 1905).

Matheson, C. *A Catalogue of the Publications of Scottish Historical and Kindred Clubs and Societies* . . . *1908–27* (Aberdeen, 1928).

Mitchell, A. & Cash, C. G. *A Contribution to the Bibliography of Scottish Topography* (2 vols, SHS, 1917).

National Library of Scotland. *Catalogue of Manuscripts acquired since 1925* (2 vols, Edinburgh, 1938, 1966).

Steele, R. *A Bibliography of Royal Proclamations of the Tudor and Stuart Sovereigns* (2 vols, Oxford, 1910).

Stuart, M. *Scottish Family History* (Edinburgh, 1930).

Terry, C. S. *A Catalogue of the Publications of Scottish Historical and Kindred Clubs and Societies, 1780–1908* (Glasgow, 1909).

Thomason, G. *Catalogue of the Pamphlets . . . collected by George Thomason, 1641–1661*, ed G. K. Fortescue (1908).

II SECONDARY: ii THESES

Foster, W. R. 'Ecclesiastical Administration in Scotland, 1600–38' (University of Edinburgh Ph.D. thesis, 1963).

Kitshoff, M. C. 'Aspects of Arminianism in Scotland' (University of St Andrews M.Th. thesis, 1968).

McNeill, P. G. B. 'The Jurisdiction of the Scottish Privy Council, 1532–1708' (University of Glasgow Ph.D. thesis, 1961).

II SECONDARY: iii GENERAL PRINTED

Aston, T. (ed). *Crisis in Europe, 1560–1660* (1965).

Aylmer, G. E. *The King's Servants; The Civil Service of Charles I* (1961).

Brown, P. H. *History of Scotland* (3 vols, Cambridge, 1912).

Brunton, G. & Haig, D. *An Historical Account of the Senators of the College of Justice* (Edinburgh and London, 1832).

Buchan, J. *Montrose* (1931).

Burnet, G. *The Memoires of the Lives and Actions of James and William Dukes of Hamilton* (1677).

Burns, J. H. 'The Political Ideas of the Scottish Reformation', *Aberdeen University Review*, xxxvi (1955–6), 251–68.

Burrel, S. A. 'The Apocalyptic Vision of the Early Covenanters', *SHR*, xliii (1964), 1–24.

Burrel, S. A. 'Calvinism, Capitalism, and the Middle Classes: Some Afterthoughts on an old problem', *Journal of Modern History*, xxxii (1960), 129–41.

Burrel, S. A. 'The Covenant Idea as a Revolutionary Symbol: Scotland 1596–1637', *Church History*, xxvii (1958), 338–50.

Burton, J. H. *History of Scotland* (8 vols, Edinburgh, 1897).

Campbell, W. M. 'Lex Rex and its Author', *RSCHS*, vii (1941), 204–28.

Campbell, W. M. *The Triumph of Presbyterianism* (St Andrews, 1958).

Clarke, A. 'The Earl of Antrim and the First Bishops' War', *Irish Sword*, vi (1963–4), 108–15.

Connell, J. *A Treatise on the Law of Scotland respecting Tithes* (2 vols, Edinburgh, 1830).

Cowan, E. J. 'Montrose and Argyll', in *The Scottish Nation*, ed G. Menzies (1972).

Cowan, I. B., 'The Covenanters: A Revision Article', *SHR*, xlvii (1968), 35–52.

Donaldson, G. *The Making of the Scottish Prayer Book of 1637* (Edinburgh, 1954).

Donaldson, G. *Scotland: James V to James VII* (Edinburgh and London, 1965).

Donaldson, G. 'Scotland's Conservative North in the Sixteenth and Seventeenth Centuries', *TRHS*, 5th ser, xvi (1966), 65–79.

Donaldson, G. *The Scottish Reformation* (Cambridge, 1960).

Dunlop, A. I. 'The Polity of the Scottish Church, 1600–1637', *RSCHS*, xii (1958), 161–84.

Fleming, D. H. 'The National Petition to the Scottish Privy Council, October 18, 1637', *SHR*, xxii (1924–5), 241–8.

Fleming, D. H. 'Scotland's Supplication and Complaint against the Book of Common Prayer . . ., 18th October 1637', *PSAS*, lx (1925–6), 314–83, and published separately (Edinburgh, 1927).

Fleming, D. H. *The Subscribing of the National Covenant in 1638* (Edinburgh and London, 1912).

Forster, R. & Greene, J. P. (eds). *Preconditions of Revolution in Early Modern Europe* (Baltimore and London, 1971).

Forster, W. R. 'The Operation of Presbyteries in Scotland, 1600–1638', *RSCHS*, xv (1964–6), 21–33.

Gardiner, S. R. *History of England* (10 vols, 1883–4).

Gardiner, S. R. *History of the Great Civil War* (4 vols, 1893–4).

Hamilton, C. L. 'Anglo-Scottish Militia Negotiations, March–April 1646', *SHR*, xlii (1963), 86–8.

Hamilton, C. L. 'The Basis for Scottish Efforts to Create a Reformed Church in England, 1640–1', *Church History*, xxx (1961), 171–8.

Hamilton, C. L. 'The Anglo-Scottish Negotiations of 1640–1', *SHR*, xli (1962), 84–6.

Hannay, R. K. & Watson, G. P. H. 'The Building of the Parliament House', *Book of the Old Edinburgh Club*, xiii (1924), 1–78.

Hay, M. V. *The Blairs Papers, 1603–1660* (London and Edinburgh, 1929).

Hazlett, H. 'The Financing of the British Armies in Ireland, 1641–9', *IHS*, i (1938–9), 21–41.

Hazlett, H. 'The Recruitment and Organisation of the Scottish Army in Ulster, 1642–9', in *Essays in British and Irish History in Honour of James Eadie Todd*, ed H. A. Cronne, T. W. Moody & D. B. Quinn (1949), 107–33.

Henderson, G. D. *The Burning Bush: Studies in Scottish Church History* (Edinburgh, 1957).

Hewison, J. K. *The Covenanters* (2 vols, Glasgow, 1913).

Hill, G. *An Historical Account of the Macdonnells of Antrim* (Belfast, 1873).

Hudson, W. S. 'The Scottish Effort to Presbyterianise the Church of England during the early months of the Long Parliament', *Church History*, viii (1939), 255–82.

Kaplan, L. 'Presbyterians and Independents in 1643', *EHR*, lxxxiv (1969), 244–56.

Kaplan, L. 'Steps to War; the Scots and Parliament, 1642–3', *Journal of British Studies*, ix (1970), 50–70.

Kirkton, J. *The Secret and True History of the Church of Scotland* (Edinburgh, 1817).

Lamont, W. M. *Godly Rule. Politics and Religion, 1603–60* (1969).

Lang, A. *History of Scotland* (4 vols, Edinburgh, 1907).

Lythe, S. G. E. *The Economy of Scotland in its European Setting, 1550–1625* (Edinburgh, 1960).

McKechnie, H. *An Introductory Survey of the Sources and Literature of Scots Law* (Stair Society, 1936).

McKenzie, W. C. *The Life and Times of John Maitland, Duke of Lauderdale, 1616–1682* (1923).

McKerral, A. *Kintyre in the Seventeenth Century* (Edinburgh, 1948).

Mackie, J. D. & Pryde, G. S. *The Estate of the Burgesses in the Scots Parliament and its relation to the Convention of the Royal Burghs* (St Andrews, 1923).

McMahon, G. I. R. 'The Scottish Courts of High Commission, 1610–38', *RSCHS*, xv (1964–6), 193–209.

Makey, W. H. 'The Elders of Stow, Liberton, Canongate and St Cuthberts in the Mid-Seventeenth Century', *RSCHS*, xvii (1969–71), 155–67.

Malcolm, C. A. 'The Office of Sheriff in Scotland: Its Origins, and Early Development', *SHR*, xx (1922–3), 129–41, 222–37, 290–311.

Masson, D. *Drummond of Hawthornden: The Story of his Life and Writings* (1873).

Mathew, D. *Scotland under Charles I* (1955).

Mathieson, W. L. *Politics and Religion. A Study in Scottish History from the Reformation to the Revolution* (2 vols, Glasgow, 1902).

Mulligan, L. 'The Scottish Alliance and the Committee of Both Kingdoms, 1644–6', *Historical Studies*, xiv (1970), 173–88.

Napier, M. *Montrose and the Covenanters* (2 vols, 1838).

Napier, M. *The Life and Times of Montrose* (Edinburgh, 1840).

Napier, M. *Memoirs of the Marquis of Montrose* (2 vols, Edinburgh, 1856).

Notestein, W. 'The Establishment of the Committee of Both Kingdoms', *American Historical Review*, xvii (1912), 477–95.

Ogilvie, J. D. 'The National Petition, October 18 1637', *PEBS*, xii (1921–5), 105–31.

Ogilvie, J. D. 'The Kirkcudbright Petition, 1637: A Collotype Facsimile; with a Notice', *PEBS*, xiv (1926–30), 47–8.

Ogilvie, J. D. 'A Bibliography of the Glasgow Assembly, 1638', *RGBS*, vii (1918–20), 1–12.

Ogilvie, J. D. 'The Aberdeen Doctors and the National Covenant', *PEBS*, xi (1912–20), 73–86.

Ogilvie, J. D. 'A Bibliography of the Bishops' Wars', *RGBS*, xii (1936), 21–40.

Ogilvie, J. D. 'Church Union in 1641', *RSCHS*, i (1926), 143–60.

Ogilvie, J. D. 'The Story of a Broadside of 1641', *PEBS*, xii (1921–5), 78–83.

Ogilvie, J. D. 'The Cross Petition, 1643', *PEBS*, xv (1930–5), 55–76.

Oldmixon, J. *The History of England During the Reign of the Royal House of Stuart* (1730).

Pearl, V. 'Oliver St John and the "Middle Group" in the Long Parliament, Aug. 1643–May 1644', *EHR*, lxxxi (1966), 490–519.

Pearl, V. 'The "Royal Independents" in the English Civil War', *TRHS*, 5th ser, xviii (1968), 69–96.

Rait, R. S. *The Parliaments of Scotland* (Glasgow, 1924).

Ranke, L. *A History of England, principally in the Seventeenth Century* (6 vols, Oxford, 1875).

Reid, J. S. *The History of the Presbyterian Church in Ireland*, ed W. D. Killen (3 vols, Belfast, 1867).

Scot, H. *Fasti Ecclesiae Scoticanae* (9 vols, Edinburgh, 1915–50).

Shaw, D. *The General Assemblies of the Church of Scotland, 1560–1600. Their Origins and Development* (Edinburgh, 1964).

Shaw, D. (ed). *Reformation and Revolution. Essays presented to the Very Reverend Principal Emeritus Hugh Watt* (Edinburgh, 1967).

Smout, T. C. *A History of the Scottish People, 1560–1830* (1969).

Smout, T. C. *Scottish Trade on the Eve of the Union, 1660–1707* (Edinburgh, 1963).

Sprott, G. W. *The Worship of the Church of Scotland during the Covenanting Period, 1638–61* (Edinburgh, 1893).

Stevenson, A. *History of the Church and State of Scotland* (Edinburgh, 1840).

Stevenson, D. 'Conventicles and the Kirk, 1619–37. The Emergence of a Radical Party', *RSCHS* (forthcoming).

Stevenson, D. 'The Covenanters and the Court of Session, 1637–51', *Juridical Review* (1972), 227–47.

Stevenson, D. 'The Covenanters and the Scottish Mint, 1639–41', *British Numismatic Journal*, xli (1972), 95–104.

Stevenson, D. 'The Financing of the Cause of the Covenants, 1638–51', *SHR*, li (1972), 89–123.

Stevenson, D. 'The King's Scottish Revenues and the Covenanters, 1625–51', *Historical Journal*, xvii (1974—forthcoming).

Stevenson, D. 'The Radical Party in the Kirk, 1637–45', *Journal of Ecclesiastical History* (1973—forthcoming).

Stone, L. *The Causes of the English Revolution, 1529–1642* (1972).

Terry, C. S. 'Charles I and Alexander Leslie', *EHR*, xvi (1901), 115–20.

Terry, C. S. *The Life and Campaigns of Alexander Leslie, First Earl of Leven* (1899).

Terry, C. S. *The Scottish Parliament, its Constitution and Procedure, 1603–1707* (Glasgow, 1905).

Trevor-Roper, H. R. 'Scotland and the Puritan Revolution', in *Religion the Reformation and Social Change* (1967), 392–444.

Wedgwood, C. V. 'Anglo-Scottish Relations, 1603–40', *TRHS*, 4th ser, xxxii (1950), 31–48.

Wedgwood, C. V. 'The Covenanters in the First Civil War', *SHR*, xxxix (1960), 1–15.

Wedgwood, C. V. *The King's Peace* (1955).

Wedgwood, C. V. *The King's War* (1958).

Willcock, J. *The Great Marquess. Life and Times of Archibald . . . Marquess of Argyll* (Edinburgh and London, 1903).

Wodrow, R. *Analecta, or Materials for a History of Remarkable Providences*, ed M. Leishman (4 vols, Maitland Club, 1842–3).

Wodrow, R. *The History of the Sufferings of the Church of Scotland*, ed R. Burns (4 vols, Glasgow, 1828).

Wodrow, R. *Selections from Wodrow's Biographical Collections: Divines of the North-East of Scotland* (New Spalding Club, 1890).

Zagorin, P. *The Court and the Country. The Beginning of the English Revolution* (1969).

Maps

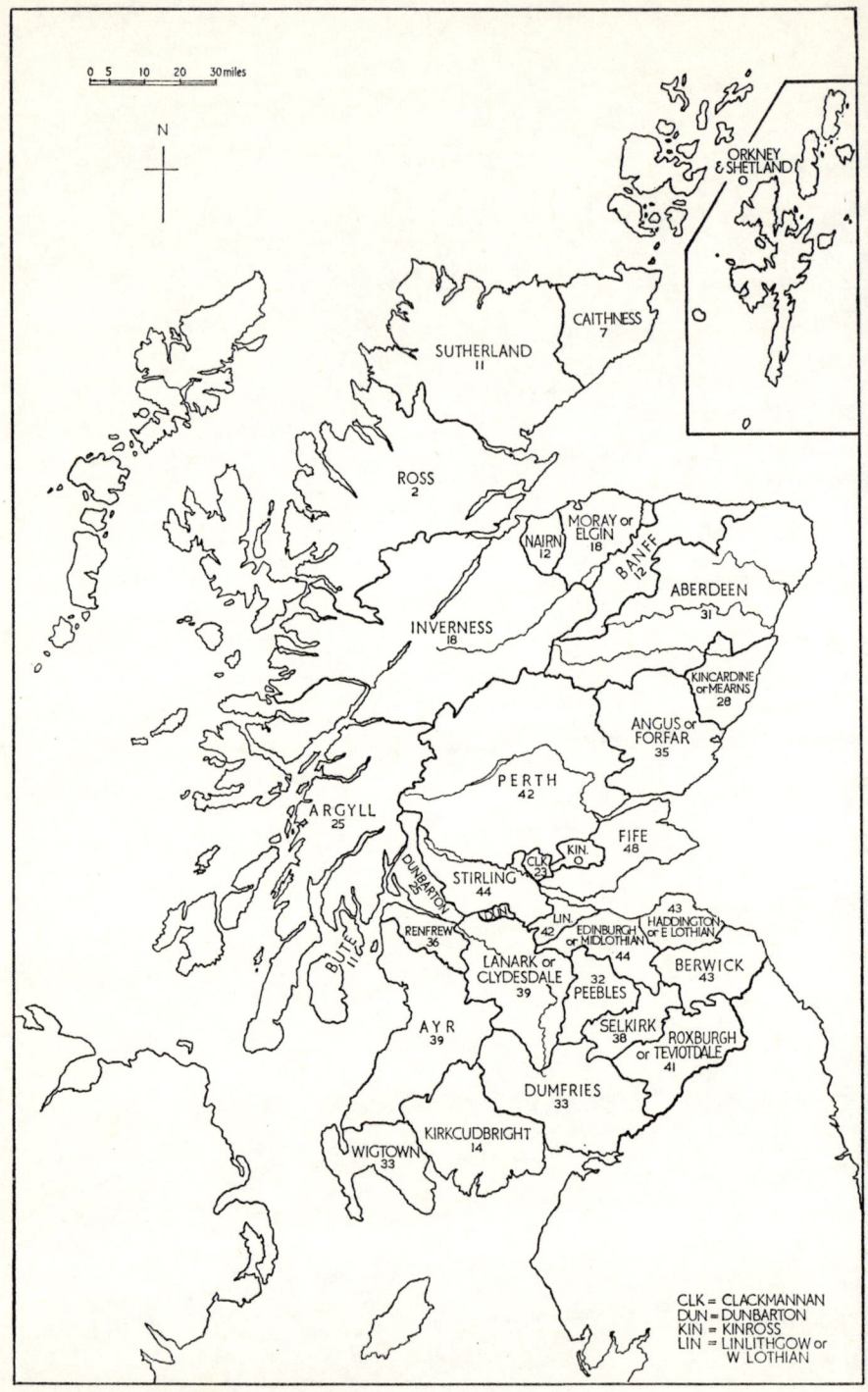

MAP 1: SCOTLAND—SHIRES
Shire representation in the parliaments of 1639–41, 1644–7 and 1648–51, and in the convention of estates of 1643–4.

See notes to maps, p. 401

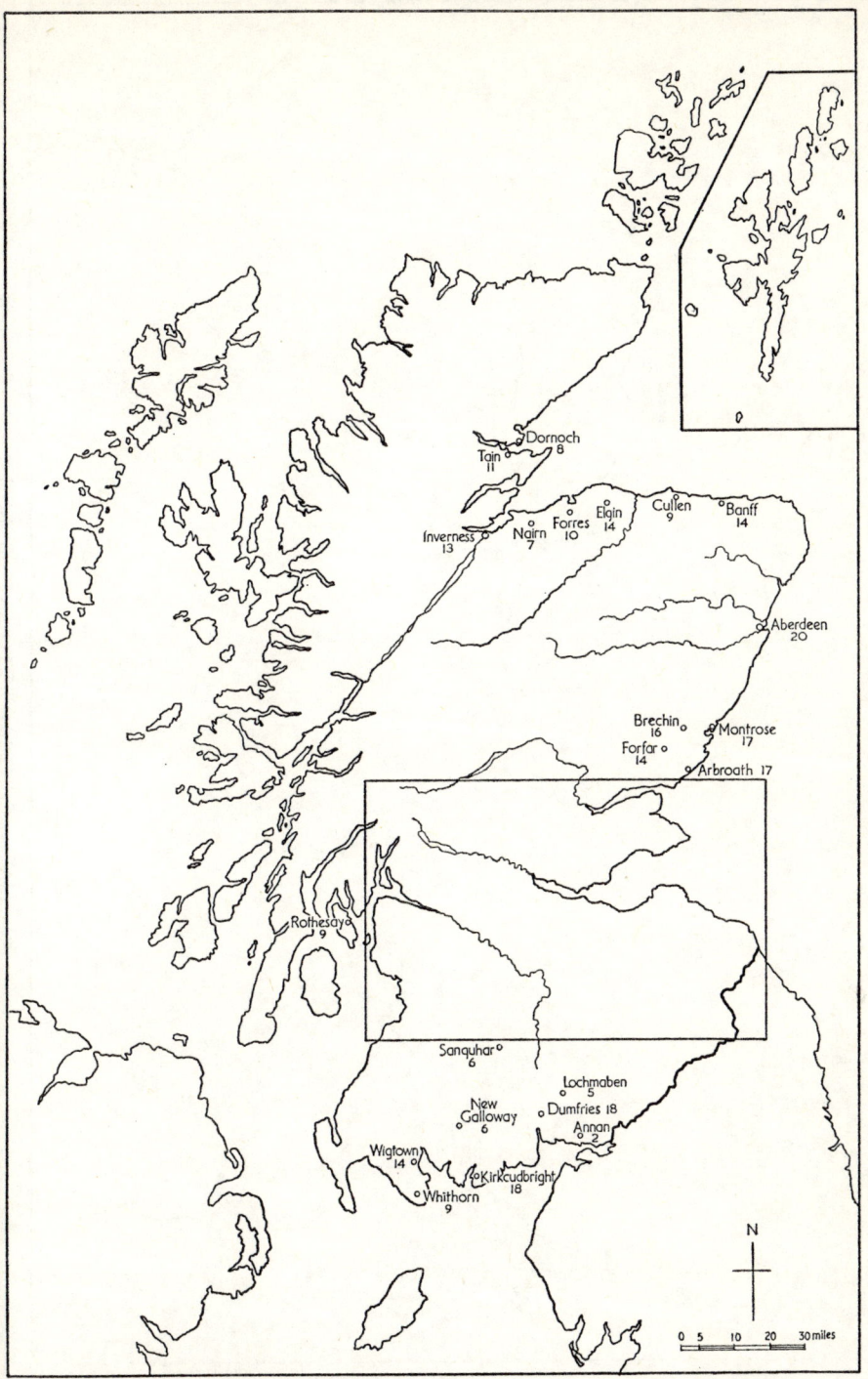

MAP 2: SCOTLAND—BURGHS
Burgh representation in the parliaments of 1639–41, 1644–7 and 1648–51, and in the
convention of estates of 1643–4. For central Scotland see map 3.

See notes to maps, p. 401

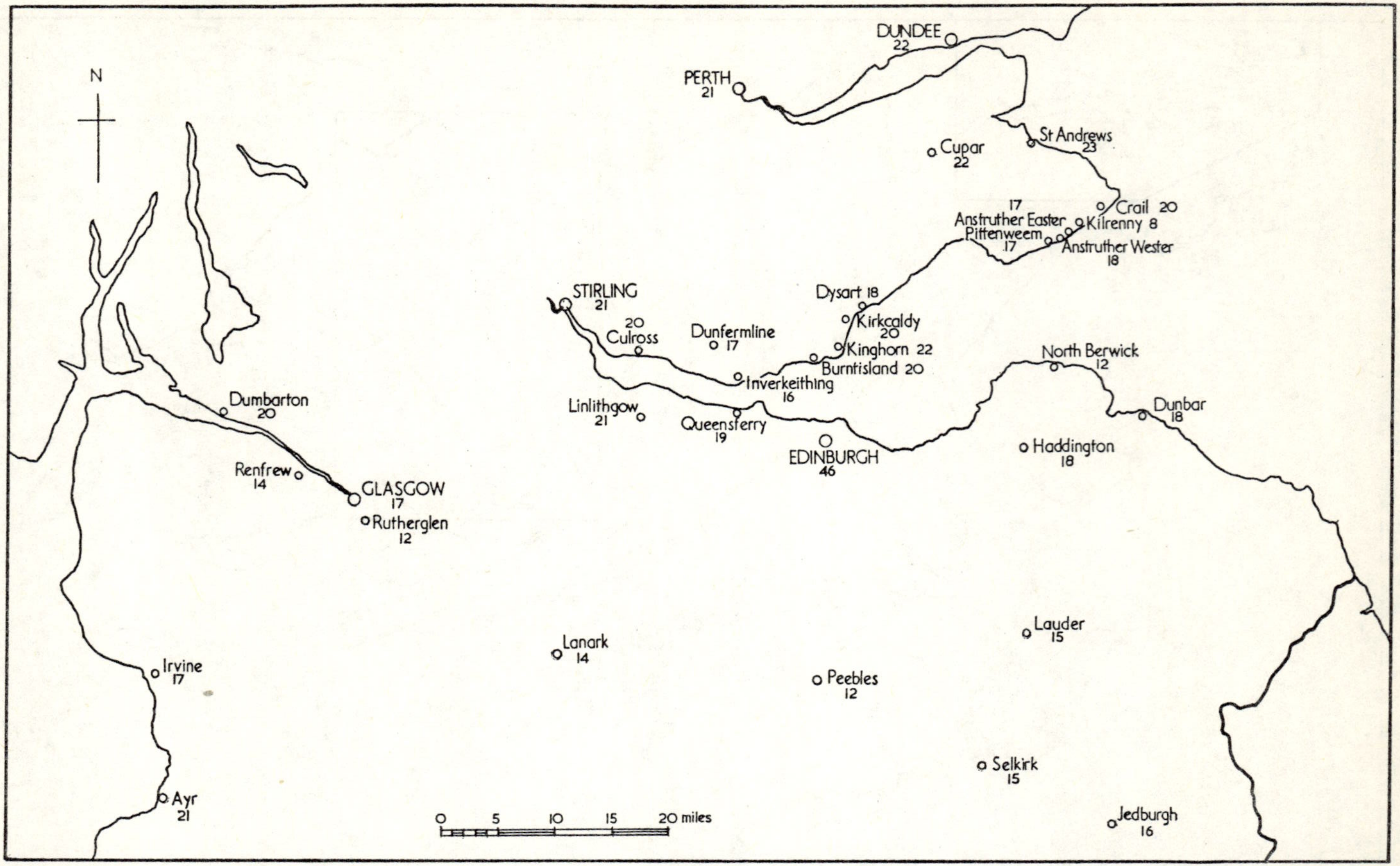

MAP 3: CENTRAL SCOTLAND—BURGHS

DUNDEE
22

PERTH
21

St Andrews
23

Cupar
22

Crail 20
Anstruther Easter 9 Kilrenny 8
17 Pittenweem 0
17 Anstruther Wester
18

STIRLING
21

Culross
20

Dunfermline
17

Dysart 18

Kirkcaldy
20

Kinghorn 22

Burntisland 20

Inverkeithing
16

Queensferry
19

Linlithgow
21

EDINBURGH
46

Dunbar
18

North Berwick
12

Haddington
18

Lauder
15

Jedburgh
16

Selkirk
15

Peebles
12

Lanark
14

GLASGOW
17

Rutherglen
12

Renfrew
14

Dumbarton
20

Irvine
17

Ayr
21

N

0   5   10   15   20 miles

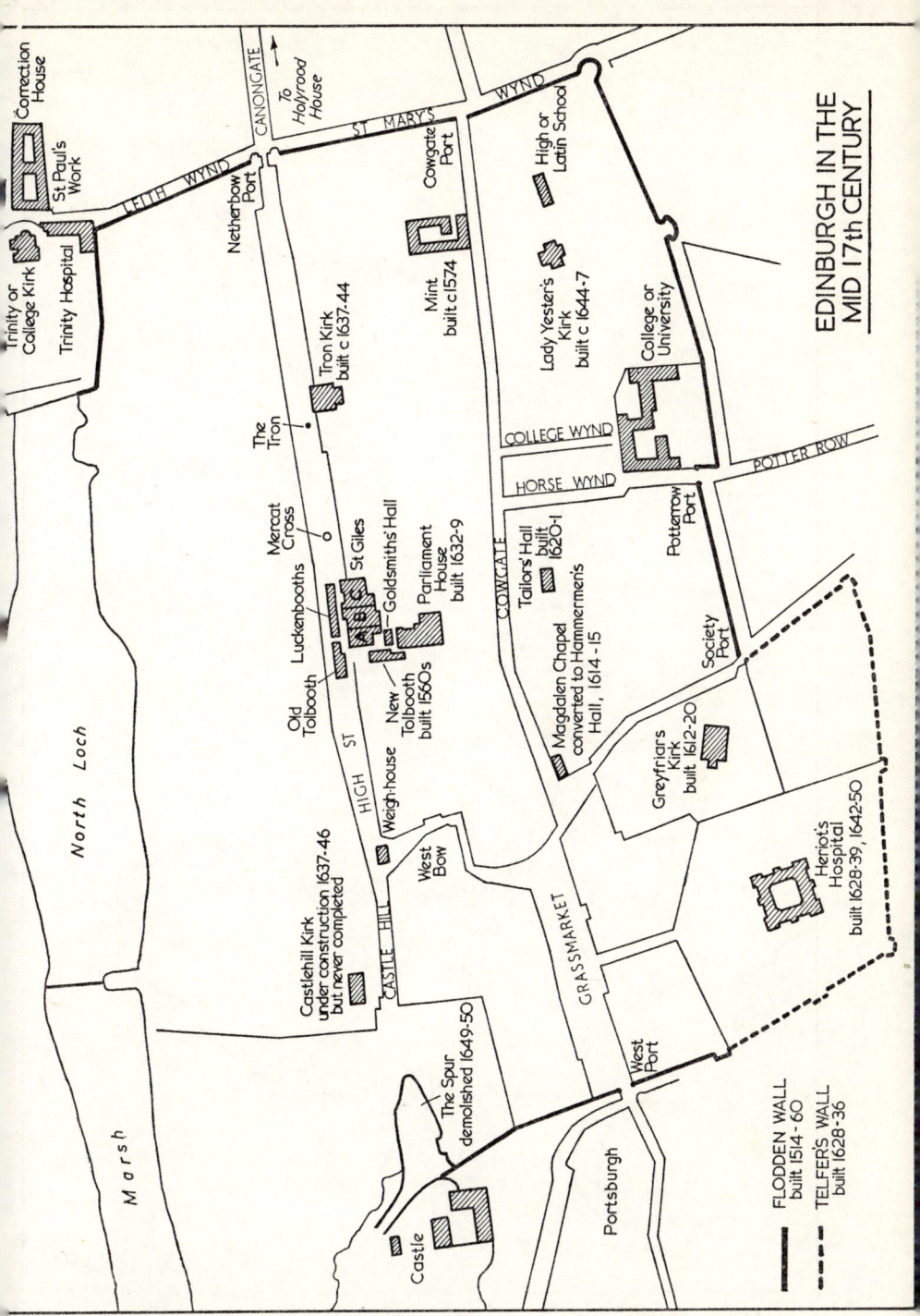

MAP 4: SKETCH MAP OF EDINBURGH IN THE MID SEVENTEENTH
CENTURY   See notes to maps, p. 401

Map labels:

Correction House

St Paul's Work

Trinity or College Kirk

Trinity Hospital

CANONGATE

To Holyrood House

ST MARY'S WYND

LEITH WYND

Netherbow Port

Cowgate Port

High or Latin School

Mint built c1574

Tron Kirk built c 1637-44

Lady Yester's Kirk built c 1644-7

College or University

The Tron

COLLEGE WYND

HORSE WYND

POTTER ROW

Mercat Cross

St Giles

Goldsmiths' Hall

Parliament House built 1632-9

Tailors' Hall built 1620-1

Potterrow Port

Old Tolbooth

Luckenbooths

New Tolbooth built 1560s

COWGATE

Magdalen Chapel converted to Hammermen's Hall, 1614-15

Society Port

HIGH ST

Weigh-house

Greyfriars Kirk built 1612-20

North Loch

Castlehill Kirk under construction 1637-46 but never completed

West Bow

CASTLE HILL

Heriot's Hospital built 1628-39, 1642-50

Marsh

The Spur demolished 1649-50

GRASSMARKET

West Port

Portsburgh

Castle

FLODDEN WALL built 1514-60

TELFER'S WALL built 1628-36

EDINBURGH IN THE MID 17th CENTURY

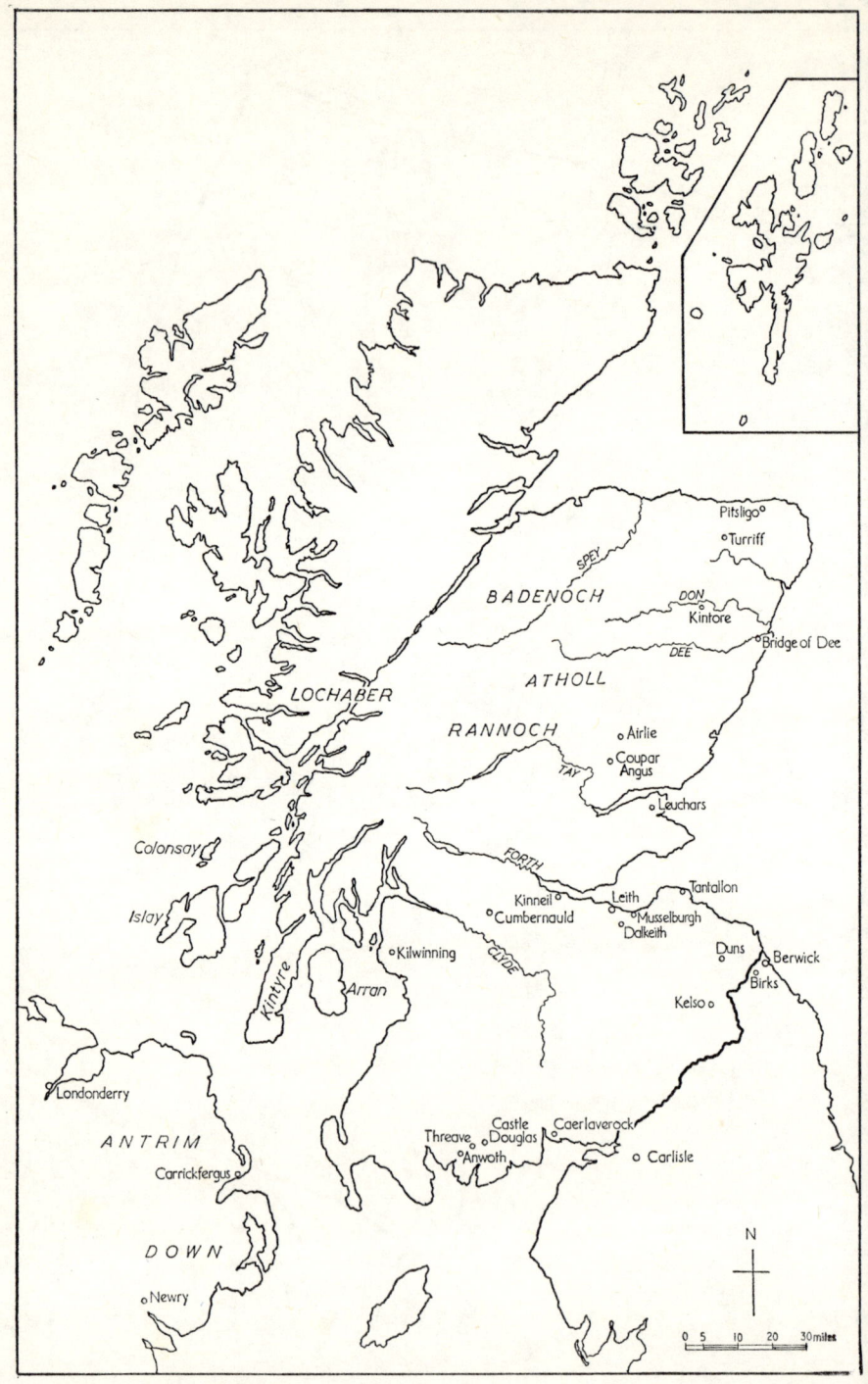

MAP 5: SCOTLAND
Showing all places mentioned in the text and not shown on maps 1–4.

MAP 1: Shire representation in parliament and the convention of estates. The figures indicate the number of times commissioners for each shire appear in the twenty-five surviving lists of members; for these lists see Stevenson. 'The Covenanters and the Government of Scotland' (PhD thesis, Glasgow, 1970), 871–3. The seven lists for 3–11 January 1644 have been combined and treated as one. As each shire was entitled to send two commissioners (except for Kinross and Clackmannan, which could each send one) the maximum possible figure is 50 (25 for the two smallest shires) though exceptionally two commissioners did sit for Clackmannan in 1639 and 1640.

MAPS 2 and 3: Burgh representation in parliament and the convention of estates. Compiled in the same way as map 1. The maximum possible figure for each burgh is 25, except for Edinburgh (50) which sent two commissioners.

MAP 4: Sketch map of Edinburgh in the mid seventeenth century. Based on William Edgar's plan of 1742, modified by reference to James Gordon's view of 1647, the *Inventory of the Ancient and Historical Monuments of the City of Edinburgh* (Edinburgh, 1951), *Edin Recs*, articles in the *Book of the Old Edinburgh Club*, and the various histories of the burgh.

The kirks of Edinburgh
In 1598 the burgh was divided into four parishes, which worshipped as follows.

South West Parish. Worshipped in High or Upper Tolbooth, which was the partitioned-off west end of St Giles (A). This congregation moved to the new Greyfriars Kirk in 1620.

North West parish. Worshipped in the choir of St Giles (C), variously known as the New, East, Little, or High Kirk. In 1634 when St Giles became a cathedral the wall dividing the choir from the nave (B) was demolished, and this congregation took over the nave as well. Nave and choir together were now sometimes called the Great Kirk. The wall was rebuilt in 1639 and this congregation confined again to the choir.

North East parish. Worshipped in the Trinity or College Kirk.

South East parish. Worshipped in the nave of St Giles (B), known as the Old or Great Kirk. Evicted in 1634 when the wall between choir and nave was demolished, the congregation moved to the Tolbooth Kirk (A) in the west end of St Giles. It moved back to the nave (B) in 1639.

In 1641 the burgh was re-divided into six parishes, as follows.

North West parish. Worshipping in West St Giles (A).

North parish. Worshipping in East St Giles (C).

North East parish. Worshipping in the Trinity or College Kirk.

South East Parish. Worshipping in Mid St Giles (B) until the Tron Kirk was completed.

South parish. Worshipping in the Parliament House or the College Hall until the South East parish moved to the Tron, when it took over Mid St Giles (B).

South West parish. Worshipping in Greyfriars Kirk.

Acknowledgements

In writing a book of this sort one inevitably incurs great debts, which it is easier to acknowledge than repay. My greatest are to Professor A. A. M. Duncan and Dr I. B. Cowan, both of the Department of Scottish History of Glasgow University. They gave me their help, encouragement and patience freely when I was working on the thesis on which this book is based. John Imrie, Keeper of the Records of Scotland, was also most helpful in the early stages of my work, while in the later stages the constructive criticism of Conrad Russell, Bedford College, University of London, has been very useful.

The libraries and record offices I have worked in most are the libraries of Aberdeen and Glasgow Universities, the National Library of Scotland, the Scottish Record Office, the British Museum, the Bodleian Library and the Public Record Office. To their staffs my thanks are therefore due. My thanks are also due to Mrs Anne Naylor for her accurate typing of the thesis from which this book grew.

It is customary at this point for the author to take the blame for all the errors and limitations of his book on himself. This I do, but following Gilbert Burnet's example (in the preface to the *Memoires of . . . Hamilton*) 'I shall not stand longer on laboured and formal Apologies, which are more used to shew the Wit of the Writer, in making them gracefully, than from any humble opinion they have of their own Performances who make them. If I have not done this to the best advantage, it is because I could not do it better'.

The following have kindly given permission for the reproduction of copyright photographs of items in their collection:

Aberdeen University Library, pp 50, 272
British Museum, p 118
Central Public Library, Edinburgh, pp 68, 185, 203
National Museum of Antiquities of Scotland, p 254
The Faculty of Advocates (Parliament House, Edinburgh), p 117 (Spottiswood)
Scottish National Portrait Gallery, pp 49 (Stirling), 67, 135, 186 (Montrose), 204, 253
P. Maxwell Stuart (Traquair House), p 136
The Earl of Haddington (Tyninghame House), p 49 (Rothes)
University of St Andrews, p 117 (Rutherford)
The photographs reproduced on pp 186 (Argyll) and 271 are my own.

Index